STALIN'S
AMERICAN
POLICY

Also by William Taubman

Governing Soviet Cities: Bureaucratic Politics and Urban
Development in the USSR

Globalism and Its Critics: The American Foreign Policy Debate
of the 1960s (Editor)

The View from Lenin Hills: Soviet Youth in Ferment

STALIN'S AMERICAN POLICY

From Entente
to Détente
to Cold War

WILLIAM TAUBMAN

W · W · Norton & Company
New York   London

Copyright © 1982 by William Taubman
Published simultaneously in Canada by George J. McLeod Limited, Toronto.
Printed in the United States of America
All Rights Reserved
First Edition

Library of Congress Cataloging in Publication Data

Taubman, William.
  Stalin's American policy.
  Includes bibliographical references and index.
    1. United States—Foreign relations—Soviet Union.   2. Soviet Union—
Foreign   relations—United   States.   3. Stalin,   Joseph,   1879–1953.
4. United   States—Foreign   relations—1945–1953.   5. Soviet   Union—
Foreign   relations—1945– .   6. World   War,   1939–1945—Diplomatic
history.   I. Title.
  E183.8.S65T38   1982   327.73047   81-38333
  ISBN 0–393–01406–1   AACR2
W. W. Norton & Company, Inc. 500 Fifth Avenue, New York, N.Y. 10110
W. W. Norton & Company Ltd. 25 New Street Square, London EC4A 3NT

1 2 3 4 5 6 7 8 9 0

To Alex and Phoebe

Contents

Preface	ix
1 / Now and Then	3
2 / Roots and Portents: 1917–1941	10
3 / The Origins of Entente: June 1941–June 1944	31
4 / Entente Stalinist-Style: June 1944–April 1945	73
5 / From Entente to Détente:	
April 1945–December 1945	99
6 / Détente Stalinist-Style: January 1946–April 1947	128
7 / From Détente to Cold War:	
April 1947–December 1948	166
8 / Cold War Stalinist-Style: January 1949–March 1953	193
Conclusion / After Stalin: To Brezhnev and Beyond	228
Notes	256
Index	283

Preface

This book is the result of living in two worlds. One is a small liberal arts college where I began teaching in the tumultuous late 1960s. The other is the world of international politics and, particularly, Soviet foreign policy, which I have studied professionally for nearly twenty years and encountered firsthand in Moscow and Washington. Several generations of idealistic Amherst students have by now challenged me with a question which I would have put to myself anyway: Why can't America have a more humane foreign policy, one which would help us find a way to keep the peace (and to defend interests and ideals worth defending) without inviting hot or cold war, without the arms races, interventions, and East-West confrontations that have disfigured the postwar era and still continue today? The answer given by many in my other world is brief: "Be realistic!" The very nature of the nation-state system, they say, a Hobbesian realm in which no one will defend you unless you defend yourself, puts a premium on national security and the need to use power—if necessary, military power—to protect it. What's more, peace and freedom have been threatened and still are by the Soviet Union, a country about which Abram Tertz has said, "So that prisons should vanish forever, we built new prisons. So that all frontiers should fall, we surround ourselves with a Chinese Wall. So that work should become rest and a pleasure, we introduced forced labor. So that not one drop of blood be shed any more, we killed and killed and killed."[1]

I began this book to see which of my two worlds is right. Since the issues have cosmic dimensions, I reduced them to a somewhat more manageable scale: How and why did the Cold War begin? What in particular was the Soviet contribution? Could the Cold War have been avoided or mitigated? Are we fated to relive the past once again? But although these questions have been much studied and debated, just as often we are told that there can be no definitive answers in the absence of more information about the Soviet viewpoint. It is not accidental, as the Soviets would say, that accounts of Stalin's foreign policy in the crucial Cold War years are conspicuous by their rarity. For it is no secret, as the Russians also say, that Soviet archives on those years have not been thrown open nor are they likely to be soon. It is difficult enough to understand and explain the foreign relations of a relatively open society like the United States. Shall the focus be on the domestic roots or external sources of foreign policy? If the former, shall the spotlight play on presidents and their worldviews (or lack of same), on wider circles of bureaucratic and electoral politics, or on deep-seated social and economic forces which shape all the rest? How much more difficult must it be to illuminate the past of a country in which history itself is often a state secret.

Oddly enough, in some ways it is easier. One need not fear being overwhelmed by the masses of data through which historians of American diplomacy have to wade. More important, even if Joseph Stalin was not the all-seeing genius he made himself out to be, or the omnipotent tyrant of others' accounts, still, any serious treatment of Soviet policy in his time must sooner or later focus on him. Troubles begin when one asks what his foreign policy was. And they multiply rapidly when the question becomes, Why? Psychobiography seems a promising approach to a man of Stalin's personality, but it risks reducing the behavior of a vast transcontinental empire to the psyche of one man. Kremlinology (the nonscience of guessing who is "doing-in" whom) beckons, even though Stalin did-in nearly everyone by the end of the 1930s. Intramural warfare among Stalin's political lieutenants apparently continued until his death, but tracing its impact on foreign policy almost immediately becomes too speculative for comfort let alone historical truth. As for deep-seated, structural forces, the Soviet Union has more than its share of these (a state-socialist economy, a Marxist-Leninist ideology, a need for warm-water ports, even, some say, a characteristically Russian soul), but the danger is that such things too easily explain everything and therefore nothing.

We cannot, however, afford to be put off by the difficulties. The meaning of the recent past, the shape of the present, the prospect for the future—all depend on Soviet relations with the United States. So even before the Soviet archives are opened (if indeed they ever are, or still exist, or ever existed), one must make the attempt. My focus is on Stalin's conception of America—the threats the United States posed and the opportunities it offered—and the policies he devised for dealing with the United States. My method is not psychohistory, although I have profitted from the use others have made of it.[2] Nor is my approach Kremlinology or its close cousin, the study of bureaucratic politics viewed as the primary determinant of policy. I lay great stress on structural elements like ideology and political culture that influenced Stalin and, as we shall see, ensure that his legacy is still with us. But I rely mainly on a close reading of the diplomatic record, along with such other evidence as can help to reconstruct Stalin's thinking. I make no exclusive claims for my method. Indeed, I am depressed by some of my own conclusions. I invite others to harrow the ground using other devices.

To those who have worked in this vineyard before me, and to those who helped me to do so, I owe thanks (along with the customary disclaimer that they bear no responsibility for my views and especially for any misinterpretations contained herein). The Council on Foreign Relations enabled me to spend a year during the early seventies as a participant-cum-observer specializing in Soviet affairs on the U.S. State Department's policy planning staff. The transition from a hotly antiwar campus was a shock for me—one which proved productive of thought. Shortly thereafter, the American Friends Service Committee included me on two consecutive bilateral seminars (one in the United States, the other in the USSR) with Soviet foreign policy specialists. On these occasions, as well as several other trips to Moscow, I was able to try out my views on official and unofficial Soviet sources, whom I cannot name but to whom I owe much. I am grateful to Amherst College, which has provided me not only with stimulating colleagues and challenging students but with two extended occasions to ponder what they have taught me, and with resources needed to get it all down on paper.

Colleagues and others, at Amherst and elsewhere, from whom I have learned are too numerous to mention but not to thank. I particularly acknowledge the inspiration of the late Earl Latham, who provoked me to begin this project but died before it was concluded, and of George Kateb, whose political wisdom has I hope rubbed off on me. Special thanks to Pavel Machala, who has been a painstaking and constructive critic, and to others who read earlier drafts and gave me their comments: N. Gordon Levin, Jr., Robert H. McNeal, Strobe Talbott, and Ronald Tiersky—and to Joel Paul, research assistant extraordinary, and Dianne Kaplan, whose typing miraculously transformed raw drafts into finished products.

Amherst, Massachusetts   W.T.
May 1981

STALIN'S
AMERICAN
POLICY

I

Now and Then

CONSIDER THE FOLLOWING SCENARIO. AFTER A PERIOD OF RELATIVELY good feeling, tensions are rising between Moscow and Washington. The situation falls short of cold war. But genuine cooperation, which both sides have pledged themselves to promote and attain, seems even more distant, perhaps a mirage altogether. Not long ago, détente held sway in U.S.–Soviet relations, but no more.

To an increasing number of Americans, the Soviet Union appears intent on expansion. How else to explain its aggressive probing for greater power and influence, especially in the Eastern Mediterranean and Southwest Asia, where a number of countries have either just fallen into the Soviet orbit or seem about to do so? These and other Soviet gains demonstrate, say the hawks, that when you treat the Soviets fairly they take advantage of you. When you arrive at understandings, they break them. If they are prepared to negotiate, it is to lull you into unconcern, to stall while Western troubles spread and deepen. The only thing the Kremlin understands is strength, but Western strength is lacking. A build-up of Western power and confidence is urgently needed. Only then will Moscow contemplate meaningful concessions. Even then, however, progress will be limited until the Soviet system itself, which has hostility and expansionism built into it, changes in fundamental ways.

Making matters worse, in the view of the hawks, has been the situation in America. After a period of vigorous internationalist action, a kind of isolationism has been gaining ground. Many Americans have no illusions about Soviet benevolence, but they have been neither sufficiently alarmed about the danger nor ready to pay the price to resist it. The administration itself has been waffling, apparently unsure whether to pursue compromise and conciliation or to draw a line and dare the Russians to cross it. The world has been watching. America's adversaries have been encouraged and its friends made uneasy by Washington's irresolution.

But other observers are not so sure. The Soviets are not saints, say the doves, but not devils either. Moscow's primary concern is not world revolution, but its own national security. Soviet leaders are careful and even conservative in their diplomacy; they are alarmed by what they regard as "the American threat." If the United States recognized legitimate Soviet interests, the Kremlin would reciprocate. In any event, argue the soft-liners, the USSR is far weaker and more vulnerable than alarmists contend. Not Soviet designs, but deep-seated social ills at home and abroad threaten America's long-term security. Americans ought to be addressing themselves to pressing global and domestic problems instead of to a largely mythical Soviet threat.

Not too long ago, our story continues, the American government seemed disposed to put an acceptable light on Soviet behavior. But a crisis along the southern border of the USSR has galvanized the administration into action. The president has gone before the Congress to warn that vital American interests are threatened. He has resolved to defend peace and freedom. The United States must and will take the lead in containing further Communist expansion.

Does the administration's new firmness mean that cold war is at hand? Not necessarily. The momentum in American policy may be moving that way. Military and other voices warn that the president's brave new words will prove empty unless bolstered by stepped-up military strength. But if the handwriting is on the wall in Washington, the Soviets seem not to realize it. The Soviet press has mounted a slashing attack on the new American doctrine but, at the same time, suggested that Washington forgive and forget or at least live and let live. Soviet leaders seem confident they can ride out the storm. They apparently view what may be a crucial historical turning point as a blowup that will soon blow over, leaving the field to détente-as-usual.

Events are developing fast. But they raise more questions than they answer. What *are* the Soviets up to? What does their geopolitical probing represent? Are they, as they claim, on the defensive, having become genuinely alarmed by Western threats to their security? Or are they on the attack, emboldened by what they see as Western weakness and irresolution? Have the Americans misplayed their hand? Have they unwittingly led the Kremlin to underestimate Washington's will and ability to defend its interests? If the United States hardens its position even further, if it begins to put increased political, economic, and even military muscle behind its words, will the Soviets back off or merely match American militance? If, on the other hand, Washington moves to defuse the tension, will Moscow retreat? Or will the Kremlin take conciliation for weakness of which it can take advantage? Will the superpowers find a way to rebuild détente and, eventually, move toward genuine cooperation? Or will they descend into cold or even hot war?

The scene is the year 1980, but the scenario fits the mid-1940s as well. This will probably come as a surprise to many. We are accustomed to thinking that the Cold War evolved more or less directly out of the wartime Grand Alliance. We would not think of describing any transition period in-between as détente. This is not only because the literal meaning of détente (relaxation of tensions) makes it awkward to apply it to a period preceding rather than following a cold war, but, more importantly, because we associate détente with Stalin's more or less "reasonable" successors rather than with the notorious dictator himself. If, however, we employ the nonliteral meaning that détente came to have in the 1970s—that is, as a competitive (and not especially peaceful) sort of coexistence characterized by less tension and more negotiation than during a cold war and by the most serious sort of rivalry—then détente is not merely a phenomenon of the 1970s; it is a recurring aspiration of Soviet diplomacy. Lenin, in his time, promoted a form of détente only partially requited by the Western powers. Stalin pursued a species of détente in the 1930s and again after World War II. Of course, the various would-be and actual "détentes" have differed depending on the circumstances, including the special character traits of successive Soviet leaders. But the variation is not as great as one might expect. Stalin, for example, is well known for (to put it gently) being suspicious. But suspiciousness, particularly about capitalist motives, is also built into Marxist-Leninist ideology and Soviet political institutions. No Soviet leader has endorsed détente out of trust in Moscow's adversaries. All have acted out of a deep sense of distrust. And yet, Stalin, the most distrustful of all, actually hewed to postwar détente longer than the United States did. Nonetheless, in the 1940s, our scenario ended in cold war.

Entente (a French word for 'understanding between allies'), détente (another French term), and cold war (why do the French get all the nice ones?)—together with "hot war" these cover the waterfront of possible Soviet-American relationships. Moreover, questions about the nature of each and the transitions from one to another have recently sparked two separate debates about U.S.–Soviet relations. One controversy concerns the Cold War's origins; the other, its alleged end and replacement by what for a year or two used to be called a new "generation of peace." The two controversies are related: similar questions about Soviet and American intentions and capabilities, and the threats each poses to the other, are at issue. But, in fact, the past is even more relevant to the present and future than one might think. For if the prime present-day puzzle has been the nature of détente, along with its potential to develop into either fuller cooperation or renewed cold war, the forties feature all three relationships in evolution from one to another. What is détente, anyway? Why do the Soviets favor it while many Americans fear it? Why and how does it tend to unravel? Consult the lessons of 1945 to 1947. Is far-reaching, long-lasting cooperation possible between Moscow and Washington? Consider what happened when the two were allies between 1941 and 1945. And cold war itself—concerning which latter-day hawks evince a certain nostalgia—what forces trigger it, and which tend to expand or limit it? On these matters, examine the evidence of 1947 to 1953.

This book is about the past, with lessons for the present and future. But, of course, the study of history is no panacea. The times, the leaders, the circumstances both global and domestic are different enough from one age to the next to prompt legitimate doubts about "lessons of the past." Furthermore, those lessons are hard to come by in the first place—witness the bitter, long-standing, unresolved debate about the origins of the Cold War. The historical problem is not so much a lack of evidence—although "inside" sources on Stalin's American policy are lacking, and good secondary studies are few and far between. It is rather that historians cannot agree on what the evidence proves. Revisionist historians view the forties as latter-day doves do the seventies: Moscow's postwar aims were limited, they say; it was American pressure which triggered the Cold War. Orthodox or traditionalist historians charge that American policy was naïve and concessive; the United States should have applied more pressure on Moscow, not less.

Traditionalist and revisionist accounts of the Cold War's origins are virtual mirror images of each other. Traditionalists (such as George F. Kennan and W. W. Rostow) portray American diplomacy as defensive and not particularly effective—precisely the way revisionists (such as Gabriel Kolko, William Appleman Williams, and Gar Alperovitz) describe Stalin's approach.[1] Traditionalists depict the USSR as expansionist; they charge Moscow with exaggerating "the American threat," whether deliberately to cover its own designs or through "honest" paranoia. Revisionists reverse the charges. They find Washington guilty of imperialism; they say the Americans resisted reasonable Soviet claims to an East European sphere of influence, all in the name of an exaggerated notion (whether sincere or contrived is a separate question) of the Soviet threat. Revisionists find the roots of American expansionism in American society, particularly in the institutions of capitalism. Traditionalists contend Soviet imperialism reflects Marxist-Leninist ideology, traditional Russian xenophobia, and the logic of totalitarian rule. Franklin Roosevelt's accommodationist policies are models for some revisionists; Truman's hard line, climaxing in his declaration of the Truman Doctrine in 1947, is anathema. For traditionalists, Roosevelt's approach (however understandable under the circumstances) encouraged Soviet expansion; even Truman is depicted as insufficiently tough-minded until in 1947 he at last opts decisively for containing Soviet power.

The most recent development in the Cold War debate is the appearance of so-called post-revisionist histories. Post-revisionists do not exactly split the difference between previous debaters, but they do come down somewhere in the complexities in-between. Neither the Soviets nor the Americans, they say, were without responsibility for the Cold War; each was victim as well as villain. We are told, by John Lewis Gaddis, that domestic politics constrained American leaders as much or more than did economic forces—with the result that Roosevelt and Truman had less leeway to accommodate Stalin than he (being free of such constraints) to conciliate them—and, by Robert Dallek, that Roosevelt wanted to grant Stalin an Eastern European sphere of influence while at the same time containing Soviet power within that zone.[2]

Most post-revisionists, like their predecessors, have been specialists on American diplomacy. "The urgent need for cold war historiography today," declared Arthur M. Schlesinger, Jr., in a recent review of the literature, "is to get off the American base and to broaden research and analytic perspectives. We need to know more, for example, about Soviet expectations and objectives."[3] And, as our opening scenario suggests, we need to know more about how the Soviets react to American efforts to apply more, or less, pressure on Moscow. Vojtech Mastny's *Russia's Road to the Cold War, 1941–1945* is one book that answers the need. Mastny's Stalin is no superman; he is capable of confusion, forced to improvise, not always effective in his diplomacy. Nonetheless, argues Mastny, "Russia's striving for power and influence far in excess of its reasonable security requirements was the primary source of the [Cold War] conflict." Mastny's Roosevelt is not a total pushover, but if Stalin failed to limit his needs, Roosevelt failed to define his limits. Stalin "might have acted with more restraint," Mastny contends, "if . . . the Western powers had taken a firm and unequivocal stand early enough." Western failure to resist soon enough was, according to Mastny, "an important secondary" cause of the Cold War.[4]

Mastny is generally on target. But his account leaves important questions unanswered. What convinced Stalin, that most suspicious of men, that he could take advantage of what he himself regarded as implacable capitalist adversaries? The answer involves not only what Western leaders did and did not do, but also the fact that Stalin perceived them through his own ideological lens and in terms of his own Soviet political experience. The same pattern applies after 1945. But Mastny breaks off his account in August of that year on the assumption, it would appear, that the Cold War was already in train. In a sense it was, but the track leads through two years of détente, then through another year of transition, and only in 1949 into what can be called the Cold War proper.

Is it possible, after all this controversy, to add something new, if not eternally definitive? Soviet wartime and early postwar policy *was* cautious and in a sense defensive. But although Stalin's initial aims were limited, his long-term goals and the likely consequences of his policies were not. Stalin *did* want to preserve the best possible relations with the United States; he shifted from entente to détente to cold war reluctantly, each time under pressure from the West. But Stalin promoted good relations at the Americans' expense—in the quite literal sense that he expected Washington to subsidize his efforts to undermine the West. Stalin was ready and willing to bargain, even after (in fact, especially after) the Americans decided there was little to be gained from further negotiation. But Stalin's idea of a compromise was something that lasted only until an opportunity arose to get around it. If this was the essence of Stalinist-style entente and détente, who can blame Washington for refusing to play along? Least of all Stalin, who viewed the leading capitalist power as hostile, devious, and threatening. Yet the same Stalin also thought he could handle the Americans—a misapprehension to which Roosevelt and Truman unintentionally contributed. Stalin both failed to anticipate the hardening of American policy, which his own tactics provoked, and misunderstood the change when it finally occurred. Washington, meanwhile, lurched from misguided efforts to win Moscow's trust to the equally misguided conviction that the Kremlin was intent on unleashing world war. But although the Americans made mistakes, they were damned if they did and damned if they didn't: conciliation struck Stalin as trickery or naïveté, and toughness only confirmed the Soviets' image of America as an unreconstructed enemy—yet one with so many built-in weaknesses that there was no need to conciliate it. The result of this Soviet double whammy was to place American policy in a double bind. Roosevelt had been too easy on Stalin, but Truman's tougher stance produced not a Soviet retreat but rather such episodes as the Berlin blockade and the Korean War—which in turn provoked the further militarization and what might be called the globalization of the Cold War.

This descent into cold war was, alas, no accident. Deep-seated forces on both sides, along with the geopolitical vacuum between them, made a clash all too likely. But the Cold War was also the product of mutual misperception, the nature of which is surprising. We are used to thinking that Soviet and American leaders see each other as the devil incarnate. The fact is that each saw in the other the image of himself. Roosevelt expected the Soviets to act "reasonably," which is to say the way he would have in their place. Later, Truman failed to appreciate that Soviet unreasonableness expressed itself in bluff and deception—a characteristic Russian pattern—rather than in a straightforward, nononsense American-style assault. As for Stalin, he took Roosevelt's attempts at friendship as deception or debility or both—which is what such efforts would have amounted to in the dog-eat-dog politics of the Kremlin. Later, he interpreted Truman's hard line as largely an attempt to cope with and cover up internal American troubles—another projection onto the United States of Soviet experience and tactics.

Are these features of Soviet (and American) diplomacy still with us? Will history repeat itself? Might a new cold war be even more dangerous and explosive than the one Joseph Stalin conducted? How to avoid it? The last chapter, in particular, will return to these questions.

Roots and Portents: 1917-1941

THERE WAS A STRIKING PARADOX AT THE HEART OF STALIN'S AMERICAN
policy. Stalin thought of the capitalist West (and especially of the
United States) as antagonistic, powerful, and treacherous. He also
viewed his adversaries as vulnerable, weak, and susceptible to Soviet
manipulation. This dualism contributed to both the successes and the
failures of Stalin's diplomacy. But the paradox transcends Stalin's time.
Anyone who reads the Soviet press today, or better yet talks candidly
and at some length with high Soviet officials, will find them embattled
and yet cocky. Present international circumstances seem to account for
the contradiction: That Russia's military power has been rising while
the West's, relatively speaking, declines fills Kremlin hearts with glad-
ness, while a looming anti-Soviet alignment (United States, Western
Europe, Japan, China) fills them with dread. But the pattern goes back
to the very beginning of Soviet rule, and we can understand it best if
we remind ourselves of the history of Soviet diplomacy from 1917 to
1941.

Is the West to blame for the deep-seated sense of insecurity that
animated Soviet foreign policy in its very first years and has characterized it ever since? If it were not for capitalist enmity would the early
Bolsheviks have been ready to live in peace? The problem with affirmative answers to these questions, answers which persist to this day
although more often given by Westerners trying to understand the
Soviet point of view than by the Soviets themselves, is that they ignore
the state of mind with which the Bolsheviks came to power. Lenin and
his comrades needed no instruction in what they assumed to be the
inherent antagonism between communism and capitalism. Mutual

enmity was their first premise—the most axiomatic of Soviet axioms. Lenin and company hoped for, indeed counted on, the spread of revolution to the advanced capitalist countries. They expected the capitalists to resist, if necessary by moving against the infant Soviet state. "We are living not merely in a state but *in a system of states*," declared Lenin in March 1919, "and it is inconceivable for the Soviet Republic to exist along side the imperialist states for any length of time. One or the other must triumph in the end. And before that . . . there will have to be a series of frightful collisions between the Soviet Republic and the bourgeois states."[1] If the bourgeois states had embraced the Bolshevik regime and offered to live happily ever after with it, the Soviets would have considered them incredibly short-sighted or dangerously Machiavellian.

But despite contemporary alarms, and a historiography which paints the Western powers as relentless enemies, the Bolsheviks sensed that the capitalist threat could be managed and that at times Moscow could even take the offensive. This confidence reflected both Marxist-Leninist assumptions and the experience of tsarist diplomacy, which lived on despite the revolutionary character of the new regime. But most of all, it drew on the lessons learned during the first months and years of diplomacy—lessons which suggested that the imperialists' bark was far worse than what the Bolsheviks assumed would be their bite.

The tsars' legacy included a tradition of imperial expansion, an attitude toward the outside world that blended antagonism, envy and distrust, and a style of diplomacy and negotiation that reflected that attitude. Tsarist diplomacy also projected a sense of Russia's historical mission (as champion of orthodox Christianity) and a willingness to manipulate that sense in the service of expansionist aims. Like other nineteenth-century great powers, Russia played the balance of power game: she allied first with a mixed coalition against Napoleon, later with conservative Germany and Austria-Hungary, and then at the turn of the century with France and England. None of these traditions can be directly extrapolated from the tsars to the Bolsheviks; indeed, not all of them manifested themselves uniformly during tsarist times. But in one variation or another, all of them appeared in the post-revolutionary period, contributing to Soviet diplomatic difficulties and to Moscow's techniques for handling those difficulties. Beyond all this, the Bolsheviks learned a crucial lesson from the fall of the Romanov dynasty itself—that world war, which was the upshot of all the nineteenth-century diplomatic maneuvering, can destroy the Russian regime—

hence, Soviet efforts both to avert another war by playing off one set of capitalist powers against another and to use the same tactic to expand Soviet power and influence without war.[2]

Karl Marx was an unreliable guide to the international situation (and the domestic one, too, for that matter) facing the Bolsheviks in 1917: first, because Marx had relatively little to say about international relations *per se*; and second, because much of what he did say seemed contradicted by the central international development of the pre-1917 years, the First World War. "Workers of all countries, unite!" "The proletarians have nothing to lose but their chains."[3] But when war came, most workers united with their rulers for fear of losing their national honor. Marx and Engels had also implied that whatever their sins of exploitation at home, capitalists of various countries had a stake in peace with each other. But this, too, the brutal and exhausting war belied.

Lenin explained what Marx had not. His theory of imperialism made clear why the capitalists went to war, why workers followed them, and how those socialists who had not capitulated to nationalist hysteria might yet turn the war to their advantage.[4] In Lenin's view, capitalism is driven by its very nature (by the pressure of overproduction and underconsumption at home and by its need for markets and raw materials abroad) to extend its sway over the globe. Whereas English liberals like J. A. Hobson had attacked imperialism as a *policy* that capitalists found convenient but could, if they would, do without, Lenin declared it to be an inexorable *phase* of capitalist development. Imperialism solved, or at least so it appeared, not only economic but social and political problems as well. Superprofits derived from colonial exploitation were used to bribe proletarians back home—a fact that accounted for their slowness to rise in revolution and for their quickness to go to war. But policies that staved off one crisis set the stage for others. The First World War, which Lenin portrayed as resulting from a scramble for colonies, was an "inter-imperialist" conflict. And there were other "capitalist contradictions" as well, including rulers against ruled, and colonists against the colonized. Not only did the Bolsheviks take heart from these handicaps they also exploited them. The Bolshevik Revolution itself owed its success to "turning the imperialist war against the imperialists." But what if the capitalists then turned the war against the revolution? Soviet hopes for social upheavals in Europe coexisted with fears that Germany or the Western Allies, separately or together, would strangle the revolution in its cradle. Slowly, however, the Bolsheviks learned to moderate both hopes and fears. The revolution, it turned out, would not easily spread westward, but neither would the Western powers muster the unity and the will to finish off Russian communism.

In the immediate aftermath of the Bolshevik Revolution, but with the world war still on, Germany was the key. It could turn overnight, or so the Bolsheviks hoped, into a powerful revolutionary ally. But in the meantime it was an awesome military antagonist. Some of the more romantic Bolshevik leaders wished to conduct a "revolutionary war" against Germany. Lenin and those who supported him argued for a retreat, for a "breathing space" to be used to prepare for future battles. Said Lenin, justifying the humiliating Treaty of Brest-Litovsk, which had taken Russia out of the war with Germany, "[We must] make use of the respite . . . [to] heal the very severe wounds inflicted by the war upon the entire social organism of Russia and bring about an economic revival. . . ." Only then would Soviet Russia "be able to render effective assistance to the socialist revolution in the West which has been delayed for a number of reasons."[5] Stalin made the same point in the brutally frank way that was typical of him: "If we accept the slogan of revolutionary war, we shall be playing into the hands of imperialism. . . . There is no revolutionary movement in the West, there is no evidence of a revolutionary movement. It exists only in potential, and in our practical activities we cannot rely merely on potentials."[6]

Meantime, however, the Bolsheviks explored the potential for exploiting inter-imperialist differences diplomatically. Before signing on the dotted line with Berlin, they conducted a minor flirtation with the Allies. During a crisis in the Brest-Litovsk talks, Leon Trotsky, then commissar of foreign affairs, encouraged certain unofficial Allied representatives in Russia to hope that the new Soviet regime might yet continue the fight on the Allied side. But this was a fall-back position in the event the Germans refused either to sign the peace treaty or to observe it once signed. This was not, as some Westerners thought, a great missed opportunity to reconcile East and West. Pressed by militant colleagues to explain how he could contemplate cooperation with the enemy, Lenin replied, "Please add my vote to those who are in favor of receiving food and weapons from the Anglo-French imperialist robbers."[7]

But the Treaty of Brest-Litovsk did not provide as much breathing space as Lenin had hoped for. Instead, it triggered the beginning of armed intervention in Russia by the Allies. Soviet histories have portrayed the Allied intervention as monolithic in anti-Soviet intent and devastating in its consequences. In fact, neither verdict is justified, as the early Bolshevik leaders themselves in effect admitted. In the beginning, the intervention was not primarily anti-Soviet; it was designed to revive Russian resistance during a great German offensive in the West. Later, especially after the November 1918 armistice, the intervention took on a clearly anti-Soviet hue as the foreign powers supported White forces in the savage Russian Civil War. But, in the words of George F. Kennan, Allied efforts "consisted merely of a series of confused and uncoordinated military efforts, almost negligible in scale, [and] lacking in any central plan. . . ."[8] Nor did Lenin himself entirely disagree. Looking back in late 1919 Lenin asked; "How was it possible for such a miracle to have occurred, for Soviet power to have held out for two years in a backward, ruined and war-weary country, in the face of the stubborn struggle waged against it first by German imperialism, which at the time was considered omnipotent, and then by Entente [that is, Allied] imperialism which . . . had no rivals and lorded it over all the countries on earth?" His answer: "Imperialism, which seemed an insuperable colossus, has proved before the whole world to be a colossus with feet of clay. . . ." "We were victorious," Lenin remarked on another occasion, "because we could be and were united, and because we were able to win over allies from the camp of our enemies. And our enemies, who are immeasurably stronger than we are, suffered defeat because they were not, never could be and never will be united, and because every month they fought against us brought them further disintegration within their own camp."[9]

Stalin, as usual, put the matter even more simply. His speeches of 1919 and 1920 (a time when, despite his growing political power, he was not generally considered a leader on a par with Lenin and Trotsky) depict a world "definitely and irrevocably split into two camps: the camp of imperialism and the camp of socialism." The relationship between the two was, to use a modern game-theory term, "zero-sum"; in Stalin's language, the Allies were insisting that "the earth is too small for both the Entente and Russia, that one of them must perish if peace is to be established on earth." The imperialists were, he declared, as devious as they were determined; anti-intervention articles in the British press were but a "smokescreen" designed to "cover up the foul work of actual armed intervention organized by the Entente." So were other expressions of readiness for negotiations, or of concern for the Russian people. And yet, Stalin ultimately judged Allied efforts as puny and worthy of contempt. The interventionist forces proved "unfit for the purposes of intervention; [they] sickened with an inevitable disease—demoralization." The White Russian governments that the Allies supported proved, in Stalin's words, to be "soap bubbles." The Entente directed "all of its available forces against Soviet Russia," and what did it receive for its trouble? "A series of drubbings," Stalin answered, with the result that Russia's "enemies" have "even begun to fear Russia, realizing that she is growing into a great socialist people's power which will not allow itself to be ill-used."[10]

Some of these claims might be dismissed as morale-raising or after-the-fact bravado. But the conclusions which both Lenin and Stalin had reached by 1921 may not be dismissed so readily. By that time foreign forces, with the exception of the Japanese, who remained on the Siberian mainland until the autumn of 1922 and in occupation of the northern part of Sakhalin Island until 1925, had been withdrawn, and the British had even signed a trade agreement, constituting de facto recognition, with the Bolshevik regime. Our international position, said Lenin in July 1921, "is distinguished by a certain equilibrium." Having been unable to "strangle" Soviet Russia, "international imperialism has been obliged to grant her recognition, or semi-recognition, and to conclude trade agreements with her." The first years of Soviet rule had demonstrated, declared Stalin, that "we (the workers) are *not yet* strong enough to put an end to imperialism forthwith. But the struggle has also shown that they (the bourgeoisie) are *no longer* strong enough to strangle Soviet Russia." Under these circumstances, Stalin wrote in December 1921, "the period of open war has been replaced by a period of 'peaceful' struggle."[11]

The period of " 'peaceful' struggle" that began in 1921, and lasted with up's and down's through the 1930s, was a time of great Soviet vulnerability—vulnerability rooted in domestic developments. By 1921 the strain of world war, revolution, and civil war had taken a terrible toll. Victorious over their White opponents, the Bolsheviks faced rebellion from their own worker and peasant supporters. Lenin's answer was to sound a retreat in the form of the New Economic Policy, which was a domestic shift as stunning and controversial as the Treaty of Brest-Litovsk. The trouble with the NEP was that although it defused the immediate crisis (by removing Draconian economic controls and permitting a modified free market to operate), it did so at the expense of socialism as most Bolsheviks understood the term—and at a price of reduced Communist party control over the countryside. The legitimacy and future of the NEP became the major issue in the succession struggle that broke out when Lenin took ill in 1922 and died in 1924. Stalin ultimately resolved both the argument about the NEP and the power struggle, but at a terrible cost. He launched that all-out war against the Russian peasantry known as the collectivization of agriculture, and a drastic industrialization campaign as well. He defeated the last of his major rivals for power by 1929 and physically liquidated his opponents, real and imagined, in the Great Terror of the late 1930s.

These struggles of the 1920s and 1930s reveal Stalin employing against his adversaries some of the same devices he deployed in the international arena. Dividing in order to conquer and sealing the victory with force were the hallmarks of his method. First, Stalin allied himself with Grigori Zinoviev and Lev Kamenev against his primary competitor, Leon Trotsky. Next, he teamed with Nikolai Bukharin to defeat the "Left Opposition" in which Zinoviev and Kamenev had, in desperation, joined Trotsky. Finally, with the Left defeated, Stalin adopted an extreme version of its program and used it to defeat Bukharin and the "Right Opposition." For Stalin, alliances and truces were only temporary arrangements; they were superseded when circumstances changed. And the vicious political battle of the 1920s was tame compared to the frantic collectivization of agriculture and the wild orgy of purges that followed. Of course, the very nature of international relations is such that it limits the applicability of some of Stalin's favorite techniques. He could not dispose of sovereign states quite as easily as he dispatched "enemies of the people." He had to proceed with caution. But he could and did view international politics as akin to the domestic Soviet variety—as a duel to the death in which only the strong and ruthless survive—and therefore acted accordingly.

The turmoil of the twenties and thirties offered grand opportunities for the capitalist powers. But they were not able to take advantage of the situation—as Stalin himself was the first to recognize. Why did the imperialists refrain from finishing off the "land of socialism"? Stalin provided his answer in a series of speeches and interviews; it was an answer that, in good Leninist fashion, stressed the built-in contradictions of capitalism during its imperialist stage.

One major contradiction, to be found within the imperialist camp itself, came, according to Stalin, in two varieties: contradictions between the victors and vanquished of World War I, and those among the victors themselves.[12] The first variety opened the way in the early 1920s for a stunning deal between Moscow and Berlin. With Germany isolated and the Soviets also an outcast in Western eyes, the Treaty of

Rapallo of April 1922 was a natural combination. Its basic terms—providing for diplomatic relations and certain other economic agreements—were not earth-shaking, nor did the good feeling between Moscow and Berlin last very long. But the treaty was important evidence of the Soviet ability to play off one Western power against the others and thus protect itself in a hostile environment.

Stalin's description of a world divided into two camps reflected his concern about the capitalists' potential to unite against Soviet Russia. In 1925, in the middle of a speech remarkable for its generally relaxed view of the West, Stalin warned that "the very existence of the Soviet state is a deadly menace to imperialism. That is why no successes that imperialism achieves can be durable as long as the Soviet state exists and develops." Particularly ominous was the entry upon the European scene of the United States of America, which had joined in an "Anglo-American Bloc" to achieve at least a temporary "stabilization" of the postwar capitalist crisis, complete with an "end of the period of revolutionary upsurge." Stalin listed the various advantages of the United States in words that expressed envy as well as concern. The United States was now the "centre of the financial exploitation of the world." American economic power was "growing in every respect." The dollar was "the most stable of all the currencies." The captains of U.S. industry and finance had achieved "the financial subordination of Western Europe to America."[13]

But despite these trends favorable to capitalism, or at least to the American branch of same, there remained deep fissures between the capitalist nations, particularly those stemming from continuing competition for markets and raw materials. "The problem of oil," declared a prescient Stalin in 1925, "is one of the principal problems now facing the world powers." It was in this "sphere, which is the principal nerve center of the entire economic and military activities of the world powers, that America everywhere and always encounters opposition from Britain." Beyond that there was the Anglo-French "struggle for supremacy on the European continent" and for "hegemony" in the colonies. Nor did Stalin feel the need to "dwell on the opposition of interests between America and Japan—that, too, is common knowledge."[14]

These and other inter-imperialist divisions suggested to Stalin a prime task of the Soviet and other Communist parties in the mid-twenties—"to utilize to the utmost all the contradictions in the camp of the bourgeoisie with the object of disintegrating and weakening its forces. . . ." One use involved dangling Russian markets and raw materials before the competing capitalist powers. The effect on European capitalism of Russia's "dropping out of the world capitalist system" had been devastating, Stalin contended. It was partly "in order to put a stop to this alienation of European capital from our markets and sources of raw materials, [that] it was found necessary to agree to a certain period of 'peaceful coexistence' with us. . . ."[15] The use of "economic incentives" began paying dividends as early as 1921, when Great Britain signed her trade agreement with Moscow. The pact was decidedly in the Soviet interest. The Bolsheviks urgently needed assistance to rebuild the national base of what was still assumed to be a world revolution. If part of the deal was a Soviet pledge of noninterference in the internal affairs of the British Empire, that promise was clearly tongue-in-cheek. But the British bought the package and later, after the Labour party came to power in 1923, extended full diplomatic recognition as well. Italy, France, and Japan followed suit within the year. The United States took ten more years to do likewise, but that gave Stalin ample opportunity to perfect his technique for wooing the Americans—a technique he was to apply both during and after the Second World War.

In his own way, Joseph Vissarionovich Stalin was an Americanophile. He considered the United States a determining factor in world politics at a time when Americans thought themselves, in a verdict supported to this day by many historians, isolationists. He appreciated U.S. economic power and envied American efficiency. He continued the Bolshevik tradition of considering the United States the least warlike of the imperialist powers.[16] Having seen less of the West than Lenin and other Bolshevik leaders who spent considerable time in emigration, and having never been to the United States, Stalin was avid for information, which he went out of his way to gather from visiting Americans to whom he readily, although somewhat defensively, admitted his ignorance of the United States. He was not above offering ideological eyewash to his visitors along with an endorsement of improved political and economic relations; he certainly did not emphasize for capitalist guests the temporary nature of "peaceful coexistence" that he stressed to Communist audiences. But he was rarely if ever challenged by his credulous Western interlocutors, some of whom were convinced that socialism and capitalism were about to converge in one common political-economic system.

Meeting with a sympathetic American labor delegation in September 1927, Stalin endorsed one thing in which he quite sincerely believed, namely, the value of U.S.–Soviet commerce, and another in which he almost certainly did not: "an agreement on disarmament, even including the complete abolition of standing armies." More striking was the series of questions with which he peppered his guests. How did they account for the small percentage of American workers organized in trade unions? "I merely wanted to clear up for myself," he said, "the difference between the situation in America and that in the USSR." Was there state insurance for workers in America? How about unemployment insurance? How to explain the absence of a workers' party in the United States, when (liberals like Franklin Roosevelt who later sought to win Stalin's trust should have noted this well) "the bourgeoisie in America have two parties, the Republican party and the Democratic party. . . ." Why did American labor leaders strongly resist formation of an independent workers' party? "I cannot understand this at all," Stalin remarked. But such lack of understanding paled before his guests' unsuccessful attempt to explain the workings of the American electoral college system. That really flummoxed the Soviet leader, but fearlessly he pressed on. How to explain the fact that even "a reactionary [sic!] like the late President Woodrow Wilson" had once sent a "greeting" to the Congress of Soviets in March 1918? Could it be regarded as "normal that the leaders of the American Federation of Labor want to be more reactionary than . . . Wilson?" Answered one of the American visitors: "I cannot give an exact explanation." Nor, apparently, could Stalin, but that did not prevent him from hewing to his inexact Marxist-Leninist sense of the "real," which was to say, sinister, meaning of American foreign policy.[17]

Early in 1929, Stalin welcomed to the Kremlin Thomas W. Campbell, a Montana wheat tycoon who was gathering material for a book entitled *Russia: Market or Menace?* Judging by his conversation with Stalin, which the Soviets were to publish three years later in order to correct "fictitious statements" in Campbell's book, Mr. Campbell could not yet answer his own question. He accused the Soviet government of "trying to sow discontent" in the United States. But he also "particularly liked the projects for the development of Soviet agriculture," and he went on to say that "if we could have official recognition everybody would be anxious to get here to do business. . . ." The potential for U.S.–Soviet trade, Stalin agreed, was "unlimited." The Soviets would "like scientific and technical people in America to be our teachers in the sphere of technique and we their pupils." Stalin asked Campbell for advice on how to make contact with American industry but at the same time, needled his visitor. Beware of British competitors, he warned, who, under the cover of an anti-Soviet campaign designed to frighten away the Americans, were plotting to monopolize the lucrative Soviet trade. Stalin informed Campbell, in strictest confidence, about a big loan being offered by a group of British bankers. "May I tell Hoover about this?" asked Campbell, referring to the recently elected American president with whom he had met before leaving the States. "Of course," agreed the genial dictator, "but don't give it to the press." As for that alleged sowing of American discontent by Soviet agents, Stalin insisted he could not "answer for the actions of persons not known and not subordinate to us" (such as the members of the American Communist party), but he could and would "give maximum guarantees . . . as regards interference by persons employed in our institutions abroad." This was a distinction that would not make much difference since the Soviets had plenty of unofficial access to American opinion, but Mr. Campbell was excited nonetheless. "May I tell that to Mr. Hoover?" asked Mr. Campbell. "Of course," answered Mr. Stalin.[18]

Mr. Hoover remained unimpressed. Mr. Stalin grew more eager. A December 1931 interview with German author Emil Ludwig found Stalin waxing rhapsodic on "the efficiency Americans display in everything—in industry, technology, in literature and in life," on the fact that so many Americans "are mentally and physically healthy," are "healthy in their whole approach to work, to the job at hand," on the "element of democracy" and the "sound and comparatively simple habits in American productive life," especially when compared to Europe, where the "haughty spirit of the feudal aristocracy is still alive." But not as rhapsodic as some Americans waxed about the USSR. Col. Raymond Robins had been one of those unofficial Western representatives who, in early 1918, had taken seriously Lenin's pre–Brest/Litovsk flirtation with the Western powers. Meeting with Stalin in May 1933, Robins stressed, "I am not a Communist and do not understand very much about communism," but he lavished such praise on Soviet progress that it was left to Stalin to note certain "difficulties" that had arisen in the course of collectivization—difficulties that Robins dismissed by remarking, "every advance involves certain outlays, and this we take into account and include in our calculations." Bidding his host goodbye, Robins expressed his conviction that "there is nothing greater and more magnificent than to participate in the making of a new world. . . . Participation in the creation and building of a new world is something of paramount significance not only now, but thousands of years hence." "All the same," replied a "smiling" Stalin, "this matter presents great difficulties."[19]

What did Stalin make of non-Communists like Robins? Did he not find their extravagant praise as unnerving as it was useful—considering that the capitalists had their own self-interested reasons for improving relations with Moscow? All this apparent credulity in the face of Soviet claims could not be entirely on the level. It must indicate either innocence, which one might exploit, or some dangerous design. Nor were such reflections provoked only by unofficial visitors. They must have been prompted by Franklin Roosevelt himself, who moved quickly in 1933 to recognize the USSR partly in return for a solemn, but largely empty, Soviet pledge "to respect scrupulously the indisputable right of the United States to order its own life within its own jurisdiction in its own way and to refrain from interfering in any manner in the internal affairs of the United States, its territories and possessions." In a December 1933 interview with *New York Times* correspondent Walter Duranty, Stalin praised Roosevelt as a "determined and courageous politician." To H. G. Wells, visiting the Kremlin in July 1934, Stalin hailed Roosevelt's "initiative, courage and decisiveness." But for all that, FDR remained in Stalin's eyes a "captain of the modern bourgeois world." When Wells suggested that Roosevelt's New Deal was edging the United States toward a convergence with Soviet-style socialism, Stalin replied that Roosevelt could not undermine the bases of American capitalism even if he wanted to—the economy remaining in private rather than state hands—and that in fact it was doubtful FDR had any such intention. Not only did Wells fail to understand the nature of capitalism, Stalin suggested, he failed to appreciate the nature of human beings. "You, Mr. Wells, apparently assume that all people are good. But I don't forget that many are evil. I do not believe in the goodness of the bourgeoisie." In answer to newspaper executive Roy Howard's question about the basic cause of the threat of war in 1936 Stalin said: "Capitalism, which, in its imperialist phase, . . . considers war to be a legitimate method of resolving international contradictions."[20]

According to Stalin, two other sorts of capitalist contradictions posed dangers to the USSR in the twenties and thirties. Paradoxically they also offered possibilities for the USSR to ward off threats from non-Communist nations. One involved tensions between imperialists and what we nowadays call the Third World. Gains by "national liberation forces" were a double-edged sword. They provoked heightened capitalist hostility toward a Soviet Union perceived as the source of colonial unrest. Yet they also distracted Western attention that otherwise might have been devoted to making life miserable for the Soviets. Moscow's role in China in the mid-1920s, which involved encouraging an anti-imperialist alliance of Communists and Nationalists, can be understood in these terms. It directly reflected the political battle between Stalin and Trotsky, who disagreed about China as well as so much else. But it was also designed to undermine a weak link in the imperialist chain.

Yet another contradiction, indeed the most important of them all, was that between capitalists and workers of the advanced Western countries. Stalin was not the type to get carried away by prospects for revolution in the West; indeed, he eventually developed a positive aversion to the idea of Communists whom he could not control coming to power in other countries. But using foreign Communists and others sympathetic to the USSR to advance Soviet interests was another matter entirely. Speaking in June 1924, Stalin credited Soviet diplomatic success in "isolating the [British and French] isolators" to the "growing resentment which the policy of bellicose imperialism is evoking among the people." The Western masses did not want war "for they have not forgotten the sacrifices they had to make for the sake of the capitalists' profits." The imperialists knew, Stalin added in late 1927, that war against the USSR could "unleash revolutions in their own countries." The fact that "the revolutionary part of the proletariat of Europe, having adopted our state, and regarding it as its child, is ready to defend it and fight for it if need be" was, said Stalin, "the fundamental antidote to imperialism and its interventionist machinations." The Soviet "peace policy," as Stalin called it in 1924, that is, the strategy of portraying the USSR as "the only country in the world which is capable of pursuing, and actually is pursuing, a policy of peace—pursuing this policy not hypocritically, but honestly and openly, resolutely and consistently," was designed with "broad masses in capitalist countries" in mind.[21]

But so, paradoxically, was what might be called the Soviet "war scare policy," that is, the policy of deliberately exaggerating the danger of war. Suddenly, in July 1927, only a year and a half after he had proclaimed "a whole period of respite" including "a sort of 'collaboration'" with the capitalist world, Stalin descried "the threat of a new imperialist war. It is not a matter of some vague and immaterial 'danger' of a new war, but of the real and actual *threat* of a new war in general, and of a war against the USSR in particular." The puzzling thing about Stalin's apparent alarm is that, as Adam Ulam suggests, "the world in

1927 appeared more peaceful than at any time since 1918"; moreover, Stalin must have thought so too since he soon launched his country on an internal upheaval which he never would have begun had he believed war to be imminent. True, British-Soviet relations had deteriorated to the point that the British government actually severed diplomatic ties in May 1927, having previously raided the premises of the Soviet Trade Delegation and the Soviet trading company ARCOS. But that hardly seems sufficient to account for Stalin's warning. A more likely explanation is that Stalin was seeking to discredit his Bolshevik opposition (by charging them with disloyalty at a moment of great national crisis) and was getting ready to justify the sacrifices he would soon be demanding from the Soviet people. But the fact that Stalin was to repeat this tactic again in the 1940s suggests another, international dimension. By warning of an imperialist attack on the Soviet Union, Stalin stoked the Western antiwar fires, which he counted on to restrain anti-Soviet statesmen. It was not that he expected war tomorrow or the next day. He was rather using a plausible occasion to stage a fire drill, "to sound the alarm," as he himself put it, "in all the countries of Europe over the threat of a new war, to rouse the vigilance of the workers and soldiers of the capitalist countries, and to work, to work indefatigably, to prepare the masses to counter with the full strength of revolutionary struggle every attempt of the bourgeois governments to organize a new war."[22]

Relying on, indeed playing on, these and other capitalist contradictions, the young Soviet state successfully navigated into the 1930s. According to Stalin, the temporary stabilization of capitalism gave way, in the late 1920s, to an intensification of capitalism's general crisis, and by the same token, "the period of 'peaceful coexistence' " (note well how Stalin places the term in quotes) began "receding into the past." Setbacks in Europe and China (where in 1927 the Nationalists turned against and just about destroyed the Communists, whom Stalin had been urging into a united front with Chiang Kai-shek) combined with the beginning of collectivization to produce a kind of Soviet isolationism, accompanied by Western Communist attempts to distract attention from Soviet turmoil by destabilizing the capitalist status quo. Addressing the party Central Committee in June 1930, Stalin gloated over the onset of the Great Depression, while warning that the imperialists might submerge their contradictions in a united campaign against the Soviets. So throughout this turbulent period Moscow kept its peace policy in play. Western fears that in the event of war the workers would "attack the capitalists in the rear" meant, said Stalin, that the imperialists would continue to be susceptible to the lure of "peace and increasing trade connections with all countries."[23]

Toward the end of the 1920s another ominous cloud had appeared on the Soviet horizon: the Nazi movement in Germany. But, again, the Russians managed to see a silver lining. The threat in Hitler's openly expressed anti-Communism was obvious. But for a variety of reasons—personal and ideological as well as political and diplomatic—Stalin encouraged tactical alliances between German Communists and Fascists in the years before the Nazis took over, and then, once Hitler was in power, hesitated to reverse course and oppose him.[24] The pattern was to be repeated both in 1941, when Stalin could not bring himself to admit that the Molotov-Ribbentrop Pact was dead and that a Nazi invasion loomed, and in 1947, when he only reluctantly acknowledged that his scheme for continued détente with the United States was no longer viable.

By 1934 Stalin was ready to oppose Hitler, in partnership if possible with the Western democracies. But since in Soviet minds Nazi Germany and the democracies were all capitalist states, the Soviet search for collective security was but a variation on the old theme of divide and survive (if not yet conquer) by exploiting inter-imperialist contradictions. And so, for that matter, was Moscow's about-face in 1939 in the form of the Molotov-Ribbentrop Pact. "In our times," Stalin warned the 17th Party Congress in January 1934, "it is not the custom to take any account of the weak—only the strong are taken into account."[25] A united front with the democracies was one way to accumulate strength. But so was an arrangement with Hitler. Some historians blame the Western powers for the 1939 pact, arguing that the West's failure to stop Hitler left Stalin no alternative. Others have Stalin contemplating his unholy alliance long before 1939. Both versions are too simple. In all probability, as Ulam has argued, the highest Soviet priority was to avoid war. At worst, war would pit Germany and the Western powers against the USSR, but a conflict which matched Russia and the West against Hitler would still be a war and, therefore, undesirable given Soviet weakness. Moscow's best bet, toward which its diplomacy was directed between 1934 and 1939, was to cooperate with Britain and France in order to deter Germany. As hope for that dimmed, Stalin began to explore his other option—a pact with Hitler which would leave Russia on the sidelines while Germany battled the West.[26]

The dualistic Soviet view of the West underwent an ironic reversal in the 1930s. In the face of fascist danger, the formerly unnerving strengths of the Western democracies offered comfort to Moscow while their weaknesses were a source of Soviet dismay. The Russians at first overrated the power of the British and their willingness to use it. Foreign Commissar Maxim Litvinov assured American Ambassador William C. Bullit in 1935 that the British had "decided to eliminate Mussolini." He believed Britain would "blockade the Suez Canal if and when necessary," and that as soon as the British had "finished" Mussolini they would "finish Hitler." Soviet confidence reflected not only faulty intelligence on Western military strength, but also Stalin's continuing respect for capitalist political and economic power. As late as March 1939, he announced that "Peaceful, democratic states, taken together, are without doubt stronger than the fascist states both militarily and economically." On the night of August 23, 1939, as Stalin closed his deal with German Foreign Minister Ribbentrop, he expressed an opinion of the British that differed significantly but not entirely from his previous assessment. The British army was "weak," the German minutes report Stalin as saying. The British navy no longer deserved its previous reputation. England's airforce was improving, but lacked pilots. If England dominated the world in spite of this, this was due to "the stupidity of the other countries that always let themselves be bluffed." It was "ridiculous" that a few hundred British should control India. Nevertheless, Stalin said that England, despite its weakness, would "wage war craftily and stubbornly."[27]

Soviet doubts about Western intentions and capabilities grew as the decade advanced. Soviet histories depict Western statesmen as trying to turn Hitler against Russia. Some were. But there were also other considerations that led some Westerners to advocate appeasement: the hope to avoid war, a genuine sense that Germany's case against the Versailles Treaty was legitimate, divisions in Western public opinion, doubt fostered by the Soviet purges that the USSR could be a strong and stable (let alone an admirable) partner. To the extent the Soviets appreciated these factors, and it is unlikely that they did so with quite the sympathy of liberal historians, they must have grouped them together under the category of weakness and irresolution.

Moscow continued negotiating with Britain and France until the very last minute in August 1939, that is, until it was certain the Hitler deal would go through. That it did go through owed much to the fact that Germany possessed (but the West did not) certain key prerequisites for dealing with the Soviets: a powerful negative incentive (the credible threat to attack the USSR); an irresistible positive inducement (the division of Eastern Europe into Soviet and German spheres of influence); and the ability to move quickly and decisively to embrace yesterday's mortal enemy. As for the Soviets, their tactics for coping with the Germans were also prototypical. Given that the Germans made Stalin an offer he couldn't refuse, it is not surprising that he didn't. What is surprising is the way he negotiated the deal and the way he acted afterwards—boldly pushing while at the same time placating his awesome ally.

Moscow began to test the waters in earnest in the spring of 1939. Soviet representatives in Germany suddenly became effusively friendly, a sure sign (as it still is in the 1980s) that the Kremlin was worried enough to contemplate making concessions. The Soviet ambassador expressed Moscow's hope to live with Berlin "on a normal footing. And from normal, the relations might become better and better."[28] The Kremlin read the German press as signaling Hitler's attitude and took heart from its reciprocal moderation. This deduction made sense in the case of a government-controlled press, whereas the same technique, later applied to the Western press, led the Soviets seriously astray. Moscow proceeded cautiously even after Berlin indicated eagerness to move quickly toward a deal. The Nazis tried to ingratiate themselves with the Soviets (as the latter would with the Americans later on) by minimizing ideological differences and implying that a kind of convergence between the two systems was taking place. But despite their own vulnerability and the Germans' eagerness to parley, or rather because of these conditions, the Soviets moved slowly. Hitler, with his invasion of Poland scheduled for September 1, was in a hurry. Stalin, seemingly, was not. In August, when Berlin wanted to send Ribbentrop to Moscow immediately, Soviet Foreign Commissar Vyacheslav Molotov (whose replacement of Litvinov—a Jew—on May 3 had signalled Stalin's interest in exploring a German connection) stalled. Stalin let Nazi anxiety build and then suddenly, with the Germans about to tear out their hair in frustration, he authorized the Ribbentrop trip and shortly thereafter the pact itself.

The Treaty of Nonaggression between Germany and the Union of Soviet Socialist Republics, with its public clauses and its Secret Additional Protocol establishing spheres of influence in East Europe, was signed in Moscow on August 23, 1939.[29] Having supped with the devil (and thereby antagonized his Western enemies), the Soviets had every reason to appease him, especially when Hitler showed his strength by crushing Poland almost overnight. According to historians this is precisely what Stalin did. Vojtech Mastny describes Stalin's "frantic effort to secure [German] good will," citing Khrushchev's comment that Stalin "literally groveled before Hitler." In Ulam's account, "Stalin now went about removing every possible point of future friction with his terrible ally."[30] But the documentary record suggests otherwise. The Soviets were surprisingly stubborn in their dealings with Berlin between August 1939 and June 1941. They bent and broke agreements and gave empty excuses when the Nazis called them to account. It may be, as Ulam suggests, that some of this orneriness was designed to convey an image of strength and confidence lest the Germans be tempted to attack. But the fact that Stalin was not prepared for the attack that eventually did come on June 22, 1941, suggests that as formidable as the Germans were, Stalin still thought he could con them.

What made Stalin think Hitler would play along? Who knows? Perhaps the Soviet dictator projected his own caution onto his more erratic German colleague. Perhaps, having settled with Hitler and thereby established a personal stake in good relations, Stalin could not admit to himself or to others that things might turn sour. In any event, the dualistic pattern of insecurity-blended-with-confidence, which had characterized the Soviet approach to the West, reemerged in Stalin's two-year dalliance with Hitler.

At the very beginning, on September 18, 1939, Stalin revealed his suspicions about Nazi trustworthiness to the German ambassador. He said ("somewhat suddenly," according to German minutes of the conversation) that "on the Soviet side there were certain doubts as to whether the German high command at the appropriate time would stand by the Moscow agreement and would withdraw to the line [in Poland] which had been agreed upon." But it was not long before the Soviets themselves began stretching the agreement and exploiting the new relationship. There were, the Germans complained, "repeated wrangles" on the boundary between German- and Soviet-occupied Poland. Taking advantage of their allied status, "the Russian delegation in Berlin," in the words of a German Foreign Office memo, "expected too much in the way of inspection and procurement of German materials of war." The Führer himself laid down the law as to what sorts of equipment might be shown or sold to the Soviets, but a month later it was reported that the Russian schedule of requests for deliveries of German products was growing "more and more voluminous and unreasonable." The negotiations with the Russians would "necessarily, therefore, become more and more difficult." Soviet moves to crush the Baltic states' independence and incorporate them into the USSR— moves that were not barred by the protocol but not envisioned by it either—surprised the Germans. So did Moscow's attempt to grab Rumanian Bessarabia, in which the Soviets had previously indicated only an "interest" (as it was labeled in the secret protocol). Berlin had expressed its "complete political disinterestedness" in all Southeastern Europe but had not meant by this to license Soviet seizure of Bessarabia or Bukovina—another Rumanian region not mentioned at all in the agreement of August 23, 1939, but coveted by Stalin. Far from petitioning politely for a change in agreed-upon spheres, the Soviets greedily demanded one. Molotov told the German ambassador on June 26, 1940, that the Bessarabian question was "particularly urgent and could brook no further delay." In a preview of tactics to be used on the Americans and British—tactics that the Germans themselves had deployed against the West—Molotov said that Bukovina "is the last missing part of a unified Ukraine" and that for this reason the Soviet government "must attach importance to solving this question simultaneously with the Bessarabian question."[31]

When Berlin objected, Stalin kindly reduced his demand (to Bessarabia plus only Northern Bukovina) and then, having issued an ultimatum to Rumania, occupied the disputed areas. The Germans acquiesced, but in August 1940, the Axis Powers guaranteed the continued existence of the rest of Rumania. In the meantime, Hitler told his generals of his desire to settle accounts with the Soviets by force the next spring. Under the façade of continued cooperation, German-Soviet tensions grew to the point where Molotov was invited to Berlin in November 1940 to talk things through. Hitler and Ribbentrop recommended to him that the Kremlin try to satisfy its expansionist ambitions in the vicinity of the Indian Ocean; in the meantime, presumably, the Germans would mop up in Eastern Europe, thus positioning themselves to attack the USSR when the opportunity arose. Needless to say, Molotov was not enthusiastic, although he later did suggest a formulation for a Nazi-proposed treaty between the USSR and the Axis; it provided (Afghans, Iranians, and others seeking to understand the roots of Soviet policy in the eighties take note!) that "the area . . . in the general direction of the Persian Gulf is recognized as the center of the aspirations of the Soviet Union." But the surprising thing is how stubbornly Molotov stated his case. When Ribbentrop, trying to get the Soviets to join the Tripartite Pact with Italy and Japan, raised the subject of a vaguely defined "Great East Asian Sphere," Molotov objected that "precision" was necessary in a "delimitation of spheres of influence over a rather long period of time." The Soviet foreign commissar insisted on discussing East Europe instead of the Indian Ocean. He complained to the Führer that Berlin had not responded to the Soviets' renewed request for Southern Bukovina; by guaranteeing the rest of Rumania, he said, Germany had "completely disregarded Russia's wishes." That guarantee was "aimed against the interests of Soviet Russia, if one might express oneself so bluntly." But that did not prevent Molotov from seeking German approval of a Russian guarantee to Bulgaria, something to which Hitler was not about to agree. Molotov departed Berlin having promised to consider the draft treaty dividing most of the globe into Axis and Soviet spheres of influence. But a week later, when Moscow conveyed its acceptance, it was only with conditions that Hitler had rejected during the Berlin discussions. [32]

In the following months, the German stance stiffened palpably. Hitler stalled on Molotov's requests. Instead of turning over Bulgaria to Soviet protection, the Nazis moved to occupy it themselves. When the Russians announced their intention to sign a treaty of friendship and nonaggression with Yugoslavia, Berlin occupied Yugoslavia as well. The Soviets got the message. By this time (April 1941) they were obviously nervous. A tell-tale sign was that Moscow began manifesting particularly thoughtful concern for the well-being of the Axis and its representatives. The German Foreign Office reported on April 5 that "after an initial lag, Russian deliveries at the moment are quite considerable, and the Commercial Agreement . . . is being observed on the Russian side." On April 13, Stalin and Molotov unexpectedly appeared at the railroad station to bid farewell to the visiting Japanese Foreign Minister Matsuoka in what German Ambassador Schulenberg characterized as a "remarkably friendly manner." Count Schulenberg continued, "Then Stalin publicly asked for me, and when he found me he came up to me and threw his arms around my shoulders: 'We must remain friends and you must now do everything to that end!' Somewhat later Stalin turned to the German acting military attaché, Colonel Krebs, first made sure that he was German, and then said to him, 'We will remain friends with you—in any event.' "[33]

Stalin's feeble efforts to reassure the Germans, and probably himself as well, continued at the May Day Parade when he had the Soviet ambassador to Berlin, Vladimir Dekanozov, stand next to him on the reviewing stand. Soviet officials conducted further economic discus-

sions in what a German report called "a notably constructive spirit"—
even though the Russians had shown "no extreme willingness to give
way which might have been construed as weakness."[34] Translation: The
Soviets were worried but not panicky. They knew the Soviet-German
connection was in trouble, but did not expect a German attack. Stalin
still thought, and apparently did so up to the very moment of the Nazi
invasion, that he could handle Hitler. Just as he thought, during both
world war and cold war, he could handle Roosevelt and Truman.

3

The Origins of Entente: June 1941-June 1944

WHEN GERMANY INVADED THE USSR ON JUNE 22, 1941, SOVIET RELA-tions with Great Britain and the United States were in a rather parlous state. The Molotov-Ribbentrop Pact had paved Hitler's way into Poland. Moscow had carved up Eastern Europe in cahoots with Berlin and had cheered the Nazis on as they blitzed the continent and bombarded England. Communist parties around the world opposed the Western war effort, further kindling resentment against their Soviet sponsors. If Stalin or Roosevelt had been told in early 1941 that the great question four years hence would be how to preserve the entente between them, and that the historical issue a generation after that would be why that entente fell apart, they would have been astonished: How could such an alliance begin, let alone endure?

And yet, by June 1944, Stalin was not only hopeful that Anglo-American-Soviet entente would endure, he was planning to use it to achieve far-reaching Soviet goals at his allies' expense. His maximum goals at the beginning of the war were now his minimum aims. What accounts for this startling turnabout? How did it happen? The course of the war itself was crucial. In 1941, Soviet armies were reeling before the Nazi onslaught. In June 1944, eventual victory over the Germans seemed assured. Soviet troops would end up occupying much of Eastern Europe. Western Europe, too would be open to increased Soviet influence if not hegemony.

But there were other sources of Stalin's optimism, and one was his view of the West—in particular, the United States. It is conventional revisionist wisdom that Stalin's suspicions about his allies increased as the result of Western actions, for example, the long delay in the promised second front. True enough: Stalin's trust certainly did not grow with the second front's delay. But Stalin had little faith to lose since he began by thinking the worst of his imperialist allies. And if his suspicions did deepen during the war, so did his confidence that he could joust with the West. In June 1941 he feared the British and Americans would not come to his aid against Hitler, or that if they did they would drive the cruelest of bargains. By 1944 he had received extensive aid and support without obvious strings attached. Stalin assumed Western largesse had an ulterior motive (which it did), but it was invaluable while it lasted. The meaning of Western actions, in other words, was in the eye of a Soviet beholder. To a Marxist-Leninist-Stalinist, capitalists were dangerous by definition. To one accustomed to Kremlin politics, apparent generosity meant either deviousness or infirmity or both.

On the morrow of the Nazi invasion, Stalin apparently went into a dark decline. He is said by Nikita Khrushchev to have cried that "All Lenin created we have lost forever." According to the Soviet ambassador in London, Ivan Maisky, Stalin "locked himself in his office, saw no one, and took no part in deciding matters of state." Some of this testimony is probably hyperbole reflecting the enthusiasm of a later, all too brief period of de-Stalinization. Khrushchev was in Kiev, and Maisky in London on June 22, 1941. Those who were on the scene confirm only that, in Marshal Georgi Zhukov's words, Stalin was "somewhat depressed," or that, according to another Soviet general, the supreme leader was "depressed, nervous, and of uneven disposition." But there is no denying Stalin's defensive tone when he finally addressed the nation via radio broadcast on July 3; he himself felt compelled to ask aloud: "How could it happen that the Soviet government went so far as to conclude a non-aggression pact with such perfidious monsters as Hitler and Ribbentrop?"[1]

Hitler, whom Stalin had trusted not to attack him, at least not so soon, had betrayed him. Knowing how the Soviet Union had reacted during the West's desperate hours, Stalin apparently expected to receive his own medicine in return. Not that he admitted it. For the most part, the Soviets acted as if all the aid the West could muster, and more, was their due. But, especially in the beginning, Moscow's underlying unease was apparent. Shortly before June 22, British Foreign Secretary Anthony Eden had indicated Britain would be prepared to aid the USSR in the event of Nazi attack. But when the attack came, Ambassador Maisky nervously plied Eden with questions: Could a guarantee be given that Britain would fulfill its pledge? Could he be assured that the British war effort would not slacken? "Behind this Russian interrogation," suggests Eden in his memoirs, "was the fear that we would stand inactively watching their life-and-death struggle, as they had watched ours. It was almost as much for this reason as because they needed help, that the next six months were filled with Soviet requests, even demands, for a second front, for enormous quantities of material aid, for British troops to fight in Russia and for a political treaty."[2]

On June 30 Maisky asked Eden whether Anglo-Soviet cooperation was to be military only, or military and economic—this although Eden and Churchill had made clear on the radio and in the House of Commons that all possible military and economic help would be given. Soviet Ambassador to the United States Konstantine Umansky began an interview with Acting Secretary of State Sumner Welles on June 26 by asking, "if I [Welles] would announce to him what the policy of my Government might be in the war which had broken out between Germany and Russia." When Welles pointed to a State Department announcement of June 24 freeing Soviet funds previously frozen in the United States, Umansky confided that the license was far less restrictive than he had feared. The ambassador, who had a well-earned reputation as even more cold and inflexible than his job presumably required him to be, apologized for his stubbornness during the past year. But Umansky did not press specific requests for aid in this first interview. Molotov explained why to American Ambassador Lawrence Steinhardt on June 29, saying there had been some "doubt" in his mind as to the extent of the aid that could be expected. Such doubt was apparently on the wane when Umansky presented "the immediate requirements of the Soviet government" on June 30. But there was still the question of credits. Toward the end of an interview with Welles "the ambassador then hesitated and said that he had forgotten a very important part of the conversation which he had been instructed to have with me and that was the method of financing the order which the Soviet Government desired to place here. He stated that he had been instructed to ask whether this Government would be willing to give favorable consideration to the granting to the Soviet Union of a five-year credit. . . ."[3]

Umansky's explanation does not ring true. A veteran Soviet diplomat does not forget a key point of his instructions. Was the reason, perhaps, that Umansky could not bring himself to beg for aid from a government he and his bosses had been castigating for years? How painful to be turned down flat! But such was not to be the case. In which event, Umansky's response was to express "for the first time in my [Welles's] long association with the ambassador . . . complete satisfaction with everything that was being done." He later lapsed back into a more familiar pattern—complaining vehemently about delays in aid; pressing Washington to share military secrets; heaping abuse on former Baltic diplomatic and consular officials in the United States ("He said they were Nazis, pro-German, dishonest, hypocritical, slimy, and so forth"); and even adding to the brew a dash or two of the goodwill that Washington fervently hoped would be a fruit of American assistance to the Soviet war effort.[4]

Soviet fears were not entirely unfounded. It occurred to some, including Senator Harry S. Truman, that the West could do worse than follow Stalin's example by standing aside, or even fanning the flames, while its two totalitarian enemies killed each other off. But as was often to happen, both during the war and after, the Western powers proved less ruthless than Stalin imagined they would be. Winston Churchill yielded to no one in his anticommunism. But Britain was on its knees on June 22, 1941, and its very existence depended on successful Soviet resistance. Churchill would "unsay no word" he had spoken in opposition to communism over the course of twenty-five years. "But all this fades away before the spectacle which is now unfolding," he told the nation on radio. "Any man or state who fights on against Nazidom will have our aid. Any man or state who marches with Hitler is our foe. . . . That is our policy and that is our declaration. It follows, therefore, that we shall give whatever help we can to Russia and the Russian people. We shall appeal to all our friends and allies in every part of the world to take the same course and pursue it, as we shall faithfully and steadfastly to the end. . . ."[5]

Nor was Churchill's friend in Washington enamored of the Soviets. Nonetheless, despite the fact that the United States was not yet at war with Germany, and in the face of political opposition and bureaucratic foot-dragging, President Roosevelt moved to aid the Soviet cause. Military shipments promised to Moscow in the summer and early fall encountered considerable delays, until the president proclaimed in November that "the defense of the Union of Soviet Socialist Republics is vital to the defense of the United States," thus rendering the USSR eligible for lend-lease aid. FDR refused to attach political conditions to American aid. To give the Soviets whatever the United States could spare (and more)—to "give and give and give," as W. Averell Harriman, FDR's special emissary and future ambassador to Moscow, put it in September 1941, "with no thought of a *quid pro quo*"—was how to convince Stalin of American sincerity and thereby obtain the close collaboration that would win the war and safeguard the peace.[6]

Roosevelt's approach flew in the face of recommendations (about which more momentarily) prepared by the State Department before the Nazi attack. Nor was this atypical. For the most part, FDR cut the State Department's Soviet specialists out of the wartime foreign policy action. He and his advisers thought the diplomats' anti-Soviet animus colored their judgments. Moscow embassy officers predicted the Red Army would crumble within weeks after the Nazi attack, whereas Joseph Davies, an informal presidential adviser, foresaw that the Soviets would prevail. The irony was that the embassy was wrong for the right reasons (the Red Army *was* in a state of disarray; the mass of Soviet peasant-soldiers *were* beaten down and woebegone; but still they would defend Mother Russia). Whereas Davies, a lawyer and Democratic politician who had managed to misinterpret the Great Purge trials as legitimate and on the level while serving as American ambassador in Moscow in 1937–1938, was right for the wrong reasons. In 1943, when Davies visited the State Department to be briefed before undertaking a special presidential mission to Moscow, he admitted that it was because of his "lucky predictions" regarding the Soviet Union and particularly the prowess of the Red Army that he had gained the reputation of being "an expert on the Soviet Union."[7]

Roosevelt's aversion to State Department "cookie pushers" has been sustained by post-revisionist historian Daniel Yergin, who indicts the department's "Riga axioms" as contributing to the Cold War. (Riga was the home base of Foreign Service Soviet watchers before Washington recognized the USSR in 1933.) The Riga view of the Soviet Union as inexorably expansionist, as committed to and capable of fomenting world revolution, did indeed become the heart of Cold War orthodoxy in the late 1940s and 1950s.[8] But leading "Riga-ites" like George F. Kennan and Charles Bohlen contested that orthodoxy on the basis of other axioms, such as that the Soviets are as realistic as they are nasty, and as ready to do business with an enemy who sees through them as they are to take advantage of one who misunderstands them.

These latter premises underlay a summary of do's and don't's for dealing with Moscow that Secretary of State Cordell Hull cabled to London for the edification of the English about ten days before German troops crossed the Soviet border. No man was to prove himself more in need of this wisdom and less receptive to it in the years to come than Hull himself. "We have adopted," he wrote, "the following policies:

· to reject any Soviet suggestions that we make concessions for the sake of "improving the atmosphere of Soviet-American relations" and exact a strict *quid pro quo* for anything which we are willing to give the Soviet Union.
· to make no sacrifices in principle in order to improve relations.
· in general, to give the Soviet government to understand that we consider an improvement in relations to be just as important to the Soviet Union as to the United States, if not more important to the Soviet Union.
· to base our day-to-day relations so far as practicable on the principle of reciprocity."[9]

These maxims, strikingly reminiscent of those championed by Henry Kissinger (especially when out of office and in opposition), reflected not just the strained mood of the moment, but years of diplomatic experience with matters large and small. (The value of hardnosed, *quid pro quo* bargaining, for instance, was demonstrated in an exchange, reminiscent of a 1979 spies-for-dissidents deal, of American-born Soviet citizens imprisoned in Russia for Soviet agents convicted in New Jersey. During this particular transaction, the Soviets showed themselves to be utterly nonideological horsetraders. Propaganda went out the window as they sat down to dicker. When an American court—drat that Constitutional separation of powers!—freed one set of Soviet spies before American negotiators could obtain suitable compensation from Moscow, Soviet negotiators immediately reduced the number of Americans they were willing to free. When the Americans nabbed another batch of agents—a brilliant move if linked to the Moscow bargaining, but doubtless it was a coincidence—the Soviets put the additional would-be emigrés back on the bargaining table. When Ambassador Steinhardt asked Assistant People's Commissar for Foreign Affairs Solomon Lozovsky whether he preferred "a limited trade" or to "clean the slate," the latter answered that "in principle" he preferred the latter course. But when the ledger was totalled up, Lozovsky objected, "That would be six for one" and tried to add three previously unmentioned Soviets in trouble with U.S. authorities to the slate.)[10]

Steinhardt, a lawyer-turned-diplomat, but not himself a Soviet specialist, set down his Soviet primer for the secretary of state on June 17, 1941. Some of Steinhardt's observations are arrogant and overstated, and the bitterness that is an occupational hazard for American diplomats stationed in Moscow is painfully evident. Six days later, with the Red Army staggering from Hitler's assault, Steinhardt's potshots would seem especially ungenerous, and in the era of détente they seem to confirm the charge that the Riga axioms led to cold war. But there is real insight, too, in Steinhardt's summary, especially into the Soviet tendency to see both deviousness and weakness in a policy of goodwill:

My observation of the psychology of the individuals who are conducting Soviet foreign policy has long since convinced me that they do not and cannot be induced to respond to the customary amenities, that it is not possible to create 'international goodwill' with them, . . . and that they are not affected by ethical or moral considerations, nor guided by the relationships which are customary between individuals of culture and breeding. Their psychology recognizes only firmness, power and force, and reflects primitive instincts and reactions entirely devoid of the restraints of civilization.

It has been my own experience that on every occasion either the Department or the Embassy has made concessions to the Soviet Government, or has approached it in a spirit of friendly cooperation or goodwill, these gestures have been received by Soviet authorities with marked suspicion and a disposition to regard them as evidence of weakness, whereas on each occasion that our attitude was stiffened, the Soviet authorities have regarded our demeanor as evidence of self-confidence and strength and have promptly reacted by a more conciliatory attitude. . . . Nor have I found any resentment or bitterness at the reciprocal application of unpleasant measures. As in the case of all primitive people it is important, however, that retaliation should not be carried to the point at which it may be regarded as provocation, and every such act should be clearly identifiable in each instance as retaliation for something the Soviet Government has done or failed to do. If so identifiable, it does not appear to provoke further retaliation, but on the contrary, frequently results in a relaxation or complete withdrawal of the action which provoked the retaliation.[11]

On June 21, the very eve of the Nazi invasion, the State Department's Division of European Affairs suggested what the American stance should be in the event of German attack.

· We should offer the Soviet Union no suggestions or advice unless the Soviet Union approaches us.
· If the Soviet Government should approach us . . . requesting

assistance we should so far as possible, without interfering in our aid to Great Britain and to victims of aggression or without seriously affecting our own efforts of preparedness, relax restrictions on exports to the Soviet Union, permitting it even to have such military supplies as it might need badly and which we could afford to spare.

· We should steadfastly adhere to the line that the fact that the Soviet Union is fighting Germany does not mean that it is defending, struggling for, or adhering to the principles in international relations which we are supporting. [12]

These recommendations, too, must have seemed coldhearted and strategically in error once the bloodbath in Western Russia began. Must one not come immediately and strongly to the aid of people fighting and dying against the common enemy? Would not the defeat of Russia leave only England standing between Hitler and the Western Hemisphere? One can still feel the weight of such questions forty years later. They seemed even more urgent at the time. I grant that the United States and England, in their own interests, had to support the Soviet Union, which for most of the war would bear the brunt of the battle against Hitler—but would that they had done so without self-delusion, an attitude that initially puzzled Stalin, later tempted him to take advantage, and, ultimately, fostered illusions of his own.

The prime American illusion was that Soviet politics were somehow akin to American. President Roosevelt thought of the USSR as an authoritarian society—but one that was becoming more like the United States. That Stalin had scoffed at this idea of convergence in his 1934 interview with H. G. Wells did not prevent Roosevelt from believing, as Sumner Welles recalls it, that "if one took the figure 100 as representing the difference between American democracy and Soviet Communism in 1917, with the United States at 100 and the Soviet Union at 0, American democracy might eventually reach the figure 60 and the Soviet system might reach the figure of 40." The president acted as if genuine cooperation, as the Americans understood the term, were possible both during and after the war. Roosevelt apparently had forgotten, if indeed he ever knew, that in Stalin's eyes he was not all that different from Hitler—both of them being heads of powerful capitalist states whose long-term ambitions clashed with those of the Kremlin. To FDR, Stalin was "Uncle Joe" ("UJ" for short), a man difficult to get along with, surrounded by advisers even more difficult than he, but a no-nonsense leader with whom one could do business—especially once he was exposed to a little old-fashioned American warmth and charm. On the last morning of the Tehran Conference, at a time, we shall see, when Stalin was waiting with trepidation for Roosevelt to lodge a stern protest about Soviet treatment of Poland, the president naturally found the Soviet leader "stiff, solemn, not smiling, nothing human to get hold of." Whereupon FDR tried to break the ice by teasing Churchill "about his Britishness, about John Bull, about his cigars. . . . Winston got red and scowled, and the more he did so, the more Stalin smiled," FDR later told Frances Perkins. "Finally Stalin broke into a deep, hearty guffaw, and for the first time I saw the light. I kept it up until Stalin was laughing with me, and it was then that I called him 'Uncle Joe.' . . . From that time on, our relations were personal. . . . The ice was broken and we talked like men and brothers."[13]

But American attempts at collaboration, including more serious efforts and substantive concessions, aggravated rather than dispelled deep-seated Soviet suspiciousness; moreover, they invited Stalin to seek gains at the West's expense which, in the long run, the United States would not abide. A crude but accurate way of putting it is that Roosevelt did not realize that Stalin and his men were, ultimately, bastards—bastard being defined, in this context, as one who in the name of the people murders millions of them; who to defend against Hitler signs a pact with him, divides the spoils of war with him, and like him expels, exterminates, or enslaves neighboring peoples; who stands aside and fulminates against the democracies as Germany moves West and then blames them for not helping enough when Hitler moves East. But if Roosevelt failed to realize what manner of men he was dealing with, Stalin and company were guilty of *being* bastards, which, in the sense I have used the term, the Americans were not. And furthermore, Stalin assumed his Western allies were more or less like him and acted accordingly. He knew, of course, there were differences between "capitalist" and "socialist" regimes, but not necessarily those trumpeted in Communist propaganda. Capitalist claims to freedom and democracy were a sham to Stalin, but Soviet boasts were obviously exaggerated, too. Stalin's interpretation of Marxism taught him that in the so-called democracies, the capitalist ruling class called the shots. But "calling the shots" had meaning for him derived from his own experience. He viewed Roosevelt and Churchill as adversaries who would do unto him approximately what he would unto them, assuming they got the opportunity.

Of all the tricks of which Stalin's ally-adversaries were capable, none was more insidious than their repeated declarations of warmest friendship. They could not possibly be sincere. And yet, as reliant as Stalin was on the West, the Americans and British seemed to feel even more dependent on the Red Army, which was bearing the brunt of battle against the Nazis. As alarmed as Stalin was that his allies might hold back and let Moscow and Berlin finish each other off, the Western powers seemed equally fearful of a separate peace between him and Hitler. Stalin was ready to cooperate as long as collaboration was in the Soviet interest. But the British and, especially, the Americans sounded as if civilization itself would come to an end if the allies did not continue the closest possible collaboration—even after the war was won. Stalin assumed the capitalist countries would remain his dangerous enemies; for the moment, however, Western anxiety and illusions offered tempting opportunities to the Soviet leader.

That this was Stalin's view is confirmed by what he told Tito's emissary Milovan Djilas in the spring of 1944.

> Perhaps you think that just because we are the allies of the English that we have forgotten who they are and who Churchill is. They find nothing sweeter than to trick their allies. During the First World War they constantly tricked the Russians and the French. And Churchill? Churchill is the kind who, if you don't watch him, will slip a kopeck out of your pocket. Yes, a kopeck out of your pocket! By God, a kopeck out of your pocket! And Roosevelt? Roosevelt is not like that. He dips in his hand only for bigger coins. But Churchill? Churchill—even for a kopeck.

Djilas had come to Moscow to consult with Stalin on the progress of Tito's Yugoslav partisans, who were by then gaining the upper hand against both Nazi occupiers and the non-Communist resistance. Flushed with victories, Tito was anxious to proclaim his communism to the world, but Stalin urged caution. "The substance of his suggestions," Djilas recalled, was "that we ought not to 'frighten' the English, by which he meant that we ought to avoid anything that might alarm them into thinking that a revolution was going on in Yugoslavia or [that there was] an attempt at Communist control. 'What do you want with red stars on your caps? The form is not important but what is gained, and you—red stars! By God, stars aren't necessary!' Stalin exclaimed angrily."

What about a possible compromise with the Yugoslav Royal government's representative, Dr. Ivan Šubašić? "Do not refuse to hold conversations with Šubašić," answered Stalin, "on no account must you do this. Do not attack him immediately. Let us see what he wants. Talk with him. You cannot be recognized right away. A transition to this must be found."

Later, pausing before a map of the world on which the Soviet Union was colored in red: "Stalin waved his hand over the Soviet Union and, referring to what he had been saying just previously against the British and Americans, he exclaimed, 'They will never accept the idea that so great a space should be red, never, never!' "

Stalin's words came after Roosevelt and Churchill had gone to great lengths to convince him of their good faith. In their efforts to win his trust he detected sinister strategems. Churchill, more open and frank about his anticommunism, was more understandable and therefore less dangerous. Roosevelt, who insisted there need be no obstacle to intimate and lasting friendship, seemed to be a bigger trickster. But despite their tricks, the Western leaders might themselves be conned. The West would never accept that "so great a space should be red," Stalin had said, but, provided they moved cautiously, the Yugoslavs could pick a pocket or two themselves. Stalin's cautionary advice was tactical and temporary. When, as had happened before, the West proved accommodating, the "transition" could and would be found.[14]

In the end, Stalin found his transitions not wisely but too well. He succeeded in creating the all-out American hostility that he erroneously had assumed to exist all along. To be sure, anti-Communism ran deep in the United States; it had been present since before 1917 and it lived on even after June 22, 1941. But whereas Stalin continued to think of his allies as mortal enemies, Roosevelt and company did not. Compared to the anti-Sovietism that was to develop after World War II in America, and in contrast to Stalin's own deep and undiminished hostility toward the West, American leaders (and to a lesser extent, British leaders) were remarkably, even naïvely, well-disposed toward the USSR throughout the war.

Harry Hopkins, Roosevelt's chief all-purpose confidant and troubleshooter, showed himself to be particularly agreeable, but not entirely discerning, when he visited Moscow in July 1941. Soviet anxiety was on display. As usual, it took the form of extreme reasonableness: Stalin was as considerate as he had been toward German representatives in the spring of 1941. Soviet nastiness, which the Americans have encountered many times but never fully understood to this day, means either that things are going so well for the Russians that they do not have to be polite and can play the bully instead, or that things are going so badly that even sweet reasonableness cannot rescue the situation—in which case a show of anger may either frighten an adversary into acquiescence or, at the least, give vent to Soviet frustration.

Stalin struck Hopkins as coolly confident. But if the Soviet leader had been as serene as he seemed, he would never have asked for American troops to fight on Soviet territory. Once the tide of war turned, any such Western presence on Soviet soil would be anathema, but in July 1941 Stalin wanted Roosevelt to know that he would "welcome the American troops on any part of the Russian front under the complete command of the American Army." Stalin flattered FDR (He noted that the "world influence" of the president and the government of the United States was "enormous"); he phrased the lesson of Hitler's treachery in terms likely to appeal to Americans ("Nations must fulfill their treaty obligations, or international society could not exist"); and he emphasized the identity of outlook between the USSR and the United States ("Therefore, our views coincide").

Few East-West meetings during the war went so swimmingly. And why not? Hopkins expressed at the outset the president's belief that the most important thing to be done was to defeat Hitler and Hitlerism and "the determination of the President and [the American] government to extend all possible aid to the Soviet Union at the earliest possible time." In addition, Hopkins manifested a deference toward Soviet censorship that must have seemed to him mere politeness, but may well have seemed meekness to his Soviet host. Hopkins asked if Stalin would prefer that he not give an interview to British and American newsmen, and he reminded the Soviet dictator (in case Stalin had forgotten?) "that under any circumstances the correspondents' stories would be subject to the control of [Stalin's] censorship." To this Stalin replied with that great magnanimity he was so often to display when offering Western leaders what they might well have considered their due: "Anything I might have to say," Hopkins was told, "would require no censorship by [the Soviet] Government."[15]

The next window onto Stalin's attitude and his tactics for dealing with the Anglo-Americans came in late September when Churchill's representative, Lord Beaverbrook, visited Moscow accompanied by Harriman, who was representing President Roosevelt. Their purpose was to find out how the Soviets were doing, and how to help. The British were particularly eager to please—to make up for their inability to open a second front on the continent. Early in September, Churchill had reacted angrily to "the air of menace" with which Maisky had delivered Stalin's request for a British landing "somewhere in the Balkans or France." "Remember," he told the Soviet ambassador, "that only four months ago we in this Island did not know whether you were coming in against us on the German side." Churchill added; "You of all people have no right to make reproaches to us." But the British tone had changed by the time Beaverbrook arrived, and it was to stay changed, for both Washington and London were nervous about the possibility of a separate German-Soviet peace.[16]

The Beaverbrook-Harriman mission demonstrated its good faith in unusual ways. In a move that Richard Nixon was to repeat in Moscow in 1972, Beaverbrook suggested dispensing with Anglo-American interpreters and relying instead on Soviet translation. Nixon's purpose, apart from avoiding leaks to the American press, was to encourage Brezhnev to "speak more freely." Beaverbrook's unspoken message was: If I show I trust you, then you will trust me. Harriman recalls assenting to this strategem with "some misgiving," but he went along readily with another one: "Both Beaverbrook and I felt that Stalin would be franker with us if we didn't take the Ambassadors along," Harriman recalled. "We knew that Stalin had no very high regard for either of them, so there was nothing to be gained by taking them."

Relinquishing his own interpreter was something Stalin would never do. That the British and Americans would do so was likely to evoke his puzzlement and, to the extent he guessed the motive, contempt. On the American side of the misunderstanding, being invited to the Kremlin immediately on arrival in Moscow struck Harriman as "in itself, encouraging." But why shouldn't Stalin have hastened to see those whose assistance was so important to him? Once in his presence, Harriman and Beaverbrook were greatly reassured by Stalin's determination to defend Moscow against the nearby Nazis, an enterprise that was, to say the least, in Stalin's own interest. Somewhat less encouraging was Stalin's response to Harriman's report that Roosevelt was anxious about Catholic opposition to prospective lend-lease aid for Russia. The president felt, Harriman recalls saying, that "American public opinion would be favorably affected by official assurance that Section 124 of the Soviet Constitution meant what it said about guaranteeing freedom of conscience and of worship for all citizens." One problem with this was that the Soviet Constitution did *not* mean what it said, but Stalin let that pass. He replied that he did not "know much about American public opinion," leaving the impression on Harriman that this was a matter "best discussed with underlings and of no interest to him." Harriman did not press the issue.[17]

Stalin's response, for all its apparent innocuousness, hinted at an attitude toward American politics that later would stand at the center of mutual miscalculation. Shortly before Harriman's arrival in Moscow, Roosevelt had explained to Ambassador Umansky "the extreme difficulty of getting the necessary authority from Congress [for applying lend-lease to the USSR] on account of the prejudice or hostility to Russia and the unpopularity of Russia among large groups in this country who exercise great political power in Congress." The president also referred to "the fact that Russia does have churches and does permit religious worship under the Constitution of 1936." He suggested that if Moscow could "get some publicity back to this country regarding the freedom of religion during the next few days . . . it might have a very fine educational effect before the next lease-lend bill comes up in Congress." The ambassador agreed to attend to this matter.[18]

This conversation is a classic. FDR blithely recognizes guarantees of freedoms in the USSR that the Soviet ambassador knows are not respected in his country. As if confiding in a co-conspirator, the president thinks "some publicity" (not much, a little will have "a very fine effect") might sway congressional opinion. Stalin's response to Harriman shows that he did not think much of American public opinion. But before long he would have to think more of it. For this was but the first of many times Roosevelt would advert to such opinion to explain why he could not accommodate Moscow on issues of the highest importance to the Soviets. The question, for Stalin, was what to make of Roosevelt's excuses. Stalin's exchange with Harriman suggests that the Soviet leader assumed American opinion could not be as important as FDR had said it was. Not only Stalin's image of a dominant capitalist class, of which Roosevelt was a powerful captain, but also the president's own string of electoral victories showed that Roosevelt had little to fear from the public. But if so, why did the president act as if he had to consult the American people? Was he, like Stalin, using alleged public and parliamentary sentiment as an excuse for not doing what he did not want to do anyway? That this was how Stalin saw it is suggested by his pointed reminder to Hopkins four years later that in contrast to the Americans, he, Stalin, did not use public opinion as an excuse. A second interpretation, however, also may have seemed plausible to the Soviets. Perhaps Roosevelt faced some opposition but honestly underestimated his own ability to overcome it. In a crucial exchange between the two leaders at Tehran in November 1943, Stalin urged Roosevelt to do "some propaganda work" on the American people. At Yalta, in response to Bohlen's warning that the American people would oppose the Soviet position on United Nations voting procedures, Soviet Deputy Foreign Commissar Andrei Vyshinsky (he who had been chief prosecutor at the murderous purge trials of the thirties) replied that "the American people should learn to obey their leaders."[19]

Neither image of Roosevelt (as conniving or as unaware of his own political strength), however, was likely to foster the respect that the president sought to evoke. Both interpretations, which in our time have been deployed in a valiant (but largely unsuccessful) Soviet effort to fathom Jimmy Carter, reflected Marxist ideological assumptions and projected Soviet patterns onto the United States. But Roosevelt himself was also to blame for Stalin's misperception. When FDR cited adverse public opinion in America to justify his resisting of Soviet designs on Eastern Europe, he was *not* being entirely frank; Roosevelt had other reasons as well, but it was easier to cite Congress as the excuse. Simultaneously, after portraying public opinion as decisive, the president sounded as if a dash of Soviet propaganda might be enough to neutralize it. One line contradicted the other.

If Americans could play games, so could the Soviets—as Stalin showed on the second evening of the Beaverbrook-Harriman visit. The first meeting went so well that Beaverbrook talked afterward of settling things in one more session. But Stalin showed an entirely different face the next day. "Stalin gave the impression," Harriman recalls, "that he was much dissatisfied with what we were offering. He appeared to question our good faith." Said Stalin, "The paucity of your offer clearly shows that you want to see the Soviet Union defeated."

Stalin was deliberately rude. "When Beaverbrook handed him a letter from Churchill, Stalin ripped open the envelope, barely glanced at it, and left it lying on the table, unread, throughout the meeting." Upon leaving the Kremlin, Beaverbrook fell into a state of depression, while Harriman puzzled over the sudden turn of events. Was this some bargaining ploy on Stalin's part? Was he reacting to pressure from hardline associates? Or feeling the strain of the war? The mission requested a third meeting; to their "great relief," Stalin agreed. Not only that, but the Stalin who had been so rude to them was once again friendly and serene. When Beaverbrook asked him if he were pleased with the help offered, "Stalin smiled and nodded." Stalin even regaled his guests with a sumptuous, evening-long feast the next night—despite the fact that the Russian people were going hungry (or perhaps just because they were, to impress his visitors with Soviet power in the midst of war). Along with the evening's multiple courses, thirty-two toasts, and two motion pictures, Stalin treated his guests to at least one barefaced lie (saying that it was only after Moscow had protested the Nazi attack on Poland that Hitler had invited the Soviet to occupy the Eastern portion of the country), and to taunts about British fear of opening a second front—which Beaverbrook and Harriman forbore to answer in kind.

By mission's end, the emissaries were elated. Beaverbrook, according to Harriman, "made the discovery that Stalin was 'a kindly man,' one who 'practically never shows any impatience at all.' " Harriman himself left the final meeting "feeling that he [Stalin] had been frank with us, and if we came through as had been promised, and if personal relations were maintained with Stalin, the suspicion that has existed between the Soviet Government and our two governments might well be eradicated."[20]

The Beaverbrook-Harriman visit was not the last time the Soviets pulled the nasty-second-session ploy; it happened when Eden visited Moscow in December 1941 and, again, when Churchill and Harriman came to town in October 1942. Nor is it unknown in our day. On the second full day of the 1972 Moscow summit meeting, Brezhnev, without warning, spirited Nixon away to his dacha, where, after a high-speed hydrofoil ride on the Moscow River, he, Prime Minister Alexei Kosygin, and President Nikolai Podgorny browbeat the president (and Henry Kissinger, who had with great difficulty managed to catch up with and rejoin his boss) for three hours on the subject of Vietnam. In 1973, when Brezhnev was Nixon's house guest at San Clemente, the Soviet leader, after retiring for the night to the absent Tricia Nixon's lavender and blue wall-papered bedroom, suddenly requested a meeting that turned into another three-hour (Is the duration of the session also standard Soviet operating procedure?) tirade—the apparent purpose of which was to convince the president to impose a pro-Arab peace settlement on Israel. Brezhnev's performance on these occasions was not unimpressive, although somewhat marred by the incongruous surroundings in which they took place. But Stalin's version—played out in his large but austere Kremlin office, and usually in the dead of night (which was when the Soviet leader transacted state business)—was the real thing: a *tour de force* with devastating impact on his unsuspecting guests. Stalin's was the old nice-cop–tough-cop routine with Joseph Vissarionovich himself playing both roles on successive nights. The pattern was by no means pure theater. A man who would liquidate his closest associates for fear they were plotting against him was capable of exaggerating British and American malevolence. Stalin was notorious among his old Bolshevik comrades for his moodiness and ill temper, yet what came so naturally to Stalin was also something he could simulate: the calculated display of genuine emotion. Stalin was, as his biographer Robert C. Tucker notes, a consummate role-player. In any case, the results of Stalin's second-session nastiness were unquestionably favorable to his cause. There was a sense of relief on the part of his interlocutors when the storm passed—relief accompanied by a disposition to accommodate Stalin lest his mood suddenly shift again. There was the hope that if the West tried hard enough, overall Soviet suspiciousness could be dispelled just as Stalin's momentary mood had been washed away.[21]

One of the most important things the West could do to please Stalin was to resolve what he called "the main question for us in this war." This was the question of the USSR's western frontiers. Only five days after the German assault, Molotov proposed to the British "a political agreement to define the basis of cooperation." In September, the Soviets endorsed the Atlantic Charter (in which Roosevelt and Churchill had proclaimed their devotion to national self-determination) but added that account had to be taken of "the circumstances, needs and historic peculiarities of particular countries." These and other signs indicated the direction of Soviet thinking. Still, Eden was not prepared for the full and frank exposition of Soviet war aims which awaited him in Moscow in December 1941. The British foreign secretary brought with him a rather general draft declaration on Anglo-Soviet cooperation—the major purpose of which was "to exorcize certain suspicions from Stalin's mind." Stalin counter-proposed a detailed secret protocol on frontiers. The border between Poland and the USSR would be roughly the Curzon Line, leaving to Russia the bulk of the Western Ukrainian and Western Byelorussian lands seized from Poland in 1939. From Rumania, Moscow would obtain Bessarabia and Northern Bukovina. Poland would be compensated with formerly German lands, while Rumania would be mollified with disputed territory that Hitler had awarded to Hungary. Thus reconstructed, both Poland and Rumania would depend on Soviet protection against newly truncated neighbors. As for the Baltic states (Latvia, Lithuania, and Estonia), they would get more than protection; having snuffed out their independence in 1940, only to lose them to Hitler, Stalin would reincorporate them into the USSR. The Soviets had other proposals, too. They would regain their June 1941 frontier with Finland, which would also be obligated, as would Rumania, to provide Soviet military bases on its territory. Stalin was greedy but not unilateral. The Soviet government would have no objection to British bases in Denmark and Norway. He also raised the issue of German reparations and suggested an armed council of the victorious powers to keep the peace following Germany's defeat. [22]

Eden was, to put it mildly, taken aback. In retrospect, Stalin's demands seem even more stunning. For the aims Stalin outlined, at a time when a Nazi victory was still anticipated by many in the West, were those he had pursued in partnership with Hitler—and would continue to pursue throughout the war and beyond. How to explain Stalin's boldness? [23] Was he attempting to obscure Soviet vulnerability by putting on a show of confidence complete with post-victory plans? Did he really expect Britain and the United States to comply with these demands? Stalin's move was reminiscent of the way he had handled Hitler. In 1939 he had parlayed a position of weakness into a seemingly profitable pact. Now he would confirm those ill-gotten gains. For all their high-flown talk about self-determination, the "democracies" were capable, or so Stalin seemed to assume, of the most cold-blooded *Realpolitik*.

But such was not the case—at least not yet. Britain was bound, Eden told Stalin, by the Atlantic Charter. Another reason for British caution, apart from a genuine preference not to settle borders and regimes—except in the British Empire—over the heads of the people involved, was that the Americans were even more adamant. Two days before Eden left for Moscow, the American ambassador to London, John G. Winant, had conveyed Washington's view that "the test of our good faith with regard to the Soviet Union is the measure to which we fulfill the commitments our representatives [that is, Harriman and Beaverbrook] made in Moscow. Insofar as our postwar policies are concerned, it is our belief that these have been delineated in the Atlantic Charter, which today represents the attitude not only of the United States but also of Great Britain and of the Soviet Union." The message continued: "In order not to jeopardize the aims we all share in common looking to enduring peace, it is evident that no commitments as to individual countries should be entered into at this time. It would be unfortunate if we should approach the peace conference thus hampered. Above all there must be no secret accords."[24]

Just as Stalin's proposals became wartime fixtures, so formal American opposition to them was to be repeated again and again—even when Roosevelt later moved quietly to acquiesce in most of them. American reasons for not granting Stalin's territorial demands have been treated at length in numerous histories: a commitment to self-determination; the desire to avoid a scramble among allies for territory and influence; the hope that Germany's defeat plus the establishment of a new international organization would render spheres of influence unnecessary; and the fear that the American public and Congress would not support the proposed United Nations if it were accompanied by British and Soviet land grabs.[25]

So Eden stalled. Germany would have to be tamed, but "exactly how this was to be done would have to be gone into carefully." He could certainly not sign such a document "without consulting my colleagues, and we have not as yet applied our minds to these problems." Furthermore, the Americans would have to agree. Stalin said he regarded the vague draft declaration that Eden had brought to Moscow as "algebra," whereas the specific agreements he had proposed were "practical arithmetic." "I do not wish to decry algebra, but I prefer practical arithmetic."

What did Stalin make of the English (and American) preference for algebra? He did not say. But his lines, especially at nasty second (and third) sessions with Eden, beg to be read between. Like Beaverbrook before him, Eden had anticipated no difficulties after such a cordial first meeting, especially since Maisky, himself, had predicted smooth sailing. Not so. Stalin demanded immediate recognition of the Soviet Union's 1941 frontiers; either that or no agreement at all! (Since the Soviets had as great a stake in reaching agreement as the British had, was this threat not Stalin's invitation to bargain?) To Eden's reply that the Cabinet would pursue Stalin's proposals further in London, Stalin answered; "If you say that, you might well say tomorrow that you do not recognize the Ukraine as forming part of the USSR." (British designs were far more sinister in Stalin's imagination than they were in fact.) Eden explained that the dominions would have to be consulted and that no British foreign minister who unilaterally settled an issue like the Polish-Soviet frontier "could survive for twenty-four hours." But Stalin assumed that the British dominions were no less under Churchill's thumb than the Soviet republics were under his: "I certainly do not want to demand the impossible from you and I fully realize the limitations of your powers, but I am addressing myself to the British Government and I am genuinely surprised." At the third meeting, Stalin added; "I am surprised at you having a treaty with Turkey and now creating a difficulty as to having a treaty with us. If you have any difficulty in entering into a treaty with us, then it is much better to say so." (Translation: Dammit, why won't you British get down to business? There is no need to pretend that we like each other. We have been adversaries before and will be again, but there is no law against a mutually profitable alliance. No one expected our first positions in these negotiations to coincide, but one at least assumed you would be willing to bargain. We cannot even do that if you won't state your terms.)

But how could Eden bargain? Could he offer a Polish-Soviet border somewhere between Curzon's Line and the 1920–1939 frontier? Neither the Poles nor the Americans would stand for that. Could he reject Soviet aims out of hand? Of course not, since for the beleaguered British, Soviet resistance to Hitler could not be put at risk. The foreign secretary did not complain to Stalin directly. He vented his frustration instead to the microphone that the British assumed had been hidden in Eden's hotel room. Whether Stalin got that message or not, he kindly agreed at the next meeting to accept the military and economic aid he so badly needed (and initially had not anticipated)—without, moreover, British concessions on frontier questions. There followed the obligatory, all-night banquet (lasting until five o'clock in the morning), after which Eden telegraphed home: "We have allayed some at least of the past suspicions."[26]

Anglo-Soviet negotiations continued after Eden returned home. Although Churchill was strongly opposed at first to accepting Stalin's proposals (especially the reincorporation of the Baltics into the USSR), he reluctantly changed his mind. "Under the pressure of events," Churchill recalled later, "I did not feel that this moral position could be physically maintained. In a deadly struggle it is not right to assume more burdens than those who are fighting for a great cause can bear. My opinions about the Baltic States were, are, unaltered, but I felt that I could not carry them farther forward at this time."[27]

But Washington lobbied against Stalin's secret protocol and in May 1942 prevailed. The Soviets dropped their demands for practical arithmetic. They would make do with the algebra of an Anglo-Soviet Treaty (signed in May 1942)—an agreement that avoided the question of Stalin's claims to East European territory and military bases. But the Western victory was Pyrrhic. It marked the beginning of Stalin's effort to achieve his aims on his own, and it was the start of a great Soviet-American misunderstanding. As Mastny suggests, either a clear acceptance of Stalin's war aims or outright rejection of them would probably have been preferable to what actually occurred. What happened was that having persuaded Britain to stand firm (and the Soviets to sit still) for what Washington insisted was high principle, Roosevelt seemed to signal that he would privately accept the East European arrangements that the administration publicly opposed—provided the Kremlin supplied a suitable "fig-leaf" for American public opinion. FDR's intimations did not put Stalin's mind at ease. But the president's hints encouraged the Soviets to think they might yet get away with what it turned out the United States would not accept.

May 1942 to June 1944: Soviet war aims escalate, along with Soviet confidence that their aims can be achieved. But the change comes slowly. Winning the war is still Moscow's top priority. Moreover, Western resistance to Soviet aims in Eastern Europe, particularly in Poland, is still anticipated in Moscow. As a result, Stalin proceeds with great caution in relations with East European Communist parties, on the one hand, and European governments-in-exile on the other.

Immediately following the Nazi attack, these parties, like their Soviet patrons, had to concentrate on sheer survival. By May 1942 Moscow was encouraging the formation of Communist-led partisan units but still extending official diplomatic recognition to non-Communist exile governments. The Comintern (the Soviet-dominated international organzation of Communist parties) called for "national fronts" throughout Europe, by which it meant broad alliances with all enemies of fascism whatever their political coloration. Yugoslavia's Communist partisans, as bold ideologically as they were effective militarily, were warned against "the sovietization of Yugoslavia." Mastny documents "Stalin's reluctance to commit himself in a fluid situation that was beyond his control." For the time being, Moscow restrained its Communist allies, who saw in the war a chance to foster long-delayed revolution.[28]

Poland, which was to become a crucial test case in U.S.–Soviet relations, illustrates this pattern. In the winter of 1941–1942 Stalin was at his most moderate. Having destroyed the former Polish Communist party (in a sideshow of the Great Terror of the late thirties), Stalin moved to recreate it around a core of loyalists parachuted into Poland from the Soviet Union. But the focus of Stalin's attention in late 1941 was the Polish government in London, which has been an invisible presence in our account because its refusal to recognize the Soviets' 1939 land grab largely explains British and American unwillingness to do so. The Polish government-in-exile, formed after the Nazi-Soviet partition of Poland, included a mixed group of politicians none of whom looked kindly on the Soviets, even though most were ready to hold their noses and work with Moscow against Nazi Germany. The list of contentious issues between Poles and Soviets was lengthy: for example, in addition to the frontier, there were the release of more than a million Poles arrested by the Soviets between 1939 and 1941 and deported to the USSR and the formation on Soviet soil of a Polish Army loyal to the London government. Nonetheless, Stalin seemed to broach a deal—no bargain for the Poles in 1941, but it looked rather different when the London Poles' exile had become permanent.

It happened at dinner during exile Polish Prime Minister Wladislaw Sikorski's visit to Moscow in December 1941. "What I want," said Stalin, "is only a very slight alteration of your prewar frontier—one which would hardly change your territorial status and would in no way seriously affect it." All he asked, he said, was "*chut' chut'* "—only the tiniest of alterations. In return, the Poles could have German territory in East Prussia and elsewhere. But Sikorski rejected the offer. He would not even discuss it. The whole world would laugh at him, he said, if he made such a deal. His own government would disavow it. Stalin persisted, "Would you not enter into a very little agreement with me?" "Don't worry," Stalin had said earlier. "We will not harm you." But Sikorski was adamant. Stalin dropped the subject and did not mention it again.[29]

If the London Poles had accepted, would the United States have gone along? (Washington later took the line that territorial settlements agreed to by the parties involved need not await the defeat of the Axis.) Would Stalin have kept his word? (He need not have, once his troops moved into Poland, but perhaps his continued dependence on allied military cooperation might have restrained him.) If Stalin had kept his word, thus settling for the "Finlandization" of Poland (that is, the establishment of a regime whose foreign policies are made with deference to Moscow's wishes but whose domestic order is not), he might have obviated the Cold War. But that did not happen. Instead, there began the Soviet pressure campaign which was ultimately to produce a Communist Poland. In the summer of 1942 Moscow rejected the idea of a postwar Polish-Czechoslovak confederation, which Sikorski had endorsed as a way of adding weight to Warsaw's voice in European affairs. The Soviets halted further recruitment by the Polish Army in the USSR. Moscow also harrassed and arrested Polish exile-government representatives in Russia, charging them with espionage. In January 1943 the Kremlin announced that inhabitants of Polish lands seized in 1939, including people of Polish origin, would henceforth officially be considered Soviet citizens.

Soviet pressure only stiffened the exile government's resolve. Whereupon Moscow speeded development of an alternative to the recalcitrant London regime. In March 1943 Moscow approved the formation on Soviet soil of the Union of Polish Patriots (UPP), an organization that was dominated by Polish Communists and pronounced itself in favor of the Curzon Line as the Polish-Soviet border. About the same time, a new, pro-Soviet Polish army was set up in the USSR. The London Poles triggered the next step themselves by requesting, in April 1943, that the Red Cross investigate Nazi charges that Soviets had massacred ten thousand Polish army officers in Katyn Forest. This gave Moscow an excuse for breaking relations with the London government, shortly after which the UPP declared that the London government was unrepresentative of the Polish people and took over the exile government's former embassy in Moscow. Meantime, in Poland, Communists took the lead in forming a National Council of the Homeland (NCH) with a mandate, according to Communist leader (and future party boss of Poland) Wladislaw Gomulka, to name a provisional government.

In January 1944 Soviet troops crossed the prewar Polish border. By now Stalin was demanding not only Polish recognition of the Curzon Line, but also wholesale reconstruction of the London government itself. When the Poles refused to comply, Stalin received a National Homeland Council delegation in Moscow. Final talks with London Poles broke off in June. July saw the creation in Moscow of the Polish Council for National Liberation. In August and September, having called for a Warsaw uprising against the Germans, the Soviets stood by while forces loyal to the London government were decimated. Late in 1944 Stalin recognized the National Liberation Council, now based in Lublin, as the new government of Poland.

This whole sequence has an air of inevitability about it.[30] In fact, however, Soviet policy was erratic and *ad hoc*. Pro-Soviet Poles would later complain that by autumn 1943 they should have prepared an "administrative apparatus" capable of governing Poland, but they "did not have the agreement of the Kremlin." Moscow may have hoped for a "Czechoslovak solution," that is, the formation of a Polish regime that, although non-Communist, would be willing to accede to Soviet wishes. Stalin told Czechoslovak President Eduard Beneš that he was seeking "Poles one could talk to." Stalin acted, according to Mastny's description, "as if he believed that other Poles, more respectable than the [Polish] Communists, could somehow be found to help him run the country if only he could impress upon them brutally enough that *they* had no choice. . . ."[31]

In January 1944 Moscow rebuked Gomulka and company for excessive radicalism. In the spring the Red Army's relations with pro-London Polish resistance forces were elaborately correct. In April and May, Stalin sounded out two visitors from America about possibilities for participation by Polish-Americans in a future coalition government in Poland. The Reverend Stanislaw Orlemanski was a parish priest from Springfield, Massachusetts, who had helped to organize the pro-Soviet Kosciusko Polish Patriotic League in the United States. That Stalin considered the lowly Orlemanski a sufficiently important personage to invite him to the Kremlin confirms that the Soviet leader's grasp of the nuances of American politics left something to be desired. In any event, Orlemanski got VIP treatment, including a two-hour Kremlin conversation in which Stalin offered a pledge of noninterference in postwar Polish internal affairs, along with a further installment of that pro-religion "publicity" that Roosevelt had once requested, namely, a promise to support religious freedom in the USSR. Oskar Lange, a Polish-born Marxist economist then teaching at the University of Chicago, was Stalin's second guest. Somewhat more important than Orlemanski, Lange was to become Poland's first postwar ambassador to the United States.[32]

Meantime, National Homeland Council representatives arrived in Moscow on a visit they thought would establish *de facto* Soviet recognition for them. But in initial talks Stalin avoided political discussions, and Molotov added that if the Soviets recognized the NCH there could be "trouble from the Western allies." Stalin sent the delegation off on a long tour of Polish army camps in the USSR, saying, "The NCH has no army and the Polish army in the Soviet Union has no government." In London at this time the Soviets contacted the Polish government-in-exile on May 23; a second meeting was held on May 31. The Soviet representative indicated that a resumption of relations might be possible without immediate, formal Polish recognition of the Curzon Line. The atmosphere, the Poles reported, was good. Only in mid-June did the Soviets seem to lose interest.[33]

Other examples of Moscow's relative moderation in the period before June 1944: the Kremlin's respectful treatment of the Czechoslovak exile government led by President Beneš; Moscow's refusal to support a Hungarian Communist plan to overthrow the pro-Nazi regime of Admiral Horthy; Molotov's pledge, issued as the Red Army crossed the pre-June 1941 Rumanian frontier, not to alter Rumania's social system.[34] For the time being, Moscow was keeping options open. The outcome would depend not only on events, but also on Western, and particularly American, policy. Developments on two fronts—the war and American policy—were increasingly encouraging, but the clinchers, which account for the hardening of Soviet policy in Poland and elsewhere, came only in June 1944.

Even as Stalin stepped up pressure against the London Poles between 1942 and 1944, he feared the Americans might somehow come to their rescue. That fear partly accounts for his caution. American diplomacy at first deterred Stalin and later encouraged him—in ways that Roosevelt never understood. Officially, the Americans opposed the Soviet position on Polish frontiers. But their opposition took strange and ineffective forms, and Roosevelt himself seemed to signal that he could live with Soviet terms even though he could not say so publicly. At Tehran in November 1943, Roosevelt appeared to sanction Soviet designs on Poland, in direct contradiction to what Washington had been telling the Poles. But in the spring of 1944, Roosevelt seemed ready to double-cross Stalin. That was when Stalin took out insurance in the form of renewed secret talks with the London Poles. But instead of dropping the other shoe, FDR confirmed the deal.

What explains Roosevelt's apparent inconsistency? The president was not unconcerned about the likely growth of Soviet power in postwar Eastern Europe, but he tried to channel rather than stop it outright. He conceded expanded Soviet influence, which in any case, he thought, the United States was in no position to prevent. But Roosevelt never spelled out the extent—either geographic or political—of the Soviet gains he was prepared to accept. This hesitation reflected both his own uncertainty and the potential explosiveness of the issue in American politics. Both Polish-Americans, who were widely (although wrongly) assumed to be likely defectors from the Democratic party in the 1944 elections, and key senators whose support for the president's internationalist postwar plans was deemed crucial would have reacted violently to any clear signal that the great powers were divvying up Europe into spheres of influence. And so, what the president conveyed to Stalin was a vague invitation to unspecified aggrandizement, along with a plea that Soviet gains somehow be rendered palatable to American opinion.[35] How did Stalin react to Roosevelt's blend of weak protests and Delphic reassurances? With fear, concern, puzzlement, eventually, perhaps with gratitude, but with little more understanding of Roosevelt than FDR had of him.

Among the more ineffective protests on Poland's behalf were those made by American ambassador to Moscow, Admiral William Standley. Standley's hard-line predecessor, Lawrence Steinhardt, had been transferred at Harriman's suggestion—just as, thirty-six years later, Harriman helped persuade Jimmy Carter to replace hawkish career ambassador Malcolm Toon with IBM executive Thomas Watson. Standley was chosen more for his military experience than for his diplomatic skill, and he lived up to that billing. Several times during 1942 he expressed American regret at deteriorating Polish-Soviet relations—as if the deterioration did not stem from Polish (and American) unwillingness to resolve the frontier issue on Soviet terms. Each time, Standley apologized in advance by making it clear that the American government did not wish to "interfere in the internal affairs of the Soviet Union or in Soviet-Polish relations." Soviet responses ranged from Assistant Foreign Commissar Lozovsky's advice that not interfering was "the best thing for [the American government] to do," to Molotov's irritation that the American government kept raising the subject if, indeed, it did not wish to interfere.[36]

But if the ambassador's representations were feeble, those of special presidential emissaries were worse. Wendell Willkie arrived in Moscow in September 1942. The defeated 1940 Republican presidential candidate had himself proposed the goodwill visit. FDR endorsed it as a means of demonstrating to Stalin the extent of bipartisan American support for the Soviet Union. It probably never occurred to FDR, but it surely did to Stalin, that such a demonstration clashed with Roosevelt's warnings that political opposition at home limited what the administration could do to help the Russians. If that was the message, a more conservative Republican would have made a better medium. As it was, off went Willkie, having been requested by the president "to express to

Mr. Stalin the hope of this government that an improvement in Polish-Soviet relations may be effected."

What followed was a textbook exercise in how *not* to treat with the Kremlin. The Russians took advantage of Willkie's determination (like that of so many presidential emissaries before and after him unto the Nixon administration) to deal one-on-one with the Soviets without the American ambassador. Willkie's Soviet hosts laid on an inspection tour of an "ordinary" airplane factory near Kuibyshev. ("The factory in question," cabled Standley, who was chagrined at being left in the lurch and therefore acted as a one-man truth squad, "had been evacuated from Moscow last fall and was the identical one visited by members of the Harriman-Beaverbrook Mission in October 1941.") At the factory, Willkie was "spontaneously" asked when the promised second front would be delivered. And everywhere else Willkie went the party line was sure to go—even to the ritual banquets at which the presidential representative was wined and dined without mercy.

And Willkie fell for it. Speaking at a formal dinner given by Deputy Foreign Commissar Vyshinsky, Willkie admitted (according to Standley's perhaps less than impartial paraphrase) that "during the two days he had been in the Soviet Union he had come to realize how unfairly the Soviet Union had been represented in the past to the American people." Enemies of the Soviet Union "had caused many Americans to believe that the Soviet government did not permit freedom of religion in the Soviet Union. . . . He now knew that the stories of religious persecution in the Soviet Union were false. It was now his understanding that the Soviet Government was opposed to priest-craft as distinct from religion. He personally also had little respect for priest-craft . . . and he hoped the American people could be brought to understand what the real situation was in the USSR."

Willkie's two days also added his name to the roster of Western believers in Soviet-American convergence. "From a social point of view," he announced, the two nations were "approaching each other," a view which even Vyshinsky and Lozovsky, disposed though they were to encourage Willkie's illusions, greeted coldly. Willkie assured his hosts that if they would let him travel freely he would not betray their trust. "The Soviet authorities could be sure that if he saw something he did not like . . . he would remain silent about it."

But his pledge not to knock the USSR when he returned to the United States did not hold the other way round, and it certainly did not apply to America's other great ally. Willkie said that "the United States was in favor of a second front but Great Britain was not." At the Vyshin-sky dinner, Willkie offered his frank opinion that only two countries could be counted on to win the war: the United States and the Soviet Union. He continued; "Without mentioning any other country—and I am sure you will know the country to which I refer—I am convinced from my recent travels that imperialism is as dead as a dodo bird." That was testimony even the former Great Purge trial prosecutor could not handle; Vyshinsky gaped in astonishment, then rose to remark that win-ning the war would require the united efforts of all three great allies.

Nor, one supposes, was Stalin much less surprised at the way Willkie raised the issue of Poland. Roosevelt's message was basic boiler plate: "It is in the common interest of the United Nations that there should be . . . the least possible cause for friction between the different nations fighting the Axis." When Stalin pressed him to be specific, Willkie replied that he did not wish to discuss the details of the case. As pressure designed to moderate Moscow's stance toward the Poles, this was worthless. But as proof positive of America's good faith, Willkie's visit was not much better. Its most likely upshot was genuine astonish-ment (Could Willkie be for real?), mixed with suspicion (He was too good to be true), mixed with contempt (Whatever he was, his naïveté could be exploited).[37]

Nor was Willkie one of a kind. In early 1943, as Soviet harrass-ment of the Polish government escalated, the president sent word to the London government to "Keep its shirt on!" They must trust him to decide when, where, and how to defend Polish interests. But the Polish ambassador kept coming around to the State Department, and after fobbing him off with sweet nothings for a while, the president rolled out another special representative—one who, the Poles were assured, had the president's "entire confidence" and who "in the course of his conversations with Stalin would be instructed to do what might be pos-sible . . . in the interest of an improvement in Soviet-Polish relations."[38]

Before departing for Moscow, Joseph Davies confessed to his own growing uncertainty about Stalin's intentions. Davies's public declara-tions that Stalin could be trusted, he now told State Department Soviet specialist Elbridge Durbrow, had been made "to counteract the all too prevalent feeling" to the opposite effect. He had been, he admitted, "whistling by the graveyard." But when Davies arrived at the graveyard, for that is what the terror and the war had made of the Soviet Union, he was still whistling. According to Standley, who was once again left behind in his embassy and was less than ecstatic about it, Davies accused American correspondents in Moscow of playing into the hands of Hitler by "picking up pins, by their criticizing the Soviet Union." To which one reporter replied by asking whether Davies was not an advocate of the "Kick me, I like it school of thought" on the Soviet Union. It may be because Davies jilted him that Ambassador Standley characterized Stalin's banquet for Davies as "the dullest Kremlin dinner I have ever attended." But his report that "Stalin's greetings were pleasant but unenthusiastic and later his movements appeared heavy" has the ring of truth. Davies's effusive efforts, which included showing Soviet leaders the uncritical film *Mission to Moscow* based on his ambassador's memoirs of the same name, must have irritated even as it pleased his hosts. What to make of an adversary who seems capable only of flattery? How to negotiate with one who insists there are no real differences? There had to be a joker in the deck. The likes of Willkie and Davies would have to be endured until the Americans showed their real hand.[39]

But even the secretary of state was not showing it. To be sure, Cordell Hull was not authorized to show much of anything. Hull, like the department he had headed longer than any other secretary of state, did not exactly formulate Roosevelt's Soviet policy. Things got so bad that Hull had to offer lame excuses to Molotov to explain why he was not *au courant*.[40] When Hull did get a piece of the action, he revealed a credulity and a passion to please that rivalled even those of Willkie and Davies. When the Soviets got the chance to negotiate with him, they fed his illusions.

Typical of Hull was a comment he made to President Beneš in May 1943. As recorded in the fractured prose of an official memorandum of conversation, the secretary "urged the necessity for a fuller and most friendly conference with Mr. Stalin on the question of prevailing on him to abandon his aloofness, secretiveness and suspicion and bring his Government more into the world family of nations in the way of international relations and international cooperation along the lines that other Governments like Great Britain and the United States are preaching." About the same time, Hull emphasized to Churchill "the extreme importance of our two countries proceeding systematically through carefully selected persons [like Willkie and Davies?] to talk Mr. Stalin out of his shell." No wonder the secretary of state was pleased when, in the fall of 1943, high Soviet officials addressed him in kind. Presenting his credentials as the new Soviet ambassador to Washington on October 6, 1943, Andrei Gromyko (sic!) assured Hull that there was "no serious divergence of interest between the Soviet Union and the United States," that their main interests were "in common," and that there were no questions which could not be "settled amicably and without serious difficulty." According to Hull's own account of this conversation, "I echoed and reechoed this view." A few weeks later at the Moscow Foreign Ministers Conference, Vyshinsky took Hull aside during an intermission at the ballet. "Vyshinsky expressed the warmest conviction that the future hope of the world rested in collaboration with the United States, Great Britain and the Soviet Union, and that without such collaboration he feared there would be no future. He said that the first task was the utter defeat of Germany and after that Japan and then there would be no trouble in the world."[41]

Vyshinsky could not have meant what he said. It was an article of Marxist-Leninist-Stalinist faith that "trouble in the world" was built into competition between rival social systems and indeed among capitalist countries themselves. Vyshinsky was mimicking a gullible American, conning him by telling him what he wanted to hear. Molotov, phlegmatic and deadpan, had a different tactic. He listened politely to Hull's most extravagant statements and then, laconically, agreed. The secretary suggested that, as a way of breaking down misunderstandings and suspicions, "it might be a good idea if the subordinate members of the American Delegations might be put in touch with their opposite numbers in the Soviet Government . . . merely to get to know each other. . . ." "Mr. Molotov agreed that this would be a good idea." Hull declared his conviction "that if we could emphasize to both our peoples that they are in fact allies and comrades in the common struggle, that nothing could prevent them from becoming fast friends." Mr. Molotov "entirely agreed." Hull engaged in a flight of internationalist fancy: What was needed, he told Molotov, was "cooperation to preserve the peace permanently and to provide for the maximum of economic advantages and benefits to each country for the equal enjoyment of their respective peoples, to preserve world order under law so as to avoid international anarchy, to provide relief against starvation in many nations, . . . to relieve the postwar German situation, to deal with dependent people, to deal with stabilization as a basis for suitable international trade and like relations, etc., etc." Molotov "agreed."[42]

As the Moscow Conference progressed, "Mr. Molotov was even more sociable, friendly and agreeable in every way, if possible, than before." As for Stalin, he "was in a most agreeable state of mind and no matter what subject was discussed he seemed to overlook nothing that might make more clear my [Hull's] understanding of his situation present and prospective." At the banquet that closed the conference, Stalin "referred to our two countries and the great necessity for collaboration and cooperation in the most sympathetic and favorable manner." Stalin had resisted Hull's plea to set a date for a Big Three summit meeting. But Hull wrote Roosevelt that the Marshal would surely agree to meet him and Churchill "unless his entire sincerity, including both words and acts here are false and this is incredible. . . ."[43]

Hull's notion that Stalin was either entirely sincere or not at all suggests the secretary was not totally credulous. But it was a seriously mistaken notion. Of course the Soviets would cooperate with the Americans to defeat Germany, and afterward, too, if it suited their interests. But if Stalin and Molotov seemed to share Hull's liberal perspective, if they ladled out so freely sentiments Americans longed to hear, there was an ulterior reason—a reason which takes us back to Poland.

The Soviets, it will be recalled, were feeling their way forward on the Polish question in the fall of 1943. By October, Moscow could be fairly certain that Britain was both sympathetic to the Soviet position on frontiers and exasperated with the London Poles for not accommodating to that position. But the American stance was not at all clear to the Soviets. Washington was exerting pressure in Moscow (such as it was) on the Poles' behalf. But Roosevelt was also hinting he would be more understanding of the Soviet position if it were not for American public opinion. In the midst of the Katyn Forest controversy, the president cabled Stalin that Sikorski had "made a mistake" in appealing to the Red Cross. But he added; "In the United States, incidentally, I have several million Poles . . . and the situation would not be helped by the knowledge of a complete diplomatic break between yourself and Sikorski."[44]

Stalin had just recently mentioned Soviet public opinion in a telegram to Churchill. The man who had dispatched millions of Soviet citizens to their deaths with a wave of the hand, the man before whom generals and other high officials trembled in fear, informed Churchill that "I was obliged also to take into account the public opinion of the Soviet Union which is deeply indignant at the ingratitude and treachery of the Polish Government." This was a distortion, to put it mildly. More important, it appears Stalin thought Roosevelt's excuses were similarly distorted. Confirmation of this view comes from Maxim Litvinov, former Soviet foreign commissar and Gromyko's predecessor as ambassador to Washington, who let down his hair to Undersecretary of State

Welles on May 7, 1943. Litvinov spoke of Stalin's underestimation of the role of public opinion in the United States: "The Ambassador emphasized in very clearcut and blunt terms the fact that Stalin was entirely unaware of the fact that public opinion in the United States was a determining factor in the creation of government policy. He himself had time and again tried to persuade him that public opinion must be reckoned with, but Stalin had apparently paid no attention whatever to the recommendations which he had sent in this regard."[45] This was not the last of Litvinov's confidential warnings to Americans about Stalin. In 1946, he was to say Stalin's appetite for power was insatiable and that any American concessions would only produce more Soviet demands.

So Roosevelt too, Stalin must have concluded, was conjuring up public pressure to cover other motives. If this was the president's game, Stalin could understand—likewise, Roosevelt's agitation for a summit conference. The president was proposing the meeting in a most reassuring manner. In May, through Joseph Davies, he had proposed a Soviet-American tête-à-tête: FDR and Stalin, each accompanied by an adviser, interpreter, and stenographer, would "talk very informally and get what we call 'a meeting of minds.'" But it might be a trap. Stalin did not know that Roosevelt had recommended a Big Three meeting to Churchill as a way "to increase the confidence of Stalin in the sincerity of our intentions." Nor did he know that the president resisted a pre-conference, Anglo-American military staff get-together without Soviet participation because, as he wired Churchill, "I have held all along— as I know you have, that it would be a terrible mistake if UJ thought we had ganged up on him on military action." To the suspicious Soviets, a face-to-face meeting would seem the perfect place for Roosevelt to drop the other shoe on Poland.

The meeting was delayed. The military situation required Stalin's presence at home. The President declined to meet in Tehran (which was Stalin's preference) given the Constitutional requirement that, as he informed Stalin, "laws and resolutions must be acted on by me after their receipt and must be returned to Congress physically before ten days have elapsed." But after insisting on the sanctity of the Constitution, Roosevelt reversed himself and said he *could* meet in Tehran. That implied both that the Fundamental Law, allegedly even more sacred than public opinion, could be gotten around and that FDR was extremely anxious to parley—which was not a good sign if the Americans were indeed up to something.[46]

Once a summit meeting appeared inevitable, the Soviets insisted on a prior meeting of foreign ministers in October. They demanded that the agenda for that and the summit session to follow be drawn up and circulated in order to minimize surprises. And while the preparations proceeded and the foreign ministers met, the Soviets put on their most reasonable faces. They assured the Americans, Hull in particular, that efforts to win Moscow's goodwill were succeeding and could only be spoiled by an attempt to play rough on Poland.

The October Foreign Ministers Conference went particularly well. Not only was Hull impressed by protestations of friendship, he also played into Soviet hands by making the major item on the American agenda a classic piece of "algebra," a vague Four-Power Declaration on international cooperation in war and peace. Hull's plan was "to keep the exchange of views on the broad basis of general world security within which framework, if the Soviet Government is willing to cooperate, many of the detailed questions would more easily be solved."[47] Any graduate of the Riga school could have warned against such a course. Moscow's draft agenda stressed concrete issues—for example, the second front and how to get Turkey into the war on the Allied side—but the Soviets obliged Hull by agreeing to general principles that could be interpreted as they wished later on. Likewise, Molotov acceded to the American desire that China be a signatory of the Four-Power Declaration. Moscow's initial resistance to this was sincere (Who really needed a China that was weak and divided and governed, if at all, by Chiang Kai-shek?) and, at the same time, expedient. In return for yielding on China, and even more for indicating that they would someday join the war against Japan, the Soviets hoped to receive greater "understanding" from the Americans and the British on matters that counted then and there.

Understanding (if that is the right word), along with further evidence of inter-imperialist contradictions, is what they got. When Eden pressed for Soviet concessions on the Polish question, Hull declined to support him. Molotov said he preferred not to discuss the issue of Poland. Hull alternately either remained silent or preached the virtues of a Polish-Soviet settlement without himself taking sides in the dispute. Harriman was dismayed and urged Hull "to apply his considerable leverage with the Russians in attempting to work out agreements to safeguard the independence of Poland and other nations in Eastern and Central Europe. . . ." Harriman's strategy might well have failed; it might have produced Yalta-like language with results little different from Yalta's. But Hull demurred (for the wrong reasons): "I don't want to deal with these piddling little things," he said. "We must deal with the main issues."

Harriman feared that Molotov would take Hull's silence for acquiescence. But the evidence of Tehran and after suggests that despite (or perhaps because of) Hull's performance the Soviets were still anxious. They knew that the president himself was still to be heard from—and, for the first time, in person. Speaking with Harriman in August, FDR sounded ready for some hard bargaining with Stalin. But as the summit approached, Roosevelt indicated to other advisers that he would appeal to the dictator "on grounds of high morality." The president would say "that neither the British nor we would fight Russia over the Baltic States, but that in Russia's own interests, from the viewpoint of her position in the world, it would be a good thing to . . . have a second plebiscite, since while she is satisfied that the earlier plebiscite was conclusive, the rest of the world does not seem to think so. The same idea might be applied to Eastern Poland." The president "did not seem to realize," Harriman wrote later, "that once the Russians occupied a territory, the plebiscite would almost certainly go their way." But Stalin did not realize that Roosevelt did not realize this. It was only at Tehran that Roosevelt managed to convince the Soviet leader that the president of the United States did not know enough or care enough about Eastern Europe to stand in Moscow's way.[48]

A classic "non-meeting" of the minds came late in the conference, which opened in Tehran on November 28, 1943. Earlier the president had resorted to several gambits that were designed to foster Soviet-American intimacy but instead illustrated intra-Western divisions. FDR joined with Stalin in disparaging the French: The president said he was "100 percent in agreement with Marshal Stalin," who had argued that "France should not get back Indochina and that the French must pay for the criminal collaboration with Germany." Roosevelt also denounced the British Empire: "The President said that at some future date, he would like to talk with Marshal Stalin on the question of India; that he felt the best solution would be reform from the bottom, somewhat on the Soviet line." To which the more knowledgeable Stalin replied that the India question was "a complicated one with different levels of culture and the absence of relationship in the castes," so that "reform from the bottom would mean revolution."

It was one thing for Stalin's sycophants to flatter him (that, he expected), but it was quite another matter for the political chief of

American capitalism to do so. One can deduce from Stalin's own behavior what he expected from the other side—hard bargaining. When he took the floor at the first plenary meeting, Stalin reaffirmed that the Soviet Union would, in due course, fight against Japan. He pressed in return for an absolute and final Western commitment to an invasion of France.

The face Stalin presented at Tehran was calm and confident. But his concern that the Americans would challenge his East European plans showed through vividly at the first formal dinner—so vividly that apparently no one noticed. It happened when Roosevelt innocently raised a pet postwar project of his own—guaranteeing free access to the Baltic Sea either through international trusteeship or an "international state" in the vicinity of the Kiel Canal. From this point in the conversation, Charles Bohlen's minutes continue as follows: "Due to some error of the Soviet translator, Marshal Stalin apparently thought the President was referring to the question of the Baltic States. On the basis of this understanding, he replied categorically that the Baltic States had, by an expression of the will of the people, voted to join the Soviet Union and that this question was not therefore one for discussion. Following the clearing up of the misapprehension, he, however, expressed himself favorably in regard to the question of insuring free navigation to and from the Baltic Sea."

More was involved than an error of translation. When Stalin heard the word "Baltic," he jumped. But poor FDR had not even meant it. Later in the evening, after the president had retired, Churchill rather tentatively raised the Polish issue with Stalin. But by this time the marshal had regained his equilibrium. Churchill said that if Marshal Stalin "felt any desire to discuss the question of Poland," he was prepared to do so and he was sure the president was "similarly disposed." Marshal Stalin replied that he had not yet "felt the necessity nor the desirability of discussing the Polish question."

The next afternoon the president and the general secretary met alone. Roosevelt said he had a great many other matters relating to the future of the world that he would like to talk over informally with the marshal. There was nothing to prevent them from discussing anything they wished, Stalin replied. Roosevelt brought up his notion of a postwar organization to preserve the peace. FDR told Stalin that Churchill did not like the proposal because the British Empire had only two votes, the United Kingdom itself plus "one British Dominion." Thus, probably, was planted the idea with which the Soviets stunned FDR in

1944—that the Soviet empire (otherwise known as the Union of Soviet Socialist Republics) ought to have sixteen votes, one for each of the constituent republics. Roosevelt also volunteered that except for "a terrible crisis such as at present," Congress would be unlikely to dispatch American troops to Europe once the war was won. Stalin pressed for details. He pointed out that the world organization suggested by the President might also "require the sending of American troops to Europe." The most he had envisaged, the president replied, was the sending of American planes and ships to Europe; Britain and the Soviets "would have to handle the land armies in the event of any future threat to the peace."

This was big news. But could it be credited? How could Congress deny a president who by then would have been elected four times? At dinner that evening Stalin's conversation had a "sharp edge." Churchill was the apparent target of what note-taker Bohlen took to be Stalin's teasing. But there was a message for Roosevelt as well when Stalin "told the Prime Minister that just because Russians are simple people, it was a mistake to believe that they were blind and could not see what was before their eyes."

But what *was* happening before their eyes? By the afternoon of December 1, the conference was almost over. It had been decided there would be no more plenary sessions—only a wrap-up session that evening. Roosevelt had toasted the success of the conference at dinner the night before, but he had still not raised the issue of Poland. Could it be that he would remain silent? What, then, had been the meaning of Harry Hopkins's hint at lunch with Molotov and Eden the day before? Speaking of Poland, Hopkins had said he was "under the impression that the President had spoken openly and frankly with Marshal Stalin and that he had told him or would tell him all that he had on his mind on this subject. . . ."

The moment of truth came at 3:20 P.M. on December 1. Responding to the president's invitation, Stalin entered Roosevelt's quarters. He was accompanied only by Molotov and an interpreter. Waiting with Roosevelt were Harriman and Bohlen. The president began by saying that he had asked Marshal Stalin to come to see him as he wished "to discuss a matter briefly and frankly."

Poland! Or was it? The president said that the matter he wished to discuss "referred to internal American politics." The conversation continued as follows:

[The President] said that we had an election in 1944 and that while personally he did not wish to run again, if the war was still in progress, he might have to.

He added that there were in the United States from six to seven million Americans of Polish extraction, and as a practical man, he did not wish to lose their vote. He said personally he agreed with the views of Marshal Stalin as to the necessity of the restoration of a Polish state but would like to see the Eastern border moved farther to the west and the Western border moved even to the River Oder. He hoped, however, that the Marshal would understand that for political reasons outlined above, he could not participate in any decision here in Tehran or even next winter on this subject and that he could not publicly take part in any such arrangement at the present time. Marshal Stalin replied that now the President explained, he had understood.

The President went on to say that there were a number of persons of Lithuanian, Latvian, and Estonian origin, in that order, in the United States. He said that he fully realized the three Baltic Republics had in history and again more recently been a part of Russia and added jokingly that when the Soviet armies re-occupied these areas, he did not intend to go to war with the Soviet Union on this point.

He went on to say that the big issue in the United States, insofar as public opinion went, would be the question of referendum and the right of self-determination. He said he thought that world opinion would want some expression of the will of the people, perhaps not immediately after their re-occupation by Soviet forces, but some day, and that he personally was confident that the people would vote to join the Soviet Union.

Marshal Stalin replied that the three Baltic Republics had no autonomy under the last Czar who had been an ally of Great Britain and the United States, but that no one had raised the question of public opinion, and he did not quite see why it was being raised now.

The President replied that the truth of the matter was that the public neither knew nor understood.

Marshal Stalin answered that they should be informed and some propaganda work should be done.

He added that as to the expression of the will of the people, there would be lots of opportunities for that to be done in accordance with the Soviet constitution but that he could not agree to any form of international control.

The President replied it would be helpful for him personally if some public declaration in regard to the future elections to which the Marshal had referred, could be made.

Marshal Stalin repeated there would be plenty of opportunities for such an expression of the will of the people.[49]

A brief exchange. But so significant! The president had not even called it the Polish question but, rather, an issue of American politics. He had given Moscow the go-ahead on the Polish frontier, and although Roosevelt had not mentioned the future Polish regime, his discussion of the Baltic situation seemed to apply to Poland as well. What Roosevelt seemed to be saying was that the Soviets were free to do as they wished as long as they supplied another plebiscite for Western public opinion. FDR apparently admitted what Stalin had all along suspected, namely, that the American public could be conned. What else could the president have meant by: "The truth of the matter was that the public neither knew nor understood"? Such a view was close to Stalin's own; falling in with the spirit of the exchange, he had replied with advice from one benevolent despot to another: "Some propaganda work should be done." Roosevelt, of course, was not Hitler. But he might yet make an even better partner. He had been roundabout in coming to the point. But he might keep his word longer than Hitler had.

The discussion at the final tripartite meeting on the evening of December 1 showed Stalin triumphant—a sore winner! When Roosevelt urged Soviet reconciliation with the London Poles, Stalin "replied that the Polish Government-in-exile were closely connected with the Germans and their agents in Poland were killing partisans." Now that Roosevelt had conceded in private there was no need to mince words. When Churchill said he would "be through" with the Polish government if it refused to go along with a new Polish-Soviet border, Stalin, who in 1941 had virtually begged the British to accept the Curzon Line and then waited two years for Churchill's blessing, magnanimously upped the ante. He said that if the Russians were given the northern part of East Prussia, running along the left bank of the Niemen and including Tilsit and the city of Königsberg, he would be "prepared to accept the Curzon Line as the frontier between the Soviet Union and Poland."[50]

The Tehran Conference was the highpoint of East-West wartime cooperation. Soviets and Americans were both satisfied but each for different reasons—reasons that, to complicate matters further, the other did not fully understand. The Americans thought Moscow had renounced unilateralism. To the Soviets, it seemed Roosevelt had approved of Soviet aims, at least as far as Poland and the Baltic States were concerned. Washington never did comprehend the Soviet perception of Tehran but, nonetheless, sensed in the spring of 1944 that something had gone wrong. In turn, American (and British) uneasiness suggested to Stalin that Roosevelt and Churchill were welshing on commitments made at Tehran if, indeed, they had not been out to trick him in the first place.

Roosevelt and Hull oversold entente even more than Nixon and Kissinger were to oversell détente in the 1970s. Even at their most Pollyannish, they retained doubts about Stalin's intentions. But they gave the public a diet of heady optimism, especially after the Moscow and Tehran conferences. Reporting to Congress upon his return from Moscow, Secretary Hull declared, "There will no longer be a need for spheres of influence, for balance of power or any other special arrangements through which, in the unhappy past, the nations chose to safeguard their security or to promote their interests." Roosevelt's report to the American people on Tehran was no less up-beat. [51]

Soviet assessments of Tehran also registered special gratification. In the press and at public meetings in factories and in farms, Tehran's "historic decisions" were extravagantly praised: the allies had reached a new understanding; the Soviet Union had been recognized to be a world power equal in importance to Britain and the United States; security in the postwar world had been assured. Even more revealing were impressions President Beneš gleaned on a visit to Stalin and Molotov in mid-December. Beneš told Harriman that as a result of the Soviet leaders' "evident sense of security and self-confidence, modesty and calm have taken the place of their previous aggressiveness and excitability." Stalin expressed to Beneš his "great satisfaction" with the new relationships with his allies. According to Harriman's paraphrase of Beneš's account, "Stalin had been much impressed with the President and felt that complete agreement had been reached with him at Tehran on all questions, not of course in detail but in approach. He gave Beneš the impression that he now felt completely at ease with the President." [52]

Soviet satisfaction manifested itself in two apparently contradictory ways. In person, Harriman reported, Molotov had never been more friendly and cordial. But the Soviet foreign minister had never been rougher on the Poles (he was now insisting that the Polish government itself be drastically reorganized), and it was not long before the Soviet press began accusing the Americans and British of duplicity. London was charged with plotting a separate peace with the Germans. The attack on Washington came in a blast at, of all people, Wendell Willkie. Upon his return from Moscow in 1942, Willkie had boasted of having had a "frank, heart-to-heart discussion" with Stalin, who had "looked at me like an old friend. . . ." But in January 1944, Willkie's friend scented in his more recent writing what *Pravda* called "the rotten smell of anti-Soviet slander." Willkie had warned his fellow American politicians not to "stir distrust" of the Russians, whether to pressure Moscow or to advance their own domestic political ambitions. But the Kremlin was not fooled. "Under the guise of strengthening trust," Willkie was himself "sowing suspicions." Willkie had cautioned that the issue of Soviet intentions toward smaller European states—Poland, Finland, the Baltics, and the Balkans—might someday produce a crisis between East and West. The Baltic states, *Pravda* reminded him, were now "an internal affair" of the USSR; as for the others, the Soviets would make necessary arrangements with them "without any assistance from Mr. Willkie."[53]

Cordell Hull regarded the harder Soviet line as a post-Tehran turn-about. He failed to realize that Stalin was implementing Tehran, as he understood it. The attack on Willkie was probably meant to warn those who, feigning support for Soviet-American cooperation, tried to under-mine it. Hull himself had complained, while in Moscow, about ene-mies of the USSR in America. The Soviet press was only doing some of the "propaganda work" that Stalin had recommended to Roosevelt. The fact that Moscow moved with unseemly haste and crudity was nothing special—only par for the Soviet course.

Yet Stalin moved cautiously withal. At their first meeting in Jan-uary 1944, Molotov told Harriman that the toughest Soviet statement yet on the Polish frontier "would be found to conform to the spirit of the conversations at Tehran." Molotov "showed he was most anxious and hopeful that [FDR] would react favorably" to the statement.[54] The Soviets knew how much stock the Americans put in a cordial and friendly personal approach. Being nice was a good way to keep the fran-chise in the event the president were to have second post-Tehran thoughts.

But Soviet stock was not quite so high in American eyes in early 1944. During January, Harriman was instructed to warn the Soviets that "the effect of any hesitancy or refusal by the Soviet Government [to reopen talks with the Polish Government] would adversely affect the cause of international cooperation." Harriman was told to underline the danger of an anti-Soviet swing in American opinion, and Roosevelt returned to the latter point in a telegram dispatched on February 7. The British, meantime, were pressing the Poles to settle with the Soviets on the kind of terms discussed at Tehran. But when the Poles refused (in part because, unaware of how much Roosevelt had conceded at Tehran, they still hoped for American backing in a showdown with Moscow), Churchill, contrary to what he had told Stalin, did not wash his hands of them. Rather, he proposed a compromise solution, which, though unacceptable to the Poles, was not acceptable to the Soviets either.[55]

Stalin characterized Churchill's plea for a compromise as "interspersed with threats in regard to the Soviet Union." "I cannot but remind you," he wrote to Churchill on March 23, "that in Teheran you, the President and I came to agreement regarding the rightfulness of the Curzon Line." Stalin continued, "In your message you express the hope that the failure of the Polish question will not influence our cooperation in other spheres. As to me, I stood and continue to stand for cooperation. But I am afraid that the method of threats and discreditation, if it will be used in the future as well, will not favor this cooperation."[56]

Two could warn that the other side's action jeopardized long-term cooperation—especially since the British and, particularly, the Americans counted so much on collaboration. Stalin's tone of bitter, injured innocence was typical of him. But so was the way he took Western warnings into account by opening those secret talks with the London Poles in May 1944. The fact that those talks were soon broken off by Moscow can be traced to two events that took place early in June. One, the allied invasion of France, the long-delayed second front, ensured Soviet conquest of much of East Europe and, at the same time, removed a major reason for Stalin to conciliate his allies. The second event was, for the Americans who played a role in it, a non-event; for the Soviets, however, it provided a signal they had been waiting for. On June 7, Harriman informed Molotov that Roosevelt and Mr. Hull were firm in their determination to carry out the understandings reached at Moscow and Tehran and that "no minor difficulties would affect this determination to work out agreements on all questions." Harriman was going on to say that the president expected the Svoiet government to carry out its commitments, too, when Molotov asked whether Roosevelt's attitude was still "the same as expressed at Tehran." "Of course," Harriman replied. Molotov said that he would "inform Marshal Stalin at once" and that the Marshal would be "gratified." Five days later Harriman met with Stalin, after which the ambassador reported to Roosevelt that the marshal "appeared pleased to learn of your attitude and said that he appreciated your position at the present time. . . ." Concluded Harriman: "This was the first friendly talk I have had with Stalin about the Poles and I got the feeling that he saw a solution in the making which would be acceptable all around."[57]

Stalin's smiles were a bad omen. Harriman had merely restated the obvious. But to Stalin, reconfirmation of FDR's views opened the way to a final solution to the Polish problem. As for the London Poles, they also received what they thought was a Roosevelt signal on the same June day Harriman met with Stalin. After months of trying to arrange an audience, Polish Prime Minister Stanislaw Mikolajczyk was received at the White House. The president told the prime minister that he thought the Poles "could trust the Russians to give them fair treatment." Roosevelt added that at most the Poles would have to give up "a little something" in the way of territory. He did not think the Soviets would insist on the Curzon Line. Was the president deceiving only his guest, or himself as well? In any event, the Polish prime minister left reassured.[58]

4

Entente Stalinist-Style: June 1944-April 1945

ON NOVEMBER 6, 1944, JOSEPH STALIN DELIVERED AN ORATION IN Moscow on the twenty-seventh anniversary of the Bolshevik Revolution. It was a triumphant account of military progress. But the speaker also discussed the political state of the allied coalition and prospects for postwar peace and security. The state of the alliance was good. Implementation of the Tehran decisions testified to that, as did successful negotiations at Dumbarton Oaks concerning the new international organization. "There is talk about disagreements among the three powers on certain questions of security," said Stalin. "Of course disagreements exist and there will be more of them on other issues. Disagreements occur even among people of one and the same party. All the more reason for them to occur among representatives of various states and parties. What is amazing is not the fact that disagreements exist, but that they are so small, and that as a rule they are resolved almost every time in a spirit of unity and agreement among the three great powers."

At the basis of the alliance, Stalin continued, were not "accidental or transitory motives, but vitally important and long-lasting interests." There could be no doubt, he said, that the entente would "withstand the trials of the last stage of the war." But the task consisted "not only in winning the war but in preventing new aggression and a new war, if not forever, then at least for an extended period of time." Would the new international organization be equal to that task? It would, Stalin answered, as long as the victors acted in a spirit of "unanimity and agreement." It would not "if they were to violate this necessary precondition."[1]

This speech has proven a trap for those who have tried to analyze it. American Communist leader Earl Browder read it at the time as confirming a new age of peace both among nations and between classes. Browder published a full-blown analysis of the new era, complete with prescription for continued Communist party alliance with the American ruling class—only to be disowned by his own party several months later after what was presumed to be a Moscow-inspired attack on him by French Communist leader Jacques Duclos. Doclos's April 1945 article, which insisted that class war would continue long after world war ended, has been cited by traditionalist historians to suggest that Stalin never meant what he said in November. But that interpretation is as simplistic as Browder's.[2]

What *was* Stalin's meaning? What were his hopes and fears as the war came to an end? Stalin did not want a cold war. Second only to a hot war between the former allies, that was his last choice. Détente was not Stalin's first preference either. What Stalin wanted was nothing less than continued entente—although, as the November speech suggests, he was not sure the "necessary preconditions" could be obtained.

This conclusion sounds like an extreme sort of revisionism. It appears to confirm that Western pressure forced the Cold War on Stalin and the world. Not so. For the entente Stalin desired was not the benign relationship revisionists depict. It was designed to foster Soviet control of Eastern Europe whether directly (in the case of Poland, Rumania, and Bulgaria) or indirectly (in Hungary and Czechoslovakia); to expand Soviet influence in Western Europe, the Near East, and Asia; to position the USSR for even greater gains when the next Western economic crisis struck; and to achieve all this while subsidized to the tune of at least six billion dollars in American credits.

This was not so much a plan, with all contingencies taken into account, as a hope. In addition to these maximum goals, the Soviets had minimum aims (ensuring Communist hegemony over East Europe and defeating, disarming, and obtaining reparations from Germany) to which they could always retreat. The winter of 1944–1945 was a period of Kremlin optimism. But even then Stalin had doubts and perhaps even moments of panic. The latent hostility of the capitalist powers was one cause for concern. The Soviet Union's own weakness was another. There was still a war to be won in which things could go wrong. Still, Stalin's maximum goals seemed obtainable, at least until Franklin Roosevelt died on April 12, 1945.

Did Stalin, that most suspicious of men, really think the West would sit still for entente Stalinist-style? He could not be sure—but was it not worth a try? His ideology, in particular his Leninist conception of capitalist contradictions, offered reasons for hope—likewise, Western behavior, as usual interpreted by Stalin in terms of Soviet experience. The conference at Yalta in February 1945 offered an opportunity to test the scenario, with results that must have seemed gratifying to Stalin. True, Yalta was followed by setbacks. And in April that hard-line article by Jacques Duclos seemed to signal a Soviet change of course. But Duclos's signal, like so much else in U.S.–Soviet relations, was not what it seemed.

Needless to say, Stalin never broadcast his maximum and minimum aims for Western consumption. Nor did he elaborate frankly and fully in any private conversation which has since come to light. That leaves historians to deduce his thinking from the pattern of Soviet foreign policy: a ruthless but not reckless clamping down in Rumania, Bulgaria, and Poland; more restrained manipulation in Czechoslovakia and Hungary; even more tentative maneuvering in France, Italy, and Greece; plus probing for advantage at various other points in Europe and Asia.

In Rumania and Bulgaria, the Soviets moved quickly. The Red Army entered both countries without resistance in the late summer of 1944. An anti-Nazi coup d'état led by King Michael opened the gates to Rumania, while a Communist-led upheaval paved the Soviets' way into Bulgaria. The Western powers endorsed armistice terms that gave the Red Army the predominant military and political role in both countries. In theory, this hegemony was not to last beyond Germany's final defeat (a reservation Washington made explicit in the Bulgarian armistice but not the Rumanian), but the Soviets used their temporary predominance to make it permanent. They intimidated or eliminated politicians who opposed or might have opposed them, and thus they laid the basis for subservient regimes. The outcome was assured in Bucharest when Vyshinsky came to town in late February 1945 and bullied King Michael (in part by slamming the royal door so hard as to crack the surrounding plaster) into appointing a Communist-dominated government which would do Moscow's bidding. A similar result was reached in Bulgaria in the spring of 1945.[3]

In Poland things moved more slowly, but no less surely. In a last effort to prevent Soviet recognition of a new Polish government, Roosevelt cabled Stalin on December 30 that "neither the Government nor the people of the United States" considered the Lublin Committee representative of the Polish people. Stalin's New Year's Day reply ended with an ironic and perhaps deliberately mocking echo of Roosevelt's references to congressional opinion. "Of course, your suggestion to postpone for a month the recognition of the Provisional Government of Poland by the Soviet Union is perfectly understandable to me. But there is one circumstance which makes me powerless to fulfill your wish. The fact is that on December 27 the Presidium of the Supreme Soviet of the USSR, responding to an appropriate request of the Poles, has already informed them that it intends to recognize the Provisional Government as soon as it is formed. This circumstance makes me powerless to fulfill your wish."[4]

The Yalta accord, in which the Soviets agreed to a limited reorganization of the Polish provisional government, seemed likely to retard Poland's progress toward the status of Rumania and Bulgaria. But the Soviets resisted implementation of the accord as the West understood it. Unknown to the West, Stalin had urged caution on the Polish Communists even after June 1944. But he also had assured them that Roosevelt and Churchill would not break with him over Poland. On July 18, 1944, Communist Poles stationed in Moscow transmitted home a Soviet warning that a new Polish government "must pursue policies conducive to understanding between the Allied nations in the Tehran spirit." That meant forming a national front government and adopting moderate policies; for the international effect of radical policies "would be to make Poland a bone of contention between the Tehran powers," and "clearly such a development would not be in the interests of the USSR. . . ." But that Britain and the United States would acquiesce if the Poles would only act prudently was a message Stalin conveyed directly to a Polish delegation in October. The international situation, Stalin explained, was as follows: Since the three-power alliance was based on "a compromise involving the capitalist countries on the one side and the USSR on the other," there were certain areas of conflict, for example, the second front and the Polish question. The British sought a Polish government "dependent on them and open to their influence." But, Stalin assured his Polish listeners, "there is no possibility of a break-up in the alliance over Poland." And when the delegates reminded him of a parliamentary speech in which Churchill had seemed to take a hard line on Poland, Stalin replied that "serious politicians should ignore parliamentary gobbledygook."[5]

"Parliamentary gobbledygook"! Never had Stalin projected Soviet experience onto the West more clearly. What was said in the great

Western legislatures was not to be taken seriously by the Polish delegates and, so it appeared to Stalin, probably not even by the speaker himself. But still, Churchill kept trying to "slip a kopeck out of your pocket." Stalin later told Polish Communist leader Boleslaw Bierut that Churchill had pushed Polish Prime Minister Mikolajczyk to resign in late 1944 as a way of insinuating him into a new coalition government. Stalin swore that as long as the Red Army was in Poland, Mikolajczyk would not pass. By the summer of 1945 (to run ahead of our story), Mikolajczyk was deputy prime minister in a coalition government formed to implement the Yalta agreement. But despite Stalin's oath, and despite the opinion of Harry Hopkins and revisionist historians that Moscow yielded at Yalta, it was Stalin who had the last laugh on Poland.[6]

Czechoslovakia is often cited by revisionists as an example of Stalin's caution in that he permitted genuine coalition rule until as late as 1948. Hungary's experience with Stalin is said to be similar although its coalition was neither as genuine nor as long-lasting as that of Czechoslovakia. In fact, Prague was not all that free of Soviet machinations, while Soviet moderation in Budapest, which was more far-reaching than contemporary Western observers appreciated, reflected Stalin's ulterior motives. Limits to Czechoslovak independence were set as early as 1943 in Moscow discussions between Stalin and Beneš and in the Czechoslovak-Soviet Treaty which emerged from those negotiations. Beneš did what was necessary to satisfy the Soviets. What was necessary was to allot key posts to Communists in the Cabinet formed in the spring of 1945. Eventually those Communist ministers would seize power in 1948; in the meantime, they exerted pressure on the non-Communist leaders to conciliate Moscow. Moreover, the Czechoslovak arrangements served, as Molotov himself noted in early 1944, as a model for other countries. If Stalin's scenario had worked out, the Czech model might eventually have been copied in the West.[7]

The Hungarian regime of Admiral Horthy fought alongside the Germans even while extending feelers to Moscow. Yet Stalin did not reject those feelers out of hand. The puny size and antinational reputation of the Hungarian Communist party made him hesitate to rely on it. (Similar calculations may have explained Soviet caution in Poland and Rumania, too.) If Horthy had broken with Hitler, Stalin told a delegation of Hungarian Communists in December 1944, Moscow would have kept the admiral in office. About the same time, the Soviets encouraged the Hungarian Communists to devise a moderate political and economic program for Hungary, and they made sure that the new provisional government included only two Communists (who, however, had disproportionate influence with the occupying Red Army). In Hungary, as in other places where the Soviet watchword was caution, more militant native Communists were puzzled and annoyed. Communication with Moscow was poor during the war. Often, their only directives were the public speeches of the Soviet leaders. "When Stalin said something Communist," recalls one Hungarian ex-Communist, "we rejoiced and obeyed him. When he said something nice about the allies, we presumed he was tricking them . . . and we became even more revolutionary." Nor was this interpretation entirely unfounded. When orders came from Moscow to cooperate in a coalition government, Hungarian Communists saw this as a short-term tactic for promoting revolution. A tactic it was, but any seizure of power was to be delayed according to Stalin's scenario. Mátyás Rákosi, the Stalinist leader of post-1947 Hungary, recalled explaining to inner party circles in 1945 that "even a theoretical discussion of a goal of proletarian dictatorship would have created upheaval in the ranks of our coalition partners"; in addition, however, he explained that "if the situation changes—and in years the situation will change—then the line will change too." According to Rákosi, Stalin thought time was on his side. The Soviet leader foresaw a Communist takeover after ten or fifteen years. Why the estimate of ten to fifteen years? By then, as we shall see, Stalin expected the next great capitalist economic crisis, complete perhaps with another round of inter-imperialist conflict, in which countries like Hungary and Czechoslovakia, and perhaps even certain West European states too, might go the revolutionary way of Russia in the First World War. [8]

If Moscow was cautious in Czechoslovakia and Hungary, it was even more circumspect in areas where Western interest was intense and Western troops were present. But, contrary to revisionist claims, Stalin was not conceding a permanent sphere of influence to the Western powers. For Stalin, political arrangements were no more enduring than the circumstances that brought them about. If he was encouraging Western Communist parties to operate moderately and legally, it was to gather up influence, to press non-Communists to pay heed to Moscow, and to prepare for later and more favorable circumstances.

The pattern in France reflected the character of Charles de Gaulle and his movement. A politician as powerful and unpredictable as de Gaulle posed formidable obstacles to Soviet aims—along with opportunities that flowed from his erratic relations with Washington and London. French Communists played a leading role in the Resistance. Yet when de Gaulle asked them to turn over their arms to the new provisional government they did so—not coincidentally—after Communist leader Maurice Thorez returned from Moscow. One reason why the Soviets restrained the French Communists was the presence of allied troops, who would not have taken kindly to civil strife behind their lines. But there was a more positive motive, too, for Soviet moderation: the desire to turn de Gaulle's stubbornness and strength of will (of which Stalin had gained firsthand knowledge in Moscow in December 1944) against the French leader's Western allies. Stalin sometimes sounded as if he dreamed of eliminating France as a great power; at Tehran he said, "the entire French ruling class [is] rotten to the core" and hence should be deprived of power. But a cheap shot like that also promoted the more realistic aim of fomenting inter-imperialist animosity—a cause Stalin increasingly pursued by building up France instead of cutting it down. When de Gaulle threatened to leave Moscow without signing a Soviet-French treaty (*This* was a tactic Stalin could respect!) the Soviets agreed to one with no strings attached. At Yalta, Stalin politely inquired whether Roosevelt meant to give Paris a zone of occupation in Germany. ("Only out of kindness," FDR replied.) Stalin and Molotov objected to French participation in the Allied Control Commission for Germany, but they relented about the same time that Roosevelt and Churchill gave way on Poland.[9]

In Italy, where there was no de Gaulle, the Soviets and their Communist allies were bolder. The Western powers offered to the Soviets the sort of room to maneuver that the West and its sympathizers never received in, say, Rumania. And the Soviets took advantage of their opportunity. They bombarded British and American occupation authorities with complaints and demands. They designated Vyshinsky himself as the Soviet plentipotentiary for Italy, a sure sign that Moscow hoped for a greater voice than it was allowing to Westerners in the Balkans. With Italian Communist leader Palmiro Togliatti operating freely (compared to his anti-Communist Rumanian counterparts), Moscow rushed to recognize Marshal Pietro Badoglio's interim regime and tried to deal with it directly instead of through Western occupation channels. That Moscow failed in its attempt to serve (in Mastny's phrase) "as an indispensable intermediary between the weak government and those popular wishes which would be articulated by the Italian Communists" does not alter the fact that the Kremlin tried.[10]

In Greece, the question is whether the Soviets even tried. In the summer of 1944, the Communist-led National Liberation Front (EAM) demanded a major role in the Greek government-in-exile. But soon after a Soviet emissary arrived at its Greek mountain headquarters, EAM drastically reduced its demands. In December 1944, the Greek Communists shifted ground again and rose in revolt. But Moscow stayed on the sidelines, failing to support the Communist cause in the Soviet press and offering to recognize the George Papandreou government, which was suppressing the revolt with British help. Apparently, the Greek Communists did not begin their uprising at Moscow's behest. Whether or not they contradicted a direct Soviet order not to revolt is another question. And even if the Russians had counseled moderation, once the revolt began it was a test of Western resistance. In Greece, where the British had charge of allied interests, that resistance was swift, strong, and successful. Such was not the exception to the rule, but it was not the rule either.[11]

Germany was, of course, the country of greatest concern to both East and West. At a minimum, the Soviets wanted reparations from postwar Germany plus security against renewed German aggression. At the maximum, Stalin seemingly wanted Germany itself. To judge by what he said at wartime summit conferences, Stalin sought to dismember and cripple Germany. He was the most bloodthirsty of the Big Three. He said he would go further than the "five-Germany" solution envisaged by Roosevelt at Tehran. In an exchange that prompted Churchill to stomp out of the room, Stalin urged that from 50,000 to 100,000 Germans be liquidated, to which FDR jokingly replied that 49,000 would probably suffice. Several times Stalin warned that Germany might rise again in fifteen or twenty years. But a new Germany (or Germanies) unable to threaten the USSR would not be able to defend itself against Russia either. Stalin's motivation may have been in part defensive, but the result of dismemberment would have opened up new opportunities for Soviet penetration.[12]

Even that, however, probably understates Stalin's maximum goal. For that, to judge by a plan drawn up by German Communists under Soviet tutelage, was a Germany united under Communist rule. The "Action Program of the Bloc of Militant Democracy," prepared in October 1944 by a group led by Walter Ulbricht, anticipated "the immediate formation of a Government of the Bloc of Militant Democracy" as a step toward "consolidation of power." Astonishingly enough, as Mastny points out, the Communists not only hoped to rule all of

Germany, they hoped to do so without antagonizing the Western powers. As a colleague of Ulbricht's put it, the new Germany would have both "an especially close relationship with the Soviet Union and friendship with the West, particularly France, England and the USA." Before long, adverse military developments (an allied speed-up on the Western front and a Soviet slowdown in the East) forced a change in tactics. Having resisted formal agreements that would define their position in postwar Germany, the Soviets agreed in November 1944 to divide the country into zones, to establish three-power status for Berlin, and to create a tripartite control system. About the same time, the line about an all-German government was cut from the Action Program, and not long after that the whole program was scrapped. Thereafter, Ulbricht and company devoted their attention primarily to the Soviet zone. But whether or not that pattern would be permanent would have to await events.[13]

Communist probes extended to the smaller countries of Western Europe. In Belgium, where Foreign Minister Paul Henri Spaak was promoting a Western European bloc, Communists attempted to overturn the government. Having liberated a piece of Northern Norway, the Soviets put in a claim for Bear Island and Spitsbergen, both belonging to Oslo. European neutrals Sweden and Switzerland were likewise bullied, as if Moscow had designs on them, too. And in May 1945 the Soviets occupied Bornholm despite a Danish plea to have Eisenhower take the island. Moscow explained that, "as is well known," Bornholm was within their sphere of operations, and it might have stayed there had the Soviets not felt the political embarrassment involved in keeping a portion of a country that otherwise remained free and independent.[14]

In the Far East, the American need for assistance against Japan opened the door to Soviet ambition. Eventually, Stalin would try to parlay participation in the Pacific war into a role in Japan's occupation. In the beginning, his "needs" were largely territorial—at the expense of China as well as Japan. In December 1944, when Harriman told him FDR was anxious to know what political questions needed to be "clairified" before Moscow would fight Japan, Stalin went into the next room and brought out a map. He said that the Kurile Islands and lower Sakhalin should be "returned to Russia." He "drew a line around the southern part of the Liaotung Peninsula including Port Arthur and Dairen saying the Russians wished again to lease these ports and the surrounding area." Stalin also asked to lease, and presumably to protect with Soviet troops, the Chinese-Eastern Railway. These wishes were granted by Roosevelt and Churchill at Yalta. In return, the Soviet Union declared its readiness to fight Japan and to conclude a pact of friendship and alliance with Chiang Kai-shek's Nationalist government.[15] The Soviets fought the Japanese for a grand total of six days; their friendship and alliance with Chiang helped him on his way to Formosan exile. But the privileges gained at China's expense remained Stalin's to have and to hold until his dear comrade Mao Tse-tung managed to make him part with some of them.

Moscow had designs on North Africa and the Near East, too. In January 1945 Ambassador Gromyko said his government had a special interest in the international trusteeships that the United States was proposing for former Axis colonies. "After all," he pointed out, "as a country at war with Italy, the Soviet Union will have to assume responsibilities with regard to Italian colonies, and it may well have to assume responsibilities with regard to territories detached from Japan." The Italian colonies Gromyko coveted were in North Africa. To the East, the Soviets had been moving to extract oil concessions and perhaps even territory from Iran. Meantime, in an unsolicited gesture of goodwill, Churchill invited Stalin to contemplate a new regime for the Turkish Straits. In a fit of *noblesse oblige* at Tehran, Churchill said he felt that such a large land mass as Russia deserved access to warm water ports. Whether because he could not believe his ears, or in order not to appear overly anxious, Stalin reacted cautiously. He replied that "at the proper time" that question could be discussed, but that since Mr. Churchill had raised the question he would like to "inquire as to the regime of the Dardanelles." Churchill succeeded in postponing a fuller discussion at Tehran, but by Yalta Stalin had worked up a full head of indignation about the hand which Turkey had "on Russia's throat." By then, Churchill had thought better of his initiative and he stalled effectively, but his Tehran indiscretion was to come back to haunt his successor, Clement Attlee. Roosevelt's contribution to the Yalta discussion on the Straits, was to say that he had "one general observation to make," which was that the United States had a frontier of over three thousand miles with Canada and there was "no fort and no armed forces." This situation had existed over a hundred years and it was the president's hope that other frontiers in the world would eventually be without forts or armed forces on any part of their national boundaries.[16]

The pattern we have been tracing poses an important question. Given his assumption of irremediable capitalist hostility, how could

Stalin ever think of achieving his maximum aims? The Leninist understanding of imperialism suggests an answer. Recall that, according to
Lenin, two kinds of conflict are endemic in the modern world—conflict
between socialism and capitalism, which on the international stage
translates into the East versus the West, and inter-imperialist strife.
World War I had been an inter-imperialist war; and so, in large part,
according to Stalin, was World War II.[17] While the war was on, these
themes were not emphasized in Soviet propaganda. But to Stalin and
his colleagues, the supporting evidence was all around them. They were
alert to latent conflict between British capitalists seeking to retain an
empire and Americans seemingly wanting to inherit one. They needed
only to look across the conference table to see capitalist contradictions
on display. Roosevelt sniped at the British. He tried to meet Stalin
behind Churchill's back and refused to let Churchill speak for him in
Moscow in October 1944. The leaders of England and the United
States disagreed on a wide variety of issues, and Roosevelt thought he
could ingratiate himself with Stalin by emphasizing these differences.
Moscow could play upon inter-imperialist splits, whether by siding with
one capitalist statesman against the other or by playing the honest bro-
ker between them, and could count on the next scheduled crisis of
capitalism to produce benefits for the USSR.

    While Stalin observed Western statesmen, his experts studied the
West. To judge by wartime Soviet press coverage (as well as Litvinov's
remarks to Sumner Welles quoted earlier), the Soviet scrutiny of American politics was superficial and on the whole reassuring to the Kremlin.
Until 1943, there were relatively few articles on the U.S. political
scene. Those that did appear depicted Roosevelt as a capitalist politician, to be sure, but relatively progressive, "realistic" in his willingness
to work with the USSR, and firmly in control of his country. Beginning
in 1944, the Soviet press increased its coverage of "reactionaries" (conservative Republicans and anti-FDR Democrats), some of whom were
allegedly dreaming of a new war against the USSR. The Kremlin projected its own conception of a disloyal opposition onto America in an
Izvestia warning, issued on the eve of the November 1944 elections,
that the GOP would stage a phony assassination of candidate Thomas
Dewey and then blame American Communists for the attempt. But
Roosevelt's reelection had a soothing effect on Kremlin nerves, for afterward the president was once again portrayed in firm control, supported
by staunchly pro-Soviet public opinion, and committed to winning the
war and organizing the peace in cooperation with Moscow.[18]

If the American political scene seemed hospitable to Stalin's hopes, so did the Western economic prospect. The leading Soviet economic expert on the West was Hungarian-born Eugene Varga, who toward the end of the war completed a book entitled *Changes in the Economy of Capitalism*, chapters of which were published in 1945. According to Varga, world capitalism would emerge from the war with both gains and losses. On the plus side were an enhanced role for the state in guiding economic activity, as well as a technological leap forward; both were particularly pronounced in the United States, which had gained on its capitalist competitors by virtue of having been spared wartime destruction. Capitalist losses were particularly devastating in European countries whose colonies, to make matters worse, were increasingly restive under imperial control. Tension was built into the uneven development of European and American capitalism; meanwhile, each faced its own unique problems—over-production in the United States, under-production and under-consumption in Europe. The outlook, according to Varga, was for a two- to three-year economic upsurge ending in a "crisis of overproduction" in the relatively well-off capitalist countries, to be followed by a new industrial cycle on the model of the period 1929–1937, with its "depression of a special type." Under these trying circumstances, capitalist reactionaries would seek to "inflame the contradictions" between East and West, but they would fail. For "democratic forces" in the West would at the same time be "aiming to cooperate" with the USSR, and capitalist governments, "taking into account the forces of democracy and the might of the Soviet Union as demonstrated in the Second World War, would not lightly take the path of armed conflict."[19]

To Westerners who read Varga at the time, his analysis seemed rigid and dogmatic. But by Soviet standards, his book was daring in its stress on facts rather than ideology and in its recognition of capitalist gains as well as losses. Later, when the Cold War was on in earnest, Varga's book would come under fierce attack. But in 1945 his conclusions boded well for Stalinist-style entente. Varga predicted continued cooperation with the United States even after the warmth of wartime faded away; his analysis suggested that the Americans might try to solve their overproduction problem by exporting goods and capital to the Soviet Union. Varga foresaw Soviet opportunities to play one set of imperialists off against another, while the capitalist economic crises he predicted might bring with them the chance for new revolutionary gains. Recall Stalin's advice to the Hungarian Communists (as relayed by Rákosi) to wait a decade before attempting a full take-over. If Moscow and its Communist allies used the time carefully and well, then they would be prepared when fresh disasters struck the West.

The question of American postwar economic assistance to Russia became a matter of actual negotiation beginning in 1943. At first, Washington was inclined to offer aid without strings. But as differences arose over Poland and other issues in 1944, some Americans, Ambassador Averell Harriman in particular, thought to offer American credits in return for Soviet political concessions. Roosevelt never followed Harriman's advice, and neither did Truman. Roosevelt refused to contaminate economic relations with political conditions, while Truman, going to the other extreme, declined to sweeten his demands with credits. In the light of Nixon-Kissinger "linkage diplomacy" of the 1970s, some might wish that Harriman's strategy had been tried. But the obstacles would have been formidable. One was the American Congress with its penchant for all-or-nothing dealings with the Soviets. Another was the Soviet perception of what aid would mean for the United States. Harriman thought Washington had the Soviets over a barrel. Stalin thought the reverse.

Symptomatic of the situation was that each side believed the other first broached postwar economic cooperation.[20] As best I can tell, Americans (first a visiting businessman and next Harriman himself) raised the issue. It was this, along with the way the Americans phrased it, plus the Soviets' Marxist-Leninist image of the American economy, that led Moscow to its misconception of the American position.

Donald M. Nelson, chairman of the War Production Board, visited Moscow in October 1943, meeting with Molotov and later with Stalin. "Speaking as a business man," Nelson said he thought there was "a great future in the exchange of goods between Russia and the United States," since the United States had a great surplus of capital equipment that Russia needed, while Russia had supplies that the United States needed. Nelson's Soviet hosts played hard to get at first. Molotov asked whether Mr. Nelson thought Russia could "*count* on receiving from the United States after the war machinery and capital equipment." (Emphasis added.) Stalin appeared bored and then perked up at Nelson's reference to surplus capital equipment that the United States would want to dispose of. Both Molotov and Stalin asked whether credits could be extended (Nelson thought so), and Stalin assured his guest several times that the Soviet government could "definitely be counted on to pay its obligations." Nelson's ten-day stay in Moscow, reported the American chargé, "was marked by extreme cordiality and exceptional cooperation on the part of all the Soviet officials with whom he came into contact."[21]

On November 5, 1943, Harriman mentioned American credits for Soviet reconstruction to Minister of Foreign Trade Anastas Mikoyan. Harriman noted in passing that "it would be in the self-interest of the United States to be able to afford full employment during the period of transition from war-time to peace-time economy." Neither Roosevelt nor Stalin raised the subject at Tehran, but the president authorized Harriman to pursue it afterward. The ambassador did so in December, and in January 1944 Molotov responded by asking how the Americans wished to consider the question formally. Later that month, Mikoyan suggested a first credit of one billion dollars. But further study in Washington revealed that congressional legislation would be required both to authorize Export-Import Bank credits and to repeal the 1934 Johnson Act provision that barred loans to nations, like the USSR, that were in default of debts to the United States. Washington therefore proposed a scheme whereby Moscow could get, under the existing lend-lease system, goods usable after the war. The Soviets seemed satisfied with this approach but did not hurry to conclude a deal. They waited several months before beginning negotiations, and then they haggled over every point. The American side pressed for an early agreement. Late in 1944, after Washington had declared its last offer to be final, Ambassador Gromyko suddenly renewed the request for long-term credits apart from lend-lease, as if the nearly year-long negotiation had been a charade. In January 1945 Molotov invited Harriman to the Foreign Ministry and handed him an aide-mémoire, the arrogant tone of which stunned the ambassador: "Having in mind the repeated statements of American public figures concerning the desirability of receiving extensive large Soviet orders for the postwar and transition period, the Soviet Government considers it possible to place orders on the basis of long-term credits to the amount of 6 billion dollars."[22]

What lay behind the erratic Soviet behavior? An answer is suggested by an exchange between I. A. Eremin, assistant chairman of the Soviet Purchasing Commission in the United States, and John Hazard of the U.S. Foreign Economic Administration. Hazard complained on August 12, 1944, about the delay in negotiations. Eremin said Washington was at fault for quibbling over details. Hazard said he thought the Soviets underestimated the attention American negotiators must give to press and congressional opinion. If the United States were to offer an interest rate lower than the cost of the money to the government, "the people and, therefore, Congress would not stand for it." Eremin knew better. According to Hazard's account, Eremin "felt certain that the American people as a whole were so responsive to the part the USSR played in the war that only a small percentage would criticize special concessions. He noted that many corporation presidents had called on him recently. They said they were Republicans, but they would go farther than the Democrats seemed willing to go in broadening trade relations with the USSR. He said that I must know myself that U.S. industry was in large measure idle in the types of equipment the USSR wants, and that it is certainly to the government's interest to get business into these plants."[23]

The Soviets thought we needed them even more than they needed us. Joseph Stalin himself said so. The occasion was the October 9, 1944, meeting (mentioned above) at which Stalin summarized the state of the alliance for his Polish protégés. In addition to the second-front issue, he said, postwar economic cooperation was another bone of contention between Moscow and Washington. The nature of that problem? "The USA would already like to involve the USSR in contracts for postwar orders from America."[24]

The very idea that the American "need" to assist Soviet reconstruction was on a par with the Soviet need for a second front boggles the mind. But not Stalin's mind. Stalin assumed the capitalist countries would desperately need to export surplus capital and import scarce raw materials. He visualized imperialists in mortal combat with one another. So the Americans would be glad to learn, as Stalin told Nelson, that Moscow preferred American goods, and, as he later told Eric Johnston, head of the American Chamber of Commerce, that "the Soviet Government has never fought for foreign markets. . . . Foreign markets would be left open to Great Britain and the United States. With Germany and Japan destroyed there would be enlarged opportunities." As for raw materials, Stalin also informed Johnston about them, enumerating "the known raw materials which could be exported to the United States after the war. . . ."[25]

Actually, not only Marxist-Leninist-Stalinists but capitalists as well anticipated postwar American economic difficulties. That men like Nelson, Johnston, and Harriman—not to mention those corporation presidents who cultivated Eremin and other Soviet officials—did anticipate difficulty seemed to confirm Soviet assumptions. But the interpretation of American diplomacy that the Soviets drew from all this was off the Kremlin wall. If (as Secretary of the Treasury Henry Morgenthau vainly proposed in January 1945) the United States were to offer Moscow ten billion dollars of credits no strings attached, Stalin would see that as a sign of capitalist desperation. If, as Harriman was urging, the United States attached strings to its aid, the Soviets would wait for the Americans to come to their senses. And if, as eventually happened, the Americans refused to assist and later even to trade at all with the Soviets? That might signify real danger, for that would mean that the Americans were ready to cut off their own nose to spite Stalin's face.

In the meantime, another set of negotiations looking toward postwar cooperation gave Stalin cause for both concern and hope. The Americans presented their project for a new international organization as a way to end war. To Stalin, that was a utopian hope—and would remain so for at least as long as capitalism existed and probably (Stalin's capacity for cynicism being substantial) forever. Moreover, the American plan was positively dangerous, since the USSR would be a minority of one in the world organization with pro-Western votes stacked against them. But if the Americans insisted, the Soviets could learn to live with the United Nations, using skillful diplomacy to minimize the danger and even turn the project to Moscow's advantage. For instance, while the Americans wanted the great powers to have a veto on substantive issues before the Security Council, Washington also proposed that "a state involved in a dispute should not vote on matters affecting that dispute." But the Soviets insisted on an unlimited right to veto (that is even in their own case) because, Litvinov explained to Edgar Snow, "This was our way of demanding a guarantee of equality, a guarantee against combinations. . . ."[26]

Actually, when Roosevelt first broached his dream to Molotov in May 1942, it was not so removed from Stalin's way of thinking. The president foresaw the four great powers (China was the fourth) acting as "the policemen of the world" and enforcing disarmament on the others. Molotov said this was "quite realistic." It apparently struck Stalin's number two man as suspicious that the Americans had progressed so far in their thinking. "Molotov repeated that the subject which the President was raising was the first stage of the discussion. He asked the President whether it represented his final and considered judgment, to which the President answered in the affirmative."[27]

It was neither final, nor all that considered. Three years later the plan was quite different. The idea of a revived League of Nations, which Roosevelt had rejected in 1942, was resurrected and blended with the four "policemen" to become the germ of the United Nations. Roosevelt explained the new conception to Stalin at Tehran, adding that Churchill was unhappy to have only two votes for the British Empire. Stalin did not comment on Churchill's dilemma, but before long, made it his own. During the negotiations at Washington's Dumbarton Oaks in the summer of 1944, the Soviet delegate made a modest suggestion. "Ambassador Gromyko suggested that all of the sixteen Soviet Republics should be included among the initial members of the Organization."

"My God," was Roosevelt's stunned reaction when Gromyko's proposal was reported to him. The United States could never publicly consider, let alone accept it. The idea would be such a bombshell in domestic politics that the Americans referred to it as the "X Matter" and locked all references to it in a special safe in the secretary of state's office. (Less than a month later, FDR himself blurted out the secret to the Brazilian ambassador.) But even sixteen Soviet votes might not prevent the United Nations from acting against Soviet interests. So Gromyko insisted on the Soviets' right to sit in judgment in their own cases, and nothing Roosevelt said could dissuade him: not the president's revelation (recorded in Under Secretary of State Edward Stettinius's personal diary) that "traditionally in this country husbands and wives when in trouble never have the opportunity to vote in their own case."; not "the beautiful story" (as Stettinius described it) the president told "tracing the development of this American concept of fair play back to the days of our founding fathers"; not even the "difficulty" the Senate would have with the Soviet proposal, or the problems with smaller, particularly Latin American, powers who might not want to join an organization that so favored the great powers.[28]

Talk like that must have set off alarm bells in the Kremlin. An "all-powerful" Senate dictating to an "impotent" president? Latin American pawns terrorizing their North American masters? Husbands and wives and fair play? And yet—American plans for the United Nations offered Moscow a global role. Roosevelt's proposed trusteeships had already stirred up inter-imperialist rivalries and might drop former Italian colonies into the Soviet lap. The delegates at Dumbarton Oaks discussed distributing military bases around the world to the great powers; Moscow would get some of those too. Finally, the Americans were so eager for Soviet cooperation (and so anxious to avoid even a wisp of public disagreement) that they might pay a price in other areas. When Stalin at first hewed to a hard line on UN votes and veto at Yalta and, then, magnanimously softened his stance, the shift helped persuade Roosevelt and Churchill to accept a Polish agreement the Soviets could live with.

Stalin could also live with Anglo-American diplomacy in the Balkans. When Moscow ruthlessly exploited its position as occupying power in Rumania and Bulgaria, neither Churchill nor Roosevelt protested vigorously. In early 1945 Churchill pushed the president to take the lead on Rumania. Roosevelt replied on March 11 that Rumania was "not a good place for a test case" but that "we shall certainly do everything we can." "Everything we can" amounted to two mild sentences in a longer letter to Stalin on the Polish question. Roosevelt referred to the Yalta Declaration on Liberated Europe, a document that appeared to commit the three powers to the establishment of free and democratic regimes. Stalin must have thought that declaration (algebra, again) committed him to nothing, since its vague general formulas could be variously interpreted and since there was no mechanism guaranteeing action. If so, Roosevelt's protest on Rumania did little to change his mind: "I frankly cannot understand why the recent developments in Rumania should be regarded as not falling within the terms of that agreement. I hope you will find time personally to examine the correspondence between our two governments on this subject."[29]

In Yugoslavia, Stalin feared Allied counteraction against Tito's leftism. But his fears proved groundless. In 1943, Djilas recalls, Tito's Antifascist Council in effect declared a "new social and political order in Yugoslavia." Moscow's response to these resolutions was so negative that "some parts were not even broadcast by the radio station Free Yugoslavia, which was located in the Soviet Union. . . ." Djilas continues, "Only when it became obvious that the West had reacted to the resolutions . . . with understanding, did Moscow alter its stand to conform with the realities." As late as April 1945, the Soviets were still treating their Yugoslav comrades according to bourgeois international protocol because, remembers Djilas, "relations between the Soviet Union and the Western allies were still in their wartime honeymoon, and the Soviet Government wished, by observing this formality, to avoid complaints. . . ." But by then, Stalin was learning another lesson: "This war is not as in the past; whoever occupies a territory imposes on it his own social system. Everyone imposes his own social system as far as his army can reach. It cannot be otherwise."[30]

Contributing to this lesson was Churchill's famous attempt actually to quantify Soviet and British spheres of influence in Eastern Europe. By October 1944, Churchill was ready to reach his own meeting of the minds with Stalin. "Let us settle about our affairs in the Balkans," he invited his Kremlin host. "Your armies are in Rumania and Bulgaria. We have interests, missions and agents there. Don't let us get at cross-purposes in small ways. So far as Britain and Russia are concerned, how would it do for you to have ninety percent predominance in Rumania, for us to have ninety percent of the say in Greece, and go fifty-fifty about Yugoslavia?" While this was being translated, Churchill scribbled the ratios of Soviet and Western influence on a piece of paper: Rumania—90:10; Greece—10:90; Yugoslavia—50:50; and Hungary, also, 50:50. According to Churchill's account, Stalin quickly indicated his acceptance with a blue pencil tick next to the numbers. Whereupon, Churchill, hesitating to dispose of the fate of millions of people in such "an offhand manner," changed his mind. "Let us burn the paper," he said. "No you keep it," Stalin replied.

The full extent and meaning of this dramatic episode is uncertain. Churchill insisted later that his ratios were meant to deal only "with immediate wartime arrangements" while leaving the postwar dispensation to subsequent discussion. But it is far from certain that Stalin appreciated the distinction. Churchill implies that consideration of the percentages ended with this exchange. But British records show that Eden and Molotov continued to dicker over the ratios as the October talks proceeded. In the end, the numbers were left in limbo, but not before Molotov apparently convinced Eden to raise the Soviet share in Hungary by 30 percent (to a ratio of 80:20) and by 5 percent in Bulgaria (to 80:20), all in return for *not* raising the Soviet share in Yugoslavia above the original 50 percent. That the British claimed so little in Rumania and Bulgaria (where in any case the Soviets were in a controlling position), that they yielded so easily on Hungary (where the ground was much more favorable to the West), and that they failed to act decisively in Yugoslavia, where in theory they insisted on parity, all this must have been extremely encouraging to Stalin. The fact that the Americans declined to play the numbers games at all (saying that even temporary spheres of influence would cause rather than avoid conflict) was disturbing—but Roosevelt's later passivity was probably taken in the Kremlin, as Harriman feared, to indicate acceptance of Soviet domination of Rumania and Bulgaria.[31]

The Americans' problem on the Polish question was not passivity but ineffectiveness. FDR opened discussion of Poland at Yalta as if he were dealing with a Boston Brahmin. It would be more palatable for the American public, he told Stalin, if, having been granted the Curzon Line, Moscow would leave the city of Lwow and its surroundings to Poland. The president merely offered this as a suggestion, he said, and would not insist on it. A gentleman would have responded gallantly, but not Stalin. Churchill rightly stressed the issue of Poland's government, saying that a new provisional regime was necessary, to be followed by free elections. But when Churchill declared Poland to be a question of honor for England, Stalin replied that for Russia it was a matter of life and death. "I am called a dictator and not a democrat," Stalin continued, "but I have enough democratic feeling to refuse to create a Polish government without the Poles being consulted." He added, "I must say that the Warsaw government has a democratic base equal at least to that of de Gaulle."[32]

Soviet security needs hardly entitled Moscow to dispose of a sovereign state in the name of which England had gone to war and to which the United States was solemnly committed. Stalin's argument about consulting the Poles was obviously empty since the Lublin government had been formed without consulting most of them. As for the Warsaw government's being as democratic as de Gaulle's, that could have been turned against Stalin by pointing out that his own previous condemnation of the French ought then to apply to the Warsaw regime as well. Objections like these would not have compelled Soviet acquiescence, but they might have shaken Stalin's confidence that Washington could be manipulated by rhetorical ploys.

Speaking of ploys, Stalin had another one ready when the Yalta discussion returned to Poland. With his Western partners still pressing for a new provisional government, Stalin interrupted the discussion— allegedly so that copies of the latest Soviet proposal could be typed— and announced in the interim that the Soviet government would settle for only two or three UN votes instead of the sixteen originally requested and would accept an American-proposed compromise on Security Council voting as well. (The compromise barred council members from voting or vetoing in disputes in which they were involved, provided that the proceedings looked toward the peaceful settlement of the dispute rather than, say, the use of military force by the United Nations or the imposition of economic sanctions against the interested party.) At this news, Roosevelt and Churchill (who had been less enthusiastic about the whole United Nations project) melted in relief and gratitude.

Molotov's Polish draft turned out, when typed, to offer mere enlargement instead of a real remaking of the Polish government, yet FDR hailed that as "progress." Stalin's partners eventually settled for a limited reorganization of the existing Polish regime and for a promise of free elections without a fixed date. Roosevelt undercut Western insistence that British and American ambassadors observe those elections by remarking that this was only "a matter of words and details."[33]

No guarantees agreed upon at Yalta could be iron-clad given the Red Army's presence in Poland. Moreover, Western diplomacy at Yalta can be explained and defended in other ways—whether by referring to Roosevelt's deteriorating health, or to his conviction that the Western powers got what they wanted (a strong United Nations, an enhanced role for France, a Soviet commitment to join the war against Japan) on the issues most important to them, or even to the American assumption that having worked so long to gain Stalin's trust, they had no alternative but to play out the string. Still, the American strategy unfortunately resembled one of 'wishing (and denigrating one's fellow imperialists) will make it so.' FDR joined Stalin in privately criticizing the French and the British; the latter, FDR said, were "a peculiar people" and wished to "have their cake and eat it too." At the first plenary meeting, the president said that he felt the Allies understood each other much better than they had in the past and that month by month their understanding was growing. At dinner on February 8, 1945, Roosevelt described the atmosphere as that of "a family," for it was with a family he liked to compare the relations that existed "between our two countries." Lest one think that formal diplomatic toasts must, by their nature, leave reality behind, consider Stalin's reply: "Marshal Stalin remarked that it was not so difficult to keep unity in time of war since there was a joint aim to defeat the common enemy. . . . He said the difficult task came after the war when diverse interests tended to divide the allies."[34]

It has been suggested by traditionalist historians that Western statesmen at Yalta must have struck Stalin as weak and innocent. Yet Stalin continued to read his own deviousness into his allies. He equated Western with Soviet tactics: When Churchill mentioned Soviet treatment of Rumania and Bulgaria, Stalin said he had no intention of criticizing British policy in Greece but would merely like to know what was going on. He invited comparisons between the British Empire and the USSR, and between the de Gaulle regime and the Polish provisional government. American claims to be 'more democratic than thou' must have particularly galled him, especially when Roosevelt insisted, for the umpteenth time, that American public opinion would require an absolutely free and open election in Poland. "I want this election in Poland," said FDR, "to be like Caesar's wife. I did not know her but they said she was pure." "They said that about her," Stalin admitted, "but in fact she had her sins."[35]

Stalin's ignorance of Western politics, and his tendency to fill in the gap with home-grown Soviet images, was visible as the Yalta Conference neared its close. The "genius of all times and peoples" (as Stalin liked to be called in his own sycophantic press) informed Churchill that the Labour party would never be "successful in forming a government in England." The "coryphaeus of the sciences" (another old favorite of the dictator) asked Roosevelt whether there was any labor party in a political sense in the United States. At the last plenary session, Churchill warned that the conference declaration on Poland would be severely attacked in England. But Stalin, whose ignorance of genuine electoral politics was matched only by his certainty that they did not exist, asked whether such an attack would be "in earnest" and answered his own question: "I doubt it."[36]

All this suggests that Stalin saw method in what some traditionalist critics depict as Western near-madness. For the moment, the Americans might yield, but not for all time. Prudence, as Stalin understood it, meant seizing the present to prepare for a possibly more difficult future. What Stalin did not understand, in part because the Americans' mild and ineffective tactics misled him, was that his own machinations were bringing that future closer, and faster, than he knew. Revisionist historians (and Soviets, too) deny that. They say that anticommunism built into the American system destroyed the alliance. But the facts are that the American government was led throughout the war by men who assumed that genuine and long-term cooperation was possible, that Stalin helped disabuse the Americans of this hopeful illusion, and that Stalin's own expert on America warned that this was happening. Litvinov had a long and candid conversation with Edgar Snow in October 1944. He said that "diplomacy might have been able to do something to avoid [the growing rift] if we had made clear the limits of our needs, but now it is too late, suspicions are rife on both sides." One reason for the Soviet failure, Litvinov said, was the fact that the Foreign Commissariat "is run by three men and none of them understands America or Britain." The three were Molotov and his deputies, Vyshinsky and Vladimir Dekanozov (the former ambassador to Germany, who, Litvinov said, "sat next to Ribbentrop for a year and that's all he knows about foreign countries.")[37]

If Yalta encouraged Stalin, the weeks which followed must have quickened his doubts. Consultations on reorganizing the Polish government revealed a gap between what the Western powers thought they were getting and what the Soviets were prepared to give. More explosive was the Soviet response to a peace feeler that German commanders in Italy extended to the British and Americans in early March. Together with the Nazi failure to blow up the last bridge across the Rhine at Remagen, which enabled Anglo-American forces to race into Germany, the Bern feeler suggested to the nervous Soviets that a separate peace might be at hand. When Harriman informed Moscow that it need not participate in the Bern peace talks (since they were exploratory and involved only a limited front), Stalin fired off an abusive protest to Roosevelt. Mastny argues that having underrated his rivals, Stalin now overestimated them and in "a growing panic" chose not to retreat on the Polish question but to press ahead without regard to the alarmed Western reaction. But if this was panic, it was informed by the knowledge that Roosevelt's own counter-complaints pulled their punches. By March 1945, Roosevelt was apparently disillusioned. "We can't do business with Stalin," said FDR to a friend on March 23. "He has broken every one of the promises he made at Yalta." But the president's messages to Moscow were still conciliatory because he feared to aggravate Soviet intransigence on Poland. When Roosevelt cabled the Kremlin on April 1, he resorted yet again to arguments that had proven their inability to persuade. His warning that "our program of international collaboration" was endangered foundered on Stalin's assumption that Roosevelt was more committed to it than he was. Nor would FDR gain the day by making it "quite plain to you [Stalin] that any such solution which would result in a thinly disguised continuance of the present Warsaw regime would be unacceptable and would cause the people of the United States to regard the Yalta agreement as having failed." Roosevelt was whistling in the dark when he told Stalin, "You are, I am sure, aware that genuine popular support in the United States is required to carry out any policy foreign or domestic. The American people make up their own mind and no Governmental action can change it. I mention this fact because the last sentence of your message about Mr. Molotov's attendance at San Francisco made me wonder whether you give full weight to this factor."[38]

Roosevelt's last remark reveals a glimmer of presidential understanding. The "last sentence" to which he referred came in a message
explaining why Molotov would be unable to attend the founding conference of the United Nations. "I and Mr. Molotov regret it extremely,"
began Stalin's March 27 cable, "but the convening, on the request of
the deputies of the Supreme Soviet, in April, of a session of the
Supreme Soviet of the USSR where the presence of Mr. Molotov is
absolutely necessary, is excluding the possibility of his participation
even in the first meetings of the Conference." A likely story! The idea
that the Supreme Soviet could constrain Stalin and Molotov was an
echo of Roosevelt's congressional excuses. The real reason for holding
Molotov at home may have been to obtain a *quid pro quo* for his presence. In any event, what offended the president, and provoked fleeting
recognition of Stalin's real conception of the West, was something else.
It was the way Stalin dismissed Roosevelt's warning that world public
opinion would misinterpret Molotov's absence as a lack of interest. "As
regards various interpretations, you understand," said Stalin, "this cannot determine the decisions which are to be made."[39]

This was not quite the last exchange on Poland. The day before he
died, Roosevelt cabled Churchill, "I would minimize the general
Soviet problem as much as possible because these problems, in one
form or another, seem to arise every day and most of them straighten
out as in the case of the Bern meeting."[40]

"The Bern meeting" flap had prompted one of Roosevelt's strongest rejoinders to Stalin: "Frankly, I cannot avoid a feeling of bitter
resentment toward your informers, whoever they are, for such vile mis-
representations of my actions or those of my trusted subordinates." But
on April 11, the day before he died, FDR thanked Stalin for his "frank
explanation of the Soviet point of view of the Bern incident" and characterized the affair as "a minor misunderstanding." Before delivering
the president's message, Harriman cabled back respectfully suggesting
that the word "minor" be deleted. Roosevelt replied he did not wish to
do so "as it is my desire to consider the Bern misunderstanding a minor
incident."[41]

By the time Harriman delivered Roosevelt's last message, the president was dead. Molotov came right to the embassy when Harriman
telephoned with the news at 3:00 A.M. Molotov seemed to Harriman to
be "deeply moved and disturbed." Molotov said the Soviets would have
confidence in President Truman because he had been "selected by President Roosevelt." Added Harriman, "I have never heard Molotov talk

so earnestly." When Harriman called at the Kremlin the next day, Stalin "greeted me in silence and stood holding my hand for about 30 seconds before asking me to sit down." Stalin then asked "many questions about the President and the circumstances which brought about his death." (Did one so accustomed to liquidating his own associates suspect foul play?) When Harriman invited questions about the American situation, "the Marshal said he did not believe there would be any change in policy." (Wishful thinking?) Harriman told Stalin that the Soviet leader "could assist President Truman in stabilizing the situation in the United States and in solidifying him with the American people." But even this astonishing notion of the Kremlin vouching for the president with American public opinion did not faze Stalin. "President Roosevelt has died," he said, "but his cause must live on. We shall support President Truman with all our forces and all our will."[42]

A kopeck—even a ruble—for Stalin's real thoughts on April 12, 1945! His ideology taught him that no single person, not even a president of the United States, determines history. But his own rule over Russia argued the contrary. Would American policy remain unchanged? What would Truman's be like?

Whether or not Stalin knew it, and since there were microphones embedded in the walls of Moscow embassies and diplomatic apartments he probably did, an alternative to Roosevelt's policy had been forming for some time in the mind of the man whose hand he held so long on April 12. Averell Harriman blended traditional State Department skepticism about the Russians (which lived on in middle officers of the embassy and especially in the remarkable person of George F. Kennan, whom Harriman made his deputy in 1944) with the activist optimism of a man used to moving mountains in business and government. By April 12, Harriman had a pretty good gauge on the Soviets' thinking. They would try simultaneously to cement an East European buffer zone, to develop profitable international collaboration, and to extend their influence westward. They thought Washington had tacitly approved the buffer, was actively committed to collaboration, and might even accept Soviet inroads into the Western sphere. But a new American approach, or so Harriman thought, could yet save the day. "In spite of recent developments," he cabled home on April 6, "I am still satisfied that if we deal with the Soviets on a realistic basis, we can in time attain a workable basis for our relations. There is ample evidence that the Soviets desire our help and collaboration, but they now think they can have them on their own terms, which in many cases are completely unacceptable to us. They do not understand that their present actions seriously jeopardize the attainment of satisfactory relations with us, and unless they are made to understand this now, they will become increasingly difficult to deal with."[43]

Truer words were rarely spoken in American policy-making circles during World War II. The Soviets *did* desire American help. They *did* think they could have it on their terms. They did *not* fully understand that their actions jeopardized their own plans. They *would* become increasingly difficult to deal with. The trouble with Harriman was not in his analysis (although it, too, had some flaws), but with his prescription. He called for both the carrot (American credits) and the stick (resistance to Soviet advances in East Europe). But Stalin was not about to be impressed by either. If the United States offered aid, it would be to serve its own interests. As to the stick, its possibilities were limited given Soviet presence on the ground.

Harriman's was a voice in the wilderness of the Roosevelt administration on April 11. A few days later it was a force guiding Harry Truman's hand. Revisionists contend that Truman's get-tough policy forced Moscow to do likewise. To which traditionalists reply that the Soviets had already signaled their own hard line in Jacques Duclos's April 1945 attack on Earl Browder. But what, in fact, was the meaning of Duclos's piece? Ironically, it may have been designed to justify (rather than proclaim the end) of Stalin's moderate policies, by reassuring radical-minded Communists that the revolution would not be postponed forever. For a close reading reveals that Duclos's blast at Browder was not inconsistent with a continuation of entente Stalinist-style. Duclos's main target was what he took (erroneously) to be the physical dissolution of the American Communist party, which in the spirit of entente had rechristened itself the Communist Political Association. He also rejected Browder's proclamation of class peace in the United States. According to Duclos, the spirit of Tehran of which Browder made so much, was diplomatic and not ideological. True, Communist parties were expected to align themselves with non-Communist forces, but that was in part to oppose reactionaries seeking to destroy the grand alliance. Far from denouncing entente, Duclos was telling the American comrades how to protect it. His advice was also consistent with the détente to which Moscow retreated later in 1945. The one international constellation Duclos's prescription did not fit was the one Stalin did not want, but ultimately settled for: all-out cold war.

From Entente to Détente: April 1945 - December 1945

FRANKLIN ROOSEVELT'S DEATH WAS A TURNING POINT IN SOVIET-AMERICAN relations, but how far those relations would turn and in what direction was not immediately clear. Not only Moscow's maximum goals but its minimum ones as well encountered new resistance from the Truman administration. But there were continuing opportunities, too, including some offered by the negotiating style of Harry Truman and his new secretary of state, James F. Byrnes of South Carolina. Was entente Stalinist-style still viable? The summit conference at Potsdam must have raised serious questions in Stalin's mind, and the September foreign ministers meeting in London confirmed those doubts. The autumn was a period of Soviet reassessment. The Moscow foreign ministers meeting in December offered renewed hope to the Kremlin, but the hope was misplaced.

On April 23, 1945, President Harry Truman had a rather strained conversation with Soviet Foreign Commissar Molotov. By that time, Harriman and others of like mind had reached and instructed the new and inexperienced president. Truman's understanding lacked the subtlety of Harriman's Moscow dispatches, but that was partly because Harriman himself oversimplified when he briefed Truman and his advisers in Washington several days after Roosevelt's death. All the frustration and urgency that had been building in the Moscow embassy went into the ambassador's warning about "a barbarian invasion of Europe." But Harriman believed the barbarians might still be repelled; since the Russians needed our help, "he felt we had nothing to lose by standing firm on issues of real importance to us." Just before meeting Molotov on the twenty-third, the president remarked that agreements with the Soviet

Union had so far been "a one-way street and that could not continue; it was now or never." The United States could not of course expect to get 100 percent of what it wanted, but Truman felt that on important matters "we should be able to get 85 percent." Truman intended to go ahead with plans to set up the United Nations; if the Russians did not wish to join, "they could go to hell." When Molotov arrived, the president lectured him in what an aide described as "plain American language." Molotov is said to have complained, "I have never been talked to like that in my life"—by which he surely meant his diplomatic life, for his boss must have used even plainer language upon occasion. "Carry out your agreements," Truman replied, "and you won't get talked to like that."[1]

No one conversation could possibly turn the tide. But revisionists say this one marked a new American approach that did alter history's course. They are partly right. Truman *did* bring a new firmness to American policy; at times his approach resembled Stalin's in reverse: what's mine (in the American case, Western Europe, Japan, and other areas not heretofore open to Soviet penetration) is mine; what's yours (Eastern Europe) is negotiable; and no economic credits until you give in. But Truman's hard line coexisted with a softer one—which was open to the same interpretation Roosevelt's had been and to the sort of manipulation that Stalin had tried on FDR. The Soviets might be barbarians, but Truman still managed to picture them in American terms. He informed Joe Davies that the Soviet generals were out to get Stalin and might succeed. He thought Stalin was surrounded by "cliques" and, hence, "didn't know half the things that were going on," but he concluded that "if you could sit down with Stalin and get him to focus on the problem, Stalin would take a reasonable attitude." In October 1945 Truman described Stalin as "a moderating influence" in the Kremlin, adding that "It would be a real catastrophe if Stalin should die at the present time." As late as 1949, with supposedly all illusions gone and the Cold War raging in earnest, Truman told friend and biographer Jonathan Daniels: "I like Stalin. Stalin is as near like Tom Pendergast [the former Democratic party boss of Missouri] as any man I know. He is very fond of classical music. He can see right straight through a question quickly. . . . I got the impression Stalin would stand by his agreements and also that he had a politburo on his hands like the 80th Congress."[2]

Picturing the Kremlin this way, Truman lacked confidence in his own tough stance. He therefore reached out for a Rooseveltian solution with the aid of advisers noted for their attachment to compromise. Harry Hopkins, although dying of cancer, was dispatched to Moscow in May 1945 to revivify the good feeling as well as the diplomatic agreements of Yalta. Jimmy Byrnes's search for a good old American-style compromise extended from Potsdam in July to Moscow in December, with his uncompromising stance in September an exception to his negotiating rule.

How did the Soviets react to what a latter-day observer might describe as Truman's Carter-like inconsistency? The official party line—also reminiscent of the 1970s—was clear: Until September, the Soviet press depicted a realistic capitalist administration in charge in Washington, although one with increasing influence wielded by reactionary forces. But there was also confusion in the Kremlin, of the sort reflected in Vyshinsky's telling Davies that Moscow knew almost nothing about Truman and asking with typical lack of finesse whether Truman and Byrnes were in fact close.[3] Anger and frustration there must have been, too, when the Americans refused to play the game assigned to them and instead tried to turn the tables. But withal, there was apparently a feeling in the Kremlin that events could still be controlled.

From Roosevelt's death until Potsdam in July, Soviet strategy unfolded almost as if FDR were still alive. Moscow maneuvered (within the limits of moderation) in areas vital to the Western powers. The Soviets applied greater pressure where the West was less interested or less able to resist. And all the while, Stalin and Molotov conducted high-level, East-West negotiations in the Grand Alliance manner.

In Western Europe, local Communist parties and Soviet diplomacy moved cautiously. Both the French and Italian Communists, having laid down their wartime arms, continued to cooperate with non-Communist governments. By this time, American diplomats were warning of a Soviet plan to "reduce Italy to the level of a Balkan state under Russian influence." But that was not Moscow's intention. The Soviets supported Tito's claims in the hotly disputed Trieste area, despite the risk of gaining an anti-Italian reputation. Before long the Soviets signaled in conversations with the Italian ambassador that Italy was lower on the scale of Soviet priorities than were the Balkan states.[4]

Czechoslovakia presents a mixed picture. Stalin admitted to Beneš that Czech fears of the Bolsheviks had been "justified" but said they no longer need be. He even urged Beneš to "broaden" the Czech Communists' political outlook. But the Soviets showed their teeth on the disposition of allied forces in Czechoslovakia. Churchill, joined by the American State Department, had urged that American troops take and occupy Prague for political purposes; General Eisenhower, however, refused (on military grounds), and the Red Army marched in. (Later, Stalin would stress to Khrushchev Eisenhower's "decency, generosity and chivalry," saying that "if it hadn't been for Eisenhower, we wouldn't have succeeded in capturing Berlin," in which case "the question of Germany might have been decided differently and our own position might have turned out quite a bit worse.") Moscow demanded complete withdrawal of American troops from Czechoslovakia in advance of Russian troops but later compromised on mutual withdrawal in November.[5]

In Hungary, Americans detected intimidation ominously reminiscent of Soviet behavior in Rumania and Bulgaria. George Kennan's recommendation was characteristically incisive—either "take a strong line and back it up with . . . action" or get out of Hungary; for to stay on ineffectively would only demonstrate impotence. But stay on ineffectively the Americans did. What did Moscow make of it? The fact that Washington did not appreciate Soviet restraint was a bad sign. That the Americans did not follow Kennan's advice was a good omen.[6]

The Soviets were less restrained in Rumania, Bulgaria, and Poland. As local Communists consolidated their hold, the Americans launched a barrage of objections. But there were also hints that Washington might settle for compromises covered by a Rooseveltian fig leaf. Whether FDR himself would have so settled is not certain. Roosevelt had pledged at home that Eastern Europe would be free, while implying to Stalin that it would be his. The president would have faced the day of reckoning that he had characteristically avoided. With Roosevelt gone, State Department officials chose in favor of the Atlantic Charter. They acted as if the Charter and the Yalta Declaration on Liberated Europe were practical arithmetic, not algebra—and they convinced Harry Truman to see it that way.

The American representative in Bulgaria, Maynard Barnes, was especially militant—to the point of once engaging in fisticuffs with a Bulgarian militiaman and goading non-Communist politicians forcefully to resist Soviet intimidation. Barnes's counterpart in Rumania, Burton Berry, was more restrained; when anti-Communists approached him with plans for a coup, he urged caution. Stalin, probably thinking he was cashing in chips promised by Roosevelt, proposed that the United States recognize the new governments of Hungary, Bulgaria, and Rumania. But Truman declined, citing Communist violations of democratic principles; Winston Churchill, who had conceded majority influence in Rumania and Bulgaria to the Russians, declined likewise. As it happened, Truman's advisers were astonishingly ignorant of exactly what his predecessor had promised or implied ("There is in the Department no copy of the Yalta Agreement or of any records of conversations pertaining thereto," noted Under Secretary of State Joseph Grew on July 13 in forwarding to the secretary a department memorandum entitled "The U.S. Interpretation of the Yalta Agreement"), but that is not the point. For Roosevelt's signals had never been clear, and, in any event, Truman was adamant.[7]

Poland, as the president saw it, was the make-or-break test case. Efforts to implement the Yalta accord were in trouble. The Soviets appeared to Truman to be welshing on their word, and that provoked his tongue-lashing of Molotov on April 23. Yet the Russians responded to Truman's pressure with studied, if pained, restraint. Stalin cabled Truman on April 24 that the Soviet government had not contested the democratic credentials of the Greek or Belgian governments "as it understands the whole importance of Greece and Belgium for Great Britain." The Soviets conceded on May 2 that Mikolajczyk could come to Moscow to take part in Polish consultations. This seeming reasonableness contributed to Truman's doubts about his own hard line, to his feeling that misunderstanding, rather than malevolence, might still be the problem, and to his decision to send Harry Hopkins to Moscow to set things right.[8]

Harry Hopkins got out of a Minnesota sickbed to try to save the Grand Alliance. When he sat down with Stalin on May 26, he began with an impassioned call for cooperation and an agitated warning that American public opinion, staunchly pro-Soviet during the war, was swinging against Moscow. "If present trends continued unchecked, the entire structure of world cooperation and relations with the Soviet Union which President Roosevelt and the Marshal had labored so hard to build would be destroyed." The main problem seemed to be Poland. "President Truman feels, and so do the American public," reported Hopkins, "a sense of bewilderment at our inability to solve the Polish question."

Hopkins's approach was familiar to Stalin, who played on his guest's sensitivities no less skillfully than in their memorable first meeting in July 1941. Stalin blamed Britain, with its "desire not to see a

Poland friendly to the Soviet Union." If, as Hopkins had stated, the United States desired to see "friendly countries all along the Soviet borders" then, said Stalin, "we can easily come to terms in regard to Poland." Stalin complained that the American attitude toward the Soviet Union had "perceptibly cooled once it became obvious that Germany was defeated." It was as though the Americans were saying the Russians were "no longer needed." Hopkins's warning about American opinion was the main message he had traveled so far to deliver, and he reverted to it again and again. Stalin retorted that he himself would not attempt to "use Soviet public opinion as a screen" but would speak of the feeling that had been created "in Soviet government circles as a result of recent moves on the part of the United States Government." Later, Stalin apologized for this remark. But the irony remained that in equating the role of opinion in America with its non-role in Russia, Stalin thereby ignored its potential for complicating his own plans. This is not to say that mass public opinion was the driving force behind the postwar reorientation of American foreign policy. As Daniel Yergin demonstrates, foreign policy elites contributed importantly to shaping mass attitudes. But the fact that both elite and mass opinion turned against the USSR cannot be understood apart from the Soviet behavior that alienated and alarmed so many Americans.[9]

A similar misreading was evident when, at Hopkins's invitation, Stalin presented his own list of grievances. Stalin complained that Argentina had been invited to join the United Nations in violation of a previous agreement. He said the invitation by the UN Conference in San Francisco "raised the question of the value of agreements between the three major powers if their decisions could be overturned by votes of Honduras and Puerto Rico." In fact, Stalin had nothing against Honduras and Puerto Rico, the latter of which he probably confused with Costa Rica. Rather, he assumed the Latin Americans were creatures of Uncle Sam and acted in accordance with American instructions. In general, he may have been right. But not, apparently, this particular time. What happened at San Francisco was that the United States backed Argentina's admission in return for Latin American support for Ukrainian and White Russian membership. Judging by Assistant Secretary of State Nelson Rockefeller's reports to closed meetings of the American delegation, this was not a charade but a vigorous attempt to get Latin American support. But Molotov suspected the old Soviet trick of selling the same horse twice. So he replied in kind by demanding that if Argentina was going to be admitted then the Polish provisional government should also be admitted. But this the United States could not accept until the Polish regime itself was reorganized.[10]

Stalin's complaint about Argentina was symptomatic but not itself overly important. In any event, he added, what had been done could not be put right and the Argentine question belonged "to the past." So did the abrupt termination of lend-lease that Washington had carried out in May. But that provoked a more bitter protest from Stalin reflecting yet another projection onto Washington of Moscow's own *modus operandi*. The cancellation reflected rising American dismay over Soviet behavior. But the fact that the cutoff was precipitate (ships at sea turned back and cargos were unloaded) and without warning was the result of a bureaucratic mix-up. Stalin, however, could no more allow for such confusion in the camp of the enemy than he could for a need to accommodate the Latin Americans. The cutoff had been "unfortunate and even brutal," he said. It was obviously "designed as pressure on the Russians in order to soften them up." As such, it was "a fundamental mistake," Stalin told Hopkins, adding that if the Russians were approached "frankly on a friendly basis" much could be done, but that "reprisals in any form [will] bring about the exact opposite effect."

There was something to that. Frank talk did help with the Soviets—although, as the 1939 Nazi-Soviet negotiations suggest, a capacity for reprisals did too—hence, the irony that Hopkins's conciliatory explanation must have sounded insincere to Stalin. Hopkins explained that the unloading of ships had been "a technical misunderstanding" and emphasized that "the incident to which Marshal Stalin referred did not have any fundamental policy significance." Actually, that was to put a rather fine point on the word "fundamental." The episode did have policy significance—to the extent that it reflected growing disenchantment with Soviet policy—but the change in policy was not as great as the Soviets inferred.[11]

On the Polish question, Stalin put Hopkins on the defensive. It was Washington, he charged, which had failed to carry out the Yalta agreement. Despite the fact that they were "simple people" the Russians should not be regarded as "fools" (a mistake the West frequently made, Stalin added) nor were they "blind" people who could not "see quite well what was going on before their eyes." But Stalin also said that Poland would live under "the parliamentary system which is like Czechoslovakia, Belgium and Holland," and that talk of an intention to Sovietize Poland was "stupid." And that showed that he regarded the *Americans* as foolish or blind. It was one thing for the Russians to take title to the word "democratic" (Western statesmen might be excused if they forgot the special Soviet meaning); it was another for Stalin to pledge that Communist-dominated Poland would model itself on capitalist Belgium and Holland or even mixed Czechoslovakia. Anyone who believed that would believe almost anything.

Before Hopkins could reply, Stalin offered further reassurance. Whether the United States wished it or not, it was a world power and would have to accept world-wide interests. In fact, the United States had "more reason to be a world power than any other state." That was why Stalin fully recognized "the right of the United States . . . to participate in the Polish question." Nor did his host quail when Hopkins justified the American position on Poland by citing "certain fundamental rights which, when impinged upon or denied, caused concern in the United States." Stalin added only that such rights (freedom of speech, the right to organize political parties, and so forth) had to be limited in wartime, and that fascist parties, whose intention it was to overthrow democratic governments, could not be permitted "to enjoy to the full extent these freedoms." Doubtless Hopkins was being polite when he replied that he "thoroughly understood the Marshal's opinions." What good would it have done to be less diplomatic? Not much—except, perhaps, to challenge Stalin's illusion that the Americans could be sweet-talked indefinitely.[12]

Throughout six days of talks, Stalin listened attentively and seemed impressed. Hopkins was, to use the language of diplomacy, the *demandeur*. He pressed hard for a resolution to the Polish stalemate and was relieved when Stalin offered a formula (Western-oriented Poles would get four or five of eighteen to twenty ministries in a reorganized Polish government) that Truman could accept.

Even Harriman was encouraged. He rightly noted, in a postmortem sent to Truman on June 8, that since Stalin "does not and never will fully understand our interest in a free Poland as a matter of principle," the dictator had to assume "we have some ulterior motive." But Harriman assumed that Stalin needed Western assistance to stabilize Poland and that since Molotov was "far more suspicious of us . . . than is Stalin," the fact that "we were able to see Stalin six times and deal directly with him was a great help. If it were possible to see him more frequently, many of our difficulties could be overcome."[13]

This notion, that Stalin was less suspicious than his advisers, was an *idée fixe* of both Roosevelt and Truman. That Harriman himself believed it testifies to its hold on the Americans. Was there any truth at all to it? Did not Litvinov himself confirm to the Americans that Stalin's sycophants fed his suspicions? But those suspicions were there to be fed in the first place. Stalin's associates told him what they thought he wanted to hear. It was Molotov, not Litvinov, who prospered. Woe to him who could be charged by Stalin with having underestimated the enemy's malevolence.

What was Stalin's postmortem on the Hopkins meeting? He, too, must have been pleased. Truman had huffed and puffed and invoked public opinion, but Hopkins had settled for a pittance on Poland. Other issues—bigger than Poland in the long run—remained, but they too looked promising. The question of Germany, which precipitated the final East-West break in 1947, was in a holding pattern pending Potsdam. On the issue of Japan, Stalin made an encouraging discovery. When he remarked to Hopkins that it would "be necessary to have some talks in regard to . . . such questions as zones of occupation in Japan," Hopkins said he "thoroughly agreed." A comment like that gave Stalin hope. It should have been no surprise, but apparently it was, when Truman responded to a Soviet request to occupy part of Japan by turning it down flat.[14]

Potsdam. The next milestone. The last gathering of the Big Three. Truman approached his first summit by a Rooseveltian route. At a time when Churchill was nearly frantic over the Soviet threat and anxious to discuss it with Truman, the president suggested that the two proceed separately to Berlin "to avoid any suspicion of our 'ganging up' " on Stalin. But Truman was not adverse to ganging up on Churchill. The president sent a special emissary to ask the prime minister whether he would mind if Truman and Stalin got together for a few days before Churchill joined them. The prime minister would and did. To make matters worse, the emissary was none other than Joe Davies, who preserved in almost pristine condition illusions that had plagued American diplomacy at the height of wartime cooperation. Among other things, Davies feared the rise of a "Soviet Napoleon" who might "overthrow and destroy the present altruistic, ideological purposes of peace and brotherhood, which the present Government avows, and, in my opinion, sustains."[15]

Truman's notion of a *tête-à-tête* with Stalin, and Churchill's allergic reaction to it, reflected the suspicion that infected British-American relations. The internal policy papers in which each side expressed its irritation with the other were, of course, secret. Stalin (presumably) did not know that in 1944 the American joint chiefs of staff had treated the likelihood of a future war with Britain or Russia as six of one, and a half-dozen of the other, or that excerpts from the JCS assessment were attached to the State Department's Potsdam Briefing Book Paper on the "British Plan for a Western European Bloc"—a plan the department wanted "discouraged" lest it have "features which would place additional restrictions on trade, run counter to the principles of free access to foreign markets and raw materials. . . ."[16] But the major issues between the United States and Britain, and particularly the economic strains, were well-known and of great interest to those who intended to play upon the inter-imperialist rivalry.

On the eve of the conference, Truman took another step that pleased Stalin and annoyed Churchill. Giving the latter but a few hours notice, he recognized the new Polish government formed on the basis of Stalin's formula. And when the Big Two met at last in Babelsberg Palace at noon on July 17, 1945, Truman sounded for all the world like FDR's ghost. According to Charles Bohlen's recollection of the meeting, Truman assured Stalin that "they would have no difficulty in reaching agreement on the matters which would be before them." With a "brief jocular reference to Stalin's nickname, 'Uncle Joe,' " Truman said that he "proposed to deal directly with Stalin as a friend. . . ." Stalin replied that "the Soviet Union would always try to meet the views of the United States."[17]

Stalin and Molotov took the offensive in this first conversation, but in a curiously anxious way. Molotov urged settling on German reparations (of which Russia was to be the primary beneficiary) and defined the Polish issue as a matter of how to liquidate the government-in-exile in London (which one might have thought to be a mere formality now that Washington had recognized its replacement in Warsaw). According to Bohlen's account, "he [Stalin] thought, although this might appear stupid, that the Soviets were entitled to be considered for trusteeship of the former Italian colonies which had not been assigned." Stalin also thought "it would be proper to break off relations" with Spain in order to "give the Spanish people a chance to select a government of their choice." (Truman responded that "he held no brief for Franco," and he agreed that "the matter should be studied.") Later, the Soviets would press for gains at Turkey's expense. They wanted to replace the Montreux Convention with an arrangement under which they themselves would determine the regime of the Straits in cooperation with Turkey.* There would be a treaty of alliance between the two, for which Turkey would prove its worthiness by returning to the Soviet Union a portion of territory that, as Molotov put it, "had been torn from Soviet Armenia and Soviet Georgia" in 1921.[18]

If Stalin expected the Western leaders to accede to his wishes, and it is my contention that he did, he must have been taken aback at American firmness. Not only did Truman decline to present him with Italian colonies, the president scuttled seemingly settled East European arrangements. Despite having just accepted the Communist-dominated Polish government, the Americans refused to recognize the governments of Rumania and Bulgaria. Secretary Byrnes cited violations of the Yalta Declaration on Liberated Europe. He said the United States had "no interest in the Governments of Rumania and Bulgaria except that they be representative of the people and permit our representatives and press to observe conditions freely." With typical brusqueness, Truman said that these countries "could have diplomatic relations if they would comply with our requirements, which they had not done." "When these countries were established on a proper basis, the United States would recognize them and not before."[19]

This new American insistence on national self-determination (put forward along with assurances that the United States expected freely chosen governments to be friendly to the USSR) must have struck Stalin as transparent hypocrisy. The Americans concentrated on the formal-legal trappings of what they called freedom and independence whereas to Stalin the underlying social system was determinative. Any country that was open to capitalism risked becoming part of the capitalist world. Only with a Moscow-dominated Communist party in control could the regime be counted on to be truly friendly to the Soviets. That the Americans really believed what Stalin must have taken to be propaganda was beyond his ken entirely.

The new American firmness at Potsdam, which revealed itself across a range of issues besides Eastern Europe, owed something to the

---

* The Montreux Convention, ratified by the USSR among others in 1936, turned military control of the Dardanelles over to Turkey. Turkey was given the authority to close the Straits to warships of all countries when threatened by war, but was to permit free passage by merchant ships even in wartime—except in the case of countries at war with Turkey. The Black Sea powers, including most particularly the USSR, were allowed free passage of warships in peacetime.

fact that the United States had successfully tested its first atomic bomb on July 16, 1945. But the same news seemed to have little impact on Stalin, to whom Truman casually conveyed it (saying that the United States had a "new weapon of unusual destructive force") on July 24. Not only did the poker-faced dictator show no emotion that Churchill or Charles Bohlen, who were watching intently, could detect; Soviet diplomacy remained seemingly unaffected by the bomb. Whether because Stalin underestimated the new weapon, or already knew about it and was determined to match it, or was shocked by the news but damned if he was going to show it, he conducted negotiations as if nothing had changed. If the Americans thought, either then or after the bomb had been used against Japan, that their atomic monopoly gave them a decisive diplomatic advantage—to be used to intimidate the Soviets or to be relinquished in return for concessions in Eastern Europe or elsewhere—they were to be sadly disappointed.[20]

German reparations produced another confrontation. At Yalta, the Americans (but not the British) had reluctantly agreed to a Soviet-proposed figure for total reparations from all zones of Germany. Twenty billion dollars, of which 50 percent would go to the USSR, was listed as "a basis for discussion" in a reparations commission that was to meet in Moscow. American representatives began backing away from the $20 billion as soon as the commission began its discussions. At Potsdam, Byrnes proposed instead that the victorious powers take their reparations from their own zones of occupation. The secretary contended that conditions had changed since Yalta and pointed in particular to reports that the Soviets were dismantling and transporting to Russia vast amounts of equipment found in their zone. This was not the only reason for the American shift. Daniel Yergin traces it to growing American distrust of Moscow which produced a determination to ensure that the needs of Western Europe and Germany received high priority. Of course, the suspicious Soviets needed no American to tell them that—nor were they likely to be reassured by Byrnes's denial that the American attitude toward the USSR had in fact changed.[21]

A sarcastic new tone crept into East-West exchanges as the conference progressed. The Soviets, old hands at recrimination, met something approximating their match. Told that industrial equipment seized by Soviet troops in Rumania was German and not British, Eden remarked that he had "heard this story before" and that it had been "disproved." To Vyshinsky's assertion that the Allied Control Council in Rumania had certified the equipment was not British, Eden retorted that this was "a unilateral action of the Soviet High Command," but then, "we are used to such unilateral acts." The Soviets' own irritation also showed through. But how deep did it go, and what were they going to do about it?[22]

One Soviet reaction was to charge Western statesmen with adopting a double standard. Any violation in Rumania or Bulgaria was overshadowed, said the Russians, by Western transgressions in Italy and Greece. When Truman and Churchill insisted on international control for the Turkish Straits, and proposed it for the Danube as well, Stalin pointed out Western domination of the Panama and Suez Canals.[23] There is no reason to doubt Soviet sincerity; the Western attempt to deny the Soviets their "fair share" must have galled Stalin. But there is no reason either to think the Western stance dissuaded Stalin from a course of genuine collaboration to which he would otherwise have stayed committed. Western double standards there may have been, but there was also a Soviet double whammy. It worked this way: Roosevelt's concessions had not reassured Stalin. Yet when Truman adopted a harder line, which the Soviets themselves should have anticipated, they managed to feel betrayed. American policies, under both Roosevelt and Truman, were often unsuccessful. But there was no way to win with the Soviets. Whatever Washington did, Moscow would think the worst.

How then could Stalin emerge from Potsdam with any optimism intact? Because toward the end of the conference, the Americans began horsetrading, which made it possible for the conference to conclude with a linked series of compromises. On July 30, Byrnes proposed a package deal covering three major issues: (1) On top of reparations they took from their own zone, the Soviets would be allowed to have a certain percentage of available capital equipment from Western zones; (2) Byrnes had been trying to restrict the amount of German territory to be turned over to Poland. Now he offered to accept Polish administration over land extending all the way to the Western Neisse River; (3) Washington had been pushing Italian entry into the United Nations, but Stalin had resisted, saying, when Truman refused to recognize Rumania and Bulgaria, that the two questions would have to be postponed, since Italy could not be "dealt with alone." Byrnes now proposed to make an Italian peace treaty, including UN admission, the first order of business for the Council of Foreign Ministers (CFM), while also pledging "to examine . . . in the near future, in the light of conditions then prevailing, the establishment of diplomatic relations [with Bulgaria, Rumania, Hungary, and Finland] to the extent possible prior to the ratification of peace treaties with these countries."[24]

In Kissingerian parlance, Byrnes was engaging in "linkage" diplomacy. As they were to do in the 1970s, the Soviets played hard to get. But under "take it or leave it" pressure from Byrnes, and after further haggling, the Soviets took it. Not only that, but Stalin singled out Byrnes for special praise as one who "had worked harder perhaps than any one of us to make this conference a success. He has worked hard and he has worked very well. He has helped us to reach agreements. Those sentiments, Secretary Byrnes, come from the heart."[25]

Not just the terms of the compromise touched Stalin's heart—so did the fact of compromise itself. Horsetrading was a favorite Soviet device; they had long been frustrated by the American preference for moral and legal argumentation. But Byrnes's willingness to bargain was particularly welcome at this time. Suppose (as would happen in 1947) the West had called a halt to Stalin's game. Instead, the Americans permitted it to continue. If Western statesmen had been alert to such things, they might have gleaned the nature of Stalin's strategy from his recommendations for dealing with the defeated Axis powers. How to treat Italy? Stalin remarked, according to American minutes, that "it would be incorrect to be guided by the remembrance of past injuries. The feelings of revenge and hatred or the desire for redress was a bad adviser in politics. He said it was not for him to teach, but thought he should be guided in politics by the weighing of forces." As to Germany, Stalin assured his allies that "the less industry we leave in Germany, the more markets there will be for your goods. We have destroyed for you a competitor with low living standards and low prices. . . ." Later, when Truman hesitated to reply to a Japanese peace-feeler since he had "no respect for the good faith" of the Japanese, Stalin suggested that "a general and unspecific answer" might be returned, since "it might be desirable to lull the Japanese to sleep." That, by analogy, was Stalin's game-plan: cooly, without feelings of hatred or revenge, to lull the West with dreams of markets both in Germany and in the USSR.[26]

Following Potsdam, Moscow continued its pre-Potsdam stick-and-carrot tactics. In Rumania and Bulgaria, that meant intimidation of local non-Communists combined with gestures designed to reassure the West. Bulgarian elections likely to stamp a contrived seal of approval on the pro-Soviet regime were scheduled for August 26. Soviet representatives on the Allied Control Commission in Sofia were insisting on a "single list" of candidates as the only "democratic" way to hold an election. British and American delegates resisted a single slate as "undemocratic." On August 24, the elections were suddenly postponed as the result of a direct order from Stalin himself—an order telephoned to the Soviet commander in Bulgaria, Colonel-General S. S. Biryuzov, in the presence of British liaison officer Malcolm Mackintosh, who later recalled the occasion: As usual, the commission meeting had begun at 8:00 P.M. and would likely last until 4:00 in the morning; since Stalin's habit was to work at night, his subordinates, even in Bulgaria, had to do likewise. During three previous evenings of fruitless discussion Biryuzov had stuck stubbornly to Moscow's insistence on a single-list election. Then, according to Mackintosh, "at 1:40 A.M. the telephone rang in the anteroom of the Russian general's office, and he sent his aide, a major, to answer it. When the major lifted the telephone to his ear, he stood there, as though struck dumb. The general thought his aide had become ill, so he strode over in a masterly fashion to the phone and seized it. Immediately he came smartly to attention, and stood upright for about five minutes while we could hear a voice crackling over the line. Then he said, 'Yes, Comrade Stalin' and came back to us to declare: 'As is well known, the Soviet government has always opposed the holding of general elections on a single list. The elections will be postponed until a more democratic method can be found.' The Bulgarian prime minister was then sent for. . . ."[27]

As for Rumania, Vyshinsky assured Harriman on September 12 that the Soviet and American governments had solved harder questions than the Rumanian question in the past and that he was hopeful that "a way could be found to solve this one as well." Washington, meanwhile, complained loudly about Communist behavior in the Balkans but carried a small stick. Revisionists who argue that American pressure forced the Soviets drastically to alter their stance exaggerate both the challenge and the response. Moscow was obviously annoyed and concerned. But the Soviets were aware of Western weakness and even developed a certain contempt for it. The pro-Western Rumanian king, Michael, was informed by Soviet officials in August that "the American and British position should not be taken seriously" because no written communications had been received specifically outlining their attitude. Vyshinsky reportedly assured Bulgarian Communist leaders that "Russia and Russia alone" would run the so-called Allied Control Council, that Allied attempts to insinuate journalists into Bulgaria were "an impudence," and that although "the temperature at Berlin [that is, Potsdam] had been very high at times," the U.S. delegation left "realizing that Eastern Europe has been permanently lost to Russia by the Anglo-Americans." Asked whether the United States and the United Kingdom would try to impose a Bulgarian Mikolajczyk, Vyshinsky is reported to have replied, "What did our allies accomplish in Poland by such [a] step?"[28]

The Soviet tendency to understand Western policy in Russian terms may in this case have reassured Moscow. What was the West up to in East Europe? Well, something like what Moscow was up to in the West, that is, doing its damndest to get what it could, while being aware of limits and ready to retreat. Such, also, was the Soviet approach to Japan. The Soviets entered the war against Japan on August 8, hurrying since a declaration by Emperor Hirohito on August 6 made the end appear near. On August 11, Molotov suggested to Harriman that the Japanese surrender to a joint high command on which two Soviet generals, with power of veto, would be represented. Harriman had a quick, clear response: "Impossible." Molotov, after consulting with Stalin, saved face by claiming a misunderstanding: in fact, he said, the Soviets had only wanted a consulting role. Molotov quickly agreed to General MacArthur's accepting Japanese capitulation and to MacArthur's famous Order #1 setting the terms for Japanese occupation.[29]

Having found one door to Japan locked, the Soviets tried another. Stalin proposed to Truman that the Japanese surrender to Soviet forces in the Kurile Islands and in Northern Hokkaido. Stalin bolstered his request with an American-style argument. Such a step would have "special meaning for Soviet public opinion," he said, since Russians well remembered how Japan had seized portions of the Soviet Far East between 1919 and 1921. The Russian public would be "seriously offended" if Russian troops were not to occupy some part of "Japan proper."[30]

Stalin characterized his as a "modest suggestion," but Truman disagreed. The president nixed any Soviet role in Hokkaido; he accepted Soviet occupation of the Kuriles (which under the Yalta Agreement were to be handed over to the USSR) but asked for American air base rights in those islands. Stalin's reply was incensed. He and his colleagues had not expected a *nyet* on Hokkaido. As for the American "demand" for permanent Kuriles bases, such demands were made only of the conquered or of a weak ally, and the Soviet Union was neither.[31] But this time there had been a real misunderstanding: Truman sought temporary refueling stations in the Kuriles and not permanent bases. The quarrel was patched up. But Stalin's reaction (not to mention Truman's) is revealing. He had probably half expected the Hokkaido turndown. But a request for permanent military bases in an area allotted to the Soviets (something that the West had given no sign of permitting Moscow in its own areas of occupation) was unexpected and therefore alarming.

In the meantime, however, the British had opened yet another door to Japan by proposing that an Allied Control Council (ACC) be established on the German model. Washington countered by suggesting a more unwieldy and less authoritative body to be called the Far Eastern Advisory Commission (FEAC). This kind of Anglo-American division was just what the Soviet doctor ordered. Moscow supported London—but not, it should be noted, immediately. As late as September 7, the Soviets seemed disposed to accept the FEAC as sufficient. The Russians later came out for an ACC, but only after the United States persisted in its refusal to recognize the Communist-dominated regimes of Rumania and Bulgaria.[32]

The most important bilateral U.S.–Soviet meeting between Potsdam and London was one between Stalin and an American congressional delegation led by William M. Colmer, chairman of the House Select Committee on Postwar Economic Policy and Planning. Colmer, of Mississippi, was hardly pro-Soviet. Upon returning to Washington, Colmer's group urged a "stiffening of our collective backbone in dealing with the Soviet Republic."[33] Colmer would approve American credits only if Moscow fulfilled political conditions—for example, disclosure of Soviet military spending and other vital economic statistics, administration of East European relief aid in an apolitical manner, guarantee of fundamental political rights to Soviet citizens—which amounted to dismantling the Stalinist system along with Soviet controls in Eastern Europe. How ironic then that Colmer unwittingly buttressed Stalin's view that the United States was desperately anxious to sell to the Soviets.

Stalin reminded Colmer of the proposal for six billion in credits that Molotov had made to Harriman in January 1945 but to which no answer had yet been received. The Soviet leader ticked off American items that the Soviets "could take." If the six billion figure were "not sufficient to satisfy these needs" (whose needs, Soviet or American, was not entirely clear), "it might be increased." Colmer asked in reply what "assurances" the United States could have that if the Soviet Union became economically self-sufficient, it would "still be interested in conducting trade with other countries." The question was an innocent one; as long as he was talking trade, the American would make sure trade could be counted on. But to Stalin's ear it must have betrayed anxiety about the long-term American economic prospect.

To economic temptation Stalin added political balm. Senator Claude Pepper, who saw Stalin shortly after the Colmer group did, asked what to tell people at home who thought Russia had "aggressive intentions with respect to border countries." "Our people are tired," Stalin scoffed. "They couldn't be induced to make war on anybody any more." The real question was not whether the Soviets would make war but how they would make peace. But the senator let that pass and instead informed Stalin that he was known affectionately among the American people as "Uncle Joe." Stalin added a ritual put-down of England ("there was not really much England could do for [the United States and USSR] or they for England") plus a recipe for continued good relations: "Christ said seek and ye shall find." Charming a sympathetic senator was no great trick. But Stalin tried the same technique on George Kennan, whose skepticism should have been well-known to the Kremlin: "Tell your fellows not to worry about those Eastern European countries. Our troops are going to get out of there and things will be all right."[34]

But things would not be all right, as the Council of Foreign Ministers meeting, which opened in London on September 11, showed. The CFM had been entrusted with drafting peace treaties. In addition to the Big Three ministers, the French and Chinese were also present— although with some ambiguity regarding their role, since the Potsdam protocol specified that council membership would vary in accordance with which treaty was being drafted. The Potsdam provision that "for the discharge of each of these tasks the council will be composed of members representing those states which were signatory to the terms of surrender imposed upon the enemy State concerned" was ignored by all parties until the Soviets, frustrated by American intransigence, turned it into a rock on which the conference broke down.[35]

London picked up where Potsdam left off. Molotov informed Byrnes that the Soviet Union would like to "try its hand at colonial administration under the general trusteeship principle." Molotov had in mind "at least one" of the Italian colonies; the United States and Great Britain could likewise administer "at least one." Lest Byrnes have any doubts, Molotov added that the Soviet government had "considerable experience in bringing about friendly relations between nationals." If the Libyan province of Tripolitania were entrusted to the Soviets, "they would not lag behind any country in their development of the welfare of the people in preparing them for independence in ten years." Molotov must have thought Byrnes credulous. Nor did Byrnes disabuse him. By this time Byrnes privately feared the Soviets wanted Libya as an anti-Western wedge from which to threaten the Belgian Congo's extensive uranium deposits. What Byrnes told Molotov was much milder—that the world would regard any divvying up of Italian colonies as "a division of the spoils of war cloaked under general trusteeship agreements," and that as a result "all our reputations would suffer." Contrast that with the British foreign secretary's more candid rejoinder: "In view of the vital interest of the British Government in the North African area," Bevin was "very much surprised" that the Soviet delegation put forward this claim for Tripolitania. The British claims in that area had been advanced on the same basis as had Russian claims in Eastern Europe, namely, "security—a perfectly legitimate basis."[36]

But the Americans, and the British too, no longer regarded Russia's East European claims as legitimate. They rejected draft peace treaties that in effect recognized Soviet hegemony in the region. In response, Molotov resorted to three tactics: he tried arguing, then bargaining, and when all else failed, he stalled.

Molotov tried arguing his way through what he must have regarded as a fog of American rhetoric. The secretary of state said that a frank airing of differences would facilitate their adjustment. But in the next breath Byrnes emphasized that "the United States is not interested in any way in seeing anything but governments friendly to the Soviet Union in adjacent countries." Molotov answered that he must tell the secretary that the Soviets had their "doubts, and it would not be honest to hide it." Byrnes answered that it was essential that these doubts be "removed," and that he was prepared to do it.[37]

But Byrnes could not remove those doubts: not by characterizing the whole Polish affair as "the result of an honest misunderstanding"; nor by contrasting Western correspondents' access to Greece with their non-access to Rumania. (Molotov countered that apparently in Greece the correspondents were happy but the people were not; whereas in Rumania the people were happy, but the correspondents were not.) The Soviets' doubts could not be eased by Byrnes's finding it "impossible to believe that a temporary Rumanian government could not be formed which would be both friendly to the Soviet Union and also representative of the people." (The real impossibility, given the miniscule size and general unpopularity of the Rumanian Communist party, was a government that the West would consider representative and the Soviets would regard as friendly.) Nor could it be accomplished by denying there had been any change in American policy since Yalta. (Molotov had said the United States was "backing the British in every way," and that there had been "a change in policy from that of Roosevelt . . . , who had been friendly to the Soviet Government.")[38]

Byrnes was alarmed at his inability to convince Molotov of American sincerity and goodwill—alarmed despite the fact that neither was as unalloyed as he claimed. He regretted "that Mr. Molotov chose to take our position in such a wrong way." He could not believe that the Soviets did not believe him: "The Government of the United States was satisfied that the Soviet Union did not really believe that the United States Government wanted in Rumania a government unfriendly to the Soviet Union." The reverse side of American innocence of Soviet tactics was anxiety at the Soviet failure to accept Washington's self-conception. How could Moscow fail to appreciate America's good intentions? How was Soviet recalcitrance to be understood? It could be seen either as a willful disregard for truth or as misunderstanding, which, in its persistence, was as ominous as was deliberate misrepresentation.[39]

Molotov's frustration was equally great and, in part, self-inflicted. All they wanted, the Soviets in effect said, was a security zone on a par with the West's. Never mind that Soviet totalitarian controls were crude and brutal; the Russians assumed that Western liberties were more apparent than real. Never mind Moscow's determination to fish in troubled Western waters while barring the door to the East. Never mind that when Washington and London finally did recognize Communist Rumania and Bulgaria, Soviet suspicions were not quenched but merely found new outlets. That these contradictions helped to explain American recalcitrance carried no weight with Moscow.

Meantime, Molotov shifted to bargaining. From equating Italy and Rumania for purposes of debate, he moved to linking them in search of a compromise. If the United States refused to sign treaties with Rumania and Bulgaria, Molotov threatened Byrnes on September 19, "the Soviet Union could not sign the treaty with Italy." And when that linkage did not bear fruit, Molotov devised another and another. On September 22, he suddenly discovered "an initial mistake" that was "retarding" the work of the conference. The CFM had "violated" the

Potsdam accord by permitting France and China to discuss the East European peace treaties. Molotov now proposed to bar them from further discussion, and when Bevin and Byrnes demurred, Molotov threatened to walk out. This prompted Truman to "urgently request" Stalin that Molotov remain in London, a plea that must have revived Soviet confidence that concessions were still to be had. But although Molotov stayed, he refused to work on the treaties. Instead he spent his time proclaiming the absolute sanctity of the Potsdam provision, which he had not noticed until midway through the conference—this even after signaling Byrnes in private that the sacred provision could be buried as suddenly as it had been found if only Byrnes found a way to accommodate Moscow on Rumania and Bulgaria. If the United States were anxious to reach an agreement in regard to the Peace Conference, remarked Molotov on September 30, "then the best thing to do would be to try to get a common attitude toward the Governments of Rumania and [Bulgaria]." Byrnes did not get the hint. So Molotov made his meaning even clearer. He had, he said, "some hope for the future," since soon there would be elections as a result of which there would be new governments in these countries which "should make it easier for the United States." If it were possible for the United States to recognize these governments then the question of a conference could be decided without trouble. Molotov felt these two questions were "linked up together."[40]

The Soviet foreign minister deployed yet another bargaining chip by raising the question of Japan with Byrnes on September 24. Molotov attacked American occupation policies and requested a greater Soviet role. He supported the British-sponsored ACC and chided Byrnes for not even acting on his own proposed FEAC. Byrnes tried to brush off the whole subject—much to the dismay of Harriman, who considered it of central importance to the Soviets—and then offered vague assurances. But Molotov was not having any. On September 27, he informed Byrnes that "if the United States could agree to the setting up of an allied control council for Japan, it would be easier for the Soviet Government to be ready for the Italian Treaty." Puzzled, Byrnes asked what "connection" there was between the Italian and Japanese questions. Molotov's answer, as summarized in the conference minutes: "There were some questions which the United States wished to postpone, and there were others which the Soviet Delegation wished to postpone." But Byrnes was not prepared to act on Japan—for a variety of reasons, including the need to clear any allied role, however insignificant, with the American viceroy in Japan, General Douglas Mac-Arthur.[41]

With these linkages in place, the stage was set for the kind of compromise Byrnes had engineered at Potsdam. But this time the deal never was struck. "I do not understand your Secretary of State," a Russian official told Charles Bohlen. "We have been told that he is a practical man, but he acts like a professor. When is he going to start trading?" The Soviet hope was not entirely misplaced. On Sunday morning, September 30, Byrnes greeted a leading Republican member of his delegation in the secretary's suite at Claridge's Hotel: "Well pardner," he said to John Foster Dulles, "I think we pushed these babies about as far as they will go and I think that we better start thinking about a compromise." But Dulles disagreed. In fact, he threatened to attack Byrnes publicly as an appeaser if he compromised with the Russians.[42]

So the United States stood firm. But the Soviets did, too. The conference staggered to a tragicomic halt. The Soviets even opposed issuing a protocol registering the ministers' inability to agree. "We know very well," said Molotov, "that the Soviet Delegation considers the decision of September 11 [permitting France and China to discuss East European treaties] to be a mistake, and how is it possible for us after this to sign a protocol which embodies that statement? . . . and you cannot compel us to do that, just as no one can compel anyone to say what he does not agree to." French Foreign Minister Georges Bidault confessed, "I do not understand what is going on." Tempers flared when Bevin compared Molotov's tactics to Hitler's—but so did the giddy laughter of men who could not believe they were devoting so much time to produce so little. The council dispersed without issuing a protocol.[43]

The breakdown of the London Conference was a blow to Soviet hopes. Until September the Truman administration had been depicted in the Soviet press as a progressive capitalist government forced to contend with reactionaries trying to poison Soviet-American relations. After London, Soviet writers increasingly identified American policy with that of the reactionaries, although they did not fully and finally equate the two until June 1947. Between the fall of 1945 and the spring of 1947, the Soviet press portrayed a struggle in both Britain and the United States between two vaguely defined "tendencies": on the one hand, those "influential circles" who, with the support of "certain official circles," sought world domination for the Anglo-Saxon powers; on the other hand, "democratic forces" backing the efforts of "realistic statesmen" who were still willing, "when it came down to brass tacks," to return to "the practice of agreed [tripartite] decisions" and to shift from the "method of dictation" to "respect for the opinions and interests of others and to a readiness for . . . compromise."[44]

This Western situation, as seen by Moscow, was not unlike the scene that confronted Soviets in the late 1970s. In both cases, "realistic" Western statesmen seemed to be accommodating to or perhaps changing into more "reactionary" politicians. In both cases, the result was apparently a fairly agonizing reappraisal on Moscow's part. The two most telling indications of the post-London Conference reassessment came directly from Molotov and, even more dramatically, from Stalin himself. Molotov gave the Anniversary of the Revolution address that Stalin had delivered throughout the war. He combined complaints on a slew of issues (Japan, Germany, West European bloc, atomic weapons, Eastern Europe, Western reactionaries, and so forth) with a call for renewed collaboration: The "failure of the London Conference sounded a certain warning," said Molotov, but there had also been allied differences during the war. Those differences had always been resolved taking into account "the need for further consolidating the collaboration of the great democratic states." Molotov expressed "confidence that all peace-loving powers are deeply conscious of the need for . . . creating . . . appropriate conditions for collaboration."[45]

Stalin revealed his thinking in a long conversation with Ambassador Harriman in October. Harriman journeyed to Stalin's Black Sea vacation home in Gagra to try to break the London deadlock. Stalin greeted him warmly at the front door, ushered him into a mahogany-paneled study, and had with him a long and difficult discussion. After a particularly tense exchange on Japan, Stalin startled his guest by declaring that it might be better for everyone if the Soviets stepped aside and let the Americans have their way in Japan. "The Soviet Union would not interfere. For a long time the isolationists had been in power in the United States. He had never favored a policy of isolation but perhaps now the Soviet Union should adopt such a policy. Perhaps, in fact, there was nothing wrong with it."

Harriman understood Stalin to be considering not "isolation in the classical American pattern" but rather "a policy of unilateral action." This meant to Harriman "a policy of maintaining Soviet domination throughout Eastern Europe and using the Communist parties in Western Europe and elsewhere as a means of expanding Russian influence.

Stalin would not rely on the United States or other Western powers for economic assistance. Nor would he count on their military cooperation in the near future."[46]

Harriman was right. Stalin was contemplating the failure of entente. But the alternative need not be a complete break with the West. The diplomatic landscape during the fall of 1945, including the rest of Harriman's conversation with Stalin, suggested that a species of détente would be both feasible and, from the Soviet point of view, productive.

The Americans were still unhappy about Rumania and Bulgaria, but they were giving further ground on Poland. Truman dispatched a special representative to the Balkans (Louisville newspaper editor, Mark Ethridge), who would later write an alarming report. But after much discussion of whether to grant a Polish request for credits, and if so whether to attach political conditions, Washington opted for aid with only economic strings attached. It is conceivable that Moscow viewed such aid with alarm since it preserved American access to Poland. More likely, the Soviets were pleased to have Washington subsidize Soviet hegemony.[47]

Moscow matched American reasonableness with moderation of its own. The Soviets withdrew their troops from Czechoslovakia. They permitted free Hungarian elections in which local Communists received only 17 percent of the vote. Across the world in Manchuria, Soviet actions were ominous, yet ambiguous. During the summer, Stalin and Molotov had pushed the Chinese Nationalists into a treaty of alliance including substantial Chinese territorial and political concessions. In return, Stalin promised to support a unified China under Chiang Kai-shek. In the sort of remark that would not exactly have endeared him to Mao Tse-tung, Stalin told Harriman that he "knew little of any Chinese leader" but that he considered Chiang Kai-shek "the best of the lot and . . . the one to undertake the unification of China." Stalin pledged to Harriman that anywhere the Red Army went in its Manchurian campaign against the Japanese, Chiang's troops could be sure to follow. But the Soviet leader did not immediately keep his word. Soviet troops looted Manchuria; they admitted to the area the Chinese Communist 8th Route Army (under the guise of considering it a Nationalist force); they arrested local Nationalist officials and refused to let Chiang's forces land at Manchurian ports except in areas controlled by the Communists. But toward the end of the year, the Soviets were so helpful in facilitating Nationalist entry into Manchuria that Chiang even asked them to stay on until his troops could occupy the area.[48]

What was Stalin after in China? For the time being, at any rate, his moderate approach promoted a weak and divided China while at the same time it mollified the Americans and British. On two other major issues—peace treaty procedures and the occupation of Japan—Moscow pressed its case with particular tenacity, as if testing the possibilities of cooperation in the new climate. In that climate, the questions of who would draft which peace treaties, and which states would attend the peace conference, changed in Soviet eyes from bargaining chips to vital issues. Although the peace conference would be advisory only, leaving ratification to the great powers, the Soviets dreaded to find themselves as isolated as they had been in San Francisco. On the Japanese question, Moscow pressed all through the fall for as great a voice as Washington would allow (including a veto if possible) in the two organs (ACC and FEAC) that seemed likely to emerge in Japan.

What lessons did Stalin learn from jousting with Harriman at Gargra? Some signs were favorable: for example, the fact that Truman had taken the initiative after London, pressing for a meeting even though Stalin was on vacation (Molotov seemed "faintly incredulous" when Harriman asked permission to travel to Gagra); the fact of Anglo-American tension over Japan, tension to which Harriman alluded on October 24 and to which Stalin returned the next day; and the fact that Washington was still bargaining, seeking concessions and offering its own in return.

But there were bad omens, too: for instance, the fact that Truman's letter (which Harriman conveyed) did not even mention Japan but rather confined itself to peace conference procedures. That letter piled arrogance upon arrogance since the Japanese policies that Truman did not deign to discuss violated the rules of the game as played in Europe. In Italy and Rumania, two countries that the Soviets kept trying to equate for purposes of argument, the predominant outside power permitted its opponent official access and a modicum of room to maneuver. (In fact, the situation was assymetrical since Soviet controls were more extensive—a point Harriman made to Stalin but then undermined by saying that this was "past history.") But the Americans had still not responded to Soviet and British requests for an allied presence in Japan on something like the East European model. To make matters worse, Harriman answered Stalin's complaints by contending that the whole argument about Japan was another misunderstanding. Such it was, in part; both British-American noncommunication and intragovernmental wrangling in Washington and Tokyo accounted for American slow motion. But when Harriman said he and Stalin did not really disagree, since both accepted the principle of allied consultation, Stalin snapped that a "failure to agree" was itself a "disagreement."

Shades of past exchanges—but in a new and ominous form. With Roosevelt, Stalin could never be sure what was trickery and what naïveté. But now, apparently, he could. Months had gone by without any answer from the United States on Japan, complained Stalin. But meanwhile MacArthur took action in Tokyo. The Soviet Union had to maintain its self-respect as a sovereign state. The USSR was not an American "satellite in the Pacific." Was this "any way to treat an ally?" MacArthur never consulted Moscow. Did he "represent" the Soviet Union? It would be more honest to leave than to be "treated like a piece of furniture." Former Japanese military officers were at liberty, Stalin contended. The Japanese press was denouncing the USSR. Why was there no censorship? Harriman had suggested a Soviet representative be sent to discuss Japanese matters in Washington. That was incorrect, said Stalin. That would be a "nuisance," and would aggravate relations. It would be better to let the United States run Japan while the Soviets embarked on a "policy of isolation."[49]

Stalin's performance (a species of second-session nastiness) produced partial results. The Americans later pleaded with him to accept in Japan what Washington had long protested in Rumania and Bulgaria, namely, the appearance without the substance of allied control. But one suspects Stalin did not savor the irony, especially once it became clear, as it did in 1946, that MacArthur would begrudge the Soviets even the façade of a role in Japan.

The Stalin-Harriman bargaining on peace conference procedures harked back to Dumbarton Oaks wrangling about United Nations membership. Harriman proposed that the following countries participate in the peace conference: "(1) the five permanent members of the Security Council . . . ; (2) the European members of the United Nations; and (3) those non-European nations which had supplied substantial armed forces against the Axis. These included Canada, Australia, South Africa, New Zealand, India and Brazil. . . ." Stalin wanted to exclude, among others, China (because it had not fought in Europe); India (a colony and not a state); Belgium (welcome at a conference on Germany but not one on Italy and Rumania); and Puerto Rico, which Stalin once again confused with Costa Rica, which itself was not on Harriman's list anyway but which Stalin mentioned to show how arbitrary it was to invite Brazil but not Nicaragua, Costa Rica, and Haiti, which had declared war on Rumania. As for Norway and Holland, if they were included then all sixteen Soviet republics "should also participate. They had fought and suffered. They had more independence than India."[50]

Sparring like that was one thing when it persuaded Roosevelt to yield on the United Nations or on Poland. It was not nearly so satisfying when designed to limit Soviet embarrassment at a propaganda circus masquerading as a peace conference, or to pry loose concessions to which the Soviets felt themselves more than entitled in the first place.

Some of those concessions finally came in Moscow in December, at a special CFM session (Americans, British, and Soviets only) convened at Secretary Byrnes's initiative. Byrnes and Bevin agreed that if the Rumanian government added two non-Communists to its membership, declared that "free and unfettered elections will be held as soon as possible on the basis of universal and secret ballot," and gave "assurances concerning the grant of freedom of the press, speech, religion, and association" then, following certification by a tripartite allied commission, it would be recognized by Washington and London. They further agreed if the Soviet government persuaded the Bulgarian government to include two ministers who "(a) are truly representative of the groups of the parties which are not participating in the government, and (b) are really suitable and will work loyally with the government" then recognition would also be extended to Bulgaria. Byrnes accepted both a Far Eastern Advisory Commission and an Allied Council for Japan; he also compromised on the peace conference and on other issues.[51]

Moreover, Western concessions came despite Stalin's almost Hitlerian display of self-pity mixed with belligerence. When Bevin asked him just what he wanted, Stalin answered that "the United Kingdom had India and her possessions in the Indian Ocean in her sphere of interest, the United States had China and Japan, but the Soviets had nothing"—nothing, Bevin retorted, except a sphere extending "from Lübeck to Port Arthur." Why, Bevin continued, did Moscow insist on retaining troops in Iran despite its wartime pledge to remove them by March 1946? To thwart, said Stalin, the Iranian nationalists, who had "plans of long standing for the incorporation of Baku [the capital of Soviet Azerbaijan] because the Iranian government was "hostile" to the

USSR and there was "nothing friendly about it"; and in conformity with the 1921 Soviet-Iranian treaty that gave Moscow "the right, if conditions are disturbed or there is the possibility of danger, to put troops in Northern Iran." Concerning Turkey, Stalin continued, it was "necessary to restore, at least to some extent, the old frontier which existed in the time of the Czars because the Georgians and Armenians were putting forward claims against the Turkish Government." As for talk of war with Turkey, said Stalin, it was "rubbish."[52]

Nor were Western concessions the only dividend in Moscow. The meeting also aggravated and displayed Anglo-American differences. Alarmed at what his London conference hard line had wrought, Byrnes had unilaterally proposed the special CFM session to Molotov. This soured Bevin on the project from the start, nor did he march in step with Byrnes, for example on the Iranian question, once they got to Moscow.

Not only that, but when Byrnes returned home he was met by accusations of appeasement plus a personal dressing-down from the president of the United States. Truman was outraged by Byrnes's independent ways (the secretary had hardly bothered to keep his boss informed on developments in Moscow) and even more by his concessions. The president had just read Ethridge's report on the Balkans that Byrnes had kept from him until then. It confirmed Truman's impression of "those two police states. I am not going to agree to the recognition of those governments unless they are radically changed." As to Russia's behavior in Iran, there was "no justification for it." It was, Truman said, "another outrage if I ever saw one." Moreover, there wasn't a doubt in Truman's mind that "Russia intends an invasion of Turkey and the seizure of the black Sea Straits to the Mediterranean. Unless Russia is faced with an iron fist and strong language another war was is in the making." Truman continued, "I do not think we should play compromise any longer." He concluded, "I'm tired of babying the Soviets."[53]

Although Stalin and Byrnes each thought he had done well at Moscow, the conference led directly to a worsening of relations. Some historians, however, blame neither Stalin nor Byrnes, but rather Truman himself. "Byrnes had not babied the Russians," concludes Daniel Yergin, "he had negotiated with them. If anything, the Moscow Conference had demonstrated that force was not the only way to do business with the Soviet Union." "Byrnes proved at Moscow," Yergin continues, "that Roosevelt's approach was still viable" but was "no longer acceptable in the American government." It was not so much Stalin as American "universalism," the "belief in American purity," and an "expanded notion of national security" that led Truman, with a chastened Byrnes in tow, to a much tougher American stance.[54]

Truman's stance *did* stiffen even further in 1946. His approach *did* reflect his belief in American purity and an expanding notion of American security. But the President's policies cannot be understood apart from Stalin's, to which they were in large part a reaction. The Moscow Conference was a triumph for the Soviets. But like previous successes scored at Roosevelt's expense, it was a Pyrrhic victory.

6

Détente Stalinist-Style: January 1946-April 1947

BY EARLY 1946, IF NOT BEFORE, IT MUST HAVE BECOME APPARENT to Stalin that continued entente was no longer viable. Formally, the United States, the USSR, and Britain were still allies. But tensions churning beneath the surface and beginning to boil up into public view made for a dilemma—there could be no more pretending that relations were good enough to justify the West's underwriting its own undoing in the name of friendship and cooperation.

The alternative to entente became, for a period of about a year and a half, a mixed relationship falling somewhere between alliance and cold war. One might refer to it using the Soviet term "peaceful coexistence"—by which Stalin meant (but did not always say) a struggle encompassing whatever tricks of the trade the traffic would bear. But in effect, if not in name, this was a time of détente—détente defined (to repeat a point made at the start) not by its literal meaning but by its characteristics: a moderate amount of tension plus a good deal of negotiation, all within the context of what the Soviets, at least, regarded as inevitable, ongoing competition.[1]

Such a relationship has, in theory, both defensive and offensive advantages for Moscow. It is safer than out-and-out conflict, whether of the hot or cold war variety, with an adversary who possesses great military and economic strength and even greater potential. On the other hand, it may offer more positive gains in the form of concessions by opponents lulled into thinking that enduring accommodation, rather than a temporary equilibrium, is the goal of the game. The kind of détente that Lenin had pursued, once the initial flush of revolutionary enthusiasm died down, was clearly defensive, indeed, a matter of sheer survival. The détente that Stalin explored later in the 1920s and 1930s blended defensive and offensive aims with a stress still on the former. In 1946, détente served to avoid alarming and mobilizing an America that had just demonstrated its vast military and economic power against Hitler. But détente Stalinist-style was also a way of keeping a good thing going, of extracting further concessions in the course of extended nego-tiations while waiting for economic troubles to take their toll on the West.

Postwar détente occurred at a time of military demobilization, a process in which, to be sure, the United States went farther and faster than did the Soviet Union.[2] In that sense, 1970s détente, which devel-oped amidst an ongoing nuclear and conventional arms race, was potentially more explosive than its Stalinist forerunner. But Stalin's ver-sion was hardly benign. The Kremlin launched a strident anti-Western propaganda campaign, both as a diplomatic pressure tactic and to pre-pare the faithful for a competition which could get rough. The Soviets were merciless in East European areas subject to their uncontested con-trol, although still moderate elsewhere. Moscow negotiated not in search of a lasting accord, but rather awaiting the next "scheduled" capitalist economic crisis with its presumably devastating effect on the West.

It was the Americans (along with the British and, more reluctantly, the French) who refused to play the role which Stalin had assigned them, thus prompting him to resort to more militant tactics, which in turn further alarmed the West. Whereas the Americans concluded dur-ing the course of 1946 and early 1947 that genuine cooperation with the Soviets was for all practical purposes impossible, Stalin continued to pursue cooperation for his own purposes. To this extent, the revision-ists are correct. Truman did turn his back on Stalin before Stalin did the same to him. But the détente that Stalin pursued was a snare and delusion. The Americans may be responsible for declaring the game at an end, but it was Stalin who invented it. Was there no way to beat Stalin at his own game instead of provoking an even more dangerous one? The answer, unfortunately, is probably not.

American policy toward the Soviet Union was transformed between the end of 1945 and the spring of 1947. Byrnes returned from Moscow hopeful that compromise could reconcile conflict, or at least produce greater understanding. Fourteen months later, Secretary of State George Marshall left another Moscow foreign ministers meeting convinced—if indeed he had not been before arriving—that nothing could be gained and a lot could be lost by negotiating with the Soviets.

The landmarks of this shift in American policy have been charted by numerous diplomatic historians. George F. Kennan's famous Long Telegram from Moscow in February 1946 set out premises that rapidly became administration axioms: the Soviets were fanatically and unalterably hostile to the West; they threatened vital American interests; while Moscow was "impervious to the logic of reason," it was "highly sensitive to the logic of force" and so would withdraw when "strong resistance" was encountered.[3] The Truman administration itself was slow to convey its new consensus to the broader public, but others, like John Foster Dulles and Winston Churchill, spread the gospel. The kind of "strong resistance" that Kennan called for helped to persuade the Soviets to withdraw from Iran in the spring of 1946 and eased the pressure on Turkey in the fall. The "logic of force" hardened the American stance on Germany and Japan. Byrnes resisted any compromise until almost the very end of the 1946 Paris Peace Conference and let the resulting acrimony spill out into the public arena.

Toward the end of 1946, Truman's young assistant Clark Clifford delivered to the president a lengthy, secret report on the Soviet threat— a summary of wisdom gathered throughout the American government. The report portrayed the Soviets as even more dangerous and incorrigible than Kennan had depicted them. "The Soviet Union operates on a world-wide basis," concluded the report. "Each move in its foreign policy is carefully planned and integrated with moves on other fronts." The United States must fight fire with fire. The whole of American foreign policy, whether concerned with Europe, the Near East, or the Far East, must be subordinated to Washington's Soviet policy. Truman ordered the report "put under lock and key," saying it was "so hot, if this should come out now it could have an exceedingly unfortunate impact on our efforts to try to develop some relationship with the Soviet Union." But by now, as Yergin demonstrates, "Truman, like most other policymakers certainly accepted the image presented in the Clifford Memorandum." Marshall took that image with him to Moscow in March 1947 and, therefore, was alarmed to hear Stalin make light of the stalemate in the German negotiations. The situation was not "so tragic," said Stalin reassuringly. He was "more optimistic than Mr. Marshall." As reported in the official U.S. memorandum of conversation, Stalin regarded the talks so far as "only the first skirmishes and brushes of reconnaissance forces on this question. Differences had occurred before on other questions, and as a rule after people had exhausted themselves in dispute they then recognized the necessity of compromise. It was possible that no great success would be achieved at this session, but that should not cause anyone to be desperate. . . . It was necessary to be patient and not become depressed."[4]

To Marshall, that sounded like stalling while the Western economic crisis deepened. He returned to Washington determined to defend the West against Stalin's design. The Marshall Plan, which Stalin took as an assault on the USSR was the result.

Daniel Yergin believes Truman and company misunderstood Stalin. Kennan's Long Telegram, says Yergin, "presented Stalin as a fanatic revolutionary, rather than a careful, calculating politician bent on the consolidation of Soviet power and the reconstruction of the USSR. . . ." Kennan overlooked the devastation of war and other "great constraints" on Soviet behavior. "The contradiction in his [Kennan's] portrait of the Soviet Union and its leaders—the rational fanatic, the devastated aggressor—went unrecognized." So did the "plausible hypothesis," as Yergin puts it, that Soviet troop movements in Northern Iran in early March 1946 were "bluster and bluff." After all, "the Russians did not follow the path of the arrows [which a State Department map had shown pointing toward the Turkish border, the Iraqi border, the Iranian oil fields, and Tehran] but rather marched in the opposite direction toward home." As for Clark Clifford's report, it should have portrayed "a cruel, clumsy, bureaucratized, fear-ridden despotism, preoccupied with reconstructing a vast war-torn land." According to Yergin, "the Americans surely overestimated, giving the Soviets more credit than they deserved. Rigidity, fear, and caution certainly characterized the Soviet system; Stalin's court was at war within itself; . . ." Stalin's advisers "feared to give the dictator information he would not like. . . ." "Conservatism, not adventurism, more aptly characterized Stalin's postwar foreign policy."[5]

Yergin is right up to a point; but so was George Kennan. For one of the prime traits of Stalin's foreign policy—and indeed of Soviet policy to this day—was its dualism. The Soviets were *both* ideologues and *realpoliticians*. Their policies were simultaneously offensive and defensive. Stalin *was* a "rational fanatic." His country was devastated, but that did not prevent him from contemplating the downfall, if only on the installment plan, of others.

That Iranian example: Soviet bluster and bluff there was, but if the

United States had not resisted, would Soviet troops have marched home? Yergin's Soviets "did not need any fiery oratory in the United Nations to know that a move in any of those other directions" would have brought "a strong Western response."[6] But that is not the point. Instead of following the State Department arrows, Soviet troops might have sat where they were, intimidating and thus shaping the course of Iranian politics. To say this is not to defend the shah (who, as we know, managed with American help to reign for many more years). It is rather to point out the error of citing Soviet retreats to prove American resistance was unnecessary, when it would be just as plausible, if not more so, to view those retreats as the result of Western action.

"Rigidity, fear and caution" *did* stalk the Kremlin; Stalin's advisers *were* afraid to bear him bad tidings. But the news they feared to convey was that the West might be something less than a mortal enemy; and so their caution confirmed and intensified Stalin's paranoia. In fact, two of Stalin's top advisers indicated as much to Western listeners, Litvinov directly and deliberately, and Molotov unintentionally. Molotov was debating the Balkans with Byrnes in Moscow, in December 1945. To demonstrate that American charges of Soviet repression were accurate and sincere, Byrnes presented Molotov with a copy (complete with unofficial Russian translation) of the Ethridge report and described its author as a man who had traveled to the Balkans with "a completely open and independent mind." Molotov struck back with a put-down that clearly reflected his own strategy for soothing his savage boss. Molotov "thanked the Secretary but remarked that obviously Mr. Ethridge, when he left the United States, was aware that the Secretary of State was against the recognition of these countries and that this would have a certain influence on his opinion."[7]

Litvinov, now only a deputy foreign minister, gave the latest in the series of startlingly frank interviews granted to Americans and begun during his wartime ambassadorship to Washington—this time to newly arrived CBS correspondent Richard C. Hottelet on June 18, 1946. In addition to conversations previously referred to with Sumner Welles and Edgar Snow, Litvinov had confided in *New York Times* columnist C. L. Sulzberger as early as April 5, 1945, that he was extremely pessimistic about the world situation and entirely ignored in Soviet policymaking. "A regular Jeremiah, full of gloom," Sulzberger recorded in his diary. On May 23, 1946, Litvinov told the new American ambassador to Moscow, General Walter Bedell Smith, that "the best that can be hoped for is a prolonged armed truce." Despite the stifling heat on

June 18, a fire burned brightly in Litvinov's Foreign Ministry office grate, suggesting to Hottelet that his host had learned of a forthcoming further demotion (Litvinov was in fact dropped from his post in August) and was burning his papers. Yet despite the risk of being overheard by "bugs" in the walls, Litvinov delivered a dramatic warning to the West that established him as, in effect, the first major postwar dissident. "There once seemed a chance that the two worlds would be allowed to live side by side, but that is obviously no longer the case. There has been a return in Russia to the outmoded concept of security in terms of territory—the more you've got the safer you are." The "root cause" of East-West tension, Litvinov continued, was "the ideological conception prevailing here that conflict between Communist and capitalist worlds is inevitable." When asked by Hottelet whether he would convey his ideas for bridging the chasm to the government of which he was still a deputy minister, Litvinov replied, "I have some ideas, but I won't give them until they call on me. And they certainly will not call on me."

"Suppose," Hottelet continued, asking what has become the sixty-four-thousand-dollar question in the debate about the Cold War's origin, "the West were suddenly to give in and grant all Moscow's demands regarding Trieste, the Italian colonies, the Danube River, and the rest. Would that lead to good will and easing of the present tension?"

"It would lead," Litvinov answered, "to the West's being faced, after a more or less short time, with the next series of demands."[8]

On February 9, 1946, Joseph Stalin addressed voters of his electoral district while campaigning for reelection to the USSR Supreme Soviet. The Supreme Soviet was a rubber stamp for his will. His election was as automatic as anything in this world. But his speech was important. To watching Westerners it seemed to strip the mask from Soviet policy. H. Freeman Matthews, director of the State Department's Office of European Affairs, called it "the most important and authoritative guide to postwar Soviet policy." Supreme Court Justice William O. Douglas told Secretary of Defense James Forrestal that it was a "Declaration of World War III."[9] The speech is a favorite of traditionalist historians who note that it came a month before Winston Churchill's militant "Iron Curtain" address in Fulton, Missouri, and more than a year before Truman laid down the gauntlet by proclaiming his doctrine for defending the "free world" against Communist tyranny.

Reread thirty-four years later, Stalin's speech seems almost innocuous. Its tone is predominantly defensive. Stalin cites the Soviet victory over Germany to refute Western charges—that the Soviet social order is "a house of cards"; that the multi-national Soviet state is a decrepit "Austria-Hungary"; that the Red Army was unprepared for war—and to justify the terrible decade of the 1930s, with its collectivization and industrialization campaigns, and Great Purge.

What alarmed Westerners at the time was the way the speaker treated allied wartime collaboration, and the way he did not treat post-war cooperation. Stalin depicted the war as an inter-imperialist conflict, saying that it grew out of the general crisis of capitalism. To be sure, the struggle also had a "liberationist" character; Stalin briefly recalled the antifascist coalition. But that was all. The Grand Alliance was dead. Long live the new age of ideological militance![10]

The speech was out of keeping with entente. But it fit perfectly with competitive coexistence as the Soviets have practiced it not only under Stalin but before him and since. From that perspective, Stalin's speech was distinctive for its mildness. Except for one aspect that was ominous indeed: Stalin's stress on a series of ambitious fifteen-year industrial targets, the achievement of which could "guarantee our country against any and all circumstances." Fifteen years—that would place the peak of Soviet readiness at the same moment that Stalin antic-ipated a rising danger of another war. In the course of a dinner in April 1945, Djilas reports, "someone expressed doubt that the Germans would be able to recuperate within fifty years. But Stalin was of a dif-ferent opinion. 'No, they will recover and very quickly. . . . Give them twelve to fifteen years and they'll be back on their feet again. . . .' At one point he [Stalin] got up, hitched up his pants as though he was about to wrestle or to box and cried out almost in a transport, 'The war shall soon be over. We shall recover in fifteen or twenty years, and then we'll have another go at it.' "[11]

The timing also reminds one of Stalin's order to delay the Hun-garian takeover for ten years or more. Furthermore, in November 1946, the Americans obtained what was regarded as a reliable report on a clandestine visit to Moscow by French Communist leader Maurice Thorez. Thorez supposedly summarized Soviet advice as follows: "The international situation is favorable in general to the interests of the Soviet Union but the latter is not in the position at the present juncture of European affairs to draw the greatest possible benefit therefrom. The Soviet Union is not prepared for war and its military preparation will not be completed for a number of years. Hence, the necessity to *gain time* and to avoid situations of a highly dangerous nature while endeavoring to maintain and even consolidate positions already acquired. . . . Because the Soviet Union is in the position of having to avoid during a relatively long period participation in a major war, it follows that the French Communist Party should not advance too rapidly and above all must not endeavor to seize power by force since to do so would probably precipitate an international conflict from which the Soviet Union could hardly emerge victorious."[12]

All this suggests Stalin considered war a possibility fifteen or so years down the road. Whether he imagined repelling another German attack, or consolidating Soviet political gains, or making such gains by military means is not the point. Whatever his motives, the fact that the USSR expected and was gearing for war would make war more likely. But in the meantime, Stalin counted on making gains without war. He counted on crises of capitalism to weaken the West and open it to Communist influence.

The same analyses of Western troubles that underlay Stalin's hopes for entente grounded his hopes for détente as well. Soviet press accounts of capitalist economic difficulties and of inter-imperialist tensions were an indicator of Kremlin thinking. Continued acceptance of Eugene Varga's image of capitalism was another. Once the Cold War began, another image would be necessary—capitalism had to appear more malevolent and dangerous (in order to justify preparation for war), and yet weaker and more constrained (to prevent panic and offer hope of ultimate victory). So Varga was pilloried in late 1947 and subjected thereafter to verbal attacks of mounting violence and vulgarity. And yet, Varga did not suffer the usual fate of a heretic in Stalinist Russia. He was permitted to defend himself in public and even to hold important academic offices. Why did Varga survive? Because someone was protecting him. Was Stalin himself that someone? The question arises not only because Varga had long been connected with Stalin, but also because the dictator seems to have shared Varga's sophisticated and quite undogmatic view of capitalism's immediate prospects.[13]

Stalin's own approach emerged in three conversations with Westerners in 1946 and 1947. Of course, his words were calculated with an eye for publication. But the dictator was also apparently gathering important information for himself. Stalin's sycophantic advisers told him that the West was on its knees. But was it really? No underling could be trusted to be entirely candid. The advantage of talking to Westerners was that they were not subject to his will.

On January 3, 1946, Leo Krzycki, vice-president of the Amalgamated Clothing Workers of America, president of the American Slav Congress, and CIO delegate on an East European tour, met with Stalin for one and a half hours in the Kremlin. The ever-curious dictator began by asking about the role of Slavs in American politics and industry. But he seemed more interested in the question (to which he returned "again and again," according to Krzycki) of whether the United States would be able to solve its current and prospective economic difficulties. Krzycki did nothing to challenge Soviet orthodoxy; he foresaw a permanent army of unemployed due to the absence of economic planning in America. That prompted Stalin to dangle before American trade unionists the same vision of Russian riches with which he had tempted their capitalist bosses. Russia could use many thousands of American engineers and mechanics, he told Krzycki, even more than had worked on the great dam and tractor-factory projects of the 1930s. Those who came to help would be guaranteed "the highest possible American standard of living." Krzycki was suitably impressed, and even more so by Stalin's observation that since neither the United States nor the Soviet Union "needs anything any other nation has," they were perfectly qualified to guarantee the peace. "I got the impression," Krzycki declared upon his return to the United States, "that Stalin had never been more sincere than in this utterance."[14]

By March 1947, Europe was in serious economic trouble, trouble to which the United States would soon respond with the Marshall Plan. The urgent questions for Moscow were, How bad was the Western crisis? How quickly would it deepen? and What, if anything, could the capitalists do to stem the tide? On March 24, during a break in the Council of Foreign Ministers meeting, Bevin asked Stalin whether there was anything the generalissimo would like to ask him. Was the British coal crisis "serious," inquired Stalin, or was it "merely a noise in the press?" A noise in the press? Did Stalin think reports of coal shortages were some sort of ploy—perhaps to justify channeling German reparations West instead of East? Or was this his strange way of being politely sympathetic? Even after Bevin confirmed and explained the seriousness of the situation, Stalin asked again: Was the crisis in England now over? Was it "still serious?"[15]

On April 14, 1947, at 11:00 P.M., Stalin welcomed to the Kremlin his best source yet on the crisis of capitalism—none other than a high-ranking politician in the party Moscow regarded as most purely representative of the American ruling class. Stalin assured Republican presidential hopeful Harold Stassen of the USSR's devotion to peace. It was after midnight when Stassen, not wanting to overstay, thanked his host and rose to leave. But Stalin would not hear of it. Stalin remarked that the situation in Europe was "very bad. What did Mr. Stassen think about it?" The lengthy dialogue which followed is worth quoting almost in its entirety.

STASSEN: In general this is correct, but there are some countries which, not having suffered in the war, are better off. For instance, Switzerland and Czechoslovakia.

STALIN [probing]: Switzerland and Czechoslovakia are very small countries.

STASSEN: The big countries are in very bad shape. They face financial problems, and problems involving raw materials and production.

STALIN [sympathetically]: Europe has many factories and plants but suffers from a lack of raw materials and food stuffs. That is the tragedy.

STASSEN: Lagging coal mining in the Ruhr has created a coal shortage throughout Europe.

STALIN [only semi-convinced by Bevin]: In England, too, there is a shortage and this is very strange.

STASSEN: Fortunately coal mining is in better shape in the USA . . . as a result of which the USA can send coal to Europe.

STALIN [enviously]: Things are not bad for the U.S. America is defended by two oceans. It is bordered on the north by weak Canada, and on the south by weak Mexico. The United States has nothing to be afraid of. The USA did not have to fight for sixty years following its war for independence; it enjoyed peace. All this helped the U.S. develop rapidly. On top of that, the American population consists of people long since freed from the oppression of royal rule or of the landed aristocracy. That also made possible rapid American growth.

STASSEN: . . . now our task is to avoid depression and economic crisis.

STALIN [popping the question]: Is an economic crisis expected in the USA?

STASSEN: I do not expect an economic crisis. I believe American capitalism can be regulated so as to stabilize employment at a high level and thus avoid any serious economic crisis. . . .

STALIN [skeptically]: This would require a very powerful government prepared to act decisively.

STASSEN: That is correct. Furthermore, the people would have to understand the measures designed to stabilize our economic system. This is a new challenge since there has been no parallel to this in any economic system in the world.

STALIN [helpfully]: One condition that favors the U.S. is that two of its competitors on the world markets—Japan and Germany—have been eliminated. As a result, the demand for American goods will grow and that will create favorable conditions for American development. Markets such as Europe, China, and Japan are open to the USA. This will help. These conditions, too, have no parallel.

STASSEN [gloomier than Stalin]: On the other hand, those markets can't afford to pay; in that sense they represent a burden rather than profitable business for the U.S. . . .

STALIN [seeing the bright side; or playing devil's advocate?]: Before the war, approximately ten percent of American production was exported to other countries. I think buyers will find the means; they will buy American goods and resell them to peasants in their own countries. . . . Now American exports will increase to as much as twenty percent. Is that not correct?

STASSEN: I do not think so.

STALIN [astonished]: Are you serious?

STASSEN: Yes. If American exports go as high as fifteen percent, I will consider the U.S. fortunate. . . .

STALIN [impressed nonetheless]: If, however, you keep in mind the total volume of American production, then fifteen percent is not a small figure.

STASSEN: I agree

STALIN [neutral again; checking the facts]: They say American industry now has many orders. Is that correct? They say that American factories will not be able to cope with all their orders and that all factories are working at one hundred percent capacity. Is that correct?

STASSEN: This is so, but these orders are of domestic origin.

STALIN: That is extremely important.

STASSEN: It will be possible to meet the demand for food stuffs, women's clothing, and shoes, but production of machine tools, automobiles, and locomotives is lagging.

STALIN [back to the bottom line]: There are reports in the American press that an economic crisis will soon hit.

STASSEN: [The task is to] stabilize production, thus avoiding crisis.

STALIN: You have in mind regulating production?

STASSEN: Correct. There are those who predict a depression. I believe the people understand the need for regulation.

STALIN [skeptical, again]: But businessmen—will they want to be regulated and subjected to controls?

STASSEN: Businessmen usually oppose regulation.

STALIN: Of course, they will be opposed.

STASSEN: They understand, however, that the depression of 1929 must not be repeated; they now better understand the need for regulation. [Stassen adds that the experience of Japan and Germany demonstrates that governmental failures can harm people under any regime.]

STALIN [contemptuously]: Those economies were run by military men who knew nothing about economics.[16]

Ambassador Walter Bedell Smith found "the fundamental basis of Soviet policy and tactics" in this dialogue. "The Kremlin believes," according to Smith, "that by using delaying tactics and preventing economic stability . . . they can [cause the] United States to continue to pour considerable sums to bolster weak economic systems. They believe that the American public will rebel against these expenditures when the depression, which they hope for, finally arrives, and that we shall then be forced to withdraw our economic aid and curtail our military strength to such an extent that we shall no longer be able to offer any effective opposition to Soviet efforts to establish complete control in areas which they consider of major interest."[17]

This assessment exaggerates Stalin's sense of certainty. The fact that he had to ask Harold Stassen, and that Stalin was more optimistic than Stassen about American prospects, implies a healthy degree of caution. Stalin did not necessarily share Ambassador Smith's timetable. But neither would he be willing to settle the big issues of the day on American terms as long as Smith's nightmare might indeed be the eventual outcome. For the time being, then, the Soviets' task was to keep the negotiations going; on that the embassy was correct.

Besides Stalin's assumptions about Western economic prospects, two other elements undergirded his détente diplomacy. One was a crackdown on the domestic front; the other, Stalin's unique blend of war and peace propaganda. The tightening at home was meant to douse popular hopes for a better, freer life in the postwar world and to prepare the nation for further sacrifices. There occurred a general hardening of Soviet rhetoric (as exemplified by Stalin's electoral speech and press attacks on the West), accompanied by an ideological pogrom directed by politburo member Andrei Zhdanov. In August 1946, Zhdanov, who had a party reputation as an intellectual, did a hatchet job on some of the country's best writers. His speech, which attacked poet Anna Akhmatova as "half harlot, half nun," was only the beginning of the assault on Soviet arts and sciences to which Zhdanov gave his name (*Zhdanovschchina*). By the standards of later years, 1946 was still a liberal period. Now and then there even appeared a somewhat objective assessment of American conditions, such as that by Ilya Ehrenburg in a series of articles published in the summer of 1946.[18]

Stalin's stepped-up repression has been cited by traditionalist historians to argue he could not afford and therefore never wanted open frontiers and friendly relations with the outside world. True enough. He was not prepared, nor have his successors been, to let the Western sun shine in. But the domestic shift does not mean Stalin wanted a cold war. On the contrary, in the 1940s, as in the 1970s, the domestic counterpart of détente was increased ideological and political vigilance, for only that makes it safe for a closed society to open its doors even a little.

Stalin's war and peace propaganda went like this: He warned over and over of war unleashed by the West; but the Soviet Union sought peace, he said, and with the help of people everywhere, would prevent a new war. The domestic purpose of this two-part message was to mobilize the Soviet people while at the same time preventing panic. Stalin's foreign policy aim was less clear. The reaction abroad ranged from puzzlement to grave concern. The violence of Stalin's verbal assaults on Western "warmongers" was disturbing. If this was routine propaganda meant to blacken the West while whitewashing the East, Stalin was playing with fire. If he was sincere, how could he have arrived at such a fundamental misreading, and where would it lead?

Stalin's first high-decibel blast came in response to Winston Churchill in March 1946. Speaking to a Fulton, Missouri, audience including Harry Truman, Churchill warned that an "iron curtain" had descended across Europe. Behind it lay the Soviet-dominated East; in the West, Communist fifth columns were supported by a Soviet intimidation. The Soviets did not want war, said Churchill, only "the fruits of war and an indefinite expansion of their power and doctrine." The Western reply must not be appeasement, since "from what I have seen of our Russian friends and allies during the war, I am convinced that there is nothing they admire so much as strength, and there is nothing for which they have less respect than for military weakness." The Western democracies should therefore "stand together" and from that position of strength seek a "settlement" by "reaching now, in 1946, a good understanding on all points with Russia under the general authority of the United Nations. . . ."[19]

Stalin's answer came in a *Pravda* interview on March 14. He labeled Churchill's speech "a dangerous act designed to sow the seeds of discord among the allies and to undermine their collaboration." Churchill was a "warmonger"; he had "called for war with the USSR." The British leader resembled "Hitler and his friends." "Whether Churchill and friends will succeed in organizing a new attack against 'Eastern Europe' " Stalin did not know. If they did, they "will certainly be beaten."[20]

But this blast was followed almost immediately on March 23 by a soothing interview with Associated Press correspondent Eddy Gilmore. Stalin was "convinced that neither nations nor their armies are striving for a new war." War was entirely preventable if "public and ruling circles of states [were] to organize wide-scale counter-propaganda against the propagandizers of new war and for the maintenance of peace. . . ."[21]

George Kennan's assessment, cabled to Washington from the American embassy in Moscow, was reassuring. Stalin's attack on Churchill was "obviously drawn up for home consumption." It was tactical rather than genuine, Kennan thought. Stalin was preparing his public for tensions resulting from Soviet policy in Iran. But General Smith, who replaced Harriman as ambassador to the USSR in March 1946, was less sanguine. In his get-acquainted interview with Stalin on April 4, Smith asked: "What does the Soviet Union want, and how far is Russia going to go?" "Not much farther," replied Stalin. Did Stalin *really* view his former allies as warlike? Smith wanted to know. "Neither the American people nor the American government," said Smith, "could take seriously the possibility of aggressive action against the Soviet Union by any nation or group of nations in the world today. . . . Our entire history precludes the possibility that we would ever lend support to aggressive action." If further proof were wanted, it could be found in the speed with which the United States was demobilizing its "vast military strength." Smith was fixated on this point. He came back to it, asking why the generalissimo thought any power or powers seemed a "threat to the USSR" Later, Smith asked Stalin categorically if he "really believed" that the United States and Great Britain were united in an alliance to thwart Russia. Stalin replied that he did.

Having alarmed the ambassador by refusing to be reassured, Stalin further dismayed his guest by seeking to reassure him. When Smith restated "our desires for a closer relationship and mutual understanding with the Government of the USSR," Stalin responded: "[May God(?)] Prosper your efforts! I will help you. I am at your disposal at any time." We "should not be alarmed or apprehensive because of differences of opinion and arguments which occur in families and even between brothers, because with patience and good will these differences [will] be reconciled." Here Stalin was being too clever by half. To compare the tensions of April 1946 to those between brothers was bound to seem disingenuous—as Stalin's own reaction to Smith's affirmations of American goodwill demonstrated. In a sense, Smith was as culpable as Stalin. But Smith at least had the excuse of ignorance, of really failing to understand how Stalin could credit an American threat. Whereas Stalin's first premise was deep, mutual enmity. Stalin's détente might have lasted longer if he had not bombarded the Americans with exaggerated charges of warmongering on the one hand, and unbelievable assurances of brotherhood on the other.[22]

Stalin continued to blow hot and cooler in four more puzzling interviews that were the entire extent of his direct public communication with the West during the period we are discussing. On September 17, 1946, with tension rising over Turkey and the Soviet press hammering away at the Western powers, Stalin calmly responded to questions from *London Sunday Times* correspondent Alexander Werth. Did Stalin believe there was real danger of a "new war?" "I do not believe in any real danger of a 'new war.' " "The furor about a 'new war,' " was being encouraged by "military political reconnoiterers" who needed it to: "(a) frighten with the spectre of war certain naïve politicians from among their partners and thus assist their own governments in wresting greater concessions from these partners; (b) hinder for a certain length of time reduction of military budgets in their countries; (c) put a brake on demobilization of troops, and thus prevent rapid growth of unemployment in their countries. It is necessary to make a strict distinction between the furor about a 'new war' . . . and real danger of a 'new war' which does not exist at present time." Were Britain and America creating a "capitalist encirclement" of the Soviet Union? Stalin doubted they could do so "even if they wanted to, which, however, I cannot assert." Stalin also down-played the American monopoly of the atomic bomb: "Atom bombs are designed to frighten the weak-nerved, but they cannot determine the outcome of war. . . ." As for "possibilities of peaceful cooperation with the outside world," they would "not diminish but may even increase."[23]

On October 29, 1946, the *New York Times* hit the streets with Stalin's answers to thirty-one questions submitted by Hugh Baillie, president of the United Press. These responses, too, were relatively mild but also mysteriously curt: Did Stalin agree with Secretary Byrnes that tensions were rising between the United States and USSR? "No." What was the most serious threat to world peace? "Those who would unleash a new war, above all, Churchill and his supporters in Britain and the USA." How could war be avoided? "Those who would unleash a new war must be exposed and restrained." What was the Soviet attitude toward U.S. warships in the Mediterranean? "Indifferent." Was Russia still interested in a loan from the United States? "Yes."[24]

To deny tensions were rising when the Soviet press was fanning the flames struck American embassy analysts in Moscow as "wholly disingenuous." Warming to his portraiture, Embassy Chargé Elbridge Durbrow described Stalin's attacks on Churchill as "obvious political quackery. Stalin knows as well as an American man in the street that the most serious threat to peace is Soviet expansionism." Quackery it was, but not the obvious sort. Stalin was *not* the American man in the street; he did not see Soviet expansionism as villainous. Durbrow made Stalin into a Machiavellian pure and simple, one who, following Lenin's advice, would use " 'any ruse, dodge, trick, cunning, unlawful methods, concealment, veiling of the truth.' " But, Stalin was neither as pure nor as simple as the embassy imagined.[25]

I will cite one more example before trying to explain what the Soviet leader was up to: Elliot Roosevelt brought the world the next message from Stalin in an interview held in the Kremlin on December 21, 1946, and published in *Look* magazine on January 21, 1947. This was the most soothing exchange yet, as if the president's son had evoked the kind of no-holds-barred snow-job which the Soviets had tried on FDR's associates during the war. Did Stalin think democratic America and Communist Russia could live side by side without interfering in each other's affairs? "Yes, of course. It is not only possible. It is sensible and entirely realizable." Did the generalissimo believe expanded Soviet-American trade would strengthen the peace? "Of course, I agree with this." Did he support creation of a United Nations police force? "Of course." Did he favor UN controls over the atom? "Do you mean in general?" Stalin asked, for he was not about to accept the American-sponsored Baruch Plan which the Soviets had been lambasting in the United Nations. "Yes, . . . in principle," Roosevelt replied. Then "of course." What about a Big Three summit meeting? "I believe there should be not only one meeting, but several." Would such a conference foster warmer relations among lower-level officials, as well? "Of that there can be no doubt." To what did Stalin ascribe the deterioration of relations since Roosevelt's death? As far as Soviet and American peoples were concerned, said Stalin, "there has been no deterioration but on the contrary an improvement in relations. . . . [B]etween governments . . . there have arisen misunderstandings. A certain worsening occurred and then a great noise was raised, and people begin to shout that things will continue to ge worse, but I don't foresee anything horrible in the sense of a breakdown of the peace or a military conflict. There is not a single power which, even if its government wanted to, could now raise a great army for battle against an allied power, or another great power, for at the present time no one can fight without his people, and the people don't want to fight. The peoples are tired of war. Besides that, there are no understandable aims which would justify a new war. No one would know what he was fighting for and therefore I don't see anything terrible in the fact that some American spokesmen for the American Government talk about a worsening of relations between us. In the light of these considerations, it seems to me that the threat of a new war is not a real one."[26]

What did it all mean—this talk of war and peace? Did Stalin really believe American policy was leading toward war? Former embassy analyst and later Yale Soviet specialist Frederick Barghoorn called this question "fundamental," and yet "baffling and difficult."[27] But Stalin gave his game away in his description of what he took to be the Western strategy. He charged Churchill with crying "war" to conceal Western troubles, to retard capitalism's decline, to mobilize an anti-Soviet alliance, and to intimidate Moscow. These charges have the ring of conviction; they fit Stalin's ideological assumptions about the West; they describe the sort of thing Stalin would have done if he were in Churchill's place. In fact, I would contend, Stalin was playing this same game, or rather a variation of it, in his own war and peace propaganda. By exaggerating Churchill's warnings, by treating them as a full-fledged "call to war," he would alarm the Western masses while mobilizing the Soviet people. By mixing warnings of war with calls for peace, Stalin would invite the very Westerners he alarmed to support the Soviet Union's peace program, while calming his own people and in general keeping a lid on East-West tensions.

It was a delicate balancing act. The risk was that Stalin's talk of war would turn "the peoples" of the West against *him* rather than

Churchill, while his calls for peace failed to inspire them. In fact this is what happened. Stalin's confidence that war was unlikely permitted him to play with fire in one interview and douse it in the next. But Stalin's tactics undermined his own strategy. As in 1941, Stalin thought he could handle his enemies. Once again, he was wrong.

Stalin's détente diplomacy itself (as distinguished from the assumptions which underlay it) is best examined under four headings—domination (of Rumania, Bulgaria, and Poland); moderation (elsewhere in Eastern Europe and in West Europe and Japan); intimidation (of Iran, Turkey, and, to a much lesser extent, Greece); and negotiation (on unifying Germany and Korea, and at the Paris Peace Conference in the summer of 1946).

At first glance, the diplomatic record appears to confirm the revisionist charge that during 1945–1946 Washington "applied every kind of pressure in the diplomatic arsenal—short of land invasion—to prevent the institution of left governments" in East Europe.[28] Truman refused to recognize the new Bulgarian regime. Rumania was recognized in February 1946, in accordance with the Moscow agreement, but at later CFM meetings, and especially in Paris, the Americans pressed the cause of human rights in Rumania and sought economic and other access to Eastern Europe. Was Moscow alarmed by these American moves? If the Soviets were, they need not have been. For the United States was in an untenable situation which it managed to make worse. Truman thought Soviet behavior outrageous, but he had little leverage. Washington was constant in its complaints, but the State Department took firm positions only to ignore or abandon them. It was not just that Washington hesitated to break with Moscow; the Americans feared that getting out of East Europe would only leave the area to the Russians. Unfortunately, staying in did the same. Should Washington heed local non-Communists and self-declared moderate Communists who urged hanging on while waiting for a better day? Or would that let the Soviets have their East European cake and eat into American prestige (and credits) too? No one knew for certain.

The American Mission in Sofia—which remained there by virtue of the armistice agreement until formal diplomatic relations were resumed with the signing of a peace treaty in September 1947—fumed. "For the first time in my life," the melodramatic Barnes cabled Washington in February 1946, "I have had to hang my head with shame that my country should permit such treatment of her representatives." But while Barnes's head hung, a more important American official, Presidential Counselor Benjamin V. Cohen, assured Vyshinsky that American and Soviet diplomacy in Bulgaria both had "the same objective," that is, minor government changes that would make it acceptable to Washington. In a strict sense Cohen was correct. But the juxtaposition of comments like his with Barnes's public protests helped explain the sort of thing the secretary general of the Bulgarian Foreign Office said to Barnes in October: "Russia has taken good measure of the West and knows that continued pressure will get her most of what she wishes without any serious risks." Secretary General Altunov did not mean to be disagreeable, Barnes reported. "[The] very fact that he was not, and yet that he was expressing such contemptible estimate of two great powers, made his comment far more distasteful than had he deliberately sought to be provocative."

Barnes's mood was so sour that he might have read contempt into the most innocent comment. But similar reports came from Ambassador Burton Berry in Bucharest. There, too, the Russians seemed to be snickering. "I have heard," reported Berry, "that local Communists are now quoting with a wink the sixth point (American nonrecognition of governments imposed by foreign powers) in President Truman's . . . State of the Union message." In March 1947, Julius Maniu, the leader of the Rumanian National Peasant party brought plans for an anti-Communist coup d'état to the American Mission in Bucharest. Washington telegraphed back: "While U.S. Government does not condone dictatorial minority rule of Groza Government contrary to democratic principles to which U.S. firmly adheres, U.S. Government cannot support or advocate attempt violent overthrow with probably attendant consequences for Rum. people."[29] The American advice was realistic. It was the same sort that the Soviets were giving Western European Communists. But that did not mean that the Soviets, whose secret police surely kept track of such things, appreciated American restraint or thought the better of Washington for it. Ditto the American view of Soviet caution in Western Europe.

The major issue in Poland, with diplomatic recognition already extended and no peace treaty to be signed, was Warsaw's requests for economic assistance from the United States and from the United Nations Relief and Rehabilitation Administration (UNRRA). Equating American machinations with their own, the Soviets mistakenly assumed Washington could manipulate UNRRA at will. In February 1946, at a Soviet embassy reception in Warsaw, a tipsy Russian ambassador snorted to his American colleague, "Let's not be diplomatic. You know as well as I that the person who pays is the person who controls. It is absurd that the poor United States has not enough grain for Polish needs."[30] But even if the United States had had the power the ambassador assumed, it would not have been certain what to do with it. The American ambassador in Warsaw, Arthur Bliss Lane (later the author of *I Saw Poland Betrayed*), counseled no credits without the tightest of political strings. But the State Department preferred economic linkage only. Neither the department nor Lane knew what to think when Premier Josef Cyrankiewicz, a Socialist but nonetheless a presumed Soviet stooge, warned that if the United States cut off assistance, this "could push Poland to the East." The premier said he "wished to regain independence for Poland, but this is not possible unless Poland has closer ties with the West." Why did Polish Foreign Minister Zygmunt Modzelewski assure Lane that Polish press attacks on the United States were "merely propaganda" and should not be taken "too seriously?" And how to take Polish Ambassador to Washington Jozef Winiewicz' April 1947 description of a Warsaw split between those wanting Western ties and those who felt Poland's only option was to knuckle under completely to the Soviets? Two months later Poland tried to accept an invitation to Marshall Plan talks, only to back down under severe Soviet pressure. That daring move, which was matched only by Czechoslovakia, apparently confirmed what Polish officials had been telling the Americans. But by then it was too late to build bridges to Poland, even if Washington had wanted to.[31]

Moderation was the Soviet watchword in France and Italy, where Communist ministers held portfolios in coalition governments. The same was true of Hungary and Czechoslovakia. To nervous American eyes, the distinction between Hungary and Czechoslovakia on the one hand, the the rest of East Europe on the other, was not all that great. Hungary, in particular, appeared headed for the precipice down which its neighbors had tumbled. By the spring of 1947, American representatives in Budapest were thoroughly alarmed by Soviet arrests of non-Communist politicians. As late as April, however, non-Communist Premier Ferenc Nagy told Americans that if the Big Four foreign ministers then meeting in Moscow produced substantial agreement on Germany then Hungary would remain "a factor which could be counted on in every respect." If the Moscow conference failed, he added, "this might stimulate activity in Hungary which would prove unpleasant."[32]

Czechoslovakia was freer of Soviet controls than Hungary,

although Prague's coalition government followed Moscow's lead in foreign affairs so closely that in August 1946 Byrnes called a halt to economic assistance to punish the Czech delegation for applauding Vyshinsky's Paris Peace Conference remark that the United States was enslaving Europe by means of economic handouts. It was only after the Communists seized full power in 1948 that Washington appreciated how independent the Czechs had been.[33]

Soviet moderation extended to Asia. If Stalin had hoped for a foothold in Japan via the AC or FEAC, he was disappointed. Nonetheless, while the Soviet press attacked American occupation policies, the Soviet government limited itself to ineffective sniping in the two councils. There was not much Stalin could have done in Japan even if he had wanted to, but China was different. Moscow had helped the Chinese Communists enough in late 1945 to alarm Washington. But in 1946 and 1947 the Soviets adopted a low profile. Why? Partly to avoid antagonizing the Americans, partly because Stalin was not exactly crazy about his fellow Communists in China, and partly because Mao was doing fine without Soviet help.

Moscow's friends in Iran, Turkey, and Greece were not doing so well on their own, so the Soviets lent a helping hand—or seemed to do so. Moscow kept its troops in Northern Iran past the March 2, 1946, deadline established by treaty. The U.S. response was to insist on a showdown in the United Nations. The Soviets stepped up their Turkish demands and pressed them on Ankara. For the Americans, this was Armageddon. If the Soviets controlled the Straits, Truman's advisers warned, they would dominate Turkey; from Turkey, they would move against the whole Near East (defined as "the territory lying between the Mediterranean and India"); the United States must resist aggression by all available means. The president dispatched a task force of ships to the Eastern Mediterranean, remarking that "We might as well find out whether the Russians [are] bent on world conquest now, or in five or ten years."[34]

Washington also saw the hand of Moscow in Greece, where civil war resumed in 1946. When the British announced in early 1947 that they could no longer police the region, Truman said the Americans would assume that responsibility. It was to protect Greece and Turkey, and thereby save the Middle East and Western Europe as well, that the president announced the Truman Doctrine.

Truman's image of the Soviet Union was imperfect, but so is the revisionist picture of a USSR victimized by a Western frame-up. The

Soviets sincerely felt persecuted; it was only fair for them to covet oil and influence over neighboring Iran and Turkey. For someone who saw himself at a geopolitical disadvantage, however, Stalin was remarkably aggressive. He did not expect to lose, and if he had won, his appetite would not have decreased. As for Greece, the consensus among historians is that Moscow did *not* order the latest Communist uprising, but in a sense the Soviets were indirectly responsible and not entirely disappointed when it occurred. Here was a case of real misperception on the part of Washington, but it was not inexcusable in the circumstances.

In Iran, the Soviets played the part of a bully who protests, when restrained, that the one who restrained him is the real bully. As the March 2 deadline approached, Moscow announced that Soviet troops would remain in Iran "pending examination of the situation." The American vice-consul in Tabriz reported Soviet forces moving South in what amounted to a "full combat deployment"; when he took a closer look he was escorted away with a gun to his head. Confronted with Western protests, the Soviets offered a barrage of excuses and accusations. "We do not care what the United States and Britain think and we are not afraid of them," Stalin boasted to Iranian Prime Minister Qavam on March 11. But he complained to Ambassador Smith that Washington was being particularly "unfriendly" in insisting upon a UN confrontation rather than letting the Soviets save face. Stalin also contended that he had encountered "no objection" from Truman and Byrnes in advance. This was a classic Soviet pattern—to conceal their full intent, to take anything less than an absolute *nyet* as an invitation to proceed, and then to condemn their rival's hostile reaction as a betrayal.[35]

In the case of Turkey, the "invitation" was the Potsdam agreement to disagree while letting each capital pursue separate discussions with the Turks. On February 4, 1946, the Soviet ambassador in Ankara asked the acting Turkish foreign minister, "Why don't you make a little effort to improve our relations?" What the Soviets wanted was merely Turkey's eastern provinces plus Soviet military bases in the Straits. When the Turks gave no sign of yielding, the ambassador remarked, "We waited a long time regarding the arrangement we wanted with Poland and finally got it; we can wait regarding Turkey."[36]

While waiting, the Soviets staged heavy troop movements in Turkey's direction in Bulgaria, Rumania, and Northern Iran. When these failed to intimidate, the Soviet ambassador suddenly found it possible to "disregard" the question of those eastern provinces, if only Turkey would recognize Moscow's pressing need for bases. Until August the tension was kept from public view, though the Turks informed the Americans through diplomatic channels. On August 7, Moscow went public with its "proposals" while at the same time signaling (in a conversation between Stalin and Czech Foreign Minister Jan Masaryk) that the USSR had no intention of attacking Turkey. It was these Soviet proposals that prompted Truman to dispatch the fleet. Moscow responded in turn with a harsh note of its own but then backed off without formally dropping its demands. The Americans felt challenged. Doubtless, Stalin felt cheated.[37]

Stalin conceded that Greece fell within the Western sphere of influence. From 1944, when he assured Churchill of that concession, to 1948—when he told Djilas that "the uprising in Greece must be stopped, and as quickly as possible" since it was "nonsense" to think "that Great Britain and the United States . . . will permit you to break their lines of communication in the Mediterranean Sea"—Stalin was consistent. But while Stalin's policy was cautious, his propaganda was not. One major aim of Moscow's harsh anti-Western line on Greece may have been to mollify radicals in the international Communist movement who were impatient with Soviet restraint. But the result was to encourage the Greek Communists to fight, and the Americans to see Moscow's hand behind the fighting. Late in 1945, Moscow mounted a noisy press campaign accusing the British of crushing democracy in Greece. Early in 1946, the Soviets pressed this case in the United Nations in retaliation for the West's bringing up Iran. The Soviet delegate charged that British action constituted a "threat to the peace" under the United Nations Charter. Moscow was, quite simply, posturing. But the British were not about to write off as propaganda what the Soviets insisted was not propaganda. At a closed meeting of the UN Security Council on February 5, 1946, Bevin lost his celebrated temper: "You have raised this matter in Potsdam, in London and in Moscow," he shouted at Vyshinsky. "It must be settled here once and for all, or I shall not go on with these discussions." Whereupon, according to an American record of the meeting, "Vyshinsky then lost his temper and spoke for five or six minutes, not even pausing for the interpreter. He said this was not propaganda, and that he had a deep conviction that the validity of his case was evident. It was very distressing to him that Bevin could not see the situation the way he saw it."[38]

For the rest of 1946, Soviet accusations escalated along with the tension in Greece, especially at the Paris Peace Conference, which turned into a veritable East-West brawl. Meantime, when the United States got the United Nations to appoint a commission to investigate Yugoslav and Bulgarian Communists' support for their Greek brethren, the Soviets stalled and obstructed it. It was not surprising, under these circumstances, that Washington saw Moscow's guiding hand in Greece—nor that Stalin interpreted that charge as American propaganda.

Nonetheless, Stalin was prepared to continue détente—even after Truman proclaimed his doctrine on March 12, 1947. Revisionists say the Truman Doctrine address clinched the Cold War; traditionalists, that America was now joining a conflict Moscow had begun. The truth is that Stalin himself refused to accept, even after the Truman Doctrine, that the Cold War was on. He was prepared to treat Truman's anti-Communist oratory as propaganda, and the new Greek and Turkish assistance programs as limited in scope and confined to areas that he had either already conceded to the West (Greece) or half-expected he would be required to concede (Turkey). That this was Stalin's view is confirmed by Soviet diplomacy concerning Korea and Germany.

East-West rivalry in Korea was a tragicomedy even before it erupted in a war that proved to be easier to start than to stop, ended where it began, but managed to hasten the militarization and globalization of the Cold War. For the Americans, Korea was a sideshow until the Soviets and North Koreans made it the main event. During World War II, Washington and London devised a formula under which Korea would become free and independent "in due course," meaning after a period of international trusteeship. Roosevelt and Churchill pressed for and obtained Stalin's agreement without asking the Koreans themselves, which admittedly would have been difficult to do during the Japanese occupation. Unfortunately, however, many Koreans turned out to prefer immediate independence. But in the meantime, the war had ended with the country divided between a Soviet-occupied North and an American South, and with Moscow moving-in Communist-trained Koreans from Soviet territory. To be sure, Washington had its own man in South Korea, but Syngman Rhee turned out to resent American tutelage and his fellow non-Communist politicians almost as much as he hated the Communists. Rhee made life miserable for General John R. Hodge, whose own anticommunism was overshadowed in Rhee's mind by the American's advocacy of trusteeship. Later, Rhee undermined American efforts to reach agreement with the Soviets and went so far as to threaten unilateral military action against the North. The situation was tailor-made to spark Soviet suspicions: if Rhee was a U.S. puppet (as the Soviets must have assumed early on), his appearance of independence must be a trick; if Rhee was his own man, his American puppeteers must be less resolute than Moscow had anticipated.

The December 1945 foreign ministers meeting, which appeared for a moment to resolve other issues, seemed to settle the Korean question, too. Byrnes, Bevin, and Molotov agreed on independence and democracy as goals for Korea, with an all-Korean provisional government to be a step in that direction. That government was to be shaped by a joint Soviet-American commission that was to consult with representative Koreans from both North and South and then present its recommendations for great-power ratification. Then a period of trusteeship for up to five years would begin.[39]

This scenario combined the worst of two worlds: it applied a Polish-type formula (a joint commission trying to harness Communists and virulent anti-Communists in a genuine coalition government) to a German-style setting (a country divided into zones of occupation). Not surprisingly, the commission quickly deadlocked. The Soviets proposed that only Koreans not opposed to the Moscow agreement be consulted, a seemingly reasonable idea except that Rhee and most of his Southern colleagues, being more royalist than the king, had no use for the American compromise. American observers were divided about whether the Soviets really wanted a settlement. Late in 1946 the Soviets appeared particularly conciliatory. An American delegation visiting the North found their Soviet hosts effusively friendly: they denied any intention to control all of Korea, and they seemed unsure of their ability to hang on to the North itself.[40]

The thaw continued into 1947. In February Moscow accepted American proposals designed to speed the joint commission's work. On April 19, Molotov chided Washington for not responding to his concessions and proposed that the joint commission meet in May. When Secretary Marshall pressed Molotov to accept certain further stipulations, the Soviet foreign minister obliged. When the joint commission met, the Soviet representatives were as pleasant as they could be, though still bargaining hard on the question of whom to consult. The Americans got the impression "that the Soviet delegation [was] under some driving compulsion to complete something concrete in the way of plans for a provisional government within the next two months." That impression held until late June. Shortly after Molotov walked out of a Paris conference discussing the Marshall Plan, the Soviets in Korea turned cold and absolutely unyielding.[41]

Korea is a long way from Paris. But Soviet moves in both places appear related. Soviet reasonableness on Korea in the spring of 1947 made things interesting for the Americans; it kept them in the game of détente not only after the Truman Doctrine speech but even after the Moscow CFM conference broke down in April. It was only in July, when the Americans presented the Marshall Plan, and the Czechs and Poles rushed to benefit from it, that Stalin realized the game was up.

The negotiations on Germany fit the pattern. Stalin tried to string out the talks even after the Americans gave up on them. Despite its crucial importance to both East and West, the German question was slow to come into focus as an arena of Soviet-American competition. Washington was not certain until 1946 whether Paris or Moscow was the primary obstacle to a German solution—a situation that must have encouraged Stalin's hope to downplay East-West rivalry while playing up inter-imperialist contradictions. Some Americans, like George Kennan and Ambassador Smith, contended that Moscow was out to dominate all of Germany. But others thought the Soviets' first priority was reparations. Robert Murphy, the American political adviser for Germany, said the Soviets were so anxious for reparations in the form of current production—a step beyond Potsdam's provision for the removal of capital equipment—that they might in return grant "basic civil liberties and political equality" in the Soviet zone. But the American embassy in Moscow doubted "the possibility of obtaining any lasting political concessions . . . in return for economic ones," especially since the Russians were unlikely to deliver on their bargain even if, as was doubtful, they made one in the first place.[42]

Inside sources on Stalin's German intentions: Djilas recalls Stalin's saying, in the spring of 1946, that "all of Germany must be ours, that is, Soviet, Communist." Djilas thinks the Soviet leaders "were caught up by the flush of military victories and by their hopes for the economic and other dissolution of Western Europe." Maxim Litvinov told Hottelet that since "each side wants a unified Germany—under its control," the country "will obviously be broken into two parts." Stalin repeated this prediction to Djilas in early 1948 (by which time, to be sure, negotiations to unify Germany had broken down) when he declared, "The West will make Western Germany their own, and we shall turn Eastern Germany into our own state."[43]

The most plausible interpretation is that Moscow had both minimum and maximum aims in Germany: minimally, to hold the East but, if possible, to dominate the West as well. Washington would have wished the reverse, that is, to hold the West while extending its influence eastward. In the end, both sides settled for half a loaf—but only after negotiations that some historians think offered the opportunity for reunification on Western terms, but others see as a trap for the West.

It was not until late 1946 that the Council of Foreign Ministers, meeting in New York, turned its full attention to Germany. By that time, tensions over other issues, and German developments, too, made prospects for a settlement seem bleak. The Americans had become increasingly concerned about West European recovery and less so about Russian reconstruction. The American military governor in Germany, General Lucius Clay, went so far in May as to halt the dismantling of plants designated for delivery to the Soviets. In July, Byrnes authorized the fusion of American and British zones in the name of economic efficiency and as a response to Soviet nonimplementation of common economic policies for all Germany that had been agreed upon at Potsdam. Of course, the Soviets denied the charges.

Hoping to break the stalemate, or at least to test Soviet intentions, Byrnes had proposed a twenty-five year, four-power treaty guaranteeing against any renewed German threat. Byrnes regarded his proposal as a revolutionary departure in American peacetime diplomacy: if Moscow were truly interested in peace and security, it would accept; if not, the Russians must be intent on expansion. Byrnes's notion was simplistic. The prospect of Americans on guard in Europe for a full quarter of a century was not likely to gladden Soviet hearts even if Stalin were not in an imperial mood. Molotov declined to support the treaty on the grounds that it postponed the more pressing task of the immediate disarmament of Germany.[44]

The CFM's first task in New York was to establish procedures for drafting German and Austrian peace treaties. Byrnes proposed a preliminary stage in which the ministers' deputies would hear a report from the Allied Control Commission in Germany, canvass the views of other interested countries, and prepare draft treaties for consideration in the spring in Moscow. Molotov pressed instead for immediate consideration by the CFM itself but then relented. Thereafter, the Soviets went

out of their way to be conciliatory. Stalin's interview with Elliot Roosevelt—in which he called for not one but several summit conferences—took place on December 26. On January 5, 1947, Ambassador
Smith complained to Vyshinsky about Molotov's tactics at the Paris
Peace Conference, saying he had made "antagonistic, violent and
unjustified attacks on the United States, its representatives and its institutions." Vyshinsky said his boss had not been attacking but was
"defending." "However," he continued, "the atmosphere in New York
was much happier . . . and I am sure that in Moscow it will be happier
still."[45]

Other signs reinforced Vyshinsky's message. In January 1947, the
U.S. Central Intelligence Group (predecessor to the CIA) reported eight
instances of apparently accommodating Soviet behavior ranging from
concessions on Trieste, to Eastern European force reductions, to a
relaxed stance on the veto in the United Nations, to acceptance of
Byrnes's proposals for drafting the German and Austrian treaties. The
Moscow embassy also detected a "less aggressive international attitude
taken by Soviet authorities in recent weeks." But both the CIG and the
embassy warned that the Soviet shift was a tactical one, an interpretation supported by a crude Soviet effort, at about this time, to foment
Anglo-American divisions by pressuring London into a new bilateral
treaty, and by a rather arcane article on military strategy (published in
February 1947, although written a year earlier) in which Stalin justified
retreat under unfavorable conditions but called for counterattacks when
the situation changed.[46]

What was Moscow up to? The German negotiations themselves
provided an ambiguous answer. During the preparatory talks, the Soviet
delegates stonewalled on procedure and substance. "In the past six
weeks," reported Robert Murphy on February 26, "the Soviet deputy
made only one compromise towards the idea of Allied consultation and
participation." But intransigence in the early going was par for the
Soviet course, as Murphy recognized. So that whereas Ambassador
Smith predicted lengthy and fruitless discussions, others thought Moscow might be willing to swap all-German economic unification for
badly needed reparations.[47]

When the foreign ministers gathered in Moscow in March, Soviet
negotiators became more forthcoming. Molotov offered (in the midst,
to be sure, of a long anti-Western diatribe) to eliminate interzonal barriers "of any kind." On March 19, he said that there seemed already to
be "general agreement" on most of the points discussed and that he saw

no reason why a "compromise solution" could not be reached. The Soviet foreign minister promised to account for "every kopeck" of reparations seized by the Soviets in their zone. Molotov sounded so moderate in opposing a federal political structure for Germany (on the grounds that it would be harder for the allies to control, and because it would give German militarists a Versailles-type target) and in proposing a Weimar-style constitution complete with free elections, that Secretary Marshall acknowledged, "there is much in common in the four proposals for the future political structure of Germany," and he added that the differences were more "a question of degree than fundamental."[48]

When Stalin and Molotov met privately with Bevin on March 24, high optimism reigned, or so it seemed. Molotov hoped "to finish our work here by the end of March." Bevin found "not much difference between the Russian and British proposals" on political structure. Stalin "thought so too. It would be good to come to agreement." The sweetness and light extended to non-German matters. Stalin responded to Bevin's wish to revise the Anglo-Soviet Treaty of May 1942: "Very good. We want it also." As for Bevin's claim that the Middle East was "one of our spheres of influence," Generalissimo Stalin said that he "understood." The Soviet Union had "no intention of interfering in the carrying out of British policy in Egypt," he said. Ditto for India. In fact, Russia wished "success to Great Britain in the enterprise she has started in India."[49]

By March 26, the conference had come down to two main issues—reparations and German economic and political organization. On the surface the stage appeared set for compromise, but this time the Americans and British stonewalled. American desiderata were so far-reaching as to preclude Soviet agreement except in exchange for a most lucrative *quid-pro-quo*. But the *"quid"* was puny. In a telegram to Truman summarizing the instructions he was about to give the American delegation, Marshall proposed to seek nothing less than "a politically and economically unified Germany under a democratic government with effective safeguards of human rights and fundamental freedoms." In return, he would consider giving the USSR German reparations taken from current production but only on the following conditions: that the burden on the occupying powers not be increased; that any reparations plan not become effective until "economic and political unity are established in fact"; and that "the United States would not agree here to a definite plan involving reparations from current production but only to studies of the relevant factors."[50]

The next day, April 1, Truman cabled instructions to Marshall. If anything, the president was even more rigid than his secretary of state. He would "not necessarily exclude the possibility that, after a balance of payments was achieved or in sight, consideration might be given to the availability of reparations from current production to the USSR as well as to other claimants on a proportionate basis to be determined later." Marshall cabled back at midnight on April 2 that the Truman terms were "somewhat too restrictive and may not afford necessary elbow room for negotiation." But by then, any real negotiation was over. The climax, or rather anticlimax, had come that afternoon. Each side had restated its position. They would continue to do so for twenty-two more days before disbanding the conference.[51]

This was the situation both when Stalin met Harold Stassen and when he attempted to reassure Secretary Marshall on April 15. Stalin never again met an American secretary of state; his next meeting with the American ambassador took place in the heat of the 1948 Berlin crisis. It was only fitting that this last high-level meeting misfired as miserably as had previous Soviet-American talks. Marshall meant mainly to warn Stalin but also in part to reassure him. In fact, he achieved neither aim. Stalin meant to calm Marshall and thus get him to continue serious negotiating. Instead, he confirmed the secretary's suspicion that negotiations were a sham and a trap.

It was not one of Marshall's better peformances. According to his aide, Charles Bohlen, "There had been no particular preparation for this interview, since by that time we realized that the Soviets were not willing to move on the German question, and Marshall's only point was to tell Stalin how dangerous it was to leave Germany in a chaotic and divided state." If that was Marshall's point he got to it in a round-about way and flubbed it once he arrived. He began with a warning by now as ritualized as it was unconvincing—that American public opinion had turned against the Soviet Union. Marshall next complained about Soviet slowness to settle its lend-lease debt, as if that were the primary cause of Soviet-American tension. Marshall justified his Germany policy as a defense of the American taxpayer, which Stalin knew was not the whole story. Coming at last to his major point, Marshall said the United States was "determined to assist those countries which are suffering from economic deterioration which, if unchecked, might lead to economic collapse and the consequent elimination of any chance of democratic survival"—not so unattractive a prospect to one whose notion of democratic survival was rather different from Marshall's. In conclusion, "the Secretary stated that it was his desire to rebuild the basis of cooperation which had existed during war and that he had come to Generalissimo Stalin with that hope, feeling that if they cleared away some of the suspicion, it would be a good beginning for the restoration of that understanding."

Clearing away American suspicions was something the generalissimo had once been fairly adept at—but no more. Doodling wolf heads with a red pencil, he spoke the soothing words quoted at the start of this chapter: the situation was "not so tragic"; these were "only the first skirmishes and brushes of reconnaissance forces"; differences had "occurred before" only to be compromised, so that no one need be "desperate." According to Bohlen, "Stalin's seeming indifference to what was happening in Germany made a deep impression on Marshall. He came to the conclusion that Stalin, looking over Europe, saw that the best way to advance Soviet interests was to let matters drift." The crisis facing Europe was "the kind of crisis Communism thrived on. All the way back to Washington, Marshall talked of the importance of finding some initiative to prevent the complete breakdown of Western Europe."[52]

Had Marshall indeed grasped Stalin's true intention? Even his predecessor Jimmy Byrnes (not to mention revisionist historians) was not so sure. Byrnes later recalled an exchange he had with Molotov in mid-1946. Molotov had agreed with Byrnes in a perfectly disarming way that Soviet negotiating tactics were to blame for some of the tension. Byrnes decided to probe further. "Why then don't you tell me what is really in your heart and mind on the subject of Germany?" The Soviets, Molotov replied, wanted what they had asked for at Yalta: ten billion dollars in reparations plus four-power control of the Ruhr. Thinking back to that remark, Byrnes concluded that Molotov had spoken the truth and that those were "the real desires of the Soviet high command."[53]

If so, a great opportunity may have been missed. Historian Adam Ulam thinks Stalin came close to releasing East Germany from the Soviet grasp in return for reparations plus a guarantee of German demilitarization.[54] Or would Moscow have taken reparations while insisting on loopholes through which to work for its minimum and even maximum German aims? Extensive further bargaining would have been required to reach a settlement. In the meantime (assuming the United States held off on Marshall Plan aid), Western troubles would have deepened. No one can say how the talks would have ended since Western negotiators never offered enough to test Soviet intentions. But one way to divine how Washington and Moscow might have acted if serious talks had continued is to examine how they negotiated in 1946 on other issues, issues concerning which they eventually did manage to strike a deal, of sorts, but only after the Americans explicitly threatened to break the talks off altogether.

East-West negotiations in 1946 primarily concerned the other (that is, non-German) peace treaties and related issues that the great powers had first taken up in September 1945 with high hopes of early agreement. These talks were lengthy and frustrating. Twenty-five years later Richard Nixon would hail détente as a transition from confrontation to negotiation. But the 1970s had nothing on 1946 when it came to time spent at the negotiating table.

The CFM schedule was virtually nonstop. Arrangements for the next meeting, including a preliminary canvassing of issues by the foreign ministers' deputies, began within a week after Byrnes left Moscow in December 1945 and continued until April 1946. The so-called second session of the CFM (the first had been in September 1945; the December meeting was *ad hoc*) lasted, or rather its first part lasted, from April 25 through May 16. This session's apparently painless assignment was to prepare for the actual Peace Conference on the basis of guidelines arrived at in Moscow. Instead, the foreign ministers found themselves deep in debate on Trieste, Italian colonies, Italian reparations, and so forth—so deep that a second round was required. This second part of the second session extended from June 15 to July 12. It produced agreement on a Peace Conference date, only to erupt into debate on Peace Conference procedures. The Paris Peace Conference itself, attended by twenty-one nations, staggered along for nearly three months from July 29 to October 15 with private CFM meetings interspersed amid its public, and often acrimonious, formal sessions. The council, which retained the ultimate authority to pass on the peace treaties, met to pick up the pieces in New York from October 15 to December 12. There the same issues that divided the ministers in the spring required further hard bargaining.

In retrospect all this talking seems a tedious sideshow to the onrushing Cold War. But the record is a veritable treasure house of Soviet diplomatic style and techniques. Molotov, who has a reputation as a colorless clerk, put on a bravura performance. One can understand why the Westerners eventually fled from the negotiating table thinking, as Dean Acheson was later to put it, "There's no way to argue with a river. You can channel it; you can dam it up. But you can't argue with it."[55]

Late in the afternoon of November 23, 1946, in the Waldorf-Astoria Hotel in New York City, the foreign ministers of the United States and Britain heard their Soviet counterpart say that the council could reach an agreement on territory at issue between Austria and Italy if it could, at the same time, decide on railroads between Yugoslavia and Trieste. "This seems like horse trading to me," said Bevin. "I do not know how to horse trade," answered Molotov. "Find me a horse trader as hard as you are," said Byrnes, "and I will give him a gold medal." Molotov (modestly): "I am learning." Bevin: "God help us when you have learned!" "I am learning from you," retorted Molotov. "I guess this question remains in disagreement."[56]

Several months earlier, Bevin had paid Molotov the opposite tribute (if that is the word) of saying he had a "great legalistic mind." Whether he was horse trading or refusing to trade on grounds of strictest principle, Molotov was formidable. Herewith his how-to-do-it guide as gleaned from how he did it: At the start of negotiations, stake out an extreme position so that "mutual accommodation" gives you more than you originally wanted. Toward the end, raise new and apparently trivial issues and insist they are life-and-death matters; that way you can squeeze the last drop out of the lemon. In between the beginning and the end, try the following: Stall (whether by going round and round or forward, inch by inch) when things are not going well, even at the risk of Jimmy Byrnes's complaining that you're playing "ring-around-a-rosy." Ignore previous concessions when it suits you or—a variation—sell the same horse twice. Do not shrink from harsh words, even when they provoke a reply in kind, since words can always be smoothed over. Be suspicious when that reply in kind comes and even more so when it does not; for your adversary's most sinister device may be to deny disagreement exists or to agree in principle and then retreat, saying it was only in principle. Dole out minor concessions—not enough to clinch a deal but enough to pose the prospect of one. Avoid stupid mistakes—like the one even Molotov made when he agreed upon a date for the Paris Peace Conference without first settling on the rules, and so had to negotiate the rules without having the date to use as a bargaining chip. It is okay to stutter at tense moments, as Molotov did, as long as your tactics, and your overall political stance, show that you are not afraid.

To compile such a list is not to say Western negotiators were without guile. By 1946 they were suspicious of Soviet motives, determined not to agree for the sake of goodwill, and increasingly unwilling to agree at all. But even then, the Soviets viewed the Americans as more devious than in fact they were. Take, for example, Byrnes's proposal (which Secretary Marshall later renewed) for a twenty-five-year treaty on Germany. Coming after FDR had assured Stalin that the United States would leave Europe within two years, the proposal probably seemed a double-cross to the Soviets. Another example from the Paris Peace Conference: The Soviets feared from the start that the conference would undo agreements reached in the CFM—a prospect Moscow hedged against by insisting that a two-thirds vote be required to carry certain issues and that final treaty ratification be reserved for the great powers. Sure enough, Western-oriented small powers, Australia in particular, lit into agreed-upon arrangements, seeking, for example, to reduce Italian reparations to Moscow's East European clients and to increase Western access to the East. That small countries should raise questions at all was annoying; Molotov once inquired "how much of the world's surface" was represented by the nations who opposed him. Vyshinsky referred to the Australian delegate as "a country lad who had come to town and wanted to try everything himself, not believing in the work done by others." That the hands of Washington and London were behind Australia was axiomatic to Molotov. All the Australian amendments, he charged, were "directed against the interests of the Soviet Union." The Australian delegation had submitted so many that "it must have had help in drawing them up." The conference record suggests, however, that although Washington and London were often with the Australians and other amenders on substance, and although Byrnes thought that the small-powers' "hell-raising" could prove useful (both in showing them what he had been "up against" and in strengthening his bargaining position with the Russians), the American delegates were also exasperated by their allies' tactics. So that once again Molotov's conception of a "Western bloc" revealed more about his tight hold over his own supporters (including nominally independent delegations from the Ukraine and Byelorussia) than about relations among Western states.[57]

The reader will be spared a blow-by-blow account of these negotiations. I shall concentrate on moments when the Soviets offered serious concessions designed to keep the talks going and to avoid a break. The first moment came in June 1946, when American diplomats picked up hints of Soviet unhappiness with the course of the talks. The Soviet ambassador to France complained that Moscow had shown "a real desire and willingness to compromise," but unfortunately the West had not reciprocated. Ambassador Smith found his Soviet contacts in Moscow quite as "anxious" as Smith was "to avoid a complete break-up," a feeling that Smith thought might be "of great importance in connection with irreconcilable questions such as Trieste." Molotov himself sent a Trieste signal at a private dinner with Byrnes in Paris on June 21. The question at issue was whether Yugoslavia (the Soviet preference) or Italy (the Western candidate) should control Trieste and the surrounding territory. Molotov noted Soviet concessions on the Italian colonies, in return for which, he said, the Americans ought to meet Soviet wishes concerning Trieste. When Byrnes refused to bite, Molotov sweetened his offer. The idea of UN administration of Trieste (advanced by the French) might be acceptable if there was "reason to hope that such a decision would facilitate the solution of other questions." Byrnes was not buying that either, but he was talking Molotov's language: the secretary said that "if we could settle Trieste, the other questions would not be too difficult." The next day, Molotov took what he called "another extreme step" by agreeing to "dual Yugoslav and Italian sovereignty with two governors, one Italian and one Yugoslav." Byrnes did not find the step extreme enough. Whereupon Molotov cashed yet another chip he had been holding since the previous September; he conceded that the Dodecanese Islands, the disposition of which Molotov had been delaying for purposes of bargaining, could go to Greece after all. Byrnes asked for "a minute or two to recover." Molotov suggested that they "might make some other good agreements." Could they settle on Italian colonies? asked Byrnes half in jest. They could, indeed, and did, on the basis of the American position.[58]

These Soviet moves invited counter-concessions from the West. But when Vyshinsky pressed for American acceptance of the Soviet-proposed Italian-Yugoslav boundary line, Cohen said no deal. Told that the United States would insist on at least the French-proposed boundary, the Soviets accepted that, too—only to have Byrnes favor leaving final resolution to the Peace Conference, which "would have the advantage," he said, "of having the recommendation come from twenty-one nations." This provoked Molotov to complain that he did not know what Mr. Byrnes wanted. Yet when pressed to the wall, which is to say confronted with the prospect that the Peace Conference might not occur, Molotov yielded further ground. The Soviet delegation was prepared, he said on July 3, "to accept the [Trieste] proposal of the U.S. Delegation as a basis."[59]

This and other concessions, on both sides, unblocked the way to the Peace Conference, which managed to aggravate and dramatize the disagreements before returning them to the CFM for final disposition. By this time, moreover, the atmosphere had further deteriorated as a result of the Turkish war scare of August and the Anglo-American decision to fuse their German occupation zones into a single economic unit to be known as Bizonia. Stalin's fall interviews with Werth and Baillie were one Soviet effort to calm the waters. Molotov's tactics, when the CFM resumed meeting in New York, were another.

From the very first day (November 4) Molotov was so good humored as to invite and even apparently appreciate Byrnes's humorous reference to a "Soviet-American bloc" at the Peace Conference. Molotov assured his colleagues that "there is no enmity among us." He even tried to be amusing in a self-deprecating way by saying, when asked if he had any further "observations" (which is to say, objections), that he had "a whole box of them." But through it all Molotov was stingy with substantive concessions—until Byrnes took the drastic step of threatening to break off the talks.[60]

As Bohlen recalls it, Byrnes phoned him and said, "Come on, Chip, we'll go to see Molotov. I have an idea." Once in Molotov's suite at the Ritz, Byrnes dropped his bomb: "In thinking the whole matter over, I really believe the wisest thing for us all to do is admit failure and to disband this meeting." Byrnes added smoothly that he really had "great sympathy" for Molotov. No one could have put himself out more to "take care of the Yugoslavs." As far as Byrnes could see, the Yugoslavs were "totally ungrateful" for all the effort. Molotov's reaction was characteristic: "He began to stutter, as he always did when he was a little excited, and said, 'No, no, Mr. Byrnes, don't take hasty actions. Just wait until this afternoon's meeting and you will see developments.' As we were going down in the elevator Byrnes said, 'Well, I hope that works.' In the meeting that afternoon, Molotov handed out concessions like cards from a deck. Almost all the outstanding points were agreed to in a reasonable manner, and finally the Italian treaty was completed and a signature date set."[61]

Could the German negotiations of 1947 have ended in similar fashion? Or, if the German issue was not susceptible of compromise, because neither Washington nor Moscow could risk letting such an important piece of real estate end up under the other's control, could they not have arrived earlier, and with less *Sturm und Drang*, at the division of Germany—which they eventually agreed was less risky than unification? What if the Western powers, realizing how much Stalin wanted to avoid a break, had threatened one and proposed an attractive alternative? Suppose, like Nixon and Kissinger more than twenty years later, Truman and Marshall had offered continued détente but demanded that the Russians pay a price for it. The Nixon-Kissinger carrot-and-stick strategy (about which more in chapter nine) was to offer the Soviets positive inducements to restrain their expansionist urge while at the same time resisting Soviet adventures that the Russians themselves could not. Truman mounted effective resistance to Communism in such places as Iran, Greece, Turkey, and Japan. Truman's carrots might have included earlier acceptance of Soviet control over Bulgaria and Rumania, plus economic assistance—either credits of the sort the Soviets had asked for or a more generous stance on German reparations.

It would not have been easy. Even if Truman had opted for carrots and sticks, would Congress have followed along? Was not the all-or-nothing approach too deeply engrained in American foreign policy? Either the USSR was our friend or it was not. The idea of helping and resisting it over a lengthy period of time would have appeared, as it still does to many today, slightly mad. Moreover, it is doubtful that Stalin would have played the role assigned to him. He would have pocketed whatever carrots were offered (considering them far less than his due) while searching for ways to get around the sticks.

And yet, despite everything, it almost happened. Consider the situation in the late spring of 1947. By that time the United States had in fact, if not in rhetoric, accepted Soviet control over much of Eastern Europe; at the same time, the United States was moving vigorously to resist Communist gains outside that sphere. Stalin, moreover, had signalled his, at least temporary, acceptance of this mixed approach—most recently in his conversation with Secretary Marshall in Moscow. The American decision to offer Marshall Plan aid to Western Europe (and, however reluctantly, to Eastern Europe as well) did not mark a drastic break from this pattern, yet it apparently triggered a panicky response in Moscow, which produced a corresponding reaction in Washington.

The upshot was the Cold War. Stalin had not wanted it. Nor had he anticipated it; for although the Soviet dictator yielded to no one in his suspicions, he underestimated American determination in a way that was doubly ironic. Soviet propaganda had long depicted Western statesmen as "warmongers" who would not hesitate to break with the

USSR. Yet when that very propaganda helped provoke a break, the rupture caught Stalin by surprise. Stalin thought he could diddle the West along without provoking a severe reaction even after CFM talks on Germany broke off in April 1947. He was wrong, but his miscalculation was not unprecedented; nor was it the last time he misjudged the Americans.

From Détente to Cold War: April 1947 - December 1948

WHO DOUBTS THAT THE COLD WAR WAS ON IN EARNEST BY 1948—THE year of the Czechoslovak coup d'état and the Berlin Blockade—with the beginnings of NATO and war scares all around? But who realizes that it was also in 1948 that people who knew the Kremlin best, in both East and West, expected Stalin to broach a settlement with his capitalist enemies?

George Kennan—wartime Cassandra, postwar Paul Revere, founding father of containment—was one such expert. In February 1948, the State Department Policy Planning Staff, of which Kennan was chairman, prepared a "Review of Current Trends [in] U.S. Policy." The report called for bold action to resist the Soviet threat: "If the Russians knew that the establishment of a Communist government in Greece would mean the establishment of U.S. air bases in Libya and Crete, or that a Communist uprising in northern Italy would lead to renewed occupation by this country, . . . a restraining [Soviet] hand would certainly be placed on the Greek and Italian Communists." But Kennan also assumed that if the West would but hold firm, the Soviets would sue for peace.

> If . . . their situation outside the iron curtain does not improve—if ERP [European Recovery Program, that is, Marshall Plan] aid arrives in time and in a form to do some good, and if there is a general revival of confidence in western Europe, then a new situation will arise and the Russians will be prepared, for the first time since the surrender, to do business seriously with us about Germany and about Europe in general. . . .
>
> When that day comes, i.e., when the Russians will be prepared to talk realistically with us . . . what the Russians will want us to do will be to conclude with them a sphere-of-influence agreement similar to the one they concluded with the Germans in 1939.

Kennan was against such a pact. "It will be our job to explain to them that we cannot do this and why," he continued, and to persuade the Soviets: "(a) to reduce communist pressures . . . in Europe and the Middle East to a point where we can afford to withdraw all our armed forces from the continent and the Mediterranean; and (b) to acquiesce thereafter in a prolonged period of stability in Europe."

How to do it? Not, Kennan advised, by discussing things in the CFM or any other public forum unless such talks were preceded by "preparatory discussions of the most secret and delicate nature with Stalin." Who should conduct these discussions, which should aim to clear the ground for a later public agreement? The negotiator should be someone "prepared to observe the strictest silence about the whole proceeding," someone "thoroughly acquainted not only with the background of our policies but with Soviet philosophy and strategy and with the dialectics used by Soviet statesmen in such discussions," and someone "able to conduct conversations in the Russians' language," which was particularly important when dealing with Stalin.[1]

Kennan himself was just such a someone. Doubtless, he would have loved to parlay personally with Stalin. But lest one think Kennan's thinking wishfully unique, consider the views of some of Stalin's East European victims who had no such reason to vouch for his reasonableness. On May 21, the American minister in Hungary reported that "politically minded non-Communist Hungarians" expected the Kremlin to "seek a settlement." They assumed, and assumed the Soviets did too, that time was on the Western side. Growing Western strength plus a spreading awareness of Soviet weakness would undermine the Russian bargaining position. Before that happened, the Soviets would reduce their maximum aims in Western Europe in hope of retaining their East European empire. The Hungarians pictured the United States in the driver's seat; Washington, they thought, would "hold out for Hungary and Czechoslovakia" while acquiescing in Soviet dominance over the rest of East Europe.[2]

That *was* wishful thinking—even though the Hungarians, like Kennan, based their scenario on historical precedent, especially that of 1939. When circumstances required, and state interests dictated, Moscow had settled with sworn enemies: no matter that the Kremlin had cursed them the year, month, or even day before. No such deal had been struck in early 1947. But since then, the Marshall Plan and moves toward a Western alliance had supposedly provided new incentives for Soviet restraint. Unfortunately, however, the Nazi-Soviet Pact, or the

Brest-Litovsk Treaty for that matter, were not the only available prewar analogies. While Kennan was dreaming of a deal, others in Washington and Europe were imagining war. In their nightmare, Soviet totalitarianism was equated with the Nazi variety, and Stalin was cast in the role of a Hitler bent on armed aggression.

The American version of this image ripened quickly in late 1947 and 1948. As early as August 1947, Acting Secretary of State Robert Lovett privately described the world as "definitely split in two," thus anticipating by a month Andrei Zhdanov's famous "two camps" speech. Not only in the Soviet camp, but beyond the iron curtain as well, wrote John Foster Dulles to Dean Rusk in March 1948, Soviet tentacles were inescapable: "Today there is hardly anyone in Europe or Asia who does not feel that if he asserts himself in a manner displeasing to the Soviet Communist Party, he will be, or shortly may be, liquidated." President Truman drew the Nazi parallel in a March 17 speech in which he warned of Moscow's "clear design" to extend its sway to Western Europe. According to an interagency report, NSC 7, the "ultimate objective of Soviet-directed world communism is the domination of the world"; by March 1948, Stalin had already "come close to achieving what Hitler attempted in vain." Moscow was for the moment relying on "subversion" and other "legal and illegal political and economic methods, but might ultimately resort to war if necessary to gain its ends." When might war come? The American embassy in Moscow pictured Soviet armed forces as already "capable of taking continental Europe and key areas of Asia within a few months" and assumed that the decision whether or not to resort to military action was "under constant review." The most dangerous moment would be when Western military strength, though temporarily inferior, was likely to "increase in the future to Soviet disadvantage." This would be the situation "between one and two years from now." Then "immediate war" might be expected.[3]

"We are faced with exactly the same situation with which Britain and France were faced in 1938–39 with Hitler," Truman wrote to his daughter on March 3, 1948, in the aftermath of the February coup in Czechoslovakia and in the midst of Soviet pressure on Finland and Norway. "Things look black," he said. "A decision will have to be made. I am going to make it." Two days later, on March 5, General Clay cabled from Berlin. He had previously thought war was at least ten years away; now, a "subtle change" in Soviet attitude persuaded him that war could come with "dramatic suddenness." On March 16, the

CIA assured Truman that war was improbable only for the next sixty days; after that, all bets were off. The next day Truman went before a joint session of Congress to request universal military training and reestablishment of selective service.[4]

European leaders were, if anything, even more nervous. Italian Foreign Minister Count Sforza feared that "we are now in a stage of Russian expansion corresponding to Hitler's 1938 and 1939 inevitably follows." His French counterpart, Georges Bidault suggested to the American ambassador that Soviet thinking went as follows: "If we do not take over western Europe in the relatively near future, the Americans may wake up and then we shall be up against it. Of course, there is a little risk that the Americans may wake up sooner than we think and knock us out with some of their famous atomic bombs. However, we believe that the Americans are still 'des naïfs' and will wait too long." Bidault added, "I know that this may sound extravagant, but we are sitting here under the guns and your people are on the other side of the ocean."[5]

Other foreign leaders sounded the same note. Bevin warned Marshall on March 11: Unless the United Kingdom and United States move immediately toward "an Atlantic security system" in order to "inspire the Soviet Government with . . . respect for the West, . . . the alternative is to repeat our experience with Hitler and to witness helplessly the slow deterioration of our position, until we are forced in much less favorable circumstances to resort to war to defend our lives and liberty." Belgian Prime Minister Paul Henri Spaack at an April 5 Washington meeting looking toward an Atlantic alliance added that in contrast to the pre-1939 situation, the Soviets had no desire to fight in Europe. If they attacked any European country, it would only be to "open war against the United States." The shah of Iran as reported by the American ambassador on April 6: "He regards future with deep pessimism and evidently foresees a Russian invasion of Iran at a not very remote date."[6]

Even George Kennan nearly panicked. He followed European developments while on a mission to Asia. "I have always felt," Kennan cabled the secretary of state from Manila on March 15, "that the Russians neither wanted nor expected a military contest with U.S. and that no military complications were likely to occur in our relations with them unless: (a) their political fortunes were to advance too rapidly in Europe and they were to become dizzy with success; or (b) they were to become really alarmed for security of their power in eastern Europe and to take foolish and precipitate action to prevent its dissolution. Strangely enough, in their recent actions in Europe I think there is something of both these elements."[7]

Still a third view of the Soviet Union emerged in Washington later in 1948—that Moscow was neither disposed to settle nor poised to strike and that the Soviet threat was primarily political and could therefore be contained by other than military means. This view was associated with George Kennan but apparently shared by his chief, General Marshall. It was opposed, Kennan remembers, by the Pentagon and by "a vigorous right-wing faction which called for war with Russia—usually over China." Kennan had the impression in 1948 that "American opinion, . . . recovering from the pro-Soviet euphoria of the period around the end of war, had been restored to a relatively even keel," which was to say that "the moderate Marshall Plan approach—an approach aimed at *creating* strength in the West rather than *destroying* strength in Russia— seemed to have prevailed; and I, like others who went by the name of 'Russian experts,' felt that our view of the Russian problem—a view that accepted Russian-Communist attitudes and policies as a danger at the political level, but did not see either a likelihood or a necessity of war and did not regard the military plane as the one on which our response ought to be concentrated—seemed to have found general acceptance."[8]

Kennan's recollection is supported by the bureaucratic record. In November 1947, Marshall asked Kennan to prepare a brief overview of the world situation to present at a cabinet meeting. Kennan included such relatively optimistic judgments as: "The danger of war is vastly exaggerated in many quarters"; the political advance of Western European Communists "has been temporarily halted"; although the Soviets could be expected to "clamp down completely on Czechoslovakia," this would be "a purely defensive move"; it was "unlikely that approximately one hundred million Russians will succeed in holding down permanently, in addition to their own minorities, some ninety millions of Europeans with a higher cultural level and with long experience in resistance to foreign rule."[9]

This report of Kennan's, together with his February 1948 review of U.S. policy, were contradicted by the interagency assessment, NSC 7, which I have mentioned. Kennan and his State Department colleagues in turn challenged NSC 7, which Secretary of Defense Forrestal and the joint chiefs of staff proceeded to defend. Forrestal pushed for some "comprehensive statement" of the world situation and American grand strategy (which Kennan resisted on the grounds that the world situation was "extremely fluid" and, furthermore, was "not something which exists independently of our defense policy"); in August he got a State Department draft, which looks like a rabid Cold War piece but actually reflects Kennan's moderation. NSC 20/1 posited as American objectives a drastic reduction in the power and influence of Russia and a "basic change" in the theory and practice of Soviet international relations. It envisaged an eventual retraction of Soviet power from Eastern Europe and even possibly from the Baltic States. It counted on growing East-bloc strain of the sort revealed in the Soviet-Yugoslav dispute (which surfaced publicly in June 1948) and urged American efforts to "place the greatest possible strain on the structure of relationships by which Soviet domination of this area is maintained."[10]

NSC 20/1 was not exactly pro-Soviet. But the very fact that it envisioned a Russian retreat reflected its relatively relaxed conception of the long-term threat. NSC 20/2, a companion piece devoted to the military situation, was similarly reassuring. It listed elements militating for and against "the likelihood at this juncture of international, planned armed action which would involve this country" and came down heavily on the "against" side. None of this satisfied the armed services, who advocated increased American arms spending, along with an image of the Soviet threat that would justify the increase. But the military encountered opposition. In March, Secretary Marshall characterized a Pentagon judgment that Soviet armed forces vastly overmatched the West's as "at best nothing but guesses." In November, he responded to a Forrestal request with a prediction that 1949 would prove "neither better nor worse" than in 1948 and that "there were certain optimistic portents for the long-range future."[11]

These three views of the Soviet Union—ready to settle, poised to strike, or neither of the above—reflect the central questions of the period from mid-1947 to the end of 1948. Which image best fits reality? My answer is that the third comes closest. How did Stalin view American policies devised in the light of these images? Suspiciously, in part accurately, but with an important measure of unintended distortion. How did the resulting Russian policies influence American perceptions? They seemed to confirm the view of those who expected the worst from the Soviets.

The first thing to notice is that Stalin was in no hurry to jettison his version of détente even after the CFM broke off without reaching agreement in April 1947. The American embassy reported an upsurge in anti-Western propaganda including renewed warnings about "the intrigues of international reaction which is nurturing plans for a new war." But in mid-May a Soviet journal specifically designed for an international audience repeated the soothing line Stalin had taken in April with Stassen and Marshall. There was no need for excessive pessimism, declared *New Times*. "For the facts show that the Moscow conference performed work of no little value, bearing in mind the complexity and importance of the German problem. Unless one believes in miracles . . . agreed decisions on such a problem require time, patience, goodwill, and serious effort. The value of the Moscow conference is that the position of the powers on the disputed issues has become clarified. And this clears the way—given goodwill on both sides—for the necessary, if exacting, work of reconciling the different points of view and arriving at agreed decisions."[12]

Other signs of moderation were visible. Hungarian Prime Minister Nagy, whose April optimism we have encountered, was still hoping to avoid a Soviet clamp-down as late as May 13. By June 1, he was no longer prime minister, having been forced to resign and choose exile. But Czechoslovak non-Communists were not to meet a similar fate until early in 1948. French and Italian Communists were excluded from coalition governments in May and June, yet these parties hewed to moderation (with Togliatti even offering mild endorsement of the Marshall Plan) until Moscow ordered an about-face in September. That order, which came at the founding meeting of the Cominform, an organization devised by Moscow to keep a tight rein on its comrades and allies, led directly to a wave of strikes designed to cripple American aid to Western Europe. But even this was not the call for revolution that many in the West took it to be. Nor had Moscow totally given up on negotiations (although now more than ever it meant to use them for tactical purposes) in the way that Washington had.[13]

What prompted the Soviet shift in the fall of 1947? The failure of the West either to yield to Soviet blandishments or to confront Stalin with an offer he could not refuse, is part of the answer—so was the need to justify further postponement of the long-delayed socialist good life in the name of defense. But Stalin had been content to play out the string of détente even though the West was not biting; moreover, nothing happened on the domestic front in the summer of 1947 that would account for his sudden about-face. The remilitarization of the Soviet economy accelerated in 1948; hence, it was an effect rather than a cause of heightened East-West tension. The precipitating cause was, I believe, the Marshall Plan and the reaction to it in Eastern Europe. For this seemed to jeopardize not only Moscow's maximum postwar aims, but its minimum goals as well.

That the Soviets interpreted the Marshall Plan this way is ironic, for Marshall's intentions were primarily defensive. Marshall was exasperated with the German negotiations; he was determined to stop fiddling while Rome and other Western cities threatened to burn. Marshall's plan was not military, although NATO, the military counterpart to it, came rapidly in its wake. The American decision was to concentrate on building up Western Europe. True, Kennan and others hoped that the Soviets' East European empire would eventually unravel, and presumably the CIA later did its part to help that process along. But that effort was still to come in the summer of 1947, when Stalin reacted violently to the Marshall Plan.[14]

The policy planning staff urged that Marshall aid be offered in "such a form that the Russian satellite countries would either exclude themselves by their unwillingness to accept the proposed conditions or agree to abandon the exclusive [read "Soviet"] orientation of their economies." The Soviets feared the latter outcome. But the Americans preferred the former—out of concern that the Communists would somehow turn the program to their advantage or else cripple it either directly or by ensuring congressional rejection. The famous Harvard commencement address in which Marshall unveiled his plan warned that "any government which maneuvers to block the recovery of other countries cannot expect help from us" and that those who "seek to perpetuate human misery in order to profit therefrom . . . will encounter the opposition of the United States." But the secretary of state was not entirely disingenuous when he said, "Our policy is directed not against any country or doctrine but against hunger, poverty, desperation, and chaos."[15]

The procedure devised in Washington was for the United States to invite a joint European response to Marshall's offer, including a detailed statement of needs. Bidault and Bevin invited Molotov to meet with them in late June to discuss the American offer, though each hoped the Soviets would refuse to come, in which event they were prepared "to go ahead with full steam." The Soviet press greeted the whole project with intense suspicion. Initial reaction came in the main Ukrainian paper, which on June 11 detected "a new stage in Washington's campaign against forces of world democracy and progress." *Pravda*, itself, seconded the motion on June 16. Despite these attacks, however, Soviet diplomacy proceeded cautiously in June—enough to suggest that, until his East European clients started seeming too eager, the top man in the Kremlin thought he might turn even the Marshall Plan to his own benefit!

Molotov arrived in Paris on June 26 with a delegation one hundred strong, not all of whom could have been assigned, as Bevin suspected, to lobby against French participation in the European recovery effort. Molotov greeted Bidault with a cheery question: What had he and Bevin been doing behind his back? The next day Molotov made a proposal: The three of them should ask Washington (1) how much money the United States was prepared to put up; and (2) whether or not the United States Congress would vote such a credit. Molotov's probe (which his colleagues quickly rejected) was not necessarily designed to torpedo the project. (In any event, it marked an advance in Soviet understanding of Congress.) The Soviets still assumed that America needed capital outlets to avoid a depression and that Britain and France would be leery of American domination in the guise of benevolence. Could Moscow somehow get access to credits without unacceptable strings attached? If not, could the British and French be induced to set so many conditions of their own that they would reveal Washington's intention to dominate? On June 28 Molotov dropped his two questions of the day before and proposed instead that each European country decide on its own needs, all of which would be pooled to establish the amount the United States should provide. Bevin and Bidault opposed this, too. But although Molotov stuck to his guns he struck the French as "unusually mild" and wishing "at all cost" to avoid a break. In Bidault's view, Molotov was very "uncertain"; the Soviet diplomat clearly did not wish the talks to succeed, but on the other hand, Bidault told the Americans Molotov's hungry satellites were "smacking their lips in expectation of getting some of your money." Molotov was "obviously embarrassed."[16]

The talks broke down on July 3. But even after that, the lip-smacking continued. On June 18, the Polish ambassador in Washington had expressed his government's "great interest" in Marshall's speech; he did not think *Pravda*'s June 16 article (which he said all East Europe was studying) excluded the possibility of Soviet cooperation. As late as July 7, the Polish foreign minister was "certain" his government would work with the British and French to prepare a joint request for American aid. On July 4, Czechoslovak Foreign Minister Jan Masarysk accepted a similar Anglo-French invitation. But on July 8, he and other Czech leaders were informed in Moscow that, to put it mildly, Stalin did not agree. According to Communist chief Klement Gottwald's report to the Czech government, a copy of which found its way to the American embassy, Stalin said he was "surprised" at Prague's decision to attend the Paris meeting since the "real aim" of the Marshall Plan was to "create a western bloc and isolate the Soviet Union." Either the Americans would welsh on their promises, or their loans would "not be without decisive limitations on the economic and political independence of the recipients." Therefore, Gottwald continued, "the Soviet Union would regard our participation as a break in the front of the Slav States and as an act specifically aimed against the USSR."[17]

That was enough—more than enough—for the Czechs. They immediately sent their regrets to Paris. So did the Poles. Ambassador Smith in Moscow described the Czech refusal as "nothing less than a declaration of war by the Soviet Union," a metaphor to which his embassy resorted with dismaying frequency in those years. But the Soviet words and actions that followed during the summer and especially in the fall of 1947 were, indeed, unnerving: there was further tightening at home, plus a propaganda barrage climaxing in a diatribe equating Truman with Hitler; there was the establishment of the Cominform in September; and there was West European Communist militance (including a wave of violent strikes) as ordered by the Soviets at the Cominform meeting—this after taunting the West European comrades for their previous, Soviet-inspired restraint.[18]

All this contributed, even before the March 1948 war scare, to an American sense of crisis. The Moscow embassy predictably called the Cominform Declaration "a declaration of political and economic war against U.S. and everything U.S. stands for in world affairs." President Truman told a group of congressmen in late September that Western Europe hung in the balance: either the United States pumped in interim aid (pending congressional passage of the Marshall Plan) or "the governments of France and Italy will fall, Austria, too, and for all practical purposes Europe will be Communist. The Marshall Plan goes out the window, and it's a question of how long we could stand up in such a situation. This is serious. I can't overemphasize how serious."[19]

Even discounting for hyperbole intended to inspire congressional action, the president's words depict a Soviet Union on the offensive. Yet, in retrospect, Daniel Yergin thinks the Soviets saw the Marshall Plan as a "declaration of war by the United States for the control of Europe" and feared it would "disrupt their sphere in Eastern Europe," and Adam Ulam agrees. What were the Soviets really up to? Their own words (in the Cominform Declaration, in Zhdanov's and Malenkov's speeches at the Cominform founding in Poland, and in Molotov's Anniversary of the Revolution address) provide important clues. These pronouncements were meant to indict the enemy and rouse the faithful. But the speeches were consistent with such private statements as are available and with Soviet actions as well.[20]

The Cominform Declaration proclaimed a new and dangerous phase in international relations. During the war the allied states had formed one camp, even though the Soviet Union had aimed at a peaceful and democratic Europe, while the United States and Britain sought "to rid themselves of competitors on the world market and establish their dominant position." After the war, "two diametrically opposed political lines took shape." Now "two camps were formed—the imperialist and anti-democratic having as its basic aim the establishment of world domination of American imperialism and the smashing of democracy, and the anti-imperialist and democratic camp having as its basic aim the undermining of imperialism, the consolidation of democracy and the eradication of the remnants of fascism."

According to the Declaration, American imperialism was on the offensive in accordance with a "general plan" for "global expansion." That plan called for "simultaneous action along all lines," Zhdanov explained. On the strategic and military fronts, the Americans were spending vastly more on arms than before the war, stockpiling atomic bombs and developing bacteriological weapons, and building air and naval bases around the world. On the economic front, a search for new markets for American goods and capital was underway, while Washington used so-called "assistance" to other countries to extort economic concessions and to subjugate them politically. In the ideological struggle, the American "plan is to deceive public opinion by slanderously accusing the Soviet Union and the new democracies of aggressive intentions." The Western warmongers "fully realize," said Zhdanov, "that long ideological preparation is necessary before they can get their soldiers to fight the Soviet Union."

The Truman Doctrine and the Marshall Plan were allegedly parts of this grand design; both, said Zhdanov, had Eastern Europe as a prime target. The Truman Doctrine, with its "support of the reactionary regimes in Greece and Turkey as bastions . . . against the new democracies in the Balkans," was so crude and obvious as to evoke "dismay even among circles of American capitalists that are accustomed to anything." Hence the insidious Marshall Plan "which is a more care-fully veiled attempt to carry through the same expansionist policy. . . . Whereas the Truman plan was to terrorize and intimidate these coun-tries, the 'Marshall Plan' was designed to test their economic staunch-ness, to lure them into a trap and then shackle them in the fetters of dollar 'assistance.' " The ultimate target would be the USSR itself. According to a report by Maurice Thorez (of which the American embassy got wind), Moscow feared the United States would expand its influence in Europe to the point where it would have achieved "a dan-gerous jump-off place for attacking Soviet Russia."[21]

If American power was on the march, the Soviets depicted them-selves on the defensive. The Communists' task, according to the Com-inform Declaration, was to "close ranks . . . to frustrate the plan of imperialist aggression." Communist parties must not "let themselves be intimidated and blackmailed." The "principal danger for the working class today lies in underestimating their own strength and overestimat-ing the strength of the imperialist camp." According to Thorez's account, West European comrades were to discard the tactics of "legal-ity" as "hopelessly inadequate to cope with the new situation resulting from the Marshall Plan." As for the USSR itself, Malenkov told the Cominform meeting that it "calmly and confidently rebuffs all attempts at blackmail and keeps a watchful eye on all suspicious maneuvers of its erstwhile allies belonging to the imperialist camp, in order not to allow itself to be tricked." As described by Molotov in November, Mos-cow was practicing its own version of containment: it was seeking, both in and outside Europe, to "erect an impregnable barrier to imperial-ism . . . and to its policy of new aggression." Eventually, "if the anti-imperialist and democratic camp unites its forces and avails itself of all opportunities, it will compel the imperialists to be more sensible and restrained."

So far, so bleak. Yet the same speeches reveal a keen Soviet aware-ness of compensating advantages and opportunities. The very "imperi-alist offensive" reflected Western weakness. The declaration described "a situation marked by further aggravation of the general crisis of capi-talism . . . and the strengthening of the forces of Socialism and democ-racy." Malenkov explained that whereas Socialism and democracy had gained as a result of the war, capitalism had suffered the defeat of Ger-many and Japan, and the crippling of Great Britain and France. It was precisely these setbacks that prompted the United States to bid for "world supremacy." But Washington faced important obstacles stemming from capitalist contradictions. The "prospect of the restoration of German imperialism," said Zhdanov, "cannot be very alluring either to Britain or to France." American capitalists "trust neither the British Laborites nor the French Socialists, whom . . . they regard as 'semi-Communists,' insufficiently worthy of confidence." By the same token, "the appetites of American imperialists cannot but cause serious uneasiness in Britain and France." Even without the Soviet Union, Zhdanov continued, the Europeans themselves, "if they display will and determination . . . can foil this plan of enslavement"—especially since "America herself is threatened with an economic crisis," a crisis that accounted for "Marshall's official generosity" and could be aggravated if Europe would but reject his plan. For "if the European countries do not receive American credits, their demand for American goods will diminish, and this will tend to accelerate and intensify the approaching economic crisis in the United States. Accordingly, if the European countries display the necessary stamina . . . America may find herself compelled to beat a retreat."

Another countervailing consideration was military and psychological. The Americans would try atomic intimidation. But nuclear blackmail, like any other kind, was in the eye of the beholder, and anti-imperialist beholders need not be afraid. "The war danger hullabaloo . . . is intended to frighten the nervous and unstable elements. . . ." "Having no faith in their own internal forces," said Molotov, the Americans "put their faith in the secret of the atomic bomb, although this secret has long since ceased to be a secret." War itself was not likely since would-be Western cannon fodder would not fight. True, ideological indoctrination was underway, and "when practically every newspaper and broadcasting station is in the hands of a handful of aggressive capitalists and their hired servants, it is difficult for the people to get to know the truth." But that only emphasized the necessity for the Soviets and their allies to unmask American designs and to undermine both the false image of a Soviet threat and the empty threat of a nuclear war.

The categories of offensive and defensive blend and blur as one contemplates U.S.–Soviet relations in 1947–1948. Who was which? That depends on who answers the question and on whether one consults intention or consequence. The Americans felt embattled. The Soviets did, too. The Russians exaggerated American aggressiveness as the result of reading into American motivation the possible East European consequences of the Marshall Plan. But the Western instability Stalin fomented for defensive purposes was indistinguishable from the disruption Moscow might have fostered if it had high hopes for immediate revolution. Yergin contends Stalin "recognized that a major communist military or political assault in Western Europe would have generated an all-too-strong and unpredictable reaction in the United States." But a political assault *was* made in late 1947 and early 1948. This is not to say that Stalin wanted Western Communist parties to take power. Western turmoil sufficient to foil American designs while leaving Communist options open was good enough—but it was also enough to help explain how the Americans could become so alarmed.[22]

Stalin did not intentionally precipitate the Cold War, but he was not without resources for conducting it. Among his resources were the tactics that one associates with a time of tension and conflict: ominous warnings, political and military pressure, rigid diplomacy. But another Stalinist technique was none other than the tactical use, in a new strategic setting, of the devices of détente itself.

The Council of Foreign Ministers session in the fall of 1947 was a fitting anticlimax to abortive negotiations on Germany. Bevin's on-the-eve pronouncements about "the critical nature" of the meeting and the dangers of failure were made, a British official admitted, "to reassure the public." In fact, neither the British nor the Americans wanted an agreement; they merely went through the motions. "If we can treat the Soviet charges with the humor they deserve," Bevin said, "we can promote peace." He half hoped that if the West stood firm, Molotov might yield as he had in New York in December 1946. In the meantime, Bevin favored the "method of short answers—no comment on nonsense," while arranging things so that the break, when it did come, could be blamed on Moscow. As for Molotov, he played the same game, although at times he sounded conciliatory, as if testing to see if there was any give in Western positions. On December 15, 1947, Bidault suggested the council adjourn rather than further aggravate relations. Molotov had no objection. Bevin and Marshall hoped for a better atmosphere next time. The council disbanded without setting a date for its next session.[23]

Soviet diplomacy was cold and forbidding in the winter of 1947–1948. When Ambassador Smith met with Vyshinsky on January 7 to discuss Soviet customs procedures affecting the American embassy, the Russian was "completely intransigent." "For the first time during our many conversations," Smith cabled Washington, "[he] departed from the usual attitude of personal friendliness regardless of official subject, and showed irritability and antagonism. It is quite obvious that he had received instructions to make no concessions whatever."[24]

Moscow put pressure on Finland in early 1948. Finland had been part of the tsarist empire, had fought alongside the Nazis, and was a potentially hostile Soviet neighbor in a strategic location. Yet, perhaps because the Finns had dared to fight the Russians in 1939, and fought well, Helsinki had been spared the postwar fate of other Russian neighbors. But that seemed about to change in February 1948. Just when the Czech non-Communists were going under, the Finns got word from Stalin himself that Moscow desired a pact of friendship and military alliance along the lines of its treaties with Rumania and Hungary. And Stalin's message was accompanied by other promptings—warnings from the Soviet ambassador, threats from lower-level Soviet diplomats, demands that the Finnish president visit Moscow. The Finns, with Communists in the government, feared a Czech-style coup. London's ambassador in Helsinki saw no alternative but to make the best deal possible with the Soviets. Ambassador Smith in Moscow read the situation this way: "Only if and when [the Russians] and the countries they threaten realize that we mean business and are willing and prepared to back up our policies politically, economically, and if necessary, militarily, is there any real chance that the present Soviet policy of truculent, aggressive expansionism may be modified."[25]

More familiar trouble spots like Greece, Turkey, and Iran appeared to fit the same pattern. About the time Stalin was secretly expressing his dismay about the Greek uprising to the Yugoslavs, an equally secret American report (NSC 5) depicted "a forceful energetic effort to overthrow the present Greek Government and to achieve complete and dictatorial control over Greece." Loy Henderson, director of the State Department Office of Near Eastern Affairs, feared the Balkan Communists would "go so far before realizing the extent of our determination" that they would be unable to "draw back and there [would] be the beginnings of a new World War." Later during the summer, when the Soviets quietly proposed talks with Athens with an eye to "settling outstanding differences," the Americans feared a trick, just as they did when Moscow shifted from brow-beating to sweet-talking Turkey in September 1948. In a series of not-so-diplomatic exchanges, Moscow accused the shah's government of making Iran into an American military base for use against the USSR. The shah expected an imminent Soviet invasion—or said he did, the better to lobby for the sort of American arms aid that Greece and Turkey were getting under the Truman Doctrine. The shah told an American diplomat that dictatorial regimes, whether Nazi or Communist, had to win wars in order to continue in power. Diplomat John Jernegan rejected the Nazi-Soviet parallel, saying that whereas Nazi Germany "had always to move forward to maintain their own prestige," Moscow was not looking for a fight, especially at a time of domestic Soviet weakness and growing Western strength. His Majesty was interested in this analysis but not convinced.[26]

Those, like Kennan, who were convinced, drew hope from the Soviet-Yugoslav rift. Tito had been more Stalinist than Stalin—which was one reason why the latter had turned against him. Kennan concluded: "A new factor of fundamental and profound significance has been introduced into the world communist movement by the demonstration that the Kremlin can be successfully defied by one of its own minions. By this act the aura of mystical omnipotence and infallibility which has surrounded the Kremlin has been broken. The possibility of defection from Moscow which has heretofore been unthinkable for foreign communist leaders, will from now on be present in one form or another in the mind of every one of them."[27]

But other American officials were skeptical. It seemed to Foy Kohler (then chargé and later to be ambassador in Moscow) that "in the event of hostilities, Tito's Yugoslavia would seek to outdo all satellites in her participation in the Communist cause." Kohler reported the Moscow embassy's conclusion that "on balance we do not believe Tito's defection has as seriously reduced Kremlin's willingness to engage world hostilities as is generally believed." This despite Tito's own prediction to an American visitor that "there would not be war since Russians would not start one."[28]

This last conclusion of Tito's found support in the Soviets' own campaign against him. Moscow charged Belgrade with failing to realize that "after such a hard war the USSR could not enter another." That was why, despite Yugoslav lobbying in 1946, the Soviets had refused, as they put it, "to start a war with the Anglo-Americans over Trieste." But control without war was another and more attractive matter. Recalling (and exaggerating) Red Army help in Tito's seizure of power, the Soviet lamented that "unfortunately, the Soviet army did not and could not render such assistance to the French and Italian CP's." That the Soviets wanted not war but expanded power and influence without war is a proposition defended in this book. So is another that also finds supporting evidence in the recriminations between Moscow and Belgrade: namely, that Stalin had a gift for turning allies (whether Yugo-slavs or Americans) into enemies. Stalin insisted, the Yugoslavs charged, on crediting "inaccurate and slanderous" information pro-vided by those with a personal or political axe to grind. Projecting his own cynicism onto Yugoslav leaders, Stalin assumed they did not believe their own charges. "We doubt," said a CPSU letter to the Yugoslav Communists, "whether Comrades Tito and Kardelj them-selves believe the truth of [their own] version even though they seize on it as if it were true." Moscow treated Yugoslav restraint as weakness and reacted to it with scorn. When the Yugoslavs, like the Americans before them, forbore to answer an accusation, the Soviets took that as an admission of guilt. When Tito, like Roosevelt, attributed tensions to some vast misunderstanding, Stalin became even more suspicious.[29]

By June 1948, when the Soviets blockaded Berlin, American sus-picions almost matched Stalin's. President Truman recalls his reaction to the blockade: "The Russians were obviously determined to force us out of Berlin. They had suffered setbacks recently. . . . Their strongest satellite, Yugoslavia, had suddenly developed a taste for independent action, and the European Recovery Program was beginning to succeed. The blockade of Berlin was international Communism's counterattack. The Kremlin had chosen perhaps the most sensitive objective in Europe. . . . If we wished to remain there, we would have to make a show of strength. But there was always the risk that the Russian reaction might lead to war."[30]

Wrong again! The blockade was not designed to force the United States out of Berlin—although if the West wanted to leave, the Russians would certainly not stop them. It was primarily intended to reopen high-level negotiations on the future of Germany.[31] Those negotia-tions, in turn, were not meant to produce a settlement—unless, unex-pectedly, the West chose to settle on Soviet terms. The Soviet hope, rather, was to deflect progress toward a separate West German state. Blockading Berlin was an odd way to tempt the West. But Moscow had reason to think it might work; for even in 1948, Western governments still seemed susceptible to détentelike blandishments.

The German progress Moscow wanted to deflect was proceeding on several fronts in the spring of 1948. Meeting in London, the three Western powers were hatching plans for a West German state. They were also preparing a currency reform for the three Western zones, a change that would signal the end of four-power control over Germany even before creation of a West German government. The Brussels Pact, a "Treaty of Economic, Social and Cultural Collaboration and Collective Self-Defense" among Britain, France, and the Benelux countries was signed on March 17, 1948. The next logical step would be a North Atlantic alliance.

The Soviet response to all this was to blow hot and cold. After the CFM adjourned in December 1947, Moscow made some conciliatory gestures. But soon, new Soviet protests poured forth, climaxing in the Warsaw Declaration by Soviet and East European foreign ministers on June 24, 1948. Soviet representatives on the Allied Control Council for Germany and the Allied Kommendatura in Berlin were "comparatively friendly" during the early part of January 1948, Robert Murphy reported. "Agreement could be reached without too much difficulty on matters of second-rate importance." But by March, Russian delegates were seizing on any Western statement "no matter how simple, how friendly or how innocent, to launch violent propaganda attacks." And a month later the Soviets had given up even the pretense of "listening to or discussing points raised by their colleagues, but have rather come with prepared statements and rigidly fixed lines of argument from which they do not deviate." Things reached a new low in May: "Almost complete disintegration quadripartite government in Berlin pointed up yesterday as Allied Commandants wallowed for more than 15 hours in disagreement, abuse, charges, and counter-charges."[32]

The American response to Soviet tactics was stern on the surface but softer underneath. Soviet protests were rejected. Accusations produced counter-allegations. The Moscow embassy peppered its cables with reminders that the State Department did not need—namely, that the Soviets could not be trusted. And yet, despite all the tension, or perhaps just because of it, the American urge persisted to talk to the Russians, to try to reach at least a minimal meeting of the minds in order to prevent a slide into war. The Americans thought they were under no illusions; they took care, when approaching the Russians, to foster none on the Soviet side. But they were, and they did.

The specific event that prompted a fresh American approach to Moscow was the defeat of the Communist party in the Italian elections of March 1948. The trouble with this Western triumph, according to an "eyes-only" State Department telegram to Ambassador Smith, was that it confronted the Soviets with a dangerous choice—either to acquiesce in their failure to dominate Western Europe (which in due course might erode Soviet hegemony in the East) or to recoup by some dramatic action. If the Kremlin chose the latter course, and if it underestimated American resolve, the result might be war. Hence the need, as Washington saw it, to convince Stalin not only "that any further encroachment by the Soviet Union, by countries under its control, or by Communist Parties dominated by it, beyond the present limits of Communist power, would be regarded by this country as an act of aggression"; but also "that it is definitely not true that this Government is aiming in any way, shape or form at an imperialistic expansion of its own power or at the preparation of military aggression against the Soviet Union or any country in Eastern Europe or elsewhere."

The State Department's second point was yet another sign of the nervousness evoked by Stalin's "warmonger" charges. But the department proposed to conceal its anxiety from the Soviets by making clear that its two points were "merely a statement of U.S. position and policy and in no sense an indirect bid for agreement or even negotiation at this time." Department strategists were prepared for any eventuality. Stalin might seize upon the American approach "to offer some sort of division of the world into spheres of influence." That, said the Acting Secretary of State Robert Lovett, would be "unthinkable even to contemplate."[33]

The department invited Ambassador Smith's reaction to its plan. He, it turned out, had been about to recommend a similar approach. With the department and the ambassador "on board," why bother about the allies? Without informing the British or French, Smith met with Molotov at 2:30 P.M. (unlike his boss, Molotov transacted business in the daylight) on May 4, 1948. Smith thought he struck just the right note of calm, cool confidence. But to Molotov, Smith apparently came across as both anxious and insincere.

Smith began by recalling his 1946 warning to Stalin about alienating American public opinion. That was precisely what the Soviets had done, he continued, and now they faced the consequences. As for the Marshall Plan, it was "obviously only a measure of American assistance for reconstruction on a cooperative basis without menace or threat to anyone." Obviously to Smith, but not to Molotov. Smith was at a loss to understand Soviet charges of warmongering: "Whether, or in what degree, the members of the Soviet Government themselves believe this distorted version my government has no means of estimating." So, when Molotov repeated the charge, Smith made the same point even more urgently: "I had only to say that our entire history was refutation of any suspicion of a policy which involves aggressive war." "The United States has no hostile or aggressive designs whatever with respect to the Soviet Union. Assertions to the contrary are falsehoods which can only result from complete misunderstanding or malicious motives. United States policies . . . cannot possibly affect adversely the interests of a Soviet Union which seeks to live at peace with its neighbors." Fine words, but imagine how they struck the Soviets: Did Smith want the Kremlin to certify American innocence? Didn't Western propaganda intentionally exaggerate the so-called Soviet threat? Why were the Americans so distressed, if distressed they really were, when the Soviets replied in kind?

Ambassador Smith wished "to make plain" that American foreign policy had the overwhelming support of the American people; it would be a grave error for "others" to expect up-coming elections (in November 1948) to change that. An equally serious error would be to suppose an economic crisis would force a radical change in American policy. "It is to be hoped," the ambassador said, "that no one will be so foolish as to forfeit the chances of . . . world stability for the sake of an economic prognostication which has been proven wrong time and time again"—sensible words, designed to undermine false Soviet hopes. But the Soviets mocked those words in public. How confident could the Americans be, asked the Moscow journal, *Bolshevik*, "if they found it necessary to give assurances that their policy would not alter in connection with forthcoming elections and the possible economic crisis"? Once again the Soviets were projecting a Kremlin rule of thumb (or rather, rule of bluff) onto the Americans—that the surest sign someone is nervous is if he denies it.

The last thing Smith said to Molotov was the most reasonable of all. "We still do not despair by any means of a turn of events which will permit us to find the road to a decent and reasonable relationship between our two countries, with a fundamental relaxation of those tensions which today exercise so unhappy an influence on international society everywhere. As far as the United States is concerned, the door is always wide open for full discussion and the composing of our differences." Molotov apparently read this as a plea for negotiations that the Soviets could enter into when and if it suited them. He replied that the Soviet government would "pay the closest attention to the statement of the United States' position," that it reciprocated the wish of the U.S. to "alleviate the present situation," and that he considered there were "not a few possibilities of enabling the U.S. to go along this path toward improved relations."[34]

The moment was not yet ripe for "enabling the U.S." Instead, the Kremlin published the Smith-Molotov exchange without American permission. The American embassy analysis of this Soviet move was probably on target: Moscow was trying to spotlight Western anxiety, to sow inter-imperialist dissension, to encourage former Vice-President Henry Wallace and his supporters in America, and to allay fears of war in the USSR and Eastern Europe. And the ploy worked; at least, the British protested Washington's unilateral approach. Soon afterward, the Soviets followed up with a gambit made possible by Wallace's "Open Letter to Stalin," published in the *New York Times* on May 12. Wallace proposed a peace program partly overlapping the Soviets' own. *Izvestia* greeted the Wallace initiative as a new and "joyous fact"; Stalin, replying in an open letter of his own, called Wallace's a "very important document." Wallace's formulations needed "a certain improvement," Stalin explained, but nonetheless they could provide a "fruitful basis . . . for the development of international cooperation," for "coexistence," and for the "peaceful resolution of differences between the USSR and the USA." This resolution was "not only possible, but absolutely necessary in the interests of world peace."[35]

Apparently Stalin overestimated Wallace's third-party candidacy for the presidency in 1948, which is not surprising since many Americans did likewise until Wallace's resounding defeat in November. Not only Wallace, however, but Harry Truman himself occasionally evoked memories of Franklin Roosevelt. On June 11, 1948, in Eugene, Oregon, Truman reportedly said, "I like Old Joe. He's a decent fellow but he's a prisoner of the politburo." Then, in October, there was Chief Justice Fred Vinson's astonishing 'non-mission' to Moscow. Concern about East-West tension combined with electoral calculation to recommend to Truman a dramatic presidential initiative. He secretly summoned Vinson and proposed that the chief justice go to Moscow "for an informal exchange of views and impressions with Stalin." Truman explained that "the Russians simply did not understand—or *would* not—our peaceful intentions. . . ." He hoped that "Vinson's mission . . . might expose the Russian dictator to a better understanding of . . . our nation's peaceful aspirations for the whole world." Truman had "the feeling that Stalin might get over some of his inhibitions if he were to talk with our own Chief Justice." Truman adds in his *Memoirs*, "If we could only get Stalin to unburden himself to someone on our side he felt he could trust fully, I thought that perhaps we could get somewhere. But of course, if the Russians were hell-bent for communizing and dominating the world on a rule-or-ruin basis there was little we could do by the negotiation route. Even then we had . . . to keep trying. That was why I wanted him to go to Moscow and to see if he could not get Stalin to open up."[36]

Only in America, perhaps, could a national leader credit in one breath two such opposite, and equally erroneous, images—Stalin pouring his heart out to Fred Vinson, and Stalin hell-bent on world conquest. The Vinson mission was canceled when a leak to an "unfriendly newspaper" resulted in public cries of appeasement, and a private protest by Secretary of State Marshall. But long before that, the Soviets must have sensed an American desire somehow, someway, somewhere to patch up the quarrel and resume more peaceful relations. If only Moscow could tap that feeling and channel it into German negotiations. The need to do so became urgent in early June 1948 when the London Conference agreed on procedures for setting up the West German state, including the convening of a German assembly by September 1.

On June 18, the Western powers announced that currency reforms in Western Germany (but not West Berlin) were imminent. The Russians countered by declaring all of Berlin would come under currency regulations planned for their zone. On June 23, the West extended its currency to West Berlin. The next day the Soviets severed the overland arteries between Berlin and West Germany and cut off electricity to the city.

The fat was in the fire. Lucius Clay, American military governor for Germany, recommended "a determined movement of convoys with troop protection" even though he realized "the inherent dangers in this proposal since once committed we could not withdraw." Robert Murphy warned against a "Munich of 1948," saying "our retreat from Berlin would be tantamount to an acknowledgement of lack of courage to resist Soviet pressure short of war. . . ." British Foreign Secretary Bevin now realized "what agony Neville Chamberlain must have endured in September 1938."[37]

Were the Soviets enduring any similar agony? Or, having gauged the likely Western response, and knowing that they could retreat if necessary, were the Russians the cool masters of the situation? Stalin may have had a moment of panic; either that, or Marshal Sokolovsky, the local Soviet commander, did. On June 23, with all in an uproar, Sokolovsky's chief of liaison and protocol had a strange conversation with an American official. Colonel Vyrianov, who was usually stiffly formal on such occasions, treated his American guest to champagne and informal conversation. He spoke of "the danger of war" and offered it as his "strictly personal observation" that "possibly an adjustment of present zonal lines in Germany should be made with a view of eliminating the friction over Berlin." Although the Soviet officer did not elaborate, Murphy took the comment to indicate a "desire to bargain and a disinclination to force the issue." Murphy had a similar reaction to a letter Sokolovsky sent shortly before the Western powers announced their response to the blockade.[38]

If the Soviets were anxious, the Western announcement put their minds at rest. There would be no armed convoy. Instead, Truman announced an airlift of supplies to Berlin, the transfer of American bombers to bases in Britain, and America's determination not to be forced out of Berlin—which was not the main Soviet objective in the first place. The Western powers followed on July 6 with a note insisting on their rights in Berlin, but also proposing talks. That put the Soviets in the driver's seat. The Soviet government, "while not objecting to negotiations" (how nice of them not to oppose their own heart's desire), considered it necessary to state that it could not link the inauguration of these negotiations with "the fulfilling of any preliminary conditions whatsoever" (in other words, the West would have to talk under the gun of the blockade) and that "in the second place, four-power conversations could be effective only in the event that they were not limited to the question of Berlin, since that question [could] not be severed from the general question of the four-power control in regard to Germany" (meaning that the agenda for negotiations would revert, if the Soviets could manage it, to 1947).[39]

The Western powers rightly took this as the first, not the last, Soviet word on the subject and proceeded to prepare their own agenda. But the omens were not favorable. The three-way Western talks brought out serious tactical disagreements; at one point the State Department secretly characterized a British draft as "redolent of appeasement." Meanwhile, Bevin delivered himself of two off-the-wall judgments: He hesitated to approach Stalin directly for fear of "aggravating prejudices in the Soviet Foreign Office" and he thought the Soviets so troubled that they might agree to "retire to the Oder." On July 30, the three Western ambassadors, having been informed that Molotov had chosen the height of the crisis to go on vacation, met separately with Deputy Minister Valerian Zorin. They sought a meeting with Stalin, but Zorin said he saw no sign of the sort of positive Western attitude that would merit a discussion with the generalissimo, or even with Mr. Molotov.

However, he graciously agreed to transmit the request to his government for their consideration.[40]

Surprise! Stalin, whose purpose all along had been to prompt talks, agreed to meet the Western spokesmen on August 2. He began with a typically direct question: Were they authorized to negotiate? Assuming Berlin issues could be settled, were they prepared to discuss Germany as a whole? Stalin proposed that in return for Moscow's lifting the blockade, the West accept Soviet-zone currency in Berlin and delay implementation of the London decisions until the four powers met and tried to resolve "fundamental questions affecting Germany." The generalissimo explained that "the only real issue" he had in mind was the formation of a German government in the Western zones. He said he did not mind the unification of the three Western zones, and even considered it "progress." (One would never have guessed from Soviet pronouncements on the subject!) But unless they began talking by September 1, Stalin added, there would be nothing to talk about. If the talks failed, so be it. The Soviet government would, however, be "embarrassed" if a German government were set up now in the Western zones. If the United States wanted to negotiate, it would have to postpone this.

Stalin admitted that the strictly Berlin issues were "insignificant conflicts." After disposing of them, a CFM meeting or its equivalent should take up reparations, demilitarization of Germany, the formation of a German government, a Germany peace treaty. This *was* the 1947 agenda. Stalin even harked back to what he told Secretary Marshall in April 1947: "He had always been confident that after much skirmishing they could return in the end to a basis for agreement." But it was 1948, and Ambassador Smith said the United States would not negotiate under duress. Stalin wanted to know, referring to the looming London program, who was pressuring whom. But he was prepared to be reasonable. The London problem "could be handled confidentially by an oral statement which need not be published. . . . He did not want anyone to be placed in an embarrassing position. There would have been no restrictions if it were not for the London decisions. The Soviet Government was not seeking conflicts but trying to find a solution."

This did not satisfy Stalin's guests, and neither did his suggestion that they adjourn and meet again the next day; whereupon, Stalin suddenly asked if they wanted to settle the matter that very night. If so, he had another proposal: He would no longer insist on suspending the London program but would simply ask that this be recorded as "the insistent wish" of the Soviet government. The Western representatives agreed to recommend to their governments that this proposal be accepted. The meeting broke up in what Smith called "a very friendly atmosphere."[41]

Even Smith, no Pollyanna he, thought Stalin was "undoubtedly anxious to settle." Molotov had never been so cordial, and Stalin invited Smith in for "a couple of drinks" before his scheduled departure from Moscow. The Soviet attitude had been "literally dripping with sweet reasonableness and desire not to embarrass." Smith cabled home that he was almost certain that the Western powers could have obtained their original formula, that is, lifting the blockade in return for the promise of negotiations, without any concessions on currency. Instead, because the British wanted to "keep us on the soft side as far as possible," the Westerners had agreed to accept Soviet-zone currency throughout Berlin.[42]

Was Stalin ready to lift the blockade right then and there? If so, the Americans might have balked anyway for fear that the prospect of new negotiations would unravel painfully achieved Western unity on Germany. But the test never came. Instead, complications cropped up, which provoked a new round of disagreements, which propelled Stalin toward the conclusion that the Americans had reached in 1947—that there was no longer much point to high-level East-West negotiations.

Ambassador Smith and his Western colleagues had muffed a key issue on August 2. If Soviet-zone currency were to be used throughout Berlin then its issuance must be subject to quadripartite controls. The Western draft agreement presented to Molotov on August 6 added that insistence and, to make matters worse, failed to record the Soviet government's "insistent wish" to suspend the London decisions. This amounted, complained Molotov, to an alteration in "the agreed decision" of August 2. Not so, since the Western negotiators had agreed only to *recommend* acceptance to their governments. But the Soviets may have been genuinely perplexed on that point. (Asked by Stalin on August 2 whether they were authorized to negotiate, Smith had answered: Not "to negotiate but to attempt to work out a formula which might lead to negotiations.") "Tell me," demanded Molotov on August 6, "Do you or do you not intend to postpone the convocation of the [West German] Parliamentary Council on September first?" The ambassadors answered that September 1 would mark only the beginning of a process that could be reversed when and if four-power talks succeeded. But Molotov reverted again and again to the date's pivotal importance. The foreign minister gave the impression he was more willing than Stalin to settle for a two-Germanies solution. And perhaps he was. He knew Stalin had told Djilas in February that "The West will make Western Germany their own, and we shall turn Eastern Germany into our own state." Stalin could always abandon his new negotiating game if it did not pan out, but in the meantime Molotov had to play it.[43]

If Molotov's secret desire was to be spared this game, his wish seemed granted when Western representatives came calling on August 9. With the West hewing to its London timetable, the Soviets resurrected Berlin issues that Stalin had dismissed as unimportant on August 2. Since quadripartite control over Germany had lapsed as the result of Western actions, claimed Molotov, the Western powers had no juridical rights in Berlin. The foreign minister was as tough as he had been cordial on August 2. But the clouds lifted on August 12; once again Molotov was mellow, reasonable, and anxious to explore areas of possible agreement. On August 17, the Soviets agreed to let the military governors in Berlin resolve some relatively minor disagreements. On August 24, Stalin himself accepted quadripartite control over Soviet-zone currency with details to be worked out later. But on August 27, the Soviets tried to sneak language postponing the London program into an almost-agreed-upon communiqué. And at the last minute, Western negotiators sought to alter an agreed-upon directive to the military governors in order to strengthen controls over the Soviet Bank in Berlin. This jockeying was a bad sign—but an accurate one.[44]

The scene now shifts to Berlin, where the military governors are doing the negotiating: the Soviets up the ante by demanding controls over hitherto unregulated air traffic even after the overland blockade has been lifted; next comes some crude stalling (Sokolovsky complains of being too tired to negotiate) and some even cruder threats (he says that the Berlin *magistrat* is now a tool of the West but will not be forever—this while a mob is denying it access to City Hall); finally, the Soviets turn amiable and jocular again—without yielding anything of real significance.[45] All this to-ing and fro-ing is standard Soviet procedure; Henry Kissinger encountered it over and over again in his negotiations with the Russians some twenty years later. But what was the point? If Stalin wanted Western negotiators to plead with him to resolve the stalemate, he was disappointed. They offered no concessions, either in Berlin or in further talks with Molotov in Moscow. The West was adamant. But neither would it go to war to lift the blockade—that much the summer's negotiations had made clear: hence, Stalin's decision to leave the blockade in place and let events take their course.

The result was a further poisoning of relations. But was there any alternative? George Kennan thought there was. He proposed a plan for reunifying Germany that supposedly would protect Western interests, but might be acceptable to the Soviets. The main points of Kennan's plan, which he suggested be set before the Council of Foreign Ministers, were: establishment of new, veto-free four-power control machinery; free elections under international supervision in all zones; creation of a provisional government; simultaneous withdrawal of occupying garrisons to positions on the periphery of Germany; and continued demilitarization of Germany. Kennan's plan reflected certain pessimistic assumptions—that Berlin could not survive continuing blockade; that the Western zones alone could not mount a viable economy; that the irritants of occupation would eventually trigger an explosion; that since a divided Europe offered no exit for East European peoples, they would one day rebel and thus raise the specter of World War III. On the other hand, there was one overriding *positive* advantage of Kennan's plan. It was designed to produce a united Germany that would be both free and democratic, and linked to the West through the European Recovery Program. Had they bought the plan, the Soviets would have had to withdraw to the East.[46]

Kennan admits in his *Memoirs* that he was overly pessimistic about Germany. In any event, his State Department colleagues feared his plan would frighten the British and French. America's allies would not know which to dread more—the failure of Kennan's project (resulting in the Soviets' somehow coming out on top) or success (in the form of a reborn and potentially threatening Germany). All three Western capitals could imagine Moscow turning further talks to its own advantage. Why should Stalin *not* negotiate if Kennan's terms were offered to him? The talks could drag on indefinitely—until the West gave up on them once again. Such an outcome, which appears quite plausible in retrospect, would only have delayed the onset of what might be called the "Cold War proper." The hallmark of the Cold War proper was that Stalin himself gave up on negotiations.

8

Cold War Stalinist-Style: January 1949-March 1953

IN EARLY 1948 GEORGE KENNAN WAS THE REIGNING RUSSIAN EXPERT IN the United States government; his view of the USSR as primarily a political challenge rather than a military threat had found, he felt, general acceptance. "Two years later," Kennan recalls, "all this was rapidly changing." Kennan himself went on leave in the fall of 1950 at the Institute for Advanced Study in Princeton, after having become, as he notes in his *Memoirs*, "increasingly worried over the growing evidence of difference in outlook between myself and my colleagues . . . including the Secretary of State." Kennan had retreated from Washington. But "a number of disturbing trends were now detectable," he recalls, "as a result of which I found myself increasingly concerned over the course of American opinion and policy precisely in the area where I was thought to have, and fancied myself to have, the greatest influence."

Particularly distressing to Kennan was the fact that, even before the Korean War, a Nazi-like image of the Soviet threat had found great favor in Washington. In vain had Kennan argued that the parallel with "Hitler and his timetables" was a chimera, that "the Russians were not like that; that they were weaker than we supposed; that they had many internal problems of their own; that they had no 'grand design' . . . for the early destruction of American power and for world conquest." And of course, Kennan recalls, the Korean War "greatly heightened the danger." It seemed to validate the view of the Soviet threat as primarily military. It led not only to the fuller militarization but also to the globalization of containment—which Kennan, the founder, had intended to be neither a military doctrine nor global in scope.[1]

And yet, until the Korean War, American military preparedness did not match the administration's agitated view of the Soviet threat, nor did it meet the various overseas defense commitments into which Washington had entered. Postwar demobilization had dropped American armed forces to a level of about 1.3 million in early 1948. Although Truman called for resumption of the draft in March 1948, the big jump in American manpower came after the outbreak of the Korean conflict, not before. The defense budget for the fiscal year 1949, presented to Congress in January 1948, called for military spending of $10 billion— a dip from $10.5 billion for fiscal 1948. Early in 1948, Truman requested a $3 billion military supplement but, intent on balancing the overall budget, he limited defense spending to $15 billion for fiscal 1950 and beyond—this compared to the $20 to $50 billion dollar price tag attached to NSC-68 (the interagency assessment of the Soviet threat and how to confront it), which was presented to the president in April 1950. Furthermore, the nuclear weapons that Truman counted on to deter Soviet attack in the absence of conventional forces capable of doing so were themselves apparently less numerous and less likely to be effective than one might have supposed. And an area like South Korea, to which not a great deal of American attention was paid until the North Koreans invaded it, was a particularly inviting target—especially when the Americans pulled their troops out while at the same time expressing public doubts about the importance of South Korea to U.S. security.[2]

Exactly how much the Soviets knew about American nuclear readiness is uncertain, although they may have known quite a bit thanks to Soviet agents like Donald Maclean, who from 1946 to 1948 had access to atomic stockpiling information as Britain's Washington-based joint secretary of the Combined Policy Committee on Atomic Energy, and Kim Philby, who beginning in the fall of 1949 served in Washington as London's liaison with the CIA.[3] But most of the gap between American rhetoric and reality was visible in the public records and debates of an open society—which is strikingly reminiscent, or so hard-liners might say, of the situation facing the United States in the 1980s. Such critics charge that the United States lacks the wherewithal to meet its commitments, in particular to defend the Persian Gulf in line with the Carter Doctrine. They warn that American weakness could tempt Moscow to press forward with the result either a damaging American retreat or a hot war. Of course, American nuclear and conventional arsenals are now vast in comparison with those of 1949. On the other hand, the Soviets have come even farther—all the way from an American nuclear monopoly to what some see as Soviet strategic superiority. These and other differences complicate any effort to draw parallels. But there may be important lessons. American military weakness, along with the ambiguity of Washington's commitment to South Korea, did encourage Moscow to authorize if not initiate the North Korean invasion. Yet just as important to Stalin, I shall argue, was his overall image of the West—particularly his personal conviction, which clashed with his public position, that capitalist statesmen neither wanted war themselves nor thought that the Soviet Union wanted war. Moreover, this conviction, which apparently sustained Stalin despite moments of near panic at the height of the Korean conflict, was one of which the Americans, including George Kennan, were unaware. This increased the danger of miscalculations that could have transformed a limited war into an all-out conflagration.

In 1952 President Truman called Kennan back from Princeton to serve as American ambassador to the USSR. But the appointment only brought Kennan further frustration. Isolated in Moscow, ignored by both host and home governments, the ambassador pondered a kind of "cosmic misunderstanding between the Kremlin and the Western powers." The Soviets knew they planned no attack on the West and, hence, were surprised and alarmed when the West acted as if they were about to strike. Why, the Soviets must have asked themselves, "were they being accused of precisely the one thing they had not done, which was to plan . . . to conduct an overt and unprovoked invasion of Western Europe?" Assuming the West knew the falsity of its own charges, and observing Western military preparations, the Soviets must have reached an ominous conclusion—that its enemies were determined on "a military conflict with the Soviet Union as soon as the requisite strength had been created on the Western side." The Korean War clinched this "misunderstanding between adversaries" because neither side "understood very well the motives underlying the behavior of the other side."[4]

Kennan was right that the Kremlin and the Western powers misunderstood each other. But the noncommunication was assymetrical and therefore more complicated than he thought it was. True, the West was mesmerized by the false specter of an all-out Soviet attack. But for the most part, Stalin did *not* assume that the West was intent on war; rather, he believed that capitalist statesmen were deliberately exaggerating "the Soviet threat" in order to mobilize their own people and intimidate the Soviet Union and its partners. Stalin hoped to foil this strategy by convincing the peoples of the West that their own governments were in fact plotting war; for if they believed that, they might rise up and restrain their leaders—some of whom might themselves shrink from high tension, or at least fall to blaming each other for it. Stalin's tactic, in other words, was to counter what he perceived to be propaganda with propaganda of his own. Instead, his behavior confirmed the Western impression that he was either willfully ignorant or dangerously misinformed about the West's true intentions. And that ultimately had the effect of reinforcing the Hitler-like image he had already gained in the West. Stalin hinted at his actual strategy throughout these years, and he offered a fuller explanation in his political testament in 1952. But it is not clear that even his closest aides understood what he was up to, let alone the West.

Nikita Khrushchev, for example, portrays Stalin as nervously fearful of American aggression throughout the postwar period—as "very worried [in 1945] that the Americans would cross the line of demarcation" in Germany; as "terribly concerned that the clouds of war were gathering over Bulgaria"; as in a "white heat of worry" for fear that the "United States might send its troops into Czechoslovakia and try to restore the capitalist government which had been overthrown by the working class under the leadership of the Communist Party"; as "afraid of a new round of destruction" resulting from the creation of a West German state; as "obsessed with shoring up our defenses against the West" as a result of "exaggerating our enemies' strength and their intention to unleash war on us." But Khrushchev's charge that for Stalin, "foreign policy meant keeping the antiaircraft units around Moscow on 24-hour alert," like his picture of Stalin at bay on June 22, 1941, need not be credited without serious qualification—for Khrushchev, that arch de-Stalinizer, had a good reason to exaggerate his former leader's failures of nerve. Moreover, Nikita Sergeyevich, who was not privy to Stalin's full range of foreign policy calculations, may have projected his own nervousness onto his boss. Khrushchev admits that Stalin "jealously guarded foreign policy . . . as his own special province" and that "the rest of us in the leadership were careful not to poke our noses into these matters. . . ." "The rest of us were just errand boys," Khrushchev continues (another self-vindicating disclaimer?), yet when the boss did reveal his basic foreign-policy assumptions in a political testament designed to enlighten his associates and heirs, Khrushchev, at least, found these last writings too theoretical to be worthy of much interest and attention.[5]

Granting that Stalin viewed the West as hostile, stubborn, and devious but neither itself eager for war nor convinced that the Kremlin wanted war, what sort of policy flowed from his assumptions? Marshall Shulman, like Kennan, a scholar-statesman specializing on the USSR, has analyzed Soviet behavior from 1949 to 1953. Some time before assuming the Kennanesque role of Secretary of State Cyrus Vance's chief Soviet adviser in Jimmy Carter's administration, Shulman rejected what had been the conventional American view of late Stalinist policy. The prevailing view, he wrote, depicted Stalin's death, in 1953, as "the great watershed event, from which is charted the shift toward a more flexible policy broadly known by the term, 'peaceful coexistence.' " Shulman dates the change from 1949 instead. "The use of détente, of divisive action, nationalism, the peace movement, and anti-imperialism, [of] an indirect policy of maneuver to strengthen the Soviet bloc and weaken the Western bloc in place of a direct advance toward social revolution"—the "emergence of this combination in the late-Stalin period, and its further development in the post-Stalin period, represent a qualitative change in the direction of Soviet policy."[6]

But the tactics Shulman lists do not date from 1949 *or* from 1953. They were features of Stalinist-style détente that had begun in 1946; indeed, they had been employed off and on, in very different contexts of course, ever since 1918. What 1949 did mark was not a shift toward "a more flexible policy" but, rather, a move to a more rigid one; it marked a further turning away from serious negotiations and even, for the most part, from the convincing pretense of same—a kind of hunkering down for the long haul punctuated by occasional (but forceful) probing for advantage and by peace propaganda even more crude and manipulative than it had been before 1949.

One more question must be considered before we examine in detail, first, Washington's image of Soviet policy and, second, Soviet policy itself. It is the question of Stalin's psyche and its influence on Soviet strategy during his last years. The question arises because some of his actions (including apparent preparations for another round of high-level purges) suggest—his daughter, Svetlana, as well as his disciple Khrushchev do too—that Stalin was progressively losing his grasp on reality. According to Svetlana, her father "saw enemies everywhere. It had reached the point of being pathological, of persecution mania. . . ." Khrushchev speaks of "the sickness which began to envelop Stalin's mind in the last years of his life." But seeing enemies all around him was nothing new for Stalin, and there is evidence that he was of clear mind (as well as clearly in control of his colleagues) until almost the very end. Joining her father on a vacation by the Black Sea in the summer of 1951, Svetlana found him to be physically fit. Khrushchev depicts Stalin not only dictating his last writings to his aide, Alexander Poskrebyshev, but also dictating to his frightened associates a revised Politburo roster that seemed to signal the end for at least some of them.[7] And so, the questions remain: How *did* Stalin's intensified suspicions influence foreign policy? If a main feature of that policy was an ever-increasing retreat from serious negotiations with the Western powers, is that to be explained by Stalin's psychological state or by his experience with the Western powers? The most likely answer is both, but we really do not know. There was, in any event, a pattern to Soviet policy, and it was that with which the Americans and their allies had to deal.

Early in 1949 the National Security Council Staff prepared yet another report in response to Pentagon pressure for a comprehensive assessment of the Soviet threat along with measures, particularly military measures, required to combat it. The draft NSC report of March, 1949, "Measures Required to Achieve U.S. Objectives with Respect to the USSR," alarmed Kennan. The paper seemed to assume, he said, that "a war with Russia is necessary," which contrasted with the State Department view that "some *modus vivendi* is possible." Policy-planning staff members were reported to have "generally and roundly condemned the paper as being extremely dangerous. . . ."[8]

Kennan warred against what he regarded as militarist assumptions throughout 1949. He seemed, moreover, to have support at high levels of the State Department. The new secretary of state, Dean Acheson, thought "the weight of the evidence leads to the belief that the Russians will put their chief reliance on the cold war. It is here that we must meet the most pressing dangers and not from military aggression." But Acheson's judgment was not a sign of those to come. Early in 1950 the State Department embarked, along with other agencies, on a new national security assessment, NSC 68, that would warn of a possible atomic attack by the Soviets within the next four or five years. The NSC 68 "exercise" (as the drafting process is called in Washington) was sparked by the Communist victory in China, the detonation of the first Soviet atomic bomb, and the need for the United States to decide whether to build the hydrogen weapon. The drafting spawned poisonous bureaucratic in-fighting marked by some unlikely alignments. The Pentagon, in the person of Defense Secretary Louis Johnson, was *not* the prime proponent of increased military spending (in fact Johnson angrily resisted Acheson, who did advocate stepped-up defense outlays);

on the contrary, Johnson was committed to holding down government spending and thought Harry Truman agreed with him on the issue. Kennan and Charles Bohlen, the government's leading Soviet experts, were largely left out of the exercise. Bohlen, then stationed in Paris, returned to Washington in March to criticize the report's assertion that the Kremlin's aim was "world domination." Since this "carries the implication," said Bohlen, "that all other considerations are subordinate to this major purpose and that great risks would be run for the sake of its achievement," it "leads inevitably to the conclusion that war is inevitable." It would have been more accurate to say, Bohlen contended, that Soviet leaders sought first of all to maintain their regime and, only then, to extend it "throughout the world to the degree that is possible without serious risk to the internal regime." But while Bohlen regretted over-simplification, he understood and approved its uses. He did not wish to "belabor" his point because "it is obviously better to over-simplify in the direction of greater urgency and danger than it is to . . . [on] the side of complacency when dealing with Soviet intentions."[9]

Over-simplification was the game Acheson and others were apparently playing. Revisionists may contend that NSC 68, like the Truman Doctrine before it, presented a false rationale for expansion having little to do with any real Soviet threat. In fact, Acheson and others were deliberately overstating a case in which they genuinely believed— the better to rouse those in government whom they considered dangerously complacent or unwilling to put their money where their anti-Communist mouths were.[10]

NSC 68 was a chilling document. Consider its picture of Soviet intentions: The USSR sought "to impose its absolute authority over the rest of the world"; that goal required "the ultimate elimination of any effective opposition to [Soviet] authority"; that, in turn, demanded "the complete subversion or forcible destruction of the machinery of government and structure of society in the countries of the non-Soviet world and their replacement by an apparatus and structure subservient to and controlled from the Kremlin."

Next, NSC 68 on Kremlin capabilities: "No other value system is so . . . implacable in its purpose to destroy us, so capable of turning to its own uses the most dangerous and divisive trends in our own society, no other so skillfully and powerfully evokes the elements of irrationality in human nature everywhere, and no other has the support of a great and growing center of military power." The "demonstrated capabilities" of the Communist party and Soviet secret police were "unparalleled in history." Soviet ideology was another "great source of strength." In the "flexibility of Soviet tactics," combined with secrecy, the Kremlin "possesses a formidable capacity to act with the widest tactical latitude, with stealth and with speed." True, the USSR was not without its own vulnerabilities, the greatest of which lay in the "basic nature of its relations with the Soviet people." But none of them detracted from its most dangerous weapon of all—the weapon of war. Sounding a note often heard a generation later, NSC 68 declared that Moscow possessed armed forces "far in excess of those necessary to defend its national territory," but quite enough to provide it with "great coercive power for use in time of peace." Should war come in 1950, the Soviets could not only "overrun Western Europe, with the possible exception of the Iberian and Scandinavian Peninsulas," but also "drive toward oil-bearing areas of the Near and Middle East, . . . consolidate Communist gains in the Far East, . . . launch air attacks against the British Isles and air and sea attacks against lines of communication of the Western Powers in the Atlantic and Pacific, . . . [and] attack selected targets with atomic weapons . . . in Alaska, Canada and the United States." Such estimates were presumably based on the sort of information that General Marshall had labeled two years before as "at best nothing but guesses." Ditto the prediction that the Kremlin would have stockpiled two hundred fission bombs by 1954. Yet this last projection prompted the following doomsday speculation: "If it is assumed that [the Soviet Union] will strike a strong surprise blow, and if it is further assumed that its atomic attacks will be met with no more effective defense opposition than the United States and its allies have programmed, results of those attacks could include: (a) Laying waste the British Isles; . . . (b) Destruction of vital centers . . . of Western Europe; . . . (c) Delivering devastating attacks on certain vital centers of the United States and Canada." NSC 68 admitted that Moscow preferred to win a cold war rather than a hot one. But Paul Nitze, the chief drafter of the report (and later a leading hawk of the 1970s), contended the Kremlin did not "make a sharp distinction between 'military aggression' and measures short of military aggression. In its decision, it is guided only by considerations of expediency." That put "a premium," as NSC 68 called it, "on a surprise attack against us."[11]

How could the United States cope with this awesome threat? In typical government fashion, NSC 68 drafters offered four possible courses of action, three of which were designed to be rejected. "Isolation" and preventive war were out. And who in his right mind would opt for "continuation of current policies" after reading the report? That left only "a rapid build-up of political, economic and military strength in the Free World" as the preferred option, with "military aspects" coming first in the report's detailed recommendations. Negotiations would play an insignificant role if NSC 68 drafters got their way; for they assumed that the Kremlin had all the advantages that came from not having to take into account public or allied opinion and from having control over left-wing groups in Western countries. Western statesmen should be ready to talk with Moscow, if only to mollify those who still thought equitable agreements possible. But to propose a general settlement of the sort Secretary Acheson had proposed on March 16, 1950 (complete with reunification of Germany via free and internationally supervised elections, withdrawal of Soviet forces from satellite areas, abandonment of "indirect aggression," and so forth), "could only be a tactic" pending "such a radical change in Soviet policies as to constitute a change in the Soviet system." In the meantime, NSC 68 recommended "dynamic steps to reduce the power and influence of the Kremlin inside the Soviet Union and other areas under its control"—steps including covert operations designed "with a view to fomenting and supporting unrest and revolt in selected strategic satellite countries." This was fighting fire with fire. As NSC 68 itself said, "It would be the current Soviet cold war technique used against the Soviet Union."[12]

If the Korean War had not begun on June 25, 1950, it would have had to have been invented by the drafters of NSC 68. Which is not to say, as some critics have been tempted to say, that Washington somehow caused the war for that reason. The fact that the North Koreans used force suggested that the Soviets themselves might do so—and in a more important part of the world (as far as Washington was concerned) like Europe. A National Security Council report of July 1 foresaw no general war in the near future but admitted that its own prediction might be wrong: "It is merely the assumption that seems to have the greatest support on the basis of the available data." Chip Bohlen hedged his bet: "There is not sufficient evidence to justify a firm opinion that the Soviet Union will *not* take any one or all of the actions which lie within its military capabilities." Even Kennan was nervous and uncertain: Although the Soviets did not want war, they might consider that conflict could not be avoided, in which case their action would be "the same as though they themselves deliberately decided to unleash a general war." Moscow was unlikely to invade Western Europe, said Kennan, but "armed action by German units, along the Korean pattern," was not out of the question. If Kennan went that far, it was not surprising that others went further. The CIA, whose prognoses were generally cautious, thought the Kremlin might "deliberately provoke . . . a general war" between 1950 and 1954; the peak of danger would be in 1952. Harry Truman warned of a Soviet drive for world conquest that could be resisted only with military strength.[13]

Here was the basis for a terrible misunderstanding. Convinced that the Kremlin was contemplating general war, the Americans might have interpreted lesser Soviet moves, whether in Korea or elsewhere, as steps in that direction; whereupon they might have responded with drastic action of their own. And that would have made the no-holds-barred conflict that both sides sought to avoid even more inevitable than it seemed to be according to NSC 68. Compared to the actual use of force in Korea, Soviet propaganda was only a secondary source of concern for America. But Soviet charges that the West wanted war, or that Washington and Seoul were the aggressors in Korea, or that the United Nations troops were using germ warfare, all alarmed both those unaccustomed to Soviet propaganda and those who were familiar with it. Recall Ambassador Smith trying to convince Molotov in 1948 that America was not the sort of country that engaged in aggression. A year later, Smith's successor, Admiral Alan Kirk, was back at the same stand while preparing for a get-acquainted talk with Stalin. The State Department suggested what an appropriate response would be if Stalin accused NATO of threatening war against the USSR: "We cannot believe," Kirk was to say, "that [this] can represent a sincere view of Soviet leaders who, we must assume, receive accurate reports from their representatives abroad and are not deceived by their own propaganda." The military balance in Europe was such that invasion could only come from the East. Furthermore, "elementary acquaintance with the traditions and institutions of the Anglo-Saxon countries would suffice to reveal that it would be quite impossible for even the most rash and aggressively minded Government, if such existed, to obtain popular support for . . . an aggressive or 'preventive' war which would require years of advance planning. . . ."

As it happened, Stalin never gave Kirk his cue—or rather, the ambassador did not give Stalin an opening. Kirk told Stalin that in view of "the grave and basic character" of East-West divisions, it was "unlikely that discussion of them on such an occasion would contribute to their solution barring fundamental change of attitude on the part of the Soviet Government."[14] But even if Kirk had conveyed the State Department message, what would have been Stalin's reaction? He did not need to be told yet again about American public opinion; he knew enough, or thought he did. This is not to deny the other part of Kirk's prepared "response": that Stalin might be deceived by his own propaganda, that is, by underlings who thought they were anticipating his wishes. But the State Department misconceived an important truth when it suggested the Soviets could not possibly believe everything they said. Of course they could not, but that did not mean their hyperbole was designed to prepare the ground for a general war.

Western disclaimers continued. Said Admiral Kirk to Soviet authorities in October 1951: "I assume that the Soviet Government is receiving full and objective reports concerning . . . the attitude of the United States. . . . I wish to assure the Soviet Government that the United States has no aggressive designs on the USSR. . . ." Anthony Eden (foreign secretary again in a new Churchill government) put it this way at the United Nations in November 1951: "The most fantastic of all charges leveled against us last Thursday was that we were warmongers. Let me assure this audience—need I really do this?—that everyone in Britain, 'the people, Parliament, the Government,' deeply desire peace. . . . In all our actions we seek peace; yet our proposals are laughed to scorn. I must admit that I do not understand or accept such methods."[15] The fact that Western statesmen kept coming back to Soviet allegations confirms that they feared Moscow might attack out of a misplaced conviction that it was itself about to be attacked—or would cunningly cite such a concern to justify unprovoked aggression. But at the peak of the Cold War, just as at the height of entente, the Americans misjudged Stalin. Washington could imagine straightforward misunderstandings—whether they impeded collaboration among allies or triggered cold war tensions. The Americans could also conceive of a Soviet conspiracy to launch a general conflict. What they could not understand was the very essence of Stalin's American policy—conspiracy, but not with intent to unleash war, plus misunderstandings that were not merely coincidental but deliberately conceived and fostered.

A funny thing happened to Vyacheslav Molotov and Anastas Mikoyan on their way to the Kremlin. On or about March 3, 1949, they were relieved of their duties as foreign minister and minister of foreign trade, respectively. They did, however, remain members of the party Politburo and deputy chairmen of the USSR Council of Ministers. The changes caught the West by surprise. They left American experts gasping while at the same time, in good bureaucratic fashion, down-playing the significance of what they could not explain. "While we do not believe changes involve any fundamental shift Soviet foreign policy," cabled the Moscow embassy, "we think timing may have been influenced by desire evoke misinterpretations and sow confusion in West. . . ."[16] There was a certain exculpatory logic to deducing Moscow's intent from the confusion of American experts, but still the move remained a riddle.

George Kennan pondered the puzzle while flying to Germany on a routine inspection trip. Upon arrival in Frankfurt, he recounted his ruminations in a letter to Chip Bohlen. As so often happened, Kennan's fine antennae had picked up a key signal, even though its meaning was not clear even to him. The more Kennan thought about the removals of Molotov and Mikoyan, the more convinced he was that "this marks some sort of turning point in the attitude of the Soviet Government toward . . . the Western powers." There were two other clues. One was a recent reference in the Soviet press to Stalin's speech of March 10, 1939, in which he warned those who "are in the habit of getting others to pull their chestnuts out of the fire"; this speech had signaled Soviet interest in shifting from cooperation with the West to possible accommodation with Hitler. Another was the demise of the *Moscow Daily News* (an English-language newspaper which ceased publication on January 1, 1949); this, too, had a prewar counterpart in the suppression of the *Journal de Moscou,* a paper that perished "for technical reasons" on May 1, 1939. Kennan put these two parallels together with a third: Litvinov's fall and replacement by Molotov in 1939, now followed by the latter's transfer and replacement by Vyshinsky. All this added up, he thought, to "a gesture of disgust with the West: a gesture testifying to the futility of trying to gain Soviet objectives by dealing with us, just as the 1939 move recognized the futility of trying to gain Soviet objectives by dealing with the French and British." What had Kennan "puzzled and worried" was the alternative. In 1939 Stalin had the "tremendous and dramatically promising alternative . . . of dealing with Hitler." But what now? One possibility was "some sort of exploitation of the satellites against us, from which Russia herself would remain aloof." Whatever the Kremlin hoped to achieve, it was plain they did not expect to achieve it through negotiations with the United States. But beyond that Kennan could not see: "Somewhere Moscow must think that it has a means of bedeviling the West and promoting Soviet objectives which will not involve the Soviet Union directly. And it is toying with the idea of invoking that means at some time within the coming period."[17]

Kennan was close to the mark. Stalin had tried entente, then détente, then militance, then negotiations again. Now he would opt for another way. This would at times involve invitations to negotiate, but more for the narrow, tactical purpose of delaying specific Western projects (such as NATO and West Germany) by tempting America's allies away from Washington's embrace rather than as part of an on-going strategy of improving relations with the West as a whole. Stalin would, as Kennan suggested, exploit a satellite, North Korea, against the West. He would also "bedevil the West" without involving the USSR directly by revving up a vast international peace movement whose task it would be both to indict and inhibit the Western powers.

Yet this policy shift reflected more than the West's refusal to play the role Stalin had assigned to it. More than other Stalinist moves, this one lends itself to a psychological explanation. Svetlana Alliluyeva and Nikita Khrushchev cite the fall of Molotov and Mikoyan as evidence of Stalin's now all-encompassing mistrust. Molotov's wife, Polina Zhemchuzhina, a substantial figure in her own right as former head of the State Perfume Trust and later commissar of fish industries, was arrested and imprisoned in 1948—the victim of Stalin's long-smoldering conviction that she had contributed to his wife's (and her friend's) suicide in 1932. Molotov and Mikoyan themselves, according to Khrushchev, were suspected by Stalin of being Western agents (the former because he had traveled in the United States by private railroad car, which suggested to Stalin that his foreign minister might have been corrupted by American intelligence), although their sins could not have been too grievous since they were permitted to remain in high official posts. This was also the period of the so-called "Leningrad Affair," in which Stalin permitted the late Andrei Zhdanov's politburo rivals Georgi Malenkov and Lavrenti Beria to liquidate Zhdanov's leading associates—for reasons that are still not entirely clear. And that affair in turn was apparently linked with an orgy of purges throughout Eastern Europe. With Tito resisting Soviet efforts to depose him, other Communist leaders with (and without) histories of independence became suspect— Gomulka, imprisoned, but not liquidated, in 1948; Traicho Kostov of Bulgaria, for whom the bell tolled in March 1949; the Hungarian leader, Laszlo Rajk, accused of the wildly improbable crime (even assuming the CIA was anticipating NSC 68) of serving Western intelligence services as well as Tito.[18]

How did all this blood-letting connect with Stalin's new "non-approach" to the West? One possibility is that his lower profile in East-West relations allowed him to concentrate on resisting challenges (more imagined than real) closer to home. Another is that the same suspiciousness that turned Stalin against former friends and allies had now deepened to the point that even his enemies could not be "trusted"—in the sense that he had once trusted Hitler, Roosevelt, and Truman to acquiesce in Soviet pressures and blandishments. In any event, although Stalin's diplomats still went through the motions, their hearts did not seem in it. In January 1949, Moscow launched a peace offensive designed, apparently, to forestall the signing of the North Atlantic Treaty. But the campaign did not last long and was not very effective while it lasted. It featured such resistible temptations as: The *Information Bulletin* of the Soviet embassy in Washington stopped shouting "warmonger" and "imperialist" long enough to wish the Americans Happy New Year and to present them with a conciliatory article by a *Pravda* correspondent; French and Italian Communist leaders Marcel Cachin and Palmiro Togliatti suddenly rediscovered the blessings of cooperation, both between the great powers and with their own native non-Communists—they even went so far as to suggest that Truman revive his plan to send a personal representative (whether Fred Vinson was their first choice is not clear) to consult with Stalin. Replying to questions submitted by Kingsbury Smith of the International News Service, Stalin declared his readiness to meet with President Truman and conclude a vague and unenforceable peace pact. But even before the United States refused to bite at this bait, the Soviets jerked it out of the water. The Ministry of Foreign Affairs issued a blast at NATO just two days before Stalin's Smith interview was published. Moscow simultaneously attempted to pressure Norway out of adhering to NATO. In February the French Communists reversed their field once more by making their most militant statement yet. Maurice Thorez asked himself a rhetorical question, which he said had been put to his party by "enemies of the people": "What would you do if the Red Army entered Paris?" His answer was that the Communists would offer all-out support to the Soviets.[19]

If anything, these and other Communist actions—violent demonstrations in France and Italy, Soviet threats to annul treaties with Britain and France, hostile troop movements near Yugoslavia, border incidents with Iran—may have speeded the NATO signing, which took place in Washington on April 4, 1949. With that, the anti-NATO barrage sub-

sided and the Soviets turned their attention to delaying, if not preventing, the establishment of a West German government. September 1,
1948, had not been the turning point that Stalin and Molotov feared.
Intra-Western negotiations on Germany dragged on into 1949 and then
seemed to achieve a breakthrough in the spring. The three Western
powers reached full agreement on April 8, 1949; West German assent
as well as a timetable for forming the new government by July were
announced on April 25. It was not accidental, as the Soviets would say,
that at just this time Moscow signaled its readiness to lift the Berlin
blockade and resume all-German discussions.

Negotiations on Germany began with contacts at the United
Nations between Soviet delegate Yakov Malik and American Philip Jes-
sup and rose in May and June to the level of the Council of Foreign
Ministers. The details need not be recounted. The point is that the
Soviets failed even to make a credible show of trying to resolve all-
German questions, let alone actually seeking an equitable resolution.
The Western powers displayed no such desire either—which is one rea-
son why Moscow held back. Malik at first insisted that the West Ger-
man state's founding be delayed as long as the CFM was meeting. He
settled for Jessup's assurance that there would be no such government
in existence when the CFM session *began*. The Americans kept their
promise, but just barely; the Western powers celebrated the first day of
CFM negotiations by having the Basic Law for the Federal Republic of
Germany signed in Bonn on the very same date.[20]

That was rubbing it in. No wonder the new Soviet foreign minister, Andrei Vyshinsky, only repeated old proposals to the CFM. *Pravda*
correspondent Yuri Zhukov (still active and influential in the 1980s)
confirmed to an American at the conference that Moscow had given up
on German unification; the Soviets' main aim, he said, was increased
trade between Eastern and Western zones of Germany. But even on the
propaganda level, the Soviet effort was uninspired. On the eve of the
conference, the American chargé in Moscow, Foy Kohler, predicted it
would be the "capstone in [the] current 'peace offensive' designed to
disrupt and divide West and delay to maximum [the] formation of West
German government." But as the Americans later noted with some surprise, as a capstone it was unimpressive.[21]

Nor was Vyshinsky's lack-lustre performance in Paris unique. The
Americans again had imagined a Soviet propaganda spectacular in the
United Nations, complete with a proposed ban on regional pacts like
NATO. Much closer to the mark was Assistant Secretary of State John

Hickerson, who remarked at a meeting of American, British, and Canadian UN delegates that "we were very fortunate the Politburo did not have a hard-headed non-Communist adviser on tactics vis-à-vis the West. . . ." Instead, "the Soviets played all their cards the wrong way."[22]

That the man dealing these indifferent cards was none other than Stalin himself became clear in two of his conversations with British and American ambassadors in 1949. Sir David Kelly's July 18 visit seemed promising because he was summoned after Vyshinsky had ignored his suggestion that a courtesy call might be appropriate. The audience ended on a positive note, too, when Stalin said (with Vyshinsky looking on sourly) that the new ambassador would be given "every facility" for exploratory talks with the Soviet foreign minister. But the rest of the short talk was barren, and equally sterile was Admiral Kirk's audience the next month. Kirk's carefully rehearsed defense of American innocence turned out superfluous. The highlight of the occasion was the chance to see Vyshinsky "hopping around like a pea on a hot griddle to do [Stalin's] slightest wish." The biggest victory Kirk could claim in his report to the State Department was that "nothing transpired that would give the Politburo the chance to make propaganda."[23]

The case can be made that Soviet fortunes sank exceedingly low in the summer of 1949. Western defense preparations were marked by an Anglo-American meeting to coordinate military and economic policies, a NATO foreign ministers conference (followed by establishment of the North Atlantic Council and Defense Committee), and Senate consideration of stationing American military equipment abroad to defend against a Soviet invasion of Europe. Moscow's diplomatic isolation was evident in September when it received almost no support beyond the Soviet bloc in a series of key votes at the United Nations. Add to this, internal and East European purges plus an overall lack-lustre diplomacy.[24] But did the Soviets see themselves in disarray? The Soviet press had no such self-image, to judge by its unending accounts of capitalist crises; nor did a high-ranking Soviet academician whose public lecture was attended and reported by an American diplomat. The gist of the talk, entitled "The Further Aggravation of the General Crisis of Capitalism after the Second World War," was as follows:

> The USA is in a weaker position because it now has to occupy the front lines of imperialism, having lost the 'shock brigades' of Germany and Japan. The preponderance of U.S. economic

strength means increasing pressure to grow at the expense of the older capitalist economies, hence a responding increase of 'centrifugal forces' in the Western Bloc, which is consequently doomed to break up. This process will be accelerated as the economic crisis gets worse. The shrinking of the colonial system has continued: the loss of China alone is a major blow to the USA comparable to the loss of Japan and Germany. The heavy waves of strikes signify the sharpening of class 'contradictions': workers and peasants are less docile after heavy sacrifices imposed on them by the war. . . . The warlike aggressiveness of the imperialists indicates that they realize time is working against them.[25]

Now, speeches of this sort, and of course newspaper articles too, raise the question of how seriously to take them. Obviously they have a propaganda and morale-raising purpose. But there is reason to think the Soviet dictator shared the apparent optimism. Whatever the USSR's problems (and one result of Stalin's terrorizing his associates was that they dared not inform him fully), did they not pale before those of capitalism? However great the capitalists' hostility, were they not inhibited by their troubles? It was theoretically possible that capitalist contradictions might prove more, not less, susceptible of solution in a cold war setting in which the Soviet Union loomed as the common enemy of the rival imperialist states. And Stalin might have feared that capitalists on the run would resort to fascism—as the Germans had supposedly done in 1932—and then move, as the Nazis had, against the USSR. But apparently Stalin's forecast carried more hope than such an interpretation would indicate, for he was ready to see the Cold War escalate rather than undertake the sort of serious "peace" feelers which Chip Bohlen, who considered the Soviets' position nearly as desperate as in 1941, still half expected to encounter in 1949.[26]

If Stalin was relatively unperturbed in the summer of 1949, how did he feel in the fall? By then, the USSR had detonated its first atomic bomb, an explosion that sparked a minor panic in the West even though Stalin did his best to cushion the blow. It was one thing for him to encourage a run-of-the-mill war scare when there was little prospect of actual fighting. But the atomic bomb was different; to bluster about that might frighten the West into some irrational response. So TASS was authorized to issue a reassuring statement emphasizing Moscow's peaceful intentions—the same sort of statement that Stalin himself would make on October 16, 1951, when another Soviet bomb test raised what *Pravda* called a "hullabaloo in the Western press."[27]

The founding of the Chinese People's Republic in the fall of 1949 must have been cause for Soviet satisfaction. There had been strain aplenty between the Soviet and Chinese Communists and, as we now know, a great schism lay ahead. But Mao's victory put Moscow's Berlin retreat into perspective, and it appeared to confirm Lenin's prediction of revolution in less developed countries; not the least dividend of the Chinese revolution was that the British and Americans quickly fell to quarreling about how to treat the new Communist regime. The British were ready to recognize Peking and support its entry into the United Nations, partly in hope of benefiting from Chinese trade; the Americans, rich enough not to compromise their principles for mercenary motives, took a tougher line. Meanwhile, inter-imperialist differences on European issues were intensifying as well. Having previously feared that the United States would not defend them, many Europeans now worried that Washington would go too far in challenging the Soviet Union. The question of West Germany's relationship to NATO also provoked contention among the Western allies.

Georgi Malenkov's Anniversary-of-the-Revolution speech rang with seeming assurance on November 6, 1949. Never before had the Soviet peoples been so united, their frontiers so "just and well-ordered," their country surrounded with "neighboring countries so friendly to [their] state." The great Chinese victory had opened "a new chapter in the history . . . of all peoples of Asia." The whole capitalist world faced a "gathering crisis," which could not be concealed by a "campaign of feigned optimism." The speaker hailed the Soviet Union's peace policy, adding that "if this program is not being realized, it is solely because it does not suit the warmongers." But the "program"—which consisted of condemning war, pledging peace, and banning the bomb—was a lame substitute for the vigorous détente diplomacy of old. The major element in Moscow's program was the international peace movement: 561 national organizations and 12 international associations had attended the recent World Peace Congress; in all, "600 million organized supporters of peace" had been represented. The great goal of the movement, said Malenkov, was to prevent any repetition of Hitler's treacherous 1941 attack:

> Ever louder ring the voices raised in defense of peace, ever wider spreads the mighty movement of the masses against the aggressors and warmongers and on behalf of national independence and peaceful cooperation among nations. The time has passed when the imperialists could hatch war in profound secrecy, and when war burst suddenly on the peoples, who found themselves faced with the fact that hostilities had already begun.

The mighty movement for peace testifies that the peoples constitute a force capable of curbing the aggressors.

To be sure, the peace movement alone could not keep the peace, especially since its own successes drove "the warmongers to increasing frenzy." Other measures were needed to deter them—measures like the Soviets' own military and industrial remobilization, like the development and testing of a Soviet atomic bomb, like the psychological tactic used in Malenkov's own speech. "Let nobody think we are scared by the warmongers' sabre-rattling," he proclaimed. "It is not we but the imperialists and aggressors that should be afraid of war. . . . Can there be any doubt that if the imperialists unleash a third world war, it will mean the grave not of individual capitalist states but of the whole of world capitalism?"[28]

How confident *were* the Soviets? Was it possible that Malenkov was feigning optimism—just as he accused Western leaders of doing? There are no certain answers. One must rely on circumstantial evidence—evidence as intangible as the impression Ambassador Kirk drew from a diplomatic reception the day following Malenkov's address. It was an impression of cocky self-satisfaction exemplified by Marshal Vasily Sokolovsky's and Deputy Foreign Minister Andrei Gromyko's condescending references to the meager American war effort against Hitler.[29] There was also evidence as important as that suggested by the Soviet role in the Korean war.

Recall the Korean situation in the summer of 1947. The Soviets were being reasonable; they seemed eager for some sort of accord with the Americans. But when détente broke down in Europe, the Korean talks quickly deadlocked, and before long the Americans and South Koreans were unknowingly inviting a North Korean attack. In early 1950, Washington seemed to assume that Korea could not or should not be defended by American forces. But that judgment changed in a hurry on June 25, 1950; suddenly it seemed vital that the North Koreans be repulsed. The Soviets must have felt betrayed by Washington's sudden shift. For all his suspiciousness, we have here another instance of Stalin's counting on the Americans not to oppose him. Once again he underestimated their resolve to resist. It was not he, however, but the Americans, Chinese, and most of all the Koreans, who paid the price of that resistance.

The politics of Korea in the late 1940s were bizarre. General John Hodge considered Syngman Rhee a semi-rational megalomaniac. Rhee thought Hodge a virtual Russian stooge. The American political adviser in Korea, Joseph E. Jacobs, warned of a North-South conflict as early as 1947, but he also thought the United States could avoid involvement by getting out before the blow-up occurred. The American joint chiefs of staff concluded that Korea was not vital to American military security. Even Rhee himself, though he blew hot and cold on the subject, agreed that the United States could safely leave the South Koreans to their own devices.[30]

Add to this fermenting brew the actions of America's allies and of the United Nations. In the eyes of the international community (which does not really exist but is assumed to have eyes), Korea was to be unified and governed under the auspices of the United Nations. Washington soon despaired of unification on acceptable terms but, nonetheless, supported creation of the United Nations Temporary Commission on Korea (UNTCOK) as a means of restraining the North. Instead, UNTCOK became a forum in which supposedly friendly Canadian, Australian, and other delegates criticized American and South Korean policies. By this time (1948), the British, Chinese (Nationalists), and Japanese were also warning of a coming explosion, but the U.S. Army wanted out of Korea (both because "the U.S. has little strategic interest in maintaining troops and bases in Korea" and for fear that American strength there was so puny as to constitute a "military liability rather than an asset . . . in the event of major attack") and, of course, convinced itself there was no need to stay.[31]

By June 1950 all was in readiness. American troops were out. Dean Acheson had publicly excluded Korea from America's Pacific defense perimeter. United States Senator Tom Connally had stated in a U.S. News and World Report interview, that South Korea was being written off. American ambassador to Korea, John Muccio, complained to Assistant Secretary of State Dean Rusk on May 25 that Korea was "very frequently omitted" from "public statements attributed to the President, the Secretary or other high Government officials in which various countries [were] named as special objects of United States interest and concern."[32]

Why did the North Koreans, with Soviet blessing, attack South Korea? The more appropriate question, or so it must have appeared to Stalin, was: Why not? Nikita Khrushchev recalls that Moscow anticipated an easy victory. According to Khrushchev, Kim Il-sung initiated the idea and assured Stalin that a mere "poke" across the border would prompt the South Koreans to rise in revolution. Stalin had his doubts, reports Khrushchev, but did not try to dissuade Kim. The Soviets concluded that "if the war were fought swiftly—and Kim Il-sung assured [the Soviets] it could be won swiftly—then [U.S.] intervention could be avoided." Another aspect of the plan that, according to Khrushchev, appealed to Stalin was that "the struggle would be an internal matter that the Koreans would be settling among themselves." Or, as George Kennan put it in 1952, the Soviets might have considered "successful instigation of a civil war in a third country" to be within the rules of the game: that is, a "perfectly fair and acceptable political expedient which anyone was entitled to get away with if he had the skill and enterprise to do so."[33]

Yet, rulers, unlike mountain climbers, do not attack simply because their targets are there. Rulers have reasons; in the case of Korea, they may have involved Soviet calculations about Japan and China. Japan seemed a sideshow in the late 1940s. While Washington leisurely contemplated its peace treaty options in 1948, the Soviets' most potent weapon was propaganda potshots in the Far Eastern Advisory Commission and the Allied Council for Japan. The sizable Soviet mission in Tokyo (the fact that it numbered five hundred as compared with ninety-five Chinese and sixty-five British was justified by, among other things, the Soviets' alleged need for Russian cooks to save them from unfamiliar Japanese food) cultivated and manipulated the Japanese Communist party. But the Russians could not gain much ground in Japan as long as Douglas MacArthur treated them as pests, brushing off their charges with contempt and denying them room to maneuver in Japanese politics.[34]

As late as 1949, Washington was still not sure what sort of Japanese peace treaty it wanted, when it wanted it, and by whom it wanted the document drafted and ratified. But the Americans were sure of one thing—they wanted to deny a significant voice in the process to the USSR. *"By the middle of February 1950 at the latest,"* argues Kennan, emphasizing the time factor since it bears on the question of how much Stalin knew when he authorized Kim Il-sung to move South, "it was clear to all responsible people in Moscow (1) that the treaty for which the State Department was angling was to be a separate one (unless the Russians wished to adhere to something they had never approved and to which they had not been invited to adhere); (2) that this treaty was to mark, or be accompanied by, an arrangement that would turn Japan into a permanent military ally of the United States; (3) that the arrangement would provide for the continued use of the Japanese archipelago by American armed forces for an indefinite period to come; and (4) that

the remaining differences of opinion within the official American establishment in this matter were ones that might at best delay, but would
not prevent, the ultimate realization of such a program." This sort of
reasoning leads Kennan, Shulman, and others to a formulation of Moscow's "Japanese reasons" for approving the North Korean invasion—
that is, the interpretation that Moscow wanted to shock the Japanese
into a neutralist stance, or, if a pro-Western alignment could not be
prevented, to eliminate the Western presence on the strategic Korean
Peninsula and replace it with Communist control of all Korea.[35]

There may have been a China connection, too. Unfortunately,
Sino-Soviet-American relations *circa* 1950 are as unclear now as they
were important then. Some historians think the United States missed a
chance for an accommodation with China that might have altered the
shape of world politics. Whether or not China and the United States
could have reached a mutual accord, the Soviets might have feared it—
and seen the Korean adventure as a way to prevent it. More likely,
U.S.–Chinese tensions were a welcome consequence of the war rather
than a reason for starting it. Once the war was on, in any case, Peking's
role in it became decisive. The upshot was to poison all three relationships—Sino-American, Soviet-American, and even Sino-Soviet.[36]

If Stalin expected a quick victory, he was wrong. The Americans
had not thought Korea all that important, but the Soviet-supported
invasion of June 25, viewed through the lens of the Hitler analogy,
made it so. The Truman administration moved decisively, both in the
United Nations and on the battlefield. Although thrown back at first,
by autumn UN troops had crossed the 38th parallel into North Korea
and approached the Chinese border. The Soviet reaction to all this
confirms the view that Stalin was confident that general war could be
avoided—in part by revealing exceptions that prove that rule.

The Americans were not so confident. They assumed general war
a distinct possibility, and assumed Stalin thought so too. George Kennan, who came to share this alarm, especially when American planes
attacked close to the Soviet frontier, finds support for his image of Stalin
in documents published in 1970. The documents concern Stalin's
effort in January 1951 to persuade Togliatti to head the Cominform
and, in that connection, to take up residence in a Communist country.
Stalin cited tension between East and West and said that he thought
the danger of general war was real and imminent. Certain Soviet moves
in June and October 1950 did betray intense Kremlin nervousness. But
on the whole, Soviet diplomacy displayed remarkable cool. It seems

that by mid-1951, if not before, the most serious Soviet fears had subsided.[37]

Soviet behavior following June 25 was consistent with either of two opposite interpretations—either the Kremlin was lying low and anticipating a quick North Korean victory, or it was in shock at signs that Washington intended to resist. The American ambassador tried five times on June 27 to arrange an appointment with Gromyko. (Vyshinsky, like Molotov at the start of the Berlin crisis, was said to be out of town.) When Kirk finally saw Gromyko on June 29, the latter read a prepared statement rejecting American protests and then refused to discuss the matter further. The Soviets (having walked out earlier in protest over the non-seating of China) contended that the UN Security Council could not act in their absence and were taken aback when the Indian government charged that the Soviet walkout itself had violated the UN Charter. On July 6, Gromyko summoned the British ambassador and explored with him London's suggestion that the Soviets persuade the North Koreans to respect the cease-fire that the UN had demanded and to retreat to the 38th parallel. Gromyko said his government also wished for a peaceful settlement, and to the British call for a return to the *status quo ante*, he reportedly "nodded assent."[38]

This was not much to go on. It might have been a device for deflecting the Western reaction to the North Korean attack. But even the cynical American embassy thought Gromyko's "peace-feeler" was "genuine." The embassy thought the Soviets had concluded that the outcome in Korea could not be favorable to their cause, that they therefore wished "to localize the affair," and that they were trying "to salvage as much prestige as possible." Back in Washington, Bohlen's impression was that the Soviets were "serious" and wished "to find some means of terminating a situation which obviously has taken a turn unanticipated by them." But he also warned that "this Soviet desire is not unlimited." This analysis was correct. Both in June and October, Moscow might have offered concessions to terminate a misadventure but not the concessions the Americans were asking. Washington was determined not to yield on any important matter—such as seating China in the United Nations or turning over Taiwan to Peking—in order to get the North Koreans to cease their aggression. It was "imperative," Acheson wrote to Bevin on July 10, "that the Soviets not be paid any price whatever for calling off an attack which they never should have started." Only after the North Koreans moved out could other discussions begin.[39]

Meanwhile, as the British were pressing for a North Korean pullback *sans* preconditions, the Indian government leaped in with another proposal. Prime Minister Nehru suggested (1) that America support Chinese Communist entry into the United Nations, and (2) that the Security Council, with China now on it, support an immediate cease-fire in Korea and withdrawal of Northern troops. The two points formed a package; the first would take effect only if the Soviets accepted the second. To the Americans it seemed as though the Indian *démarche* distorted the soundings the British were taking. Nor was this attitude altered by the news that Soviet and Chinese reactions to the Indian proposal diverged dramatically: Peking reportedly "agreed to both points"; the Soviets would not accept the second. As New Delhi pointed out, American acceptance of both points would split Peking and Moscow. Nor would the United States actually have to support Chinese admission into the United Nations; "abstention," said an Indian official, "coupled with a friendly word to Ecuador and Cuba would probably do just as well."[40]

London might have been tempted, but Washington was not. The Americans hewed to their hard line. And by mid-July, the Soviets matched them. By this time, Stalin had good cause to regain his composure—if, indeed, he had lost it in June. Not only were the North Koreans winning big on the ground, but the Americans were quarreling about peace terms with the British and the Indians as well as with the Soviets. No wonder that on July 15 Gromyko insisted that the prerequisite for a Korean solution was the withdrawal of *American* troops, and that a day later Stalin informed Nehru that another precondition was Chinese membership in the United Nations plus a hearing before the Security Council of "representatives of the Korean people." To make matters worse in Washington's eyes, Nehru found Stalin's reply "most encouraging."[41]

Still, the Kremlin left the door open for a possible retreat—in a typically backhanded Soviet way. It happened when an American correspondent tried to transmit the news that the Soviets would accept no Korean solution that did not provide for seating Peking in the United Nations. Soviet censors deleted this reference. When the newsman rewrote his piece to report that "the way to peacefully settling [the] Korean question [is] not completely closed," that, indeed, as far as Moscow was concerned the door remained open, the dispatch was passed by the censors.[42]

Washington, meanwhile, was debating American war aims. The

major question was how far UN troops should go once they regained the offensive. Some officials feared that an incursion into North Korea would provoke either a Chinese or a joint Sino-Soviet counterattack, and so advocated stopping at the 38th parallel. Others, like John Allison, director of the State Department's Office of Northeast Asian Affairs, warned against "a timid, half-hearted policy designed not to provoke the Soviets to war." Allison failed to see "what advantage we gain by compromise with clear moral principles and a shirking of our duty to make clear once and for all that aggression does not pay—that . . . he who takes the sword will perish by the sword." That "this may mean war on a global scale" was no reason to shrink from it. "When all legal and moral right is on our side why should we hesitate?"[43]

The Soviets knew an American drive into North Korea was not only a possibility but perhaps even a probability. That may explain why Moscow opened the door to a peaceful settlement a bit wider in late July. Soviet UN Representative Malik resumed his seat and even assumed the Security Council presidency for the month of August, this despite the non-fulfillment of that apparent precondition for his return—the admission of the People's Republic of China. Two weeks later, American B-29s bombed the North Korean port of Rashin within seventeen miles of the frontier and not far from the Soviet naval base at Vladivostok. Whereupon Malik seemed to take a step through the door he had opened. He announced Soviet readiness to put aside for the time being its objections to the UN resolution of June 25, which had formally condemned the North Korean invasion and authorized the UN's armed response. He also withdrew Stalin's suggestion that representatives of "the Korean people" be invited to the United Nations and proposed instead that both South and North Korean governments send delegates. If these were small steps forward, Vyshinsky seemed to go backward when, in early September, he insisted that the United States rather than the United Nations accept a protest against the shooting down of a Soviet plane off the Korean coast. But this may have been Moscow's way of saying that since the Korean conflict now threatened a direct Soviet-American confrontation, Russians and Americans ought to talk directly about ending it—an interpretation supported by the fact that Gromyko went through the same procedure in October when the Soviets were exploring, via another equally indirect route, the possibility of a compromise Korean settlement.[44]

On September 15, 1950, General Douglas MacArthur's troops turned the tide of war by landing at Inchon, deep behind North Korean lines. On September 25, a British UN draft resolution proposed that "(a) all necessary steps be taken to insure conditions of enduring peace throughout *the whole of Korea*, (b) that elections be held . . . under the auspices of the United Nations to complete the establishment of a unified, independent and democratic Government of *all Korea*, and (c) that any United Nations forces entering North Korea do not remain otherwise than so far as necessary for achieving the objectives specified in (a) and (b) above." (Emphases added.) About the same time, the American joint chiefs of staff drafted presidential instructions to General MacArthur naming as his objective "the destruction of the North Korean armed forces" and authorizing him to conduct military operations north of the 38th parallel except along Soviet and Manchurian borders—provided that there was no threat of Soviet or Chinese counteraction. Meanwhile, Chinese troops were preparing for just such counteraction—which Peking had warned the Indians was coming, but which Dean Acheson refused to expect. The secretary pointed out to British officials that "the Chinese Communists were taking no risk inasmuch as their private talks to the Indian ambassador could be disavowed, that they had not made any statement directly to the United Nations, . . . and [that] if they wanted to take part in the 'poker game' they would have to put more on the table than they had up to the present."[45]

Moscow presumably knew what Peking was about to put on the table. If a Sino-American war remained limited, the Soviets could live with it and even profit from it. But what if, despite the odds against general war, the conflict spread beyond Korea and involved the Soviet Union itself? On September 26, Malik expressed publicly his government's interest in high-level Soviet-American talks. In response, a State Department spokesman demanded "deeds not words" to secure peace in Korea. On October 2, Malik submitted a UN draft resolution calling for a cease-fire, the withdrawal of American and other foreign troops, and the holding of free, all-Korean elections to be arranged by a joint North-South commission, and observed by a UN committee "with the indispensable participation in it of representatives of states [guess who!] bordering on Korea." The proposal was obviously booby-trapped. But given the Kremlin's habit of opening negotiations with extreme demands, Malik's terms were not ungenerous. Still, the prior problem was how to get the Americans to talk at all without the Soviets' having to humiliate themselves in the process. Moscow's solution, an old favorite still in use in the 1970s according to Henry Kissinger, was the

round-about approach. Its great advantage is that it can easily be disavowed if it comes to nought. The drawback is that it is likely to come
to nought because it can be so readily dismissed. The October 1950
version worked this way:[46] Vasily Kasaniev, a Soviet employee of the
United Nation's Trusteeship Division, invited Hans Engen, who was a
casual acquaintance of his and a member of the Norwegian UN Delegation, to lunch on October 4. The Russian asked what the Norwegian
Delegation thought about the Soviets' October 2 draft resolution.
Engen replied that the demand for withdrawal of American troops
showed the Soviets' "insincerity." Kasaniev answered that the eight-
power resolution (a slightly milder version of the British September 25
draft) would permit American troops to occupy North Korea, something
that the Russians could not abide; it was a question of not only their
"security," but also their prestige and their standing in the eyes of
"neighboring states."

Suppose, said Engen, the Americans stayed only long enough to
defeat the North Koreans and then gave way to Asian troops (Indian or
Pakistani, for example), who would occupy the North. This was a
wholly new idea to Kasaniev, who seemed to assume, Engen said later,
that the United States wanted to occupy North Korea permanently.
Kasaniev was so excited he "paled visibly." He asked Engen to repeat
this new scenario and then asked whether or not he, Kasaniev, might
repeat it to Vyshinsky. After that, Kasaniev outlined what the Russians
wanted: "MacArthur should agree to stop at the 38th parallel. The
North Koreans would then lay down their arms, and, third, a United
Nations Commission would be allowed to go into North Korea to hold
elections" as well as "to see to it that the surrender terms were
observed."

These terms conceded more than the *status quo ante bellum*. They
constituted a better deal than the Americans eventually achieved after
fighting their way to the Chinese border, being driven back into South
Korea by Chinese troops, scraping their way up to the 38th parallel,
and then negotiating, while sporadic fighting continued, for two more
years. To be sure, Kasaniev was a low-level official—of the United
Nations secretariat, not even of the Soviet government. But his position
was not quite as low as it seemed; he had been Soviet consul general in
New York and then a member of the Soviet UN Delegation. Furthermore, Engen, who had once been foreign editor of an Oslo newspaper,
had a history of being approached by the Russians when they had sensitive messages for his close friend, the Norwegian foreign minister.

The fact that Kasaniev himself had easy access to Vyshinsky (Engen saw the two conferring in the corridor immediately after lunch) confirmed that something potentially big was up.

The very next day, October 5, Kasaniev invited Engen to have lunch with him again on October 6. When that meeting failed to come off due to confusion about where they were to meet, Kasaniev sought Engen out later in the afternoon to report both Vyshinsky's "very great interest" in their previous conversation and the foreign minister's regret that he had not heard earlier about the idea of Asian troops occupying North Korea. Given the certain adoption by the General Assembly of the eight-power resolution, Vyshinsky said the question was "finished as far as the UN was concerned," the clear implication being, Engen thought, that "the Russians want negotiations outside the UN," that they are in "a bad way" about Korea and "want to reach the best settlement they can."

Engen kept American diplomats informed of his conversations with Kasaniev. When, therefore, the two met again on October 7, the very day the General Assembly adopted the eight-power resolution while rejecting two Soviet draft resolutions, Engen was armed with the Americans' conviction that the whole Kasaniev affair was a Soviet maneuver designed to suspend UN military operations and thus to give the North Koreans a badly needed respite. "If the Russians were really interested in getting us out of Korea," went Washington's message to Moscow (which Engen was not even authorized to admit came from Washington), "the best way would be for the Koreans to lay down their arms. Otherwise . . . we would be likely to get further and further involved." Furthermore, "since the Russians do not believe public statements made by us . . . what sort of assurances would they need?"

Negotiations never got as far as assurances because they never really began. As Engen pointed out to his American contact, there were two things that the Soviets wanted to avoid: the continued presence of American forces in North Korea and the liquidation of the North Korean regime. The first issue might have been susceptible to a compromise involving Asian troops. The second was not—if only because after all their experience with Communist regimes preparing "free" elections, the Americans would not have trusted the North Koreans not to prevail, even in the presence of a United Nations commission and non-Communist Asian troops.

Kasaniev suggested on October 7 that he and Engen meet again later in the week. But by the time they did, General MacArthur's troops had been sent into North Korea with orders to fight even "major Chinese Communist units," should they appear, as long as in his judgment, his forces had "a reasonable chance of success." On the same day, in Moscow, Gromyko "mystified" the American ambassador by attempting for a second time to present the Americans with a protest that properly should have been addressed to the United Nations. Admiral Kirk need not have been so puzzled. Moscow was emphasizing the fact that U.S.–Soviet relations were at issue in Korea—but not, this time, with an eye to opening talks. It was too late for that. When Engen and Kasaniev met on October 10, Vyshinsky sent thanks to Engen for communicating his interesting views.[47]

The rest of the Korean story, and indeed of Soviet diplomacy in 1951 and 1952, may be briefly summarized. The Americans blindly pressed northward in Korea. The Chinese intervened—in small numbers as early as October 15, in full force on November 26. With UN forces retreating in disarray, the Soviet line hardened. The Chinese, with Soviet support, demanded withdrawal of UN troops from Korea, evacuation of the Seventh Fleet from the Formosa Straits (where President Truman had placed it following the North Korean attack), and seating of Peking in the United Nations. Washington insisted that the United Nations formally find Peking guilty of aggression—which even the British resisted doing for fear of providing General MacArthur with a UN–approved license to attack China itself. Even the top man in the Kremlin must have been nervous, with his easy proxy victory now threatening to become World War III.

Yet this cloud too, like so many that we have observed darkening the Soviet horizon, had a silver lining. The British-American rift over Korean tactics was widening. The American stance also alarmed moderate Arab and Asian states. President Truman sounded tougher than ever, but he could be deterred, or so the Soviets seemed to think, by the popular antipathy to war—on which Stalin had counted all along. On February 16, 1951, Stalin told *Pravda* that "at the present time [a new world war] cannot be regarded as inevitable." To be sure, there were "aggressive forces thirsting for war," but they were "afraid of their peoples who do not want war. . . ." Peace would be "preserved and strengthened" if the peoples took the cause into their own hands and defended it "to the end." This was "the reason why the broad campaign for the preservation of peace [had become] of paramount importance."[48]

By late spring the Chinese advance had been stopped, a military equilibrium reestablished in the vicinity of the 38th parallel, and Douglas MacArthur fired. The way was now open for Soviet UN Ambassador Malik to repeat his Berlin blockade performance by hinting at Soviet readiness for Korean peace talks. Such talks soon opened, and although they were to drag on for another two years, other things were virtually back to normal. In October, Admiral Kirk again assured the Soviet foreign minister that the United States nourished "no aggressive designs" on the USSR, in response to which Vyshinsky characterized the United States as "anxious for the outcome of the military gamble it had undertaken in Korea" and, therefore, interested in "the question of improving relations between [the] two countries." The Soviets still mixed belligerent protests with invitations to negotiate on Germany and Japan. When such invitations were accepted (if only to show Western willingness to talk), Soviet negotiators proved half-hearted and ineffective— which, in a sense, was all they needed to be. When the West was sufficiently divided, as on the question of German rearmament and integration in NATO, the Soviets did not need to be effective; when the West was more or less united, as on the issue of the Japanese Peace Treaty, the Soviets could not be effective. The talks on the German question that took place in the spring of 1951 were the most fruitless yet; negotiators failed even to reach agreement on an agenda. Andrei Gromyko so "undistinguished" himself at a September conference held to conclude the Japanese Peace Treaty that the wonder was why he had bothered to come at all.[49]

By 1952 the Cold War was in a deep, dark rut. Faced with plans for a European Defense Community with West German participation, Moscow at last came up with a more interesting German offer—in fact, one that rivalled its most enticing proposals of the pre-1949 period. The Soviets offered reunification of Germany following free elections to be supervised by the four occupying powers and, for the first time, indicated willingness to see Germany rearmed provided that it agreed to remain neutral. Was Stalin really prepared to abandon East Germany? Washington did not trust the Soviets to let things come out that way, nor would it have necessarily wanted that result even if Moscow had allowed it. This time, the Soviet proposal died without even a preliminary conference.[50]

Nineteen fifty-two was also the year of Stalin's political testament as revealed in his book, *Economic Problems of Socialism in the U.S.S.R.* The book was actually a series of articles and other pro-

nouncements (some of them written in 1951) mostly on economic subjects. Yet *Economic Problems of Socialism* reveals the assumptions
behind Moscow's post-1949 foreign policy and, in particular, behind
Stalin's confidence that come what may, general war itself probably
would not.

Stalin's testament chastised his followers for failing to understand
his teaching. He accused them of interpreting him (and Marx and
Lenin) too literally. Stalin was reminding them of the brutal realism,
that blend of belief and cynicism, that was the hallmark of not only his
economics but his foreign policy as well. Consider Stalin's injunctions
on several seemingly arcane theoretical issues. Regarding the issue of
"scientific economic laws," Stalin inveighed against idealists who imagined that the Soviet regime could do "anything," that everything was
"child's play" to it, and that it could "destroy scientific laws and establish new ones." Such comrades were "deeply mistaken." Concerning
"the question of commodity production [the production of goods for
purchase and sale in the market] under Socialism," both optimists who
thought socialism meant the end of commodity production and pessi-
mists who saw no change from capitalism were "deeply mistaken,"
indeed, "completely wrong." On "The Law of Value Under Socialism," once more Stalin steered a realistic middle course between those
who said the law did not apply to Soviet socialism and those contending
it had the same scope there as it did under capitalism. Regarding "The
Antithesis Between Town and Country and Between Mental and Man-
ual Labor," Stalin said that comrades who suggested such differences
would be completely eliminated under socialism "must be basing their
stand [on] certain of my statements. . . ." If so, continued the eminent
author, his own formulation "was not precise, was unsatisfactory."

Stalin's modesty was, of course, false. And it was in the same spirit
of benevolent contempt that Stalin treated his followers to a rundown
of his main foreign policy assumptions. These, too, seem abstract and
doctrinaire. But their implications are concrete and important. Stalin
repeated what he had told his constituents in February 1946—that the
Second World War both resulted from and intensified capitalism's
crises. The "most important economic result" of the war was "the disintegration of the single, all-embracing world market"; the disintegration was further aggravated when China and the East European people's
democracies "broke away from the capitalist system and, together with
the Soviet Union, formed a unified and powerful socialist camp," so
that now there were "two parallel world markets also confronting each

other." Moreover, the capitalist states had unwittingly strengthened their rivals. Imperialist attempts to "blockade" and to "strangle" the people's democracies had forced them to rely on their own, and especially the Soviet Union's, resources. The result was that "it will soon come to pass that these countries will not only be in no need of imports from capitalist countries, but will themselves find it necessary to export their surplus products."

The revelation in this was that Stalin assumed the West was still suffering from its lack of economic access to the East. Western "opportunities for sale in the world market will deteriorate" even further, he predicted, and "their industries will more and more be operating below capacity." But even more revealing was Stalin's contention that it had been "to overcome these [economic] difficulties," that the capitalists had embarked on the Marshall Plan, the war in Korea, and the "arms race and industrial militarization." The idea that Western militarization was primarily a response to capitalism's internal difficulties, rather than a means of coping with the "Soviet threat," suggested that the imperialists did not want a war with the USSR after all; it was one thing for the capitalists to build themselves up under the guise of preparing for war, and quite another to risk all they built up in a war with a newly strengthened Soviet bloc. But had not Stalin himself been assuming that war was sooner or later inevitable?

Some comrades, their great teacher continued, believed war was no longer inevitable. They were, of course, wrong. War remained inevitable. "To eliminate the inevitability of war, it is necessary to destroy imperialism." *But what kind of war did Stalin have in mind?* The answer which is crucial to understanding Stalin's American policy, was "wars *between capitalist countries*." (Emphasis added.) Some comrades thought "that the contradictions between the socialist camp and the capitalist camp are more powerful than contradictions among the capitalist countries; that the USA has sufficiently subordinated the other capitalist countries to be able to prevent them from going to war among themselves and weakening one another; that the leaders of capitalism have been sufficiently taught by the two world wars and the serious harm they did to the whole capitalist world not to allow themselves once more to involve their countries in war with each other; and that, in view of all this, wars between capitalist countries have ceased to be inevitable." But such comrades were naïve. They saw only "the outward phenomena which come and go on the surface." Outwardly, things seemed to be going well for the West. But "it would be incorrect to think that things can continue to 'go well' for 'all eternity.' . . ." Long before that, Britain and France would "break from the embrace of the USA and enter into conflict with it in order to guarantee themselves an independent position and, of course, higher profits." To think that West Germany and Japan, now "languishing in misery under the jackboot of American imperialism . . . , will not try to rise to their feet again, will not try to smash the U.S. 'regime,' and blast their way to independent development, is to believe in miracles."

What, then, about the contradictions between capitalism and socialism, between East and West? Were they not in fact more acute than any inter-imperialist tensions? "Theoretically, of course," Stalin answered his own questions, "that is true." But the capitalists knew very well that "war with the USSR, as a socialist country, is more dangerous to capitalism than war between capitalist countries; for whereas war between capitalist countries poses only the question of the supremacy of certain capitalist countries over others, a war with the USSR would surely pose the question about the continued existence of capitalism itself." And what's more, the capitalists also knew, despite all the noise about the "Soviet threat," that the USSR would not attack them: ". . . although they clamour for 'propaganda' purposes about the aggressiveness of the Soviet Union, the capitalists themselves do not believe that it is aggressive, because they take account of the Soviet Union's peaceful policy and knew that the Soviet Union will not itself attack the capitalist countries."[51]

Eureka! Here was a clear indication that Stalin's propaganda about Western warmongering *was* mainly that, that he had assumed all along that Western alarms about the Soviet threat were as exaggerated as his own about the danger of American armed aggression. One might object that this, too, was propaganda rather than an indication of Stalin's true thinking. There is no way to prove the point beyond doubt. But it fits the pattern of Soviet foreign policy—a pattern of cautious but persistent probing that was only safe if the Americans were not spoiling for a fight. This is not to say that Stalin always kept his cool. But for the most part, the lens through which Stalin viewed capitalist statesmen provided reassurance. Why was Washington exaggerating the danger of Soviet aggression? To dominate their allies, to justify foreign expansion, and only last, and in some ways least, to intimidate the Soviet opposition. Why then did Stalin exaggerate the American threat? To turn the capitalists' propaganda against them by alarming Western peoples and thus attracting them into the pro-Soviet peace movement, whose object, Stalin wrote in *Economic Problems of Socialism*, was "to rouse the masses of the people to fight for the preservation of peace and the prevention of another world war."[52]

The situation is full of ironies. Washington took Stalin's accusations too seriously and suspected his assurances. The Americans resisted Soviet pressures politically and then militarily, but they also tried to convince Stalin of what he already suspected, namely, that the West was not hankering for a war. And that confirmed his view that as hostile as the capitalists were, they could also be manipulated. All of which recalls the Soviet-American entente of World War II. Then, too, the Americans struck Stalin as simultaneously dangerous and innocent. Then, too, his image of them reflected both his ideological assumptions and his own Soviet experience. As for the Americans, they were also consistent, in the sense that they went from one extreme to the other. Confronted in 1941 with a strange and difficult Soviet ally, they determined to think the best of the USSR. A decade later, the former would-be angel had become a devil, as malevolent as he had once been benign. The one thing that Americans, with important exceptions like George Kennan, could not conceive of, was what the Soviets actually were—allies who assumed ultimate enmity and plotted accordingly—and what they later became—enemies who did not assume that enmity necessarily meant war.

None of this is to say that the Cold War was a mistake, or to put it more formally, primarily a product of misperceptions. Cassandras on both sides were right; men like Hopkins and Litvinov underestimated the potential for trouble. But while some conflict was inevitable given East-West differences (in political and economic systems, in interests and ideologies), misperception aggravated and intensified the tension—misperception that often took the form of each side's projecting onto the other a warped image of itself.

On Christmas Day, 1952, Joseph Stalin sent greetings to the United States in the form of replies to James Reston's written questions. On the eve of a new American administration, Stalin found the sources of international tension "everywhere and in everything, wherever the aggressive actions of the 'cold war' against the Soviet Union find their expression." Yet he also insisted that war between the United States and the Soviet Union could not be considered "inevitable." Would he welcome conversations looking toward a meeting with General Eisenhower? Stalin replied that he "would regard such a suggestion favorably."[53]

Three months later Joseph Stalin was dead. A new era of hope, hope for moving from Cold War to détente and perhaps even beyond, was at hand.

After Stalin:
To Brezhnev and Beyond

IMAGINE THE SCENARIO SKETCHED IN CHAPTER ONE DEVELOPING SOME-
thing like this: Confronted with the new hard line in Washington, the
Soviets urge the Americans to return to détente. Moscow insists that the
"situation" in Afghanistan must not be permitted to poison the Soviet-
American relationship on which the peace of the world depends. The
same goes, of course, in Moscow's view, for any Soviet crackdown on
Poland "required" by the process of "counterrevolution" underway in
that keystone of the USSR's East European realm. But the Americans,
led by a new, anti-Communist president, will not oblige. Certain East-
West negotiations continue (primarily at the insistence of the West
Europeans), but this is a dialogue of the deaf. The U.S. administration
makes no serious attempt to learn what price (if any) the Soviets will
pay to ward off a new cold war. Considering any such payment to be
counterfeit, and almost grateful for the opportunity to mobilize the
West for a new round of containment, the Americans step up the pressure on the Kremlin. They launch an accelerated arms build-up in the
expectation that the smaller Soviet economy will be incapable of
matching it. They call upon NATO to close ranks and offer American
assistance to any (well almost any) Third World government that claims
to be resisting Communist aggression. They cut back trade and other
economic, scientific, and cultural contacts with the USSR. They move
to strengthen Moscow's eastern nemesis, China, by supplying the
Chinese with extensive military equipment, which American officials
emphasize is strictly defensive in nature.

This combination of moves plays the fateful role in the 1980s that
the Marshall Plan did in 1947. The Marshall Plan, along with the
Czechs' and Poles' reaction to it, threatened to unravel Moscow's hard-

won domination of Eastern Europe. Polish developments in the 1980s pose the same ominous prospect. American military assistance to China confronts the Soviets with threats on two fronts. A U. S. arms build-up coupled with a trade cut-back force the Russians to produce more guns *and* butter at a time when their domestic resources are stretched thin and getting thinner. In the face of rising tensions, some Americans play down the danger. They say that serious economic difficulties at home, and the morass Moscow faces in Afghanistan and Eastern Europe, mean that the Soviets cannot afford to respond in kind to American pressure. They say the worst that can happen is a confrontation or two, after which the Russians will accept a new, and this time "genuine," détente (meaning that at last the Kremlin will pull in its expansionist horns) in order to reduce the burden of military spending as well as the risk of war. But the Soviets have other ideas. They are determined not to concede the military superiority that Washington seems to be seeking. They count on the traditional submissiveness of the Soviet people to sustain a new round of national sacrifice. To justify that sacrifice, Soviet leaders point to the deteriorating international situation. Washington may have calculated that new East-West strains will unite the fractious Western alliance, but the Soviets mean to divide the capitalist camp by coupling counter-pressure of their own with a peace offensive aimed at the nervous West Europeans and Japanese.

Where to apply that counter-pressure? East Europe—Poland in particular, but post-Tito Yugoslavia too—is an obvious candidate for Moscow's new and more bitter medicine. A more formidable opponent, but not entirely out of the question, is China. One way to settle accounts with China would be to incinerate Chinese nuclear installations. Or, after threatening an attack, the Russians might make the Chinese an offer they cannot refuse—say, the division of Southeast Asia into Chinese and Soviet spheres of influence. Nineteen forty-seven is not the only apt analogy. Nineteen thirty-nine (with the Soviets playing the part of the Nazis and the Chinese filling Moscow's former role) has possibilities, too. Yet another region for a Soviet show of force is the Persian Gulf. With Iran continuing to disintegrate, Soviet troops could reoccupy the positions in Azerbaijan that Stalin abandoned so reluctantly in 1946, and even move down to seize Iran's oil fields. Or, Moscow could sponsor rebellions by Baluchi tribesmen in Pakistan and Iran, rebellions designed to carve out a new People's Republic of Baluchistan with a port (Gwadar) on the Arabian Sea. This project could humble Pakistan's Chinese and American allies without confronting them with the use of force by Soviet troops. It could provide a buffer for beleagured Afghanistan while positioning Moscow to reach for Persian Gulf oil either to meet its own needs or to hold the West hostage, or both. With any of these moves, Cold War II would be on in earnest. Except that this time—in a world of massive nuclear arsenals on both sides, disarray in both superpower blocs, and turmoil in the Third World—it might lead to a global nuclear conflagration.[1]

This nightmare could begin to come true tomorrow. And it will not lose its menace even if the hot spots of the early 1980s cool down. For Stalin's death did not usher in a transition from cold war to détente and beyond. Several times since 1953 a new era of good feeling has appeared ready to crystallize only to dissolve in renewed tension. And since there is every likelihood that this oscillation will continue, the major question of this chapter—whether or not patterns of the 1940s still apply—will in all probability be asked again and again.

But there are prior questions. Why should history repeat itself at all? Have not the Soviet Union and its foreign policy changed fundamentally since Stalin's death? Have not the United States and the world at large changed too? How can one apply lessons of Stalin's American policy to the final two decades of the twentieth century?

These are legitimate questions. To try to answer them fully would require another volume (or two) on post-Stalin developments—for which the kind of direct documentary evidence I have relied on for this present volume is not yet available. What follows are preliminary answers developed in two different ways: first, sketches of four post-1953 periods that reveal a pattern all too reminiscent of the Stalinist years; then, consideration of important changes that have and have *not* occurred in the Soviet Union since Stalin's death.

The post-1953 pattern is the following: Stalin's successors have pursued détente for offensively defensive reasons; like him, they have undermined their own strategy by alarming those whom they are seeking to soothe. As in the 1940s, American presidents have managed to manifest both innocence and intransigence—thus tempting and threatening the Soviets at the same time. Moreover, the Americans have put the Soviets in their own double bind by interpreting Soviet concessions as tricks or signs of weakness and Soviet refusal to concede as confirmation of the menace Moscow represents. But the American catch-22 is different. It has been neither as uniform nor as unchanging as its Soviet counterpart. It has characterized a portion of American opinion but not all of it. Many important politicians, including practically every post-1953 president, have forgotten at one time or another what the Soviets have not—namely, that the other side is by its very nature the enemy and will ever remain so. Recent American administrations have attempted the kind of deliberate mixing of cooperation and competition, of carrot and stick, which Roosevelt and Truman never tried. But the result has been, in part as a result of American failings, a new *triple* bind. Damned if you conciliate, damned if you resist, and damned if you do both simultaneously.

When Stalin died on March 5, 1953, his successors appealed for "the prevention of any panic or bewilderment." They were addressing themselves as well as the Soviet people. Stalin had vividly expressed his contempt, telling them, "You'll see, when I'm gone, the imperialist powers will wring your necks like chickens." But, as Khrushchev reports, "We had doubts of our own about Stalin's foreign policy." Stalin's erstwhile colleagues remembered something the Boss had neglected—that détente was a safer way than cold war to advance Soviet interests. But unfortunately for the Soviets, Secretary of State John Foster Dulles, who prided himself on his knowledge of Stalinism, also remembered. So while East-West tensions eased considerably, the process did not go as far or as fast as at least some Soviet leaders appeared to wish.[2]

"At present," declared Georgi Malenkov—apparently first among equals in the new collective leadership—on March 15, 1953, "there is no litigious or unsolved question which could not be settled by peaceful means on the basis of mutual agreement with the countries concerned. This concerns our relations with all states, including the United States of America."[3] Andrei Gromyko expanded on Malenkov's theme at the United Nations on March 26 and, a few days later, agreed to the appointment of Dag Hammarskjöld as secretary general, thus breaking a stalemate over who would be Trygvie Lie's successor. The Soviets urged more rapid progress in the apparently endless Korean negotiations. They praised President Eisenhower and published a speech of his in *Pravda* on April 25.

The full dress exposition of the new line came from Malenkov on August 8. The USSR's major aim, he said, was to reduce Cold War tensions. "The distinguishing feature of the international situation," he added, was Moscow's "big successes" in achieving this aim. By August, a Korean armistice had finally been signed. Moscow's relations with its immediate neighbors were on the mend. The Kremlin had proposed talks with Iran on frontier problems, financial claims, and expansion of trade. The "Governments of Armenia and Georgia" had somehow "found it possible to renounce their territorial claims on Turkey," while the Soviet government had "reconsidered its former opinion" about how best to secure the Straits. Malenkov announced Moscow's intention to improve relations with Japan and India. He pointed to the reestablishment of diplomatic relations with Yugoslavia, Greece, and Israel. These and other Soviet moves had produced, he said, "a change in the international atmosphere. After a long period of mounting tension, one feels for the first time since the war [World War II] a certain easing of the international situation."

Malenkov's message to the new Eisenhower administration sounded particularly hopeful. The Soviets stood, "as we have always stood, for the peaceful coexistence of the two systems. We hold that there are no objective reasons for clashes between the United States of America and the Soviet Union." The Soviet government welcomed President Eisenhower's April 16 declaration that no dispute " 'great or small is insoluble—given only the will to respect the rights of all nations.' " What was needed now, said Malenkov, were deeds to go with the American president's words.[4]

Alas, this was exactly what Eisenhower had demanded from the Russians on April 16. He, like Malenkov, welcomed declarations of peaceful intent. But, he added, "We care only for sincerity of peaceful purpose as attested by deeds." An honorable Korean armistice, Soviet agreement to an Austrian Peace Treaty, a new Russian policy allowing East European nations "the free choice of their own forms of government"—these and other deeds which Eisenhower requested amounted to a very mixed bag.[5] Some could be done by a Soviet leadership seeking only to reduce tensions without any fundamental shift in its long-term aims. Others would require a radical restructuring of the Soviet bloc. The lesser deeds were done in due course: the Korean armistice in 1953, an Austrian Treaty in 1955. But the Soviets did not free the East Europeans (although they did loosen the reins considerably), which came as no surprise to Dulles, who had included this test in Eisenhower's speech in the certainty that the Soviets would not pass it. Dulles did his best in the ensuing years to champion negotiating from strength, which amounted to not negotiating at all if he could avoid it. But he could not avoid it entirely given Eisenhower's rather more hopeful approach and the evident desires of allies, especially Britain, for a reduction of tension with the Soviet Union. It was only a matter of time before the United States would join the USSR in a new round of détente.

Nikita Khrushchev, who replaced Malenkov as top man in the Kremlin, pressed détente on Eisenhower and to some extent succeeded. He even got to visit the United States in 1959—only to see Ike's return trip to the USSR shot down along with Gary Powers's ill-fated U-2 spy flight. With John F. Kennedy's inauguration, however, new vistas appeared to open. Kennedy took office in 1961 vowing never "to fear to negotiate" any more than to "negotiate from fear." But instead of creating new understanding, the two leaders staged the single most anxious episode of the Cold War: the Cuban missile crisis. This ironic result owed a lot to Nikita Sergeyevich's round-about method of courtship; he operated, as Adam Ulam has pointed out, according to the old saying: Be my friend or I'll break your neck! But the same sort of mutual miscalculation that plagued Stalin lived on to foil Khrushchev. Once again, those infuriatingly inconsistent Americans seemed to invite the Russians to take advantage of them only to turn suddenly on the Kremlin, showing strength and a willingness to use it that the Soviets themselves could not match.

Khrushchev's view of the West, not unlike Stalin's, was bifurcated. Khrushchev was painfully aware, even though he did not admit it on revolutionary anniversaries, of Western strength—particularly American military, technological, and economic prowess. He was sensitive, also, to East Europe's instability (for example, in Hungary and Poland in 1956) and to Soviet economic backwardness, which he was determined to rectify even at the cost of a reduced defense effort. He was uncertain of his own ability to joust with worldly and experienced Western statesmen. But Khrushchev was also a true believer. He believed in communism despite its parlous state in the USSR; he believed in Stalin's achievements even while unmasking his crimes; he believed history was going Moscow's way, witness the Third World's apparent advance along a "non-capitalist" path. Détente recommended itself to Khrushchev as a way to inhibit the Western powers from exploiting Soviet weakness while at the same time reconciling them to Soviet gains. But Khrushchev feared his capitalist adversaries would take mildness for meekness. His fellow Soviet oligarchs might also interpret him thus (some of them apparently did charge him with being soft on capitalism)—not to mention the Chinese, who by the late 1950s were accusing the Soviets of selling out to the West. So Khrushchev blustered and bluffed even as he extended his hand in apparent friendship. He boasted of strategic rocket strength that did not exist. He issued ultimata on Berlin, trying to force the still reluctant Western powers to negotiate a German settlement. On the very eve of Kennedy's inauguration, Khrushchev gave a belligerent speech endorsing "wars of national liberation" while reaffirming the need to avoid world war. The bravado was probably meant more for Chinese than American ears, but how was Kennedy supposed to know?[6]

John Kennedy never really understood what his Kremlin counterpart was up to. But Kennedy did sense that the two-handed Soviet approach demanded an equivalent American response. To contain what he regarded as a Soviet political offensive, the president sought to demonstrate strength and the will to use it by launching a strategic military build-up (despite the alleged missile gap's having turned out to favor the United States, not the Soviet Union) and by firmness in Berlin and Southeast Asia. But Kennedy also tried to be reasonable—which led him to pull his punches at the Bay of Pigs and to spend his time at the Vienna summit meeting trying to persuade Khrushchev (in part by almost pleading with him) to eschew pressure tactics lest they provoke a direct Soviet-American clash.[7] The trouble with this dual approach was that it confirmed for Khrushchev that the United States was both threatening, and yet vulnerable to the very pressure that Kennedy had been trying to avoid. And therein lie answers to the two most often asked questions about the Cuban crisis: Why did Khrushchev place offensive Soviet missiles in Cuba? (to reduce the strategic-political threat that Kennedy's missile build-up had created) and, What made Khrushchev think he could get away with it? (The same sort of American "reasonableness" which persuaded Stalin that he could have most of Eastern Europe and continue détente as well, that he could revive all-German negotiations by blockading Berlin, and that North Korea could invade the South without provoking armed American opposition.)

In Nixon and Kissinger, the Russians found the first postwar American statesmen willing to play their game. The trouble during this period was not that the two sides disagreed but that each wanted the same thing: to use détente to contain the other while advancing its own interests. That, more than anything else, accounts for the fact that while détente seemed in full flower in 1973, by 1976 it was once again in disarray.[8]

Unlike some of their predecessors, Nixon and Kissinger entered office with a pretty good gauge on Soviet strategy and tactics—the Kremlin blend of painful insecurity and breathtaking arrogance, the preference for gradual aggrandizement rather than aggrandizement through one cosmic roll of the dice, the ruthless opportunism in service if not of a grand design then at least a rough geopolitical blueprint. Moreover, aware of lessons of the past, Kissinger employed a carefully adapted carrot-and-stick diplomacy to break the double bind that had ensnared his predecessors. "In the face of the Soviet Union's ambiguous challenge," Kissinger writes in his memoirs, "the West had paralyzed itself . . . not only by excesses of conciliation but by excesses of truculence. . . . Both these attitudes sprang from the same fallacy that there was some terminal point to international tension, the reward for either goodwill or toughness. They neglected the reality that we were dealing with a system too ideologically hostile for instant conciliation and militarily too powerful to destroy." The trouble "when conciliation becomes an end itself," Kissinger continues, is that "a ruthless Soviet policy can turn it, as it occasionally has, into an instrument of blackmail and a cover for unilateral gains." But when "the more hopeful U.S.–Soviet dialogue is closed off by our action, a price is paid in domestic support and allied cohesion," without any guarantee, one should add, that the shift will produce the intended result.[9]

What were required, Kissinger concluded, were "incentives for Soviet restraint" and "penalties for adventurism." The former included summit conferences producing not only agreements long sought by the Soviets (which to be sure Nixon and Kissinger also considered in the American interest) but also the symbolism of superpower equality and vast clouds of good feeling with which the Soviets love to beguile Americans; economic inducements in the form of expanded trade (especially in badly needed technology and grain) facilitated by credits and most-favored-nation tariff treatment; plus acceptance of Soviet hegemony in Eastern Europe—acceptance signalled by the Helsinki ratification of European frontiers, by the so-called Sonnenfeldt Doctrine (named after Kissinger's adviser on Soviet affairs, Helmut Sonnenfeldt) according to which Soviet control over the area must be allowed to change gradually and organically lest it trigger rebellions that Washington could neither direct nor protect but which might lead to war, and by the fact that Kissinger never attempted to play on East European instability except to tweak the Soviet nose with presidential trips to independent-minded Rumania and restless, Russophobic Poland.[10]

Penalties for adventurism, on the other hand, included—in addition to the grand opening of China that Kissinger counted on to alter the psychological if not the geopolitical balance of power—"firm counteraction including military assistance to friends resisting Soviet or Cuban or radical pressures."[11] Nixon and Kissinger threatened to use force in response to the Soviet-blessed (or so the White House assumed) Syrian invasion of Jordan in the autumn of 1970. They quietly but firmly insisted the Russians dismantle a nuclear submarine base they had begun to build in Cienfuegos, Cuba. Nixon tilted toward Pakistan in the Indo-Pakistan war of 1971 (signalling the preference by dispatching a carrier task force into the Bay of Bengal) to prevent Soviet-backed India from settling accounts with its neighbor by force. And most important of all, Nixon and Kissinger determined to fight on in Indochina (in the process invading Cambodia, mining Haiphong, and bombing Hanoi) so that the Thieu regime would have a chance to prevail (with the help, if necessary, of continued American bombing even after the United States withdrew), all in order to teach the Soviets especially that the United States does not shrink, no matter what the cost to itself and to others, from defending its friends and its interests.

In a sense, Nixon and Kissinger did what Harry Truman did *not* do in 1947; they held out the prospect of détente but made it conditional on Moscow's refraining from adventures that, in any event, the Americans proceeded to resist. And yet, by 1976 détente was reeling from a succession of blows. Kissinger blames Watergate for creating a climate in which Congress deprived him of both carrots (Export-Import Bank credits and MFN tariff treatment) and sticks (such as the covert American intervention that Kissinger wanted to mount against Soviet- and Cuban-supported factions in the Angolan civil war). But Watergate was only part of the story. Another was that Kissinger's strategy contained the seeds of its own disintegration. For to insist on opposing virtually any and all Communist pressures on American "friends" was to end up defending causes that were morally or practically indefensible—which sparked vigorous resistance within the United States, to which Nixon and Kissinger responded by seeking quasi-dictatorial control over foreign policy, which further guaranteed that their policies would be resisted, which then ensured that a president of Richard Nixon's character (or lack of it) would react to domestic opposition with abuses of executive authority of the sort we call Watergate.

But the Soviets, too, were responsible for détente's demise. Kissinger boasts that before Watergate struck in 1973, he had the Russians just where he wanted them. The symbol of their dilemma was that they sat still for the American mining of Haiphong and then welcomed Nixon to Moscow. The triumph of carrot and stick seemed at hand when Brezhnev formally endorsed the rules of the game as Nixon and Kissinger wanted it played. Both sides ruled out "efforts to obtain unilateral advantage at the expense of the other, directly or indirectly." Both pledged to "act in such a manner as to prevent the development of situations capable of causing a dangerous exacerbation of their relations" and to "enter into urgent consultations with each other" in the event that "relations between countries not parties to this agreement appear to involve the risk of nuclear war between the United States and the USSR."[12]

But all the while the Soviets must have thought they had Kissinger where they wanted him. They would use Nixon's vague rules of détente, as a connoisseur of the Yalta Declaration on Liberated Europe might have anticipated, to soothe and lull the Americans. It was humiliating to ignore the American bombing on the eve of Nixon's visit, but the price was acceptable in view of the benefits to be gained—benefits that went far beyond those the Soviets usually cited, that is, a reduction in the danger of war and the burden of the arms race. The Kremlin hoped détente would constrain the American arms effort, which—given the size of the U.S. GNP along with American technological supremacy—could too easily exceed the Soviets' both in quantity and quality. Politically, an atmosphere of reduced tensions might render the West more accepting of Soviet gains. Moscow expected the West to cut back on what the Soviets call "psychological warfare," while the Kremlin stepped up its "ideological struggle." Those inter-imperialist contradictions that the Soviets have relied on since Lenin's time would flower when the unifying factor of a Soviet threat was reduced—thus weakening ties among the United States, Western Europe, and Japan.

Nor did the Kremlin entirely conceal its intentions. "It is quite clear," said Leonid Brezhnev at the 25th Party Congress in 1976, "that détente and peaceful coexistence are concerned with interstate relations. This means primarily that quarrels and conflicts between countries should not be decided by war, use of force or threat of force. Détente does not in the slightest way abolish, and cannot abolish or change the laws of class struggle. We do not conceal the fact that we see deténte as a way to create more favorable conditions for peaceful socialist and communist construction." According to a leading Soviet commentator, the principle of noninterference in the internal affairs of other states bars the United States from obstructing the "natural forces of social change." But the Soviet Union is free to "support national liberation movements directed against all forms of present-day colonialism."[13] (Whereas according to Washington, Western intervention in a place like Zaire was legitimate while Soviet and Cuban intervention in Ethiopia and Angola was not.)

If this is what détente meant to the Soviets, what made them think Washington would oblige? Georgi A. Arbatov, director of the Soviet Institute on the USA and Canada, contended in the early 1970s that "objective" realities, including American political, economic and social problems plus increased Soviet power, meant that Washington could no longer dictate to other nations, especially to the USSR. "Subjective" forces—for example, American politicians' calculation that détente wins votes at home—helped reconcile them to the new realities. Arbatov admitted that the American elite was not unanimous; Cold War diehards opposed détente. In the end, however, the "objective forces" that drove America into détente would keep it there.[14]

But Brezhnev's policies, like Stalin's before them, did not make it easy for "objective forces" to do their job—especially Moscow's failure to discourage (which may be putting it mildly) the 1973 Arab attack on Israel, its dispatch of Cuban proxy troops to Angola, and its continuing nuclear and conventional arms build-up. Of course, the Soviets had their own grievances, especially about the Americans' going back on their promises of credits and MFN. But, the point is that Soviet aggressiveness provoked alarm in Washington (things got so bad that President Ford even banned use of the word détente by his administration) and thus the dilemma that Stalin had faced: How to keep Washington committed to détente?

Jimmy Carter briefly offered new hope to the Kremlin. True, he spoke during the 1976 presidential campaign of making détente more "reciprocal," but at least he was willing to use the term. Later he would boast of "challenging" the Soviet Union in its own spheres of influence. But he also called upon Americans to rid themselves of their "inordinate fear of Communism." Almost from the beginning, however, Carter's policies were a puzzle to the Kremlin. If Kissinger tried carrot and stick, Carter seemed determined to offer neither. With the Soviets hungry for a SALT II agreement, the president without warning sprang new and unacceptable proposals on them. Yet the same Carter refused to make every third world encounter with the Russians into a test of strength. Both these innovations could be defended as improvements on Kissinger's approach. The trouble was that the Russians did not see them that way. One might have expected Moscow to be gratified when National Security Adviser Zbigniew Brzezinski placed U.S.–Soviet competition lower down than has been the custom on the American foreign policy agenda (beneath relations with Western allies, for example), a move Washington hard-liners saw as a perilous underestimation of the Soviet threat. Instead the touchy Russians complained about "a desire somehow to conceal the special importance of the problem of détente."[15]

' Understanding Carter's zig-zags was a challenge for even the most dispassionate observer. For the Soviets it proved an impossible assignment. Before long they drew up a lengthy list of grievances: Carter's outspokenness on human rights; his shift on SALT and his equally sudden switch from inviting Soviet participation in Middle East peace efforts to excluding the Soviets from the process; his rush to normalize relations with Peking in late 1978 as contrasted with his apparent inability to speed ratification of SALT II; his on-again, off-again protests against Soviet combat troops in Cuba; his Vienna summit toast to "my new friend Chairman Brezhnev," followed (in the aftermath of Afghanistan) by shock and outrage that his friend had lied to him. Americans, in their post-Watergate skepticism, viewed Carter as deluded by his sincere idealism. The Soviets, in their much deeper cynicism, saw Carter as Machiavellian. Some Russians accepted the American diagnosis that the president was torn between conflicting advice from his top advisers and buffeted in other ways by the unruly American political process. But they also attributed what Brezhnev called Carter's "indecision and inconsistency" to more sinister motives and forces. What could Carter's human rights campaign be except an attempt to undermine the stability of the Soviet system? And all that American talk about congressional opposition to SALT—it might convince veteran Americanologists like Arbatov and Ambassador Anatoly Dobrynin (on the job in Washington since 1961) but not more insular types like Leningrad party boss and politburo member, Grigori Romanov, or even the apparently sophisticated Premier Alexei Kosygin. United States' Senator Abraham Ribicoff tried to explain the Senate's role to Kosygin in late 1978, noting that a recent report of new Soviet Mig-23 fighter planes in Cuba might make SALT's passage more difficult. "Thank you for explaining to me what the U.S. Senate is," Kosygin replied sarcastically. "We know what the United States Senate is. And we cannot agree with your explanation of how things will stand at the time of SALT." Romanov later informed the senator that if President Carter really wanted the treaty he could force senators to vote for it by threatening to withhold money from their campaigns. Kosygin and Romanov, like Stalin, were viewing American actions through the prism of their own experience, which made Carter look either weaker (assuming he really *could* not control his own party) or more devious (if he simply *would* not) than in fact he was.[16]

All this poisoned the well long before Afghanistan. But just as Stalin tried to keep détente on the track with a mixture of tough and soothing talk, so did his successors. *Pravda* warned in the summer of 1978 that Carter's hard line had "every chance to develop from a tactic into a dangerous and uncontrollable political course, acquire a force of inertia that is difficult to overcome, and evoke in the world a corresponding counteraction." The enemies of détente were trying to provoke the Soviets, to "draw our country into new rounds of the arms race, into political wrangling in the spirit of the Cold War, into a scaling down of economic and cultural ties, and so forth." But, the editorial continued, "we are not accepting the invitation to join the funeral of détente."[17]

As in 1947, the Soviet leaders counted on Washington's own interests to keep it in the game. Arbatov recalled America's reasons for opting for détente in the first place: "Nothing has changed really. War still remains an unacceptable alternative. The arms race still carries great threats. The national interests of America itself . . . need a policy of détente." Arbatov himself saw the historical parallel. He admitted that some American speeches made one ask: "Is it 1948 or 1978?" But, he added, the many "fruitless, dangerous and expensive decades of the Cold War . . . were not in vain. I think that all this could not be so easily crossed off and forgotten and the situation cannot be simply repeated." Central Committee official Leonid Zamiatin agreed. The Cold War period, he said, was a time of unusual American strength; it was "an exceptional period in the world's history and the political history of America, and there is no returning to it. World realities are such that a policy . . . of pressure in all parts of the world does not correspond to the realities of the modern world. And all attempts to return to these methods, which are obsolete, cannot produce any results."[18]

But words like these seemed like whistling in the dark when Chinese-American rapprochement suddenly blossomed late in 1978 into full diplomatic recognition. Even before the Chinese invasion of Vietnam, the Soviets detected a diabolical Chinese plot to instigate war between the United States and the USSR. After the invasion they detected an American plot to foment conflict between Russians and Chinese. This necessitated an ominous warning to the West: "If relations between the West and China grow into a military-political alliance directed against the Soviet Union, we would have to reconsider the whole political situation. It would create a new picture of the intentions of the Western powers, and the whole political framework would become more and more a structure of war-waging capabilities, of the use of or at least the threat of use of military force. This would hardly leave a place for the sort of understandings which led to détente. . . ."[19]

But the trouble was that this threatened exactly what the Chinese wanted. No wonder that in almost the same breath the Soviets proclaimed their determination not to be tricked. Said Brezhnev, "We shall not give in to provocation." Soviet commentator Valentin Zorin embellished, "A great political art, a firmness in defense of principles, self-control, the ability not to give in to provocations, and the ability to see far ahead are necessary in this complicated and difficult struggle."[20]

Moscow did not let itself be provoked by the Chinese invasion of Vietnam even at the risk of seeming, as Central Committee official Vadim Zagladin put it, a "weakling, a paper bear." Far from "reconsidering the whole political situation," the Soviets redoubled their efforts to complete a SALT agreement and sell it to the United States as a good bargain. Brezhnev admitted that the treaty that he and Carter finally signed in Vienna "could have been better from our point of view." He promised that it would "undoubtedly have a beneficial effect on the international climate in general." And there were other moves designed to strengthen American support for SALT—increased emigration of Soviet Jews, the release of imprisoned Soviet dissidents, and then, patient waiting while the Americans decided whether or not to ratify SALT II.[21]

Or so it seemed. For it was not long before the Soviets launched their invasion of Afghanistan—an action at the same time unprecedented and in the Stalinist mode. For the first time, Soviet troops moved *en masse* beyond the sphere of influence that had accrued to them in the aftermath of World War II. But the motives for intervention and an apparent miscalculation about the American reaction were familiar. As so often in the past, Moscow acted from a sense of threat and opportunity. The Soviets feared the loss of a pro-Soviet buffer state on a sensitive border, but once secured the buffer could become a base for further advance. The Russians were unhappy about other developments in U.S. policy including rising American defense spending, plans for a Rapid Deployment Force, and a decision to base new ballistic and cruise missiles capable of hitting the Soviet Union in Western Europe. But they were doubtless pleased by the American nonreaction to Soviet military aid to Ethiopia, to those alleged Soviet combat troops in Cuba, and to the coup d'état of April 1978, which brought pro-Soviet forces to power in Kabul. In the months before invading Afghanistan, Soviet confidence verged on arrogance. High Soviet officials lobbied against the new Euro-strategic missiles with arguments designed for a West European audience deemed gullible in the extreme. "If you suggest total disarmament of all nuclear arms," said Vadim Zagladin, "you will have our agreement to such a treaty in two hours." Speaking at the United Nations, Foreign Minister Gromyko brushed off American complaints about Soviet troops in Cuba as "propaganda totally without foundation." His "advice" to the Americans was simple: "The artificiality of this entire question must be honestly admitted and the matter closed."[22]

These and other indications of the Soviet mood on the eve of Afghanistan suggest that the Soviets did not anticipate the full American response (economic sanctions, Olympic boycott, Carter Doctrine, draft registration) to the invasion.[23] Neither did they understand that reaction once it occurred. The Soviets explained it away by charging that President Carter had used Afghanistan as a "pretext" for hard-line steps he had wanted to take all along—including, according to Zagladin, the Olympic boycott itself. What the Russians could not allow for in their propaganda, or their own minds either, was that American leaders can shift in response to Soviet actions from being disposed to compromise to being determined to resist. There were many in Washington who did use Afghanistan to justify long-standing demands for a tougher U.S. stance. But Jimmy Carter was not the only one whose view of the Russians changed more in two weeks than in three years. Still, if Stalin was misled by Roosevelt and surprised by Truman, and if Kennedy bushwhacked Khrushchev, then can Leonid Brezhnev be faulted for failing to comprehend a born-again Christian anti-Communist?

And yet, despite everything, the Soviets were not overly alarmed by Carter's Doctrine, any more than they had been by Truman's. As in 1947, they were convinced the Americans would come to their senses—a development Moscow encouraged by urging Washington to be "realistic" about Afghanistan and to reopen contacts frozen in early 1980. Meantime, the Soviets cultivated America's allies, some of whom appeared more wedded to détente and, especially, to the economic benefits thereof than were the Americans. Soviet commentators insisted that although the USSR did not want a new cold war it did not fear one either. They could not have admitted otherwise lest that tempt the Americans to blackmail them. But the bravado had the ring of truth. If Stalin could conduct a cold war from a position of relative weakness, why should his successors shrink back in an era when their military might was much greater, their adversaries more deeply divided, and the rest of the world more resistant to American control? Warned a veteran Soviet diplomat in Washington in an interview with the West German paper, *Die Welt:* "The years in which the United States had the say as to what could be done in the world and what could not are past once and for all. We can no longer tolerate Washington behaving as though it were the umpire of contemporary history. . . . The Americans are still much too conceited. Their strength is but a strength of words. If we wanted to, we could harm the United States 20 times more than it would harm us. We can also live without détente, if necessary. . . . If the rules we had with the Americans are no longer applicable, then we shall play our way indeed. If we are not treated as equals, then it will be necessary to remind the Americans to do that."[24]

The parallels in these historical sketches are apparent. But are they real? Are they surface phenomena belied by structural changes beneath? Or are they the essence of the matter? Many observers, including experienced Western analysts of the Soviet Union, emphasize the discontinuity between Stalin's Russia and that of his successors. They point to reforms and alterations in the Soviet governmental system and in the Kremlin's outlook on world affairs. But others, including leading dissidents like Aleksandr Solzhenitsyn, insist that the Soviet system has not really changed. My view is that the system *has* changed in significant ways since 1953 but the shifts are not inconsistent with, and indeed have contributed to, a foreign policy that in some ways is more expansionist and offensive than in Stalin's time.[25]

One change that most observers agree has occurred is that the Soviet system is more open and pluralistic than in Stalin's day. His successors have abolished mass murder as a political weapon while retaining a more narrowly focused terror that threatens dissidents with loss of livelihood and liberty but not usually of life. They have offered a degree of political participation to various Soviet institutions and sub-institutions that have distinct policy preferences and make themselves heard. The post-Stalin leaders have also struggled among themselves over both power and policy, although in recent years they have been either less divided or more skillful at concealing their divisions than they were previously. These developments make some difference at home, but how much abroad? Of all the groups that have emerged from Stalin's shadow, none has been more influential than the Soviet military-industrial-party-police complex with its vested interest in international tension. One result of intra-Politburo conflict is to make a far-reaching, long-lasting accommodation with the West unlikely for a new post-Stalinist reason. Whereas Stalin had the power but not the will to arrive at a settlement, his successors apparently have lacked both. Henry Kissinger sensed that much of the rigidity he encountered in Soviet diplomacy reflected the fear (even on the part of top Kremlin leaders) of appearing to give ground to the Americans.[26] Similar qualms (about seeming to appease the Russians) are not unknown in Washington. But at least American presidents have a few months of political security before having to make foreign policy with an eye on the next election. In the Soviet system, where there are no regular terms of office, there is no guaranteed surcease from insecurity or from its effect on Soviet diplomacy.

Some American Soviet specialists (who fortunately are more numerous now—another post-1953 change—than when Kennan and Bohlen were almost alone in their expertise) believe that the Politburo is split between conservatives and reformers, that American policies influence these policy struggles, and that Washington can and should attempt to shape the Kremlin outcome. Even if the premise were accepted, puzzles would remain. Will an American hard line buttress Soviet doves' contention that you cannot push Washington around, or Russian hawks' insistence that the only thing the Americans understand is strength? Will a dovish American stance help Soviet moderates lobby for accommodation abroad and reform at home, or will it invite their belligerent colleagues to step up the pressure abroad while keeping the clamps on at home? But the premise itself is faulty. Differences among Soviet leaders there may be, but any doves who find their way into the Kremlin roost are likely to have their wings clipped in a hurry. Any Westerner who thinks the Soviet leadership spectrum runs from the equivalent of Ronald Reagan to some Soviet George McGovern (or even to Jimmy Carter and Edmund Muskie, not to mention from, say, Valéry Giscard d'Estaing to François Mitterand or Georges Marchais) is mistaking an at best incipient Soviet pluralism for the genuine Western article.

A second set of changes has affected the domestic strength of the Soviet system. Now in its seventh decade, the USSR is more stable and secure than most regimes on the face of the earth. This is not only owing to the government's demonstrated willingness and ability to control the population by force but also, ironically, because despite mass discontent—expressed more in alcoholism and malingering on the job than in explicit political protest—the Soviet people consciously or unconsciously seem to have accepted the regime as their legitimate ruler and defender of their interests in the world.[27] But there are disturbing developments; especially, a chronically lagging economy and the potential for unrest among the non-Russian nationalities who make up roughly 50 percent of the overall population; not to mention the persistent and embarrassing chasm between the promise of equality and democracy and the reality of elite privilege and authoritarian rule. Both strength and weakness can conveniently be seen as conducive to a moderate foreign policy. Stability, as it has been said, reduces the regime's insecurity, which showed its face abroad as belligerence. The decision to seek economic help from the capitalists (a far cry from the Cold War pattern of autarky) gives Moscow a stake in good relations with the West. But there is a catch. The Soviets' new confidence undergirds their drive for nothing less, and possibly much more, than superpower equality, while their internal troubles provide new economic reasons for aggrandizement previously fueled by ideological and political motives. The Soviets have long justified the gap between promise and practice (not to mention the shortage of sausage) by blaming a hostile external environment, and they have distracted attention from it with foreign policy triumphs real and put-on. Now that they are trying to close that gap with the aid of imported technology and grain, a new question arises: How will the Soviets pay for it? So far the Russians have earned much-needed hard currency by selling oil and gas to the West, but what happens when domestic energy supplies run short, as the CIA and other sources predict they will, in the years ahead? It would certainly help if the Soviets had their hands directly on Persian Gulf oil— unless they want to solve their economic problems through increased domestic repression (justified of course by external danger). In the meantime, another troubling question: Whose economic difficulties give whom a bigger stake in détente: the Soviets, who could if necessary retreat toward autarky, or Western countries, whose increasing reliance on Soviet trade accounted in part for their *sotto voce* protests against Soviet intervention in Afghanistan?

Militarily, the Soviets have come a long way since Stalin was commander in chief. From a war-torn country confronted by an American atomic monopoly, the USSR has become a nuclear power second to none, with conventional forces capable of global intervention. On the other hand, Stalin's monolithic control over the international Communist movement, which meant that Communist gains anywhere could with justice be regarded as increments to Soviet power, has gone glimmering. Not only has China switched from ally to enemy number one, but East Europeans also pose a variety of real and potential challenges vividly exemplified by the unrest in Poland. It is possible, if one is optimistic by nature, to take comfort from these developments, too. With strategic parity, some say, has come Soviet willingness to cap the arms race, and troubles with their friends give the Soviets reason not to rile their enemies. But there is rather more, I think, to the pessimistic version—that is, the Soviets have been exploiting their new power not only at the West's expense, but also to score points against the Chinese and to convince the restless East Europeans that it is useless to dream of breaking away.

Next, in this abbreviated rundown, there is the most obvious change of all. Joseph Stalin has been dead for more than a quarter of a century. His successors are widely regarded as moderate, even conservative, men. They have solemnly declared that war is not inevitable and that the capitalist encirclement has ended. They are more informed about the West and apparently less suspicious of it than was Stalin. Are they not trying, in their own way, to create an environment in which East and West can compete with reduced risk of confrontation and conflict? Their détente, it has been said, is a long-term proposition—a far cry from Stalin's temporary and tactical device. One could reply that it was not Stalin who placed missiles in Cuba and invaded Afghanistan, or that the next generation of leaders, who did not experience the horrors of the second world war, may well be bolder and more forceful than was Brezhnev. But the most interesting and difficult issue posed by the contrast between Stalin and his heirs is the impact on foreign policy of a leader's personality and political style. These always count for something in politics, but they do so especially when one man is in a position to put his personal stamp on a regime and when his actions are truly idiosyncratic—not simply what others would do in his place. Stalin's political dominance was undisputed, despite whatever internecine jockeying took place among his lieutenants. And his morbidly suspicious nature was unique. But Stalin did not create the distrust so characteristic of Soviet diplomacy, he only intensified it. And although he was not equipped personally to reach lasting settlements with his capitalist adversaries, he also erected or reinforced institutional obstacles to accommodation that have outlived him. For one thing, he trained a generation of Soviet leaders, still in power in 1981, who have made key features of Stalin's political style their own. For another, he shaped Marxist-Leninist ideology and Soviet political culture in ways that perpetuate his legacy.

For nearly three decades after Stalin's death, Soviet foreign policy has been made and implemented by men whom Stalin promoted and who had worked under him for many years. The three senior leaders of the Brezhnev team had all achieved high posts by the end of the 1930s. By 1939, Brezhnev himself was Communist party secretary of a major industrial province of the Ukraine; at Stalin's death he was a Central Committee secretary and candidate member of the ruling Politburo (then called the Presidium). Alexei Kosygin became people's commissar of textile industry in 1939, then deputy prime minister of the USSR, and by 1948, a full member of the Politburo. Mikhail Suslov, first-secretary of one of the largest Russian provinces in 1939, became a Central Committee secretary in 1947. And a similar pattern holds for the USSR's top foreign policy specialists. Andrei Gromyko, named ambassador to the United States in 1943, had been head of the Soviet Foreign Ministry's American desk since 1939. Boris Ponomarev, now Central Committee secretary with special responsibilities in international affairs, became a member of the Comintern's Executive Committee in 1936, when Jimmy Carter was twelve years old. Vladimir Semenov, chief SALT negotiator in the early 1970s, learned how to joust with Americans while serving as political adviser to the Soviet military administration in Germany from 1945 to 1949.

Men like these may have modified Stalin's policies, but consciously or unconsciously they have been carriers of his creed. It is no wonder that Henry Kissinger encountered a whole panoply of patterns and ploys that had been standard in Stalin's time: insecurity, which has the effect of putting the other side on the defensive; greediness, which results in overplaying the Soviet hand; a bargaining style that holds stubbornly to "principled" extreme demands and then baldly invites the most uninhibited horsetrading; bullying when things are going well alternating with an obviously forced joviality when the other side has the clear advantage; nasty second sessions that, to judge by Kissinger's reaction ("Suddenly the thought struck me [under a barrage of Soviet protests over Vietnam at the 1972 Moscow Summit] that for all the bombast and rudeness, we were participants in a charade"), do not carry the conviction of Stalin's stellar performances.[28] Even if these are vestiges of a bygone era, they are still daunting. Kissinger says one reason he sought to exclude the Soviets from Middle East talks was that, even if they had not intended to do so, their negotiating style threatened to aggravate local divisions.

But these devices are not vestigial; they reflect habits of mind that are shaped by Soviet ideology and political culture. Many say that Marxism-Leninism has become eroded in the USSR and even that the old ideology is dead. In any event, some Westerners add, ideology now plays the conservative role of buttressing the status quo—so that if the USSR throws its weight around, say in Czechoslovakia or Afghanistan, then it does so like any other "conservative great power" whose actions "spring from fearful, extravagant notions of national security and international status that are, unlike revolutionary ideas, reasonable subjects for diplomacy."[29] There is something to this assessment. Few if any contemporary Soviet leaders seem inspired by Lenin's vision of world revolution; none has devoted his golden years to the sort of explication of Marxist-Leninist texts contained in Stalin's last writings; even the boorish Khrushchev looks like a learned ideologue in retrospect. But ideology also contributes, along with fearful and extravagant notions of national security and international status, to making genuine accommodation an unreasonable subject for Soviet diplomacy. For ideology consists of far more than "revolutionary ideas" and other fine points of doctrine to which the Soviet leaders may pay mainly lip service—although lip service often becomes more than that when people who begin by feigning belief end up convincing themselves that they actually believe. Ideology also consists of images and axioms, such as the view of capitalism as inexorably hostile and yet tantalizingly vulnerable, that make normal, peaceful relations with the West seem both impossible and unnecessary to the Soviets. Moreover, the foreign policy successes that the system needs and craves reflect ideological imperatives. Not only must Soviet power and influence expand (or at least be seen to do so) but the cause of proletarian internationalism, for which the Kremlin still claims to speak, must advance. Gains by other Communist parties are not always in Moscow's immediate interest, and the Soviets know it (witness their readiness to turn their backs on a party persecuted by a non-Communist Soviet client, or openly to prefer a receptive Western government—like the French—to a powerful Communist party that might like to replace the current regime). But if communism is officially the wave of the future, it must make inroads in the present. Soviet

Communist credibility depends on that; and even if it did not, powerful Soviet institutions built to support ruling and non-ruling fraternal parties would prompt the Kremlin to protect gains already made (whether in Afghanistan or Poland) and to seek more victories—even when the effect of doing so would be to mobilize the United States, or alarm Western Europe, or antagonize the Moslem world, or unite China and Japan against the USSR, or accomplish all these minor miracles simultaneously.

Soviet political culture reinforces the unfortunate effect on foreign policy of Marxist-Leninist ideology. A political culture consists of the ideas about politics—what it is, how it works, and what can be expected from it—that are widespread in a particular nation.[30] Stalin's conception of politics managed to fuse a vision of an ideally harmonious future with a dog-eat-dog picture of the present. But such components were not unknown in prerevolutionary Russia and indeed have deep roots in Russian tradition. Much of the pre-1917 intelligentsia dreamed of a future heaven on Russian earth. And Russian peasant proverbs, as good a window as any into the impoverished milieu from which many Soviet leaders have risen, reflect attitudes that have been not just incarnate but fully operational in Soviet foreign policy: "Politics is a rotten egg." "The world is strong like water and stupid like a pig." "Truth won't feed you." "An honest man, like a fool, is also harmful." "The more friends the more enemies. Fear your friend as you would an enemy." "Be friendly with the bear, but hang on to your axe."[31]

The Bolshevik Revolution was supposed to produce a New Soviet Man with new political attitudes. Instead, Soviet life, particularly the experience of living through Stalinism, has reinforced the outlook caught by the proverbs. What have life's lessons been for Soviet officials who clambered to high office over the bodies of Stalin's victims—at least some of whom they must have denounced on their way to the top? Can they have matured in a country scarred by revolution, civil war, famine, collectivization, terror, world war, purges again, de-Stalinization, partial re-Stalinization, and much more without becoming convinced that life (not to mention foreign policy) is an unending struggle in which only the strong, ruthless, and devious survive? The hope for the future is that a new generation of Soviet leaders will bring fundamentally new attitudes to their diplomacy. The evidence of the past is that the current generation has not done so.

Even so, the scenario for a new cold war need not be played as written. Brezhnev's pursuit of détente has been less crude than Stalin's and more credible in Western eyes; and as long as détente has champions in the West, Moscow has incentive to hew to it. Moreover, once Stalin's détente began to unravel, his hyper-suspicious nature led him to over-react in a way his successors are not likely to duplicate. The lesson of the late forties, that cold war does unite the capitalists (at least temporarily), has not been lost on Stalin's heirs. What's more, their tendency to read extreme deviousness into an adversary's motives may in this instance be a sobering, stabilizing factor, since it suggests that the Americans are inviting a break in order to solidify their own camp. A new all-out arms race might prove to be manageable for the Soviets, but it can hardly seem appealing in Moscow. Stalin forced the Soviet people to sacrifice in the name of national defense, but consumer expectations are higher now and the terror apparatus has fallen into relative desuetude. The partial pluralization and continuing bureaucratization of the Soviet system mean that any fundamental foreign policy change involves more than a single leader's changing his mind. The decision to pursue Brezhnev's brand of détente apparently required a fair amount of institutional log-rolling; any decision to abandon détente, to which the Brezhnev leadership has solemnly affirmed and reaffirmed its commitment, would require no less.

International conditions have also changed since the late forties in ways that may give Moscow confidence that it can ride out the storm without responding in kind to Washington's new challenge. The fact that the United States is no longer the world's dominant military power but must share that distinction with the USSR, the fact that America's allies no longer follow Washington's lead automatically but often oppose and obstruct, the fact that the Third World has grown dramatically in size and strength and anti-American assertiveness—all these could embolden the Soviets to take up the American gauntlet, but they could also suggest to the Russians that if they sit tight and refuse to be provoked, the American containment campaign will hurt the United States more than it will the Soviet Union. In 1947, conditions in Europe did not provide that kind of assurance. Both East and West Europe were tinderboxes then, and Germany itself was up for grabs; Moscow and Washington had, or felt they had, little margin for error in an area both deemed crucial to their security. In recent years (until Poland began to boil over) Europe has been much more stable, if only because the dividing line between East and West has been a generally accepted fact—but, on the other hand, the Middle and Far East are far more explosive now than they were in the mid-1940s. Furthermore, when and if U.S.–Soviet relations do deteriorate drastically, the divergence between Stalin's view of the most likely future war and that of his successors may prove important. The fact that Stalin considered an inter-imperialist clash more likely than an East-West conflict permitted him to take certain risks (like authorizing the North Korean attack on South Korea) that his heirs might not dare to take. But once the Korean War was on, Stalin felt less pressure than his successors might to preempt a U.S. attack on the Soviet Union—an attack that Stalin did not really expect anyway but tomorrow's politburo might indeed anticipate.

So history may not repeat itself. Indeed, one can imagine an altogether more hopeful turn of events involving a sharp break with the past. For the Soviet Union is beginning to undergo a process of leadership change unprecedented in its scope and potential impact. According to Seweryn Bialer, the age of the top leadership stratum—consisting of the party Politburo and Secretariat plus the leading members of the Council of Ministers and Supreme Soviet Presidium—is "higher than at *any* time in Soviet history and during any of the previous successions (and incidentally, higher than the age of the comparable group in any industrial society regardless of its system.)"[32] Furthermore, these aging oligarchs have presided over what the Soviets call "stability of cadres" throughout the central elite. This stability seems to have been designed to garner the support of its beneficiaries for Brezhnev and friends on the Politburo and, probably, to discourage those friends from competing among themselves to fill lesser bureaucratic posts with personal retainers. But the same stability means that not only must an aging top leader be replaced—a shift that in the past has prompted new policy directions foreign and domestic—but this time there will be a turnover of much of the central elite involving a changeover of generations as well.

This kind of upheaval has occurred only once before in the USSR (and then *not* in combination with a change in the top leaders), that is, when Stalin liquidated the ruling elite of the 1930s and replaced it with a new elite including men who have remained in power ever since. Moreover, the generation that will soon assume supreme power in the Soviet Union is the post-Stalin generation—men (but not, if the present pattern holds, women) who entered Soviet political life in the freer years after the dictator's death, leaders who some Western analysts expect to behave rather differently than have their predecessors. According to Bialer, younger Soviet officials are committed to the basic features of the Soviet system and devoted to advancing its interests abroad, but "they tend to exhibit little of their predecessors' xenophobia, and much less of their fear and deeply rooted suspicion of the outside world. Rather they display a curiosity that surely reflects intense concern with the patent inadequacies in the working of the Soviet system." Another student of Soviet leadership in transition goes farther. Jerry Hough can imagine future leaders undertaking far-reaching economic reforms, reducing the swollen military budget, opening the Soviet Union to increased contact with the outside world, and thus providing "the basis for a relationship with the West that is far less dangerous than the events of the last few years seem to foretell." One reason for such a turn-about would be an economic crunch (reflecting the looming energy crisis and a shortage of manpower) that will soon make it all but impossible to produce both guns and butter on the scale to which the Soviets have become accustomed. But in Hough's view the Soviet future also depends on whether the United States meets Moscow half way, thus making the world safe for Soviet reform, or threatens the Russians in ways that make reform seem too risky. "It is for us," Hough concludes, "to give this new generation of officials the opportunity, the excuse, to move in the direction that its instincts are pushing it."[33]

A hopeful prospect. But don't count on it. For gauging the views and predicting the behavior of an entire generation of leaders is something less than an exact science as Bialer and Hough are quick to admit. Their projections rest, for example, on the premise that different background characteristics (the post-Stalin generation is generally better educated, more urbanized, and more likely to come from working or middle class than from peasant families) and later initiation into Soviet political life (which even after 1953 has not exactly been a kindergarten) have produced a group of men with significantly more enlightened attitudes than Stalin's entourage had. Whereas others contend that the new generation contains a goodly number of politicians who, with support from segments of the intelligentsia and the masses, could take the USSR in a right-wing, Russo-chauvinist, neo-Stalinist direction featuring stepped-up coercion at home combined with renewed cold war.[34] Moreover, Hough's hopes are predicated on the assumption that Soviet reformism is indivisible, whereas Bialer cautions (rightly in my view) that even if the new leaders undertake domestic reforms they will not be "easier to deal with in the international arena." Not only since they may be "less cautious, more prone to take risks than the present leadership exactly because they have not experienced at first hand the costs of building Soviet might," but also because their country is "not a 'sated power' " but rather a "dynamic great power . . . in a phase of ascendancy" that is out to expand its influence by "fomenting conflicts, escalating conflicts, maintaining them at a high level of intensity and exploiting them. . . ."[35]

This is *not* a hopeful prospect in a world all too prone to conflict even without the Soviets fanning the flames—not only because of the danger of war but also because so many global problems (poverty, pollution, resource depletion, nuclear proliferation to name but a few) cry out for resources now spent on superpower rivalry. What's more, there is a good chance that the United States will make a bad situation worse. The fact that certain approaches to the Soviet Union have been tried and found wanting will not necessarily be held against them. Rooseveltian illusions out of favor at present could someday regain their lure. But to try to prove through concessions or sincere face-to-face encounters that the United States trusts the Soviet Union and hence merits Soviet trust in return is to invite the very confrontations that such conciliation is supposed to avoid. An equally dangerous but much more likely temptation (especially for a hard-line Republican administration) will be to follow Harry Truman's example but this time "do it right," that is, to get so tough with the Soviets (without holding down the defense budget this time and without the itch to send the chief justice to Moscow to talk Soviet leaders out of their shells) that the Kremlin is forced to sue for peace. But pressure of this kind will at best prompt Moscow to practice selective détente with America's allies (who will be all too receptive if they consider American policies to be recklessly immoderate), and at worst provoke the Kremlin into adventures posing a real risk of war.

How about an updated carrot-and-stick strategy designed to restrain Soviet expansionism? To many observers (including both Bialer and Hough) this seems a promising approach. One could even argue, invoking lessons of the past, that a president like Ronald Reagan is ideally equipped to make it work. A hard-line chief executive facing a weakened opposition on the left can credibly threaten the sort of unpleasantness (whether an accelerated arms race, economic sanctions, or warmer ties with China) that the Kremlin might find it worthwhile to try to avoid. If such a president permitted himself (and were allowed by Congress) to offer some carrots as well (say concessions in renewed strategic arms limitation talks or some other field), that might constitute a package that could be sold in Moscow. If the Soviets thought the deal were a good one, and the president in a position to deliver on it, they would have few ideological compunctions. Indeed, they would feel more comfortable with Republicans speaking the language of unadorned power politics than with liberal Democrats who let human rights get in the way of a promising relationship.

But such a scenario is also, alas, improbable. The Soviets would wait and see if domestic or allied opposition developed to such an American policy, and in the real world it probably would. Congress and the American public are not likely, short of a much greater emergency, to present the Russians with a truly united front. Nor are the West Europeans and Japanese, even if more effective efforts could be made toward inter-allied coordination than any recent president has been willing or able to mount and sustain. Meanwhile, the Third World would be full of pitfalls, especially for those so anxious to demonstrate toughness that they are likely to insist on taking a stand in the wrong place at the wrong time. And with Vietnam-style "toughness" to deter them from aggrandizement, the Soviet would have no need for encouragement! The problem, in other words, is that for "linkage" to work in East-West relations, it must also work in West-West and North-South relations, that is, Washington must be able to bring its allies along while avoiding new quagmires in the Third World. But to ask the United States to succeed in all three realms is almost surely asking too much of a country that has lost so much international leverage and has so often proved maladroit in employing the influence it has.

In such a world, yet another temptation may beckon—the urge to ignore the Soviets. Instead of accepting the competition-*cum*-cooperation model (which the Russians were the first to propose and the United States accepted only after trying the two separately), Washington could refuse to provide much of either.[36] The Americans could decline to match the Russians missile for missile and client for Third-World client (on the grounds that scoring points in this way only weakens the United States) while at the same time refusing to conduct trade and exchanges that strengthen and dignify those who are out, however gradually and gently, to do us in. But this would amount to a kind of isolationism which would invite the worst of both worlds. The Soviets would have nothing to gain from restraint and little to fear from expansion.

Other mirages can be imagined. Condominium, a kind of entente under which the United States and Soviet Union join forces to dictate to others, may seem tempting as more countries proclaim a plague on both superpower houses. But even if condominium were possible to achieve it would be unlikely to last. The Soviets, and at times the

United States too, would be unable to resist using it against their partners. And the same flaw, not to mention domestic American opposition and resistance by local powers, would doom a new spheres-of-influence deal (which could also be part of a condominium arrangement) in which, say, Moscow and Washington try to divvy up the Middle East (with the Soviets getting, say, the predominant voice in Afghanistan and part of Iran and the Americans in Saudi Arabia) the way they divided Europe after World War II, but this time without contributing to a cold war in the process.[37]

The answer is that there is no good answer. The most we can reasonably hope to do is to keep the lid on, and even that will demand skillful diplomacy backed by a strong defense. To keep the nuclear wolf from the door will require negotiations and agreements limiting the danger of war. But we must enter into these negotiations with our eyes open; we must avoid the pitfalls of Soviet-style bargaining; we must accept only specific and verifiable agreements and shun vague, high-sounding accords; we must make sure that conditions that prompt the Soviets to agree also encourage them to keep their word; and we must never pretend, even to ourselves, that any particular agreement has ended the competition. Too many American leaders, even those who prided themselves on their anti-Soviet credentials and their unblinking realism, have believed that somehow, some way they could reach a real meeting of the minds with Soviets. Meetings there have been and must continue to be. But a true meeting of the minds must await the day when it can no longer be said as it can today—Stalin's American policy lives!

Notes

PREFACE

1. Abram Tertz, *On Socialist Realism*, trans. George Dennis (New York: Vintage Books, 1960), p. 162.
2. Robert C. Tucker's *Stalin as Revolutionary, 1879–1929: A Study in History and Personality* (New York: W.W. Norton, 1973) is the first of a projected three-volume biography. Unfortunately for my project, it leaves treatment of foreign policy to later volumes. Among other biographies that do cover foreign policy are Isaac Deutscher, *Stalin: A Political Biography*, 2d ed. (New York: Oxford University Press, 1967), and Adam B. Ulam, *Stalin: The Man and His Era* (New York: Viking, 1973).

CHAPTER 1
Now and Then

1. See George F. Kennan, *Russia and the West Under Lenin and Stalin* (Boston: Little, Brown, 1961), esp. chaps. 23—25; Kennan, *American Diplomacy, 1900–1950* (Chicago: University of Chicago Press, 1951), pp. 107–28; and W. W. Rostow, *The United States in the World Arena: An Essay in Recent History* (New York: Harper and Row, 1960). Revisionist histories include Gabriel Kolko, *The Politics of War: The World and United States Foreign Policy, 1943–1945* (New York: Random House, 1968); Joyce and Gabriel Kolko, *The Limits of Power: The World and United States Foreign Policy, 1945–1954* (New York: Harper and Row, 1972); William Appleman Williams, *The Tragedy of American Diplomacy*, rev. ed. (New York: Dell, 1962); and Gar Alperovitz, *Cold War Essays* (New York: Doubleday, 1970).
2. See John Lewis Gaddis, *The United States and the Origins of the Cold War, 1941–1947* (New York: Columbia University Press, 1972), and Robert Dallek,

Franklin D. Roosevelt and American Foreign Policy, 1932–1945 (New York: Oxford University Press, 1979).

3. Arthur M. Schlesinger, Jr., "The Cold War Revisited," *The New York Review of Books*, October 25, 1979, p. 48.

4. Vojtech Mastny, *Russia's Road to the Cold War: Diplomacy, Warfare and the Politics of Communism, 1941–1945* (New York: Columbia University Press, 1979), pp. 283, 306.

CHAPTER 2

Roots and Portents

1. V. I. Lenin, *Collected Works*, 4th ed., 45 vols. (Moscow: Progress Publishers, 1960–1970), vol. 29, p. 153.

2. For a fuller account of pre-1917 Russian foreign policy and of the difficulties in tracing and explaining continuity with Soviet foreign policy, see Ivo J. Lederer, ed., *Russian Foreign Policy: Essays in Historical Continuity* (New Haven: Yale University Press, 1962).

3. Karl Marx and Friedrich Engels, *The Communist Manifesto* (New York: Appleton-Century-Crofts, 1955), p. 46.

4. See V. I. Lenin, *Imperialism: The Highest Stage of Capitalism* (New York: International Publishers, 1939).

5. Lenin, *Collected Works*, vol. 27, p. 238.

6. J. V. Stalin, *Works*, 13 vols. (Moscow: Foreign Languages Publishing House, 1952–1955), vol. 4, p. 28.

7. Quoted in Adam Ulam, *Expansion and Coexistence: The History of Soviet Foreign Policy, 1917–1967* (New York: Praeger, 1968), p. 68; see also George F. Kennan, *Soviet Foreign Policy, 1917–1941* (Princeton: D. Van Nostrand, 1960), p. 18.

8. Kennan, *Soviet Foreign Policy*, p. 29; see also George F. Kennan, *Soviet-American Relations, 1917–1920*, 2 vols. (Princeton: Princeton University Press, 1956–1958); for a recent and relatively undogmatic Soviet account, see Nikolai V. Sivachev and Nikolai N. Yakovlev, *Russia and the United States* (Chicago: University of Chicago Press, 1979), pp. 32–75.

9. "Miracle"—see Lenin, *Collected Works*, vol. 30, p. 208. "Colossus"—p. 27. "We were victorious"—p. 382.

10. "Two camps"—see Stalin, *Works*, vol. 4, pp. 240, 293. "Smokescreen"—p. 331. "Soap bubbles"—p. 242. "Drubbings"—p. 401. For a reference by Lenin to the division of the world into two camps, see Lenin, *Collected Works*, vol. 30, p. 450.

11. Lenin, *Collected Works*, vol. 32, p. 453; Stalin, *Works*, vol. 5, p. 119.

12. For Stalin's analysis of these and other capitalist contradictions, see his report to the 14th Party Congress in 1925 in his *Works*, vol. 7, pp. 267–304.

13. *Ibid.*, pp. 51–54, 272–73.

14. *Ibid.*, pp. 284–86.
15. *Ibid.*, pp. 56, 295.
16. See Stalin's 1925 reference to America's opposition to war in *ibid.*, p. 294. On the Bolshevik view of the United States, see Ulam, *Expansion and Coexistence*, p. 86.
17. Stalin, *Works*, vol. 10, pp. 128–53.
18. *Ibid.*, vol. 13, pp. 150–59.
19. Stalin's remarks to Ludwig are in *ibid.*, pp. 116–17; his exchanges with Robins are on pp. 274–79.
20. The Soviet noninterference pledge is in U.S. Department of State, *Foreign Relations of the United States: The Soviet Union, 1933–1939* (Washington, D.C.: U.S. Government Printing Office, 1952), p. 28; hereafter, the series, *Foreign Relations of the United States*, which contains multiple volumes for each year, will be cited as *FR*; Stalin's remark to Duranty is in Stalin, *Works*, vol. 13, p. 284; for the conversation with Wells, see I. V. Stalin, *Sochineniia*, 3 vols. (Stanford: Hoover Institution, 1967), vol. 1, pp. 14–24. The three Hoover volumes may be considered an extension of the official Soviet edition of Stalin's *Works*, which ended (a casualty of de-Stalinization) with volume 13 covering materials through January 1934; Stalin's answer to Roy Howard is in Stalin, *Sochineniia*, vol. 1, p. 120.
21. "Isolating the isolators"—see Stalin, *Works*, vol. 6, p. 248. Imperialists' fear of war—vol. 10, p. 295. The "fundamental antidote"—vol. 7, p. 291. "Peace policy"—vol. 6, p. 251.
22. Stalin's war warning along with his call to "sound the alarm" are in *ibid.*, vol. 9, pp. 328–34; see also Ulam, *Expansion and Coexistence*, p. 165.
23. On the wanning of "peaceful coexistence," see Stalin, *Works*, vol. 10, p. 295; for Stalin's June 1930 remarks, see vol. 13, pp. 263, 268.
24. See Ulam, *Expansion and Coexistence*, pp. 191–96, and Mastny, *Russia's Road*, pp. 17–18.
25. Stalin, *Works*, vol. 13, p. 308.
26. See Ulam, *Expansion and Coexistence*, pp. 250–79.
27. For Litvinov's comments, see *FR: The Soviet Union, 1933–1939*, p. 264. Stalin's democratic-fascist comparison—see Stalin, *Sochineniia*, vol. 1, p. 337. The Stalin-Ribbentrop exchange is in Raymond James Sontag and James Stuart Beddie, eds., *Nazi-Soviet Relations, 1939–1941* (Washington, D.C.: U.S. Department of State, 1948), p. 74.
28. Sontag and Beddie, eds., *Nazi-Soviet Relations*, p. 2.
29. See *ibid.*, pp. 105–8.
30. Mastny, *Russia's Road*, p. 27; Ulam, *Expansion and Coexistence*, p. 283.
31. Stalin to the German Ambassador—see Sontag and Beddie, eds., *Nazi-Soviet Relations*, p. 98. Negotiations on access to German materials—pp. 127–29. Baltic moves—pp. 152–54. Bessarabian tactics—pp. 155–68.
32. *Ibid.*, pp. 225, 237, 245, 259.
33. *Ibid.*, pp. 319, 324.
34. *Ibid.*, pp. 340–41.

CHAPTER 3

The Origins of Entente

1. Khrushchev's revelation, which came in his secret speech to the 20th Communist Party Congress in 1956, is in *The Anti-Stalin Campaign and International Communism*, ed. the Russian Institute of Columbia University (New York: Columbia University Press, 1956), p. 50. See also I. M. Maisky, "Days of Trial," *Novyi Mir*, no. 12 (December 1964), p. 163; *The Memoirs of Marshal Zhukov* (New York: Delacorte Press, 1971), p. 268; N. N. Voronov, "At Supreme Headquarters" in Seweryn Bialer, ed., *Stalin and His Generals* (New York: Pegasus, 1970), p. 210; and Stalin, *Sochineniia*, vol. 2, p. 3.

2. Anthony Eden, *The Eden Memoirs: The Reckoning* (London: Cassell, 1965), pp. 270–71.

3. *FR: 1941*, vol. 1, pp. 769–80.

4. *Ibid.*, pp. 785–801.

5. Said Truman (quoted in the *New York Times*, June 24, 1941, p. 7): "If we see that Germany is winning we ought to help Russia and if Russia is winning we ought to help Germany and that way kill as many as possible, although I don't want to see Hitler victorious under any circumstances. Neither of them think anything of breaking their pledged word"; Churchill speech quoted in Winston S. Churchill, *The Second World War: The Grand Alliance* (Boston: Houghton Mifflin, 1950), pp. 371–72.

6. Roosevelt's declaration, made on November 7, 1941, is in *FR: 1941*, vol. 1, p. 857; Harriman is quoted in Dallek, *Franklin D. Roosevelt*, p. 295. Actually there were conditions attached to the aid stipulating that the Soviets provide specific information pertaining to Moscow's needs. But there was no political *quid pro quo* (apart from the obviously important payoff in the form of Soviet resistance to Hitler), and in fact it was not long before the Soviets failed to provide much of the information they had promised to supply. See George C. Herring, *Aid to Russia, 1941–1946: Strategy, Diplomacy and the Origins of the Cold War* (New York: Columbia University Press, 1973), pp. 26–48.

7. *FR: 1943*, vol. 3, p. 504. For Davies's own account, see his *Mission to Moscow* (New York: Simon and Schuster, 1941).

8. See Daniel Yergin, *Shattered Peace: The Origins of the Cold War and the National Security State* (Boston: Houghton Mifflin, 1977), pp. 17–41. The fact that Yergin much prefers Roosevelt's "Yalta axioms" to the State Department's "Riga axioms" places him closer to the revisionist than the traditionalist school.

9. *FR: 1941*, vol. 1, p. 758.

10. *Ibid.*, p. 982.

11. *Ibid.*, p. 765.

12. *Ibid.*, p. 766.

13. Summer Welles, *Where Are We Heading?* (New York: Harper and Brothers, 1946), p. 37; Frances Perkins, *The Roosevelt I Knew* (New York: Viking, 1947), pp. 84–85.

14. Milovan Djilas, *Conversations with Stalin*, trans. Michael B. Petrovich (New York: Harcourt Brace and World, 1962), pp. 73–74. Khrushchev thought that Stalin was "more sympathetic to Roosevelt than Churchill because Roosevelt seemed to have considerable understanding for our [Soviet] problems." According to Khrushchev, Stalin was much impressed by FDR's sometime siding with him against Churchill, and even more by the President's refusal to drink a toast (at Churchill's suggestion) to the King of England. It may or may not be true that "Stalin's personal sympathies were definitely reserved for Roosevelt"; if so, this preference was, as Djilas reminds us, for the lesser of two evils. See Nikita S. Khrushchev, *Khrushchev Remembers*, trans. and ed. Strobe Talbott (Boston: Little, Brown, 1970), pp. 222–23.

15. Stalin's request for U.S. troops—see FR: 1941, vol. 1, p. 814. Flattery—p. 813. Deference—p. 805.

16. Churchill, *The Grand Alliance*, pp. 457–58. For more on Anglo-American fears of a separate peace, even at this early stage of the war, see Dallek, *Franklin D. Roosevelt*, pp. 294, 338.

17. W. Averell Harriman and Elie Abel, *Special Envoy to Churchill and Stalin, 1941–1946* (New York: Random House, 1975), pp. 85–88; Richard Nixon, *RN: The Memoirs of Richard Nixon* (New York: Grosset and Dunlap, 1978), p. 610.

18. FR: 1941, vol. 1, p. 832.

19. Stalin to Hopkins—see FR: *The Conference of Berlin (The Potsdam Conference)*, 1945, vol. 1, p. 32. Stalin to FDR—FR: *The Conferences at Cairo and Tehran*, 1943, p. 595. Vyshinsky to Bohlen—FR: *The Conferences at Malta and Yalta*, 1945, p. 590.

20. Harriman and Abel, *Special Envoy*, pp. 88–101. In speaking of the partition of Poland, Stalin did not, of course, mention the Secret Additional Protocol of 1939, which did not become known until after the war.

21. See Nixon, *RN*, pp. 613–14, 884–85, and Henry Kissinger, *The White House Years* (Boston: Little, Brown, 1979), pp. 1222–29. On Stalin's capacity for deception and self-deception, see Tucker, *Stalin as Revolutionary*, pp. 434–37.

22. Soviet view of the Atlantic Charter—see Mastny, *Russia's Road*, p. 41. Stalin's proposals—see Eden, *The Reckoning*, pp. 284–88.

23. Mastny's interpretation—"Precisely because [Stalin's] chances of realizing most of [his preferences] on his own seemed remote, he tried to pin down his indispensable allies to as many specifics as possible"—seems implausible, even allowing for Stalin's ingenuity. Mastny, *Russia's Road*, p. 43.

24. FR: 1942, vol. 3, p. 507.

25. See Gaddis, *Origins of the Cold War*, pp. 133–73, and Dallek, *Franklin D. Roosevelt*, pp. 317–29; see also Lynn Etheridge Davis, *The Cold War Begins: Soviet-American Conflict Over Eastern Europe* (Princeton: Princeton University Press, 1974).

26. Eden, *The Reckoning*, pp. 290–303.

27. Winston Churchill, *The Second World War: The Hinge of Fate* (Boston: Houghton Mifflin, 1950), p. 327.

28. See Mastny, *Russia's Road*, pp. 62–64.

29. See Jan Ciechanowski, *Defeat in Victory* (Garden City, N.Y.: Doubleday, 1947), p. 78; FR: 1942, vol. 3, p. 124, and *Documents on Polish-Soviet Relations, 1939–1945*, vol. 1 (London: Heinemann, 1961), p. 245. Exactly how big a territorial change Stalin had in mind, how in particular it differed from the much more than minimal change involved in shifting to the Curzon Line, is not clear from the sources. See also Ito Takayuki, "The Genesis of the Cold War: Confrontation Over Poland, 1941–1944," in Yonosuke Nagai and Akira Iriye, eds., *The Origins of the Cold War in Asia* (Tokyo: University of Tokyo Press, 1977), p. 156, and Mastny, *Russia's Road*, pp. 53–55.

30. For a fuller account, see Takayuki, "Genesis of the Cold War."

31. "Minutes of the KRN (National Homeland Council) *Delegatura* for the Liberated Territories," Moscow, July 20, 1944, as translated in Antony Polonsky, ed., *Documents on the Communist Take over in Poland* (London: Routledge and Kegan Paul, forthcoming); Stalin is quoted in Mastny, *Russia's Roadl*, pp. 143, 170.

32. See FR: 1943, vol. 3, pp. 1398–99, 1402–11; FR: 1943, vol. 4, pp. 868–69; Gaddis, *Origins of the Cold War*, p. 145; and Mastny, *Russia's Road*, pp. 173–74.

33. This account is based on Polish sources quoted in Takayuki, "Genesis of the Cold War," pp. 180–81.

34. See Mastny, *Russia's Road*, pp. 154–55.

35. See Dallek, *Franklin D. Roosevelt*, pp. 399–417, 503–8; Gaddis, *Origins of the Cold War*, pp. 133–73; and Davis, *The Cold War Begins*.

36. FR: 1942, vol. 3, pp. 148, 185.

37. *Ibid.*, pp. 638–47.

38. FR: 1943, vol. 3, pp. 329, 363, 370–71. The main aim of Davies's mission was to obtain Stalin's agreement to attend a U.S.–Soviet summit meeting with Roosevelt. See also my chapter 3, p. 62 and footnote 46 below.

39. *Ibid.*, pp. 501–4, 652, 654.

40. FR: 1942, vol. 3, p. 586.

41. Hull-Beneš—see FR: 1943, vol. 3, p. 529. Hull-Churchill—FR: *The Conferences at Washington and Quebec*, 1943, p. 49. Hull-Gromyko—FR: 1943, vol. 3, p. 582. Hull-Vyshinsky in FR: 1943, vol. 1, p. 628. Vyshinsky's mentioning of Japan signaled Soviet readiness to talk of joining the Pacific War.

42. Fraternizing of delegations—see FR: 1943, vol. 1, p. 576. "Fast friends"—p. 615. Internationalism—p. 635.

43. Molotov's mood—see *ibid.*, pp. 653–54. Stalin's state of mind and banquet remarks—pp. 685, 687. Hull on sincerity—p. 691.

44. FR: 1943, vol. 3, p. 396.

45. Stalin's April 25, 1943 message to Churchill—see *ibid.*, p. 395. Litvinov to Welles—p. 522.

46. Davies's message—see *FR: Tehran*, p. 4. When Churchill complained about Roosevelt's two-man summit proposal, the president responded with a lie of his own: "I did not suggest to U.J. that we meet alone." Stalin's confidence—see p. 42. "Ganging up"—p. 80. Constitutional requirement—p. 31. For other reasons for the delay of the Tehran conference, see Dallek, *Franklin D. Roosevelt*, pp. 368, 403–18.

47. *FR: 1943*, vol. 1, p. 521.

48. "Piddling things"—see Harriman and Abel, *Special Envoy*, p. 236. Harriman-Roosevelt Conversations— p. 227. "On grounds of high morality"—*FR: 1943*, vol. 3, p. 541.

49. Quotations from American minutes of Tehran conference meetings are in *FR: Tehran*, pp. 485–86, 510–12, 529–32, 553, 594. For Soviet minutes of Tehran plenary sessions (which differ in some detail but not significantly from the American account) but not of the crucial Roosevelt-Stalin conversation, see *Tegeran, Ialta, Potsdam: sbornik dokumentov* (Moscow: Izdatel'stvo "Mezhdunarodnye otnosheniia", 1967), pp. 5–56. The same collection contains Soviet minutes of the plenary sessions, final communiqués and protocols of the Yalta and Potsdam Conferences as well. For an inside account by a Soviet adviser-interpreter, see Valentin Berezhkov, *Tegeran, 1943: Na konferentsii bol'shoi troiki i v kuluarakh* (Moscow: Izdatel'stvo Agentstva Pechati Novosti, 1968).

50. *Ibid.*, pp. 598, 604.

51. See U.S. Department of State, *The Department of State Bulletin*, vol. 9, no. 230 (November 20, 1943), p. 343, and vol. 10, no. 236 (January 1, 1944), pp. 3–7.

52. For a sample Soviet reaction to Tehran, see "Historic Decision," *Pravda*, December 7, 1943; see also U.S. Embassy reports in *FR: 1943*, vol. 3, pp. 608–9. Beneš-Harriman—pp. 728–30.

53. Wendall Willkie, "Stalin: 'Glad to See You Mr. Willkie,' " *Life*, October 5, 1942, p. 35; Willkie, "Don't Stir Distrust of Russia," the *New York Times Magazine*, January 2, 1944, pp. 3–4; D. Zaslavskii, "Willkie Muddies the Waters," *Pravda*, January 5, 1944, p. 4.

54. *FR: 1944*, vol. 3, pp. 1218, 1223.

55. Harriman's instructions—see *ibid.*, p. 1228. Roosevelt's telegram—p. 1244. Churchill—pp. 1240–68.

56. *FR: 1944*, vol. 3, pp. 1268–70.

57. Harriman-Molotov conversation—see *ibid.*, p. 1276. Harriman-Stalin—pp. 1282–83.

58. *Ibid.*, p. 1281.

CHAPTER 4

Entente Stalinist-Style

1. Stalin, *Sochineniia*, vol. 2, pp. 164–70.

2. See Earl R. Browder, *Tehran* (New York, International Publishers, 1944)

and *Tehran and America* (New York: Workers' Library Publishers, 1944); see also Jacques Duclos, "A propos de la dissolution du P.C.A." *Les Cahiers du Communisme*, no. 6 (April 1945) as translated in the *Daily Worker*, May 24, 1945. For a traditionalist account citing Duclos, see Arthur M. Schlesinger, Jr., "Origins of the Cold War," *Foreign Affairs*, vol. 46, no. 1 (October 1967), pp. 22−52.

3. On events preceding the Red Army's entry into Rumania and Bulgaria, see Mastny, *Russia's Road*, pp. 196−204. For negotiations relating to armistice terms, see *FR: 1944*, vol. 3, pp. 415−70, and *FR: 1944*, vol. 4, pp. 161−232 *passim*. For an account of Communist progress in both Rumania and Bulgaria, see Hugh Seton-Watson, *The East European Revolution* (New York: Praeger, 1954), pp. 202−19.

4. *FR: 1944*, vol. 3, pp. 1444−46.

5. "Letter to CC of PPR (Central Committee of the Polish Workers' Party from the CBKR (Central Bureau of Polish Communists) in Moscow, July 18, 1944"; "Minutes of the CC of the PPR (Extracts), October 9, 1944"; and "The Meeting of the PKWN (Polish Council of National Liberation) with Comrade Stalin, October 9, 1944," all in Polansky, ed., *Documents*.

6. Hopkins—see *FR: Yalta*, p. 920. For a revisionist account, see Diane Clemens, *Yalta* (New York: Oxford University Press, 1970), pp. 267−91.

7. Molotov's comment—see *Izvestiia*, February 2, 1944, p. 2. See also Mastny, *Russia's Road*, pp. 133−43; Seton-Watson, *The East European Revolution*, pp. 179−90; and Paul Zinner, *Communist Strategy and Tactics in Czechoslovakia, 1918−1948* (New York: Praeger, 1963), pp. 71−96.

8. Stalin on Horthy—see Mastny, *Russia's Road*, pp. 206, 226; György Heltai's recollections and Rákosi quoted in William O. McCagg, Jr., *Stalin Embattled, 1943−1948* (Detroit: Wayne State University Press) pp. 36, 66, 348 (fn. 68); Rákosi is also cited in Charles Gati, "Two Secret Meetings in Moscow in October 1944 and the Communist Quest for Power in Hungary," paper prepared for delivery at the 1978 annual meeting of the American Association for the Advancement of Slavic Studies, Columbus, Ohio, October 1978.

9. De Gaulle in Moscow—see Mastny, *Russia's Road*, pp. 229−30. *FR: Tehran*, pp. 484−85, 510. *FR: Yalta*, p. 573.

10. *FR: 1944*, vol. 3, pp. 999−1116 *passim*; Mastny, *Russia's Road*, p. 143.

11. This account follows that of Constantine Tsoucoulas, *The Greek Tragedy* (Baltimore: Penguin, 1969).

12. *FR: Tehran*, pp. 510−11, 513, 532, 553−54.

13. See Mastny, *Russia's Road*, pp. 233−34, 254.

14. See *ibid.*, pp. 230, 232, 278−79.

15. *FR: Yalta*, pp. 378−79, 984.

16. Gromyko on Italian colonies—*FR: Yalta*, p. 75. Churchill-Stalin exchange—*FR: Tehran*, pp. 566−67. The discussion at Yalta—*FR: Yalta*, pp. 902−4.

17. Stalin emphasized the inter-imperialist origins of the Second World War in a speech delivered on February 9, 1946. See Stalin, *Sochineniia*, vol. 3,

pp. 2–4. But surely that interpretation did not dawn on him only at that late date.

18. See Frederick C. Barghoorn, *The Soviet Image of the United States: A Study in Distortion* (New York: Harcourt Brace, 1950), pp. 86–92.

19. Eugene Varga, *Izmeneniia v ekonomike kapitalizma: v itoge vtoroi mirovoi voiny* (Moscow: OGIZ, 1946), pp. 269, 319. For a Western account, see Frederick C. Barghoorn, "The Varga Discussion and Its Significance," *The American Slavic and East European Review*, vol. 6, no. 3, pp. 214–36.

20. FR: *1944*, vol. 4, pp. 1125, 1148.

21. FR: *1943*, vol. 3, pp. 710–15.

22. Harriman to Mikoyan—see FR: *1943*, vol. 3, p. 782. Soviet satisfaction—FR: *1944*, vol. 4, p. 1077. Molotov's *aide-mémoire*—FR: *1945*, vol. 5, p. 942.

23. FR: *1944*, vol. 4, p. 1115.

24. "The Meeting of the PKWN with Comrade Stalin," in Polansky, ed., *Documents*.

25. FR: *1944*, vol. 4, pp. 973–75.

26. American proposal—see FR: *1944*, vol. 1, p. 737. Litvinov, speaking privately to Edgar Snow on October 6, 1944, is quoted in Mastny, *Russia's Road*, p. 219.

27. FR: *1942*, vol. 3, pp. 568, 573–74.

28. Gromyko's suggestion and Roosevelt's reaction—see FR: *1944*, vol. 1, pp. 743–44. Roosevelt to the Brazilian Ambassador—p. 843. Roosevelt to Gromyko—p. 785. Roosevelt's reference to "husbands and wives in trouble not voting in their own case" seems to conflate and confuse two separate principles of the law—first, that no one should be a judge in his or her own case, and second, that husbands and wives may not testify against each other. If so, Roosevelt's advice, or at least Stettinius's version of it, would have sounded strange not only to Soviet ears but to American ears as well.

29. Roosevelt to Churchill—see FR: *1945*, vol. 5, pp. 509–10. FDR to Stalin—p. 528.

30. Djilas, *Conversations with Stalin*, pp. 10–11, 104, 114.

31. Winston S. Churchill, *The Second World War: Triumph and Tragedy* (Boston: Houghton Mifflin, 1953), pp. 226–28. Accounts based on British records of the Eden-Molotov discussions are in Mastny, *Russia's Road*, pp. 207–12, and Gati, "Two Secret Meetings," pp. 1–5; Harriman's fears—FR: *1944*, vol. 4, p. 235.

32. FR: *Yalta*, pp. 668–70.

33. *Ibid.*, pp. 711–16, 846. According to Inis L. Claude, Jr., the resolution of the UN voting issue was something less than a compromise since, despite Roosevelt's seeming certainty, the United States never "clearly and firmly stood for the absolute exclusion of parties from voting in their own cases, at all stages of Security Council consideration of disputes." See Inis L. Claude, Jr., *Swords into Plowshares: The Problems and Progress of International Organization*, 2d ed. (New York: Random House, 1959), pp. 144–47.

34. *FR: Yalta*, pp. 572, 574, 798.

35. *Ibid.*, pp. 781, 854.

36. *Ibid.*, pp. 923-24, 928.

37. Quoted in Mastny, *Russia's Road*, pp. 222-23. Litvinov's words were transmitted to Roosevelt, who replied he was "tremendously interested," but took no action reflecting that interest.

38. Mastny, *Russia's Road*, pp. 260, 265. Roosevelt's March 23 remark quoted in Harriman and Abel, *Special Envoy*, p. 444. *FR: 1945*, vol. 5, pp. 195-96.

39. *FR: 1945*, vol. 1, p. 165.

40. *FR: 1945*, vol. 5, p. 210.

41. *FR: 1945*, vol. 3, pp. 746, 756-57.

42. *FR: 1945*, vol. 5, pp. 826-28.

43. *Ibid.*, p. 824.

CHAPTER 5

From Entente to Détente

1. *FR: 1945*, vol. 5, pp. 232-33, 253; Yergin, *Shattered Peace*, p. 83.

2. Truman's remarks as cited in Yergin, *Shattered Peace*, pp. 104, 119, 141. The Russian composer Dmitri Shostakovich retells Soviet stories about Stalin's alleged love and understanding of great music, but he has doubts about their accuracy. See *Testimony: The Memoirs of Dmitri Shostakovich*, as related to and edited by Solomon Volkov (New York: Harper and Row, 1979), pp. 100, 126-28, 134, 232, 241.

3. Vyshinsky—see Yergin, *Shattered Peace*, p. 112.

4. *FR: 1945*, vol. 4, pp. 1018, 1100.

5. Stalin to Beneš as reported by latter to Harriman—*ibid.*, p. 430. Liberation of Prague—Mastny, *Russia's Road*, pp. 273-78. Khrushchev's comment in *Khrushchev Remembers*, p. 221. Troop withdrawal issue—*FR: 1945*, vol. 4, pp. 473, 508.

6. See *FR: 1945*, vol. 4, pp. 811, 813-14.

7. Barnes's behavior—*ibid.*, pp. 220, 257. Berry—*FR: 1945*, vol. 5, pp. 560, 609. Truman to Stalin—*FR: 1945*, vol. 5, p. 550. Grew's memo—*FR: 1945*, vol. 7, p. 935. According to diplomatic historian Ernest R. May, Barnes and Berry, along with other American diplomats stationed along the Soviet periphery, were guilty of "tendentious" reporting that contributed to prejudicing American policy toward the Soviet Union. Such diplomats "misrepresented or at least oversimplified the background of issues with the USSR." It may be the case, as May suggests, that Barnes and Berry exaggerated the democratic credentials of certain anti-Soviet Balkan politicians, but was it such a sin for Barnes to speak in a dispatch from Sofia of the Russian "record for double dealing"? See May, *"Lessons" of the Past: The Use and Misuse of History in American Foreign Policy* (New York: Oxford University Press, 1973), pp. 26-31.

8. *FR: 1945*, vol. 5, pp. 264, 272.

9. *FR: Potsdam*, vol. 1, pp. 26–32. Yergin, *Shattered Peace*, p. 171.

10. Argentina complaint—*FR: Potsdam*, vol. 1, p. 32. San Francisco situation—*FR: 1945*, vol. 1, pp. 387, 401. The Argentine accord that Stalin referred to was a Yalta agreement that the so-called Associated Nations (those that broke relations with Germany but had not declared war on Berlin) could be invited to San Francisco if they declared war by March 1, 1945. Argentina declared war on March 27, 1945.

11. *FR: Potsdam*, vol. 1, pp. 32–35. For a careful account of events leading up to the Lend-Lease cutoff, see Herring, *Aid to Russia*, pp. 180–207.

12. *FR: Potsdam*, vol. 1, pp. 32, 39, 55–56.

13. *Ibid.*, p. 61.

14. *Ibid.*, p. 43.

15. *Ibid.*, pp. 8, 89, 218–19.

16. *Ibid.*, pp. 257–66.

17. Recognition of Poland—*ibid.*, p. 733. Truman-Stalin exchange—*FR: Potsdam*, vol. 2, p. 1584.

18. Opening gambits—*FR: Potsdam*, vol. 2, pp. 1583–84. Turkish desiderata—pp. 257, 1427. The territory to which Molotov referred consisted of the provinces of Kars and Ardahan, which had been seized by Russia in 1877 but given back by the Soviets in 1918, a loss ratified in the Soviet-Turkish treaty of 1921.

19. *Ibid.*, pp. 152, 207. See also p. 359.

20. On Truman's remark and Stalin's non-reaction, see Harry S. Truman, *Memoirs*, vol. 1: *Year of Decisions* (Garden City, N.Y.: Doubleday, 1955), p. 416, Churchill, *Triumph and Tragedy*, p. 670, Harriman and Abel, *Special Envoy*, pp. 490–91, and *The Memoirs of Marshal Zhukov*, pp. 674–75. Also see Mastny, *Russia's Road*, pp. 297–98 and Gaddis, *Origins of the Cold War*, pp. 244–46. A revisionist account is Gar Alperovitz, *Atomic Diplomacy: Hiroshima and Potsdam: The Use of the Atomic Bomb and the American Confrontation with Soviet Power* (New York: Simon and Schuster, 1965).

21. Yalta stipulation—*ibid.*, p. 1671. Yergin, *Shattered Peace*, p. 96.

22. Eden's remarks—*FR: Potsdam*, vol. 2, p. 235. Soviet irritation—p. 390.

23. Exchanges on the Balkans and Italy—*ibid.*, pp. 151, 230, 1061. On straits and canals—p. 303.

24. Byrnes's linkage—*ibid.*, pp. 491–492, 512. Reparations agreement—p. 1486. Stalin links Italy and Balkans—p. 207. American pledge—p. 630. By this time, the Soviets had referred the future of Italian colonies to the Council of Foreign Ministers to which also had been delegated the task of drafting peace treaties. Stalin had set aside his Turkish requests with the ominous comment that "the Russians had interrupted their conversations with the Turks, but only temporarily." All three powers had agreed that each might conduct separate consultations with Ankara. See *ibid.*, p. 366.

25. Byrnes's pressure and Soviet resistance—*ibid.*, pp. 510, 512. Stalin's

praise—p. 601. See also James F. Byrnes, *Speaking Frankly* (New York: Harper and Brothers, 1947), p. 85.

26. FR: *Potsdam*, vol. 2, pp. 172, 221, 1588.

27. Malcolm Mackintosh, "Stalin's Policies towards Eastern Europe, 1939–48: The General Picture," in Thomas T. Hammond, ed., *The Anatomy of Communist Takeovers* (New Haven: Yale, 1975), p. 240.

28. Vyshinsky to Harriman—FR: 1945, vol. 5, p. 617. Soviets to King Michael—p. 575. Vyshinsky to Bulgarians—FR: 1945, vol. 4, pp. 295–96.

29. FR: 1945, vol. 6, p. 630.

30. *Ibid.*, p. 668.

31. *Ibid.*, p. 687.

32. *Ibid.*, pp. 679–712.

33. Quoted in Gaddis, *The United States and the Origins of the Cold War*, p. 260.

34. FR: 1945, vol. 5, pp. 882–83.

35. FR: *Potsdam*, vol. 2, p. 1500.

36. FR: 1945, vol. 2, pp. 164–65, 189. Byrnes's private fears are cited in Yergin, *Shattered Peace*, p. 118.

37. FR: 1945, vol. 2, p. 194.

38. *Ibid.*, pp. 195–97, 247.

39. *Ibid.*, p. 295. See also Byrnes, *Speaking Frankly*, p. 99.

40. Molotov links treaties—FR: 1945, vol. 2, p. 243. On peace conference procedures—pp. 313, 328. Elections and recognition—pp. 488–89.

41. *Ibid.*, p. 426. See also Harriman and Abel, *Special Envoy*, pp. 508–9.

42. Cited in Yergin, *Shattered Peace*, pp. 127, 129.

43. FR: 1945, vol. 2, pp. 496, 526, 539–40.

44. The two tendencies as described in "The Problem of International Cooperation in the Light of Practical Experience," *New Times*, no. 24 (December 15, 1946), pp. 1–8. The evolving Soviet view of Western policies and policymaking can be traced in a journal like *New Times*. A selection of particularly revealing articles would include the following: N. Baltisky, "Combating Saboteurs of Enduring Peace," no. 9 (October 1, 1945), pp. 3–7; A. Sokolov, "International Cooperation and Its Foes," no. 12 (November 15, 1945), pp. 15–19; "The Moscow Foreign Ministers' Conference," no. 1 (January 1, 1946), pp. 3–4; "The Soviet Union on the Road of Peaceful Construction," no. 7 (April 1, 1946), pp. 1–3; N. Sergeeva, "Different Attitudes toward the Vanquished Countries," no. 17 (September 1, 1946), pp. 3–5; K. Velikanov, "The American Monopolies and United States Foreign Policy," no. 20 (October 15, 1946), pp. 6–11; "American Foreign Policy," no. 12 (March 21, 1947), pp. 1–3; A. Leontiev, "American Expansion: Past and Present," no. 23 (June 6, 1947), pp. 5–9.

45. *Vital Speeches of the Day*, vol. 12, no. 3 (November 15, 1945), pp. 70–76.

46. Harriman and Abel, *Special Envoy*, pp. 514–15.

47. FR: 1945, vol. 5, pp. 411–19. The same issue (as to the Soviet attitude

toward U.S. aid) was raised in connection with possible assistance to other East European countries. Expert diplomatic opinion, both in the United States and in American embassies, was divided on the subject.

48. On Czechoslovakia—FR: 1945, vol. 4, pp. 506–8. Chinese-Soviet negotiations—FR: 1945, vol. 7, pp. 910–85. Stalin to Harriman—vol. 7, p. 890. Manchurian manipulations—pp. 1031–51.

49. FR: 1945, vol. 6, pp. 782–92. See also Harriman and Abel, Special Envoy, pp. 511–17.

50. FR: 1945, vol. 2, pp. 567–76.

51. For the final Moscow Conference Communique, see ibid., pp. 815–24. Language pertaining to Rumania and Bulgaria is on p. 822.

52. Stalin on spheres of influence—ibid., p. 776. On Iran—pp. 685, 689. On Turkey—p. 690.

53. Truman quotes in his memoirs from a letter he either gave to Byrnes or more likely used as a basis for a discussion with him. See Harry S. Truman, Memoirs, vol. 1: Year of Decisions (Garden City, N.Y.: Doubleday, 1955), p. 552. See also Yergin, Shattered Peace, pp. 160–61.

54. Yergin, Shattered Peace, pp. 161–62.

CHAPTER 6
Détente Stalinist-Style

1. On Leninist and Stalinist Soviet conceptions of peaceful coexistence, and of the role of war in international relations, see Elliot R. Goodman, The Soviet Design for a World State (New York: Columbia University Press, 1960), pp. 164–84, 285–325.

2. Between 1945 and 1947, U.S. armed forces dropped from wartime levels to about 1.4 million where they remained until after the outbreak of the Korean War. American defense spending fell from $81.2 billion in 1945 to $14.4 billion in 1947 and $11.7 billion the next year. Reliable statistics on Soviet demobilization, which proceeded in parallel with a crash program to develop atomic weapons as well as other efforts to modernize Soviet forces, are harder to come by. According to Nikita Khrushchev, the number of Soviet troops fell from a wartime high of about 12 million to 2.8 million in 1948. See Marshall D. Shulman, Stalin's Foreign Policy Reappraised (New York: Atheneum, 1969), pp. 20–30, and Thomas W. Wolfe, Soviet Power and Europe, 1945–1970 (Baltimore: Johns Hopkins University Press, 1970), pp. 9–12.

3. FR: 1946, vol. 6, pp. 696–709.

4. Clifford Report quoted in Yergin, Shattered Peace, pp. 244–55. The full text is in Arthur Krock, Sixty Years on the Firing Line (New York: Funk and Wagnalls, 1968), pp. 419–82. Pre-Moscow Conference U.S. views—FR: 1947, vol. 1, p. 715, and vol. 4, p. 524. Stalin to Marshall—vol. 2, pp. 343–44.

5. Yergin, Shattered Peace, pp. 169–70, 185, 189, 245, 286–87.

6. *Ibid.*, p. 189.
7. *FR:* 1947, vol. 2, p. 644.
8. Hottelet did not disclose his interview publicly at the time for fear of compromising Litvinov. But he did inform the American embassy in Moscow, which, finding "the extent of this statement . . . simply amazing," flashed word of it to Byrnes then meeting with his fellow foreign ministers in Paris. According to Hottelet, who published a full account in the *Washington Post* (January 21–25, 1952) after Litvinov's death on December 31, 1951, Litvinov's warning had an immense impact on those American officials who had until then hesitated to accept the hard-line views of George Kennan and others. Khrushchev contends Stalin's secret police had planned in the late 1940s to ambush and kill Litvinov while he was traveling by car from Moscow to his *dacha* in the countryside. Khrushchev does not explain why the deed was never done and Litvinov was permitted to die a natural death. See C. L. Sulzberger, *A Long Row of Candles: Memoirs and Diaries, 1934–1954* (New York: Macmillan, 1969), pp. 252–53; *FR:* 1946, vol. 6, pp. 763–65; *Khrushchev Remembers*, p. 262.
9. Quoted in Yergin, *Shattered Peace*, p. 167.
10. Stalin, *Sochineniia*, vol. 3, pp. 1–22.
11. Djilas, *Conversations with Stalin*, pp. 114–15.
12. *FR:* 1946, vol. 5, pp. 472–73.
13. The full story of Varga's incomplete fall, and of the connection between Varga's fate and internecine strife among Stalin's top political lieutenants, cannot be established on the basis of available evidence. For Kremlinological speculation on these subjects, see Robert Conquest, *Power and Policy in the U.S.S.R.: The Study of Soviet Dynastics* (New York: St. Martin's, 1961), pp. 79–94; McCagg, *Stalin Embattled*, esp. pp. 276–78; William Zimmerman, "Choices in the Postwar World: Containment and the Soviet Union," in Charles Gati, ed., *Caging the Bear: Containment and the Cold War* (Indianapolis: Bobbs-Merrill, 1974), pp. 102–8; and Paul Marantz, "Soviet Foreign Policy Factionalism under Stalin?: A Case Study of the Inevitability of War Controversy," *Soviet Union*, vol. 3, no. 1 (1976), pp. 91–107. On Varga's early career, which began as an economic analyst and theoretician of the Hungarian Social Democratic party in 1906 and ended with his death in 1964 in the Soviet Union (in which he took up permanent residence as director of the Institute on the World Economy and International Relations in 1927), see Laszlo M. Tikos, "Waiting for the World Revolution: Soviet Reactions to the Great Depression," in Herman van der Wee, ed., *The Great Depression Revisited: Essays on the Economics of the Thirties* (The Hague: Martinus Nijhoff, 1972), pp. 76–87.
14. The Stalin-Krzycki interview is recounted in *The Advance*, March 15, 1946, p. 8.
15. Bevin answered that "though the situation was still serious and we should have to be careful next winter, we were confident that we could surmount our difficulties." See *FR:* 1947, vol. 2, p. 283.

16. Stalin, *Sochineniia*, vol. 3, pp. 85–91.

17. *FR: 1947*, vol. 4, p. 553.

18. For a brief overview of the *Zhdanovshchina*, see John A. Armstrong, *The Politics of Totalitarianism: The Communist Party of the Soviet Union from 1934 to the Present* (New York: Random House, 1961), pp. 173–87. For an American Embassy reaction, see *FR: 1946*, vol. 6, pp. 774–76. Ilya Ehrenburg's six articles reporting on a recent trip to America appeared in *Izvestiia* on July 16, 17, 24, 25 and August 7 and 9, 1946, and were translated in *Harper's Magazine*, December 1946, pp. 562–76. Anna Akhmatova was convinced that she herself, or rather a meeting she had in 1945 with Isaiah Berlin (who was then temporary first secretary in the British embassy in Moscow), was a cause of the Cold War. She theorized that the meeting infuriated Stalin, who kept track of Russian poets, and later prompted him to start the cultural pogrom that was the domestic harbinger of the Cold War. See Amanda Haight, *Anna Akhmatova: A Poetic Pilgrimage* (New York: Oxford University Press, 1976), pp. 140–47.

19. *Vital Speeches of the Day*, vol. 12, no. 11 (March 15, 1946), pp. 329–32.

20. Stalin, *Sochineniia*, vol. 3, pp. 35–43.

21. *FR: 1946*, vol. 6, pp. 725–26.

22. Kennan's assessment—*ibid.*, p. 716. Smith-Stalin—pp. 732–36. See also Walter Bedell Smith, *My Three Years in Moscow* (Philadelphia: J. B. Lippincott, 1949), pp. 47–56.

23. *FR: 1946*, vol. 6, pp. 784–86.

24. *Ibid.*, p. 794.

25. *Ibid.*, pp. 795–96.

26. Stalin, *Sochineniia*, vol. 3, pp. 65–70.

27. Barghoorn, *The Soviet Image*, p. 135.

28. Gar Alperovitz, *Cold War Essays*, p. 97.

29. Bulgaria—*FR: 1946*, vol. 6, pp. 69, 76, 155–56. Bucharest report—p. 575. Maniu—*FR: 1947*, vol. 4, p. 479.

30. Tipsy ambassador—*FR: 1946*, vol. 6, p. 402. On American influence (plus the limits on same) in UNRRA, see Thomas G. Paterson, *Soviet-American Confrontation: Postwar Reconstruction and the Origins of the Cold War* (Baltimore: Johns Hopkins University Press, 1973), pp. 75–98.

31. Lane's advice—*FR: 1946*, vol. 6, p. 432. State Department position—pp. 435–36. Cyrankiewicz, Modzelewski, Winiewicz—*FR: 1947*, vol. 4, pp. 419–21. For a summary of on-again, off-again negotiations concerning the extension of credits to Poland (by January 1947 $40 million in Export-Import Bank credits and $50 million for the purchase of surplus war property had been made available to Poland, in addition to $140 million in UNRRA aid), see Paterson, *Soviet-American Confrontation*, pp. 130–36.

32. *FR: 1947*, vol. 4, p. 294.

33. The U.S. Export-Import Bank advanced Prague a credit of $20 million toward the import of American cotton in May 1946. Negotiations for further credits of $50 million were suspended. See *FR: 1946*, vol. 6, p. 216.

34. *FR:* 1946, vol. 7, pp. 840–41; Yergin, *Shattered Peace*, p. 235.

35. *FR:* 1946, vol. 7, pp. 335, 340–41, 351–52; vol. 6, p. 734. The crisis ended with Soviet troops pulling out, but Moscow continued to exert political pressure on Tehran to the point, once the Cold War began in earnest, that some American officials feared a Soviet invasion of Iran.

36. *FR:* 1946, vol. 7, p. 816.

37. *Ibid.*, pp. 818–36.

38. Djilas, *Conversations with Stalin*, pp. 181–82. Soviet press and U.S. reaction—*FR:* 1945, vol. 8, p. 148, 152. Bevin-Vyshinsky—*FR:* 1946, vol. 7 pp. 109–10. On the situation in Greece, and especially relations between Greek and Soviet Communists, see Tsoucoulas, *The Greek Tragedy*, pp. 100–101; C. M. Woodhouse, *The Struggle for Greece 1941–1949* (London: Hart-Davis, MacGibbon, 1976), pp. 159–92; George Kousoulas, *Revolution and Defeat: The Story of the Greek Communist Party* (London: Oxford University Press, 1965), p. 230.

39. For the Korean clauses in the Moscow Conference Communique, see *FR:* 1945, vol. 2, pp. 820–21.

40. *FR:* 1946, vol. 8, pp. 660–72, 743.

41. *Ibid.*, pp. 619, 632, 640, 653–97.

42. Kennan—*FR:* 1946, vol. 5, pp. 516–20, 555–56. Smith—pp. 749–50. Murphy—pp. 625, 632. Embassy—p. 628. For a fuller account see Yergin, *Shattered Peace*, pp. 95–98, 224–32.

43. Djilas, *Conversations with Stalin*, pp. 153–54; the *Washington Post*, January 23, 1952.

44. The up's and down's of Byrnes' proposed treaty can be traced in *FR:* 1945, vol. 2, pp. 267–68; and *FR:* 1946, vol. 2, pp. 62, 83, 146–47. The draft text is in the latter, pp. 190–93.

45. *FR:* 1947, vol. 4, p. 520.

46. Central Intelligence report—see Yergin, *Shattered Peace*, p. 275. Embassy view and Soviet-British relations—*FR:* 1947, vol. 4, pp. 516–17, 523–28. Stalin article—Stalin, *Sochineniia*, vol. 3, p. 30.

47. *FR:* 1947, vol. 2, pp. 108, 139–42, 215–18.

48. Interzonal barriers—*Documents on International Affairs, 1946–1947,* ed. Margaret Carlyle (London: Oxford University Press, 1952), p. 436. Molotov and Marshall—*FR:* 1947, vol. 2, pp. 264, 278.

49. *FR:* 1947, vol. 2, pp. 278–84.

50. *Ibid.*, pp. 290, 296, 298–99.

51. *Ibid.*, pp. 302–3, 306.

52. Charles Bohlen, *Witness to History 1929–1969* (New York: W. W. Norton, 1973), pp. 262–63. Marshall and Stalin—*FR:* 1947, vol. 2, pp. 337–44.

53. Quoted in Yergin, *Shattered Peace*, p. 232. See also Byrnes, *Speaking Frankly*, p. 194.

54. Adam B. Ulam, *The Rivals: America and Russia Since World War II* (New York: Viking, 1971), pp. 122–23. Ulam recognizes that the prospect of a "united but disarmed and neutral" Germany, the most anyone could have

dreamed of getting the Soviets to concede, would have struck many in the West as *less*, not more, preferable than a two-Germanies solution. For more on this see chapter seven, below.

55. Quoted in Gaddis Smith, *Dean Acheson*, vol. 16 of *The American Secretaries of State and Their Diplomacy*, ed. Robert H. Ferrell and Samuel Flagg Bemis (New York: Cooper Square Publisher, 1972), p. 138.

56. *FR: 1946*, vol. 2, p. 1259.

57. Australian tactics—*FR: 1946*, vol. 3, p. 282. Soviet comments— pp. 288, 293, 319. Byrnes's attitude—Sulzberger, *A Long Row of Candles*, p. 316. Willard Thorp, who as deputy assistant secretary of state for economic affairs and chief American delegate to the Paris Peace Conference's economic commissions voted against Australian and other amendments (see, for example, *FR: 1946*, vol. 3, p. 297), confirmed, in an August 19, 1980, interview with the author, that the Americans had *not* put the smaller powers up to their amendments and in fact *were* exasperated at having to consider so many of them at such great length.

58. *FR: 1946*, vol. 2, pp. 508, 528, 599, 615–16, 661.

59. *Ibid.*, pp. 698–732.

60. *Ibid.*, pp. 1029, 1062, 1141.

61. Bohlen, *Witness to History*, pp. 255–56. Byrnes himself recalls two separate meetings with Molotov a day apart before the Soviet foreign minister caved in. See Byrnes, *Speaking Frankly*, pp. 152–54. American diplomatic records show a first meeting on November 25 at which Byrnes said it would be better to admit frankly that they could not agree and "announce their disagreement to the world," and a second one on December 6 at which the secretary consoled Molotov on the behavior of the ungrateful Yugoslavs. American CFM minutes reveal Molotov doling out concessions after each meeting. See *FR: 1946*, vol. 2, pp. 1264–78, 1437–41.

CHAPTER 7
From Détente to Cold War

1. *FR: 1948*, vol. 1, pt. 2, pp. 519, 522.

2. *FR: 1948*, vol. 4, pp. 337–38.

3. Lovett—*FR: 1947*, vol. 1, p. 762. Dulles to Rusk (then director of the State Department's Office of UN Affairs)—*FR: 1948*, vol. 1, pt. 2, p. 544. Truman—*Vital Speeches of the Day*, vol. 14, no. 12 (April 1, 1948), pp. 1–3. NSC-7 in Thomas H. Etzold and John Lewis Gaddis, eds., *Containment: Documents on American Policy and Strategy*, 1945–1950 (New York: Columbia University Press, 1978), pp. 164–69. Embassy estimate—*FR: 1948*, vol. 1, pt. 2, pp. 551–57.

4. Truman, Clay and CIA quoted in Yergin, *Shattered Peace*, pp. 350–53.

5. Bidault—*FR: 1948*, vol. 3, pp. 629. Sforza—p. 835.

6. Bevin—*ibid.*, p. 48. Spaack—p. 76. Shah—*FR: 1948*, vol. 5, pt. 1, p. 132.

7. *FR: 1948*, vol. 3, p. 848. Thirty years later Kennan denied that his words of March 15, 1948 were meant to warn of imminent war. See his reply to Edward Mark in *Foreign Affairs*, vol. 56, no. 3 (April 1978), pp. 643–45. See also Edward Mark, "The Question of Containment: A Reply to John Lewis Gaddis," *Foreign Affairs*, vol. 56, no. 2 (January 1978), pp. 430–41.

8. George F. Kennan, *Memoirs: 1950–1963*, vol. 2 (Boston: Atlantic, Little, Brown, 1972), pp. 90–91.

9. *FR: 1947*, vol. 1, pp. 770–77.

10. Kennan *vs.* Forrestal—*FR: 1948*, vol. 1, pt. 2, pp. 589–93, 599–601. NSC 20/1 in Etzold and Gaddis, eds., *Containment*, pp. 176–77, 182.

11. NSC 20/2—*FR: 1948*, vol. 1, pt. 2, pp. 617–19. Marshall to Forrestal— pp. 541, 655. The final product of this interagency skirmishing was NSC 20/4, the definitive statement of Washington's Soviet strategy until NSC 68 was finished in April 1950. NSC 20/4 painted a mixed picture. Long-term Soviet aims were said to be emphatically and dangerously offensive, but for the moment Moscow was largely on the defensive. Soviet armed forces were capable of seizing and holding all of Continental Europe and parts of the Near and Far East, and there was "a continuing danger of war at any time," but the "probability" was that "the Soviet Government is not now planning any deliberate armed action." America's primary objectives were those listed in NSC 20/1, but the new paper gave new prominence to the importance of military readiness. See Etzold and Gaddis, eds., *Containment*, pp. 203–11.

12. *FR: 1947*, vol. 4, pp. 557–58, 562–64. "The Prospects for International Cooperation," *New Times*, No. 20 (May 16, 1947), p. 1.

13. Nagy—*FR: 1947*, vol. 4, p. 298. Togliatti—vol. 3, p. 935.

14. For an expression of hope in NSC 20/1 that the decision as to whether to accept Marshall Plan aid would strain Soviet-East-European relations, see Etzold and Gaddis, eds., *Containment*, p. 182. For an inside account by a former U.S. intelligence operative in Hungary, who makes clear that it was only in 1948 that the CIA added political subversion to its intelligence gathering activities, see Christopher Felix, *A Short Course in the Secret War* (New York: E. P. Dutton, 1963), esp. pp. 232–36. For a Washington perspective on this same period, see William Colby and Peter Forbath, *Honorable Men: My Life in the CIA* (New York: Simon and Schuster, 1978), pp. 67–77, 104–6.

15. *FR: 1947*, vol. 3, pp. 228, 238–39; Yergin, *Shattered Peace*, pp. 314–16.

16. *FR: 1947*, vol. 3, pp. 260, 295–98, 300–301.

17. *Ibid.*, pp. 260, 313, 319–20.

18. Ambassador Smith—*ibid.*, p. 327. Soviet propaganda—*FR: 1947*, vol. 4, p. 588. For an inside account of the Cominform founding see Eugenio Reale, *Avec Jacques Duclos au Banc des Accusés à la Réunion Constitutive de Kominform à Szlarska Poreba* (Paris: Librarie Plon, 1958).

19. *FR: 1947*, vol. 4, p. 596. Truman is quoted in Yergin, *Shattered Peace*, p. 328.

20. Yergin, *Shattered Peace*, pp. 317, 324. Ulam, *The Rivals*, p. 130. The Declaration and excerpts from the speeches mentioned are in *Documents on International Affairs, 1947–1948*, ed. Margaret Carlyle (London: Oxford University Press) pp. 122–46.

21. Thorez—*FR:* 1947, vol. 3, p. 813.

22. Yergin, *Shattered Peace*, p. 311. According to a French Interior Ministry report relayed to the American Embassy in Paris, Communist militance in France and Italy was designed "not to grab power by a coup d'état at this time but rather to cause the present democratic governments in Western Europe to collapse one after another under strong Communist blows . . . thus precipitating the abandonment of Europe by the U.S. and leaving the door finally open to Communism." See *FR:* 1947, vol. 3, pp. 813–14. On the Communist-supported strike movement and its significance on France, see Ronald Tiersky, *French Communism, 1920–1972* (New York: Columbia University Press, 1974), pp. 168–75.

23. *FR:* 1947, vol. 2, pp. 687, 734, 752, 762, 772.

24. *FR:* 1948, vol. 4, p. 792.

25. *Ibid.*, pp. 759–87 *passim*. The crisis died down when the Finns, standing their ground, negotiated an acceptable treaty, excluded the Communist minister of the interior from his post, and then, after July elections in which the Communists fared poorly, constituted a new government without them.

26. Greece and Turkey—*ibid.*, pp. 3, 9, 115, 148. Iran—*FR:* 1948, vol. 5, pt. 1, pp. 88–121. Jernegan quoted on p. 120.

27. *FR:* 1948, vol. 4, p. 1080.

28. *Ibid.*, pp. 1110–13.

29. *Documents on International Affairs, 1947–1948*, pp. 355, 369, 381, 383, 386.

30. Harry S. Truman, *Memoirs*, vol. 2: *Years of Trial and Hope* (Garden City, N.Y.: Doubleday, 1956), pp. 123–24.

31. That the State Department was aware of this possible Soviet motive, even if Truman did not find it the most likely one, is suggested by a department memorandum summarized in *FR:* 1948, vol. 2, p. 483.

32. January gestures—Yergin, *Shattered Peace*, p. 367. Soviet protests—*FR:* 1948, vol. 2, pp. 338–39, 345–54. Murphy reports—pp. 878, 901–2, 905.

33. *FR:* 1948, vol. 4, p. 835.

34. Smith-Molotov conversation—*ibid.*, pp. 845–50. *Bolshevik* quoted on p. 870.

35. *Ibid.*, pp. 858–59, 860. Stalin, *Sochineniia*, vol. 3, pp. 101–3.

36. On the Soviet view of Henry Wallace's Presidential prospects, see Barghoorn, *Soviet Image*, p. 221. Truman in Oregon cited in Shulman, *Stalin's Foreign Policy*, p. 31. The Vinson episode—Truman, *Memoirs*, vol. II, pp. 213–15.

37. *FR:* 1948, vol. 2, pp. 918, 926. Bevin quoted in Yergin, *Shattered Peace*, p. 378.

38. *FR:* 1948, vol. 2, pp. 915–32.

39. *Ibid.*, p. 964.

40. *Ibid.*, pp. 975, 988, 995.

41. *Ibid.*, pp. 999–1006.

42. *Ibid.*, pp. 1006–7.

43. Smith to Stalin—*ibid.*, p. 999. Molotov and the ambassadors—pp. 1018–21. Djilas, *Conversations with Stalin*, p. 153.

44. FR: 1948, vol. 2, pp. 1024–27, 1035–38, 1042–47, 1065–71, 1088–90.

45. *Ibid.*, pp. 1099–1140 *passim*.

46. *Ibid.*, pp. 1240–47, 1287–97. Also see Kennan, *Memoirs, 1925–1950*, pp. 466–73.

CHAPTER 8

Cold War Stalinist-Style

1. Kennan, *Memoirs: 1950–1963*, pp. 90–92.

2. On troop levels and defense spending, see Warner R. Schilling, Paul Y. Hammond and Glenn H. Snyder, *Strategy, Politics and Defense Budgets* (New York: Columbia University Press, 1962), pp. 29–30, 40–47, 321. On atomic strategy and capabilities, see David Alan Rosenberg, "American Atomic Strategy and the Hydrogen Bomb Decision," *Journal of American History*, vol. 66, no. 1 (June 1979), pp. 72–87.

3. On the exploits of Maclean, Philby, and also of Guy Burgess, who for a time after the war was the personal assistant to British Foreign Secretary, Ernest Bevin's right-hand man, Hector McNeil, see Andrew Boyle, *The Climate of Treason* (London: Coronet Books, 1980). Just what information these Soviet agents transmitted and how Stalin, assuming he saw their reports, reacted to it is not clear. The information apparently included such reassuring items as Prime Minister Attlee's notes on his efforts to ensure that Truman would not use atomic weapons in Korea, but Donald Maclean himself, in whose possession Attlee's notes were later found, was reported greatly to fear nuclear war in 1950. The extent to which Stalin actually credited reports from his overseas agents is a legitimate issue given his failure in 1941 to heed warnings of Nazi attack conveyed to him by Soviet intelligence. On this failure, see F. W. Deakin and G. R. Storry, *The Case of Richard Sorge* (New York: Harper and Row, 1966), pp. 227–31.

4. Kennan, *Memoirs: 1950–1963*, pp. 336–38.

5. Khrushchev, *Khrushchev Remembers*, pp. 221, 270–75. N. S. Khrushchev, *Khrushchev Remembers: The Last Testament*, trans. and ed. Strobe Talbot (Boston: Little, Brown, 1974), pp. 188–89, 191, 355–57, 393.

6. Shulman, *Stalin's Foreign Policy*, pp. 1, 264. For the opposite view, that "Stalin was *not contemplating an international détente* toward the end of his life" but was rather "defending with all the force of his autocratic authority the opposite view that no *détente* was possible," see Robert C. Tucker, *The Soviet*

Political Mind: Stalinism and Post–Stalin Change, rev. ed. (New York: W. W. Norton, 1971), pp. 98.

7. Svetlana Alliluyeva, *Twenty Letters to a Friend*, trans. Priscilla Johnson McMillan (New York: Harper and Row, 1967), pp. 196–97, 200; Khrushchev, *Khrushchev Remembers*, pp. 246, 275, 279. For a vivid fictional portrait of Stalin in his last years, see Aleksandr I. Solzhenitsyn, *The First Circle*, trans. Thomas P. Whitney (New York: Harper and Row, 1968), pp. 85–116.

8. *FR:* 1949, vol. 1, pp. 283–84.

9. Acheson's judgment—*ibid.*, p. 615. The text of NSC 68 is in Etzold and Gaddis, eds., *Containment*, pp. 385–442. The story behind the drafting is told by Paul Hammond in Schilling et al., *Strategy*, pp. 267–378. Bohlen—*FR:* 1950, vol. 1, p. 222.

10. Hammond points to evidence of deliberate overstatement in Schilling et. al., *Strategy*, pp. 309, 370–72. So does John C. Donovan in *The Cold Warriors: A Policy–Making Elite* (Lexington, Mass.: D. C. Heath, 1974), pp. 89, 98, 262. Also see Dean Acheson, *Present at the Creation: My Years in the State Department* (New York: Signet Books, 1970), pp. 454–55.

11. Soviet intentions and capabilities—Etzold and Gaddis, eds., *Containment*, pp. 385, 387, 389, 395, 398, 400, 414. Nitze—*FR:* 1950, vol. 1, p. 145. For a skeptical assessment of the various claims of NSC 68, see Samuel F. Wells, Jr., "Sounding the Tocsin: NSC 68 and the Soviet Threat," *International Security*, vol. 4, no. 2 (Fall 1979), pp. 152–57.

12. Etzold and Gaddis, eds., *Containment*, pp. 422, 435–36. Acheson's speech—*Department of State Bulletin*, vol. 22, no. 560 (March 27, 1950), pp. 473–78.

13. *FR:* 1950, vol. 1, pp. 336, 343, 361, 365, 415. Truman's 1951 State of the Union Address is in *Public Papers of the President of the United States: Harry S. Truman, 1951* (Washington: U.S.G.P.O., 1965), pp. 7–13.

14. *FR:* 1949, vol. 5, pp. 639, 646. Instead of discussing basic East-West divisions, Kirk broached "practical issues" such as repayment of lend-lease debts and Soviet jamming of Voice of America broadcasts. Stalin replied that he was poorly informed on the latter question and appeared to confuse VOA with the BBC. Kirk's impression was that "though possibly fatigued, Stalin is in good health."

15. *Documents on International Affairs, 1951*, selected by and ed. Denise Folliot (London: Oxford University Press, 1954), pp. 649, 346.

16. *FR:* 1949, vol. 5, p. 585.

17. *Ibid.*, pp. 592–94.

18. Alliluyeva, *Twenty Letters*, pp. 61, 193, 208; Khrushchev, *Khrushchev Remembers*, pp. 245–61, 278–81, 309.

19. Resistible blandishments and Thorez statement—Shulman, *Stalin's Foreign Policy*, pp. 54–58. Smith interview—*FR:* 1949, vol. 5, p. 562. NATO blast and Norway pressure—vol. 4, pp. 51, 53, 65, 91.

20. *FR:* 1949, vol. 3, pp. 712–13, 717, 733, 750–51; Shulman, *Stalin's Foreign Policy*, p. 73.

21. *FR: 1949*, vol. 3, pp. 865, 929, 979.

22. *FR: 1949*, vol. 2, pp. 72, 86.

23. *FR: 1949*, vol. 5, pp. 632–34, 651–54. Kelly reported that Stalin "appeared to be in good health but showed his age, was vigorous mentally and was keen and alert."

24. See Shulman, *Stalin's Foreign Policy*, pp. 77.

25. *FR: 1949*, vol. 5, pp. 655–56.

26. *FR: 1949*, vol. 3, p. 705.

27. *FR: 1949*, vol. 5, pp. 656–57; *Documents on International Affairs, 1951*, p. 341.

28. *Documents on International Affairs, 1949–1950*, selected by and ed. Margaret Carlyle (London: Oxford University Press, 1953), pp. 130–33. Robert C. Tucker speculates (in *The Soviet Political Mind*, pp. 94–95) that Malenkov's optimism may have been a veiled expression of a foreign policy heresy. The opposition view, according to Tucker, was that the USSR ought to call "at least a temporary halt to Soviet foreign expansion in order to diminish the degree of external danger." Yet such a relaxation of vigilance would only be safe if one assumed that the "capitalist encirclement," which, according to Stalin, mortally threatened the Soviet Union, were at an end. The fact that in 1951 the Party journal, *Bolshevik*, condemned "certain comrades" for construing "the establishment of the people's democratic system in a number of countries bordering on the USSR as liquidating the capitalist encirclement" does not prove that Malenkov was among them. After Stalin's death, Malenkov did come out for a relaxation of East-West tensions, but it is hard to imagine even someone of his stature openly pressing a line in opposition to Stalin's during the dictator's frightful last years.

29. *FR: 1949*, vol. 5, p. 673.

30. *FR: 1947*, vol. 6, pp. 804–6, 817–18, 852.

31. *FR: 1948*, vol. 6, pp. 1094, 1155, 1180, 1317, 1342.

32. Acheson's speech, delivered at the National Press Club on January 12, 1950, is in *Department of State Bulletin*, vol. 22, no. 551 (January 23, 1950), pp. 111–18. Reference to defense perimeter is on p. 116. Connolly and Muccio—*FR: 1950*, vol. 7, pp. 65–66, 88–89.

33. Khrushchev, *Khrushchev Remembers*, pp. 367–68; Kennan, *Memoirs: 1950–1963*, p. 339.

34. See Rodger Swearingen, *The Soviet Union and Postwar Japan: Escalating Challenge and Response* (Stanford, Cal.: Hoover Institution Press, 1978), pp. 23–67.

35. Kennan, *Memoirs: 1950–1963*, pp. 41–42; Shulman, *Stalin's Foreign Policy*, pp. 143–44. Also see Allen Whiting, *China Crosses the Yalu: The Decision to Enter the Korean War* (New York: Macmillan, 1960), p. 36.

36. For a statement of the "missed chance" thesis, see Michael H. Hunt, "Mao Tse-tung and the Issue of Accommodation with the United States, 1948–1950," in Dorothy Borg and Waldo Heinrichs, eds., *Uncertain Years: Chinese-American Relations, 1947–1950* (New York: Columbia University Press, 1980),

pp. 181-233; and Donald S. Zagoria, "Containment and China," in Charles Gati, ed., *Caging the Bear: Containment and the Cold War* (Indianapolis: Bobbs-Merrill, 1974), pp. 109-27. For a rebuttal, see Steven M. Goldstein, "Chinese Communist Policy toward the United States: Opportunities and Constraints, 1944-1950," in Borg and Heinrichs, eds., *Uncertain Years*, pp. 235-78. For a summary of the debate, see Steven I. Levine, "Notes on Soviet Policy in China and Chinese Communist Perceptions, 1945-1950," in Borg and Heinrichs, pp. 293-303. Also see Robert R. Simmons, *The Strained Alliance: Peking, Pyongyang, Moscow and the Politics of the Korean Civil War* (New York: Free Press, 1975).

37. Kennan, *Memoirs: 1950-1963*, p. 34. Also see Helmut König, "Der Konflikt zwischen Stalin und Togliatti um die Jahreswende 1950-1951," and "Wollte Stalin Togliatti Kaltstellen?" *Osteuropa*, no. 10 (October 1970), pp. 699-706, A703-A718.

38. *FR: 1950*, vol. 7, pp. 204, 229-30, 280, 312-13.

39. *Ibid.*, pp. 315-16, 325, 348.

40. *Ibid.*, pp. 337-42.

41. *Ibid.*, pp. 401, 408.

42. *Ibid.*, p. 445.

43. *Ibid.*, pp. 460-61.

44. *Ibid.*, pp. 485-86, 492-95, 566, 596-99, 699-702.

45. *Ibid.*, pp. 773-74, 781, 868.

46. Malik's peace talk proposal—*ibid.*, p. 784. His draft resolution—pp. 838-39. The round-about approach—pp. 877-80, 897-99, 906-11, 922.

47. *Ibid.*, pp. 915, 917.

48. *Documents on International Affairs*, 1951, pp. 293-94.

49. Kirk-Vyshinsky—*ibid.*, pp. 649-50. Gromyko's performance—Peter Calvocoressi, *Survey of International Affairs, 1951* (London: Oxford University Press, 1945), pp. 415-16.

50. See Peter Calvocoressi, *Survey of International Affairs, 1952* (London: Oxford University Press, 1955), pp. 55-57, 88-89, 109-12.

51. Scientific economic laws—Stalin, *Sochineniia*, vol. 3, pp. 189-98. Commodity production—pp. 199, 207. Town and country—pp. 222-23. Disintegration of capitalist world market and inevitability of war—pp. 223-31.

52. Robert C. Tucker suggests (*The Soviet Political Mind*, pp. 99-101) that Stalin's stress on the primacy of inter-imperialist tensions was an Aesopian argument against associates who were urging a relaxation of Cold War tensions. According to Tucker, Malenkov and others may have privately warned that the Cold War was serving to unify the capitalist camp, whereas, as Malenkov was to argue publicly after Stalin's death, détente could increase inter-imperialist strains. In Tucker's version, Stalin was teaching that "intercapitalist contradictions were so deep and powerful that eventually they would split the capitalist world wide open quite independently of any Soviet initiative to relax international tension."

53. *Documents on International Affairs*, 1952, selected by and ed. Denise Folliot (London: Oxford University Press, 1955), p. 240.

CONCLUSION:

After Stalin

1. For a scenario by a Soviet dissident in which a Sino-Soviet war leads to the disintegration of the USSR, see Andrei Amalrik, *Will the U.S.S.R. Survive Until 1984?* (New York: Harper and Row, 1970).
2. *Documents on International Affairs*, 1953, selected by and ed. Denise Folliot (London: Oxford University Press, 1956), pp. 4, 63; Khrushchev, *Khrushchev Remembers*, p. 392; Townsend Hoopes, *The Devil and John Foster Dulles* (Boston: Little, Brown, 1973), pp. 170–75. Division in the Soviet leadership was made manifest when Beria was arrested in July and later executed. The fact that the Soviets at first resisted Western proposals for a foreign ministers meeting attests to what Adam Ulam calls "considerable uncertainty in Moscow during the wanning months of 1953 . . . and a desire to probe the intentions and capabilities of the new American administration before tipping the Soviet hand." Ulam, *Expansion and Coexistence*, pp. 547–48.
3. *Documents on International Affairs*, 1953, p. 13.
4. *Ibid.*, pp. 22–33. The reference to Turkey was in a separate statement by the Soviet government issued on May 30, 1953. See *ibid.*, pp. 277–78.
5. *Ibid.*, pp. 48–49.
6. This picture of Khrushchev is constructed from his memoirs as well as studies including Carl A. Linden, *Khrushchev and the Soviet Leadership* (Baltimore: Johns Hopkins University Press, 1966), and William Hyland and Richard Shryock, *The Fall of Khrushchev* (New York: Funk and Wagnalls, 1968).
7. See the detailed account of the Vienna summit in Arthur M. Schlesinger, Jr., *A Thousand Days: John F. Kennedy in the White House* (Boston: Houghton Mifflin, 1965), pp. 343–78.
8. This section draws extensively on Henry A. Kissinger, *The White House Years* (Boston: Little, Brown, 1979).
9. *Ibid.*, pp. 123, 1254.
10. For a report on and summary of Sonnenfeldt's remarks to American ambassadors in Europe, see the *New York Times*, April 6, 1976, pp. 1, 14. For Henry Kissinger's charge that Sonnenfeldt's message had been inaccurately reported, see *The Department of State Bulletin*, vol. 74, no. 1922 (April 26, 1976), p. 546.
11. Kissinger, *The White House Years*, p. 1254.
12. These passages are from the "Basic Principles of Relations between the United States of America and the Union of Soviet Socialist Republics," of May 29, 1972 and the "Agreement between the United States of America and the Union of Soviet Socialist Republics on the Prevention of Nuclear War," of

June 22, 1973, both in Robert J. Pranger, ed., *Detente and Defense: A Reader* (Washington: American Enterprise Institute, 1976), pp. 115, 146.

13. Brezhnev's remarks—*Pravda*, February 25, 1976. Soviet commentator Valentin Zorin's Moscow Radio (North American Service) broadcast of July 1, 1978 as monitored by *Foreign Broadcast Information Service—Soviet Union* (hereafter *FBIS*), no. 128 (July 3, 1978), p. B2.

14. Arbatov developed his analysis in these articles among others: "American Imperialism and New World Realities," *Pravda*, May 4, 1971, pp. 4–5; "On Soviet-American Relations," *Kommunist*, no. 3 (February 1973), pp. 101–13; and "Soviet-American Relations at a New Stage," *Pravda*, July 22, 1973, pp. 4–5.

15. In an interview with the Magazine Publishers' Association on June 6, 1977, President Carter said: "My own inclination is to aggressively challenge, in a peaceful way, of course, the Soviet Union and others for influence in areas of the world that we feel are crucial to us now or potentially crucial fifteen or twenty years from now. And this includes places like Iraq and Somalia and Algeria, and places like the People's Republic of China and even Cuba. I don't have any hesitancy about these matters." See *Public Papers of the President of the United States—Jimmy Carter*, vol. I (January 1–June 24, 1977), (Washington: USGPO, 1977), p. 1088. For Carter's "inordinate fear" speech, see *The Department of State Bulletin*, vol. 76, no. 1981 (June 13, 1977), p. 622. Complaint about Brzezinski is in Georgi Ratiani, " 'Complexes' of American Policy," *Pravda*, December 14, 1977, p. 4.

16. Carter's Vienna toast came in reply to a Brezhnev remark reminiscent of wartime Soviet hyperbole: "It is known that the leaders of the USSR are convinced supporters of easing international tension. But détente is only the beginning. In relations with America, as well as with other states, we would like more. We would like really good neighborly relations. . . ." See *Pravda*, June 18, 1979, pp. 1–2. The senatorial visit is recounted in Robert G. Kaiser, "Soviet Talks Shook Visiting Senators," *The Washington Post*, December 24, 1978, p. D5.

17. "On the Present Policy of the U.S. Government," *Pravda*, June 17, 1978, p. 4.

18. Arbatov and Zamiatin (head of the Central Committee's International Information Department) spoke on Soviet television, as monitored by *FBIS*, no. 129 (July 5, 1978), pp. A6, A9.

19. Arbatov warning as reported in *The Financial Times*, February 3, 1979, p. 3.

20. Brezhnev quoted in *Time*, January 22, 1979, p. 25. Zorin—Moscow television in *FBIS*, no. 4 (January 5, 1979), p. A13.

21. Zagladin—*Der Stern*, March 29, 1979, in *FBIS*, no. 63 (March 30, 1979), p. CC1. Brezhnev in *Pravda*, March 3, 1979.

22. Zagladin—*Der Spiegel*, November 5, 1979, in *FBIS*, no. 217 (November 7, 1979), p. AA10. Gromyko—*FBIS*, no. 188 (September 26, 1979), p. C5.

23. See Craig R. Whitney, "Diplomats in Moscow Speculating that Moscow Misjudged West's Reaction," the *New York Times*, January 11, 1980, p. A8; and Graham Hovey, "U.S. Adviser Says Soviets Misjudged Difficulties of Afghan Intervention," the *New York Times*, January 16, 1980, p. A13.

24. "Thomas Kielinger, "A Soviet Diplomat: We Bridle Slowly But Do Some Fast Riding," *Die Welt*, January 14, 1980, in *FBIS*, no. 10 (January 15, 1980), pp. A4–A8.

25. For a clash of views concerning continuity and change in Stalinist and post-Stalinist foreign policy, see Charles Gati, "The Stalinist Legacy in Soviet Foreign Policy," and William Zimmerman, "The Soviet Union and the West," in Stephen F. Cohen, Alexander Rabinowitch and Robert Sharlet, eds., *The Soviet Union Since Stalin* (Bloomington, Ind.: Indiana University Press, 1980), pp. 279–311.

26. Kissinger, *The White House Years*, p. 815.

27. On the nature and extent of Soviet political stability, see Seweryn Bialer, *Stalin's Successors: Leadership, Stability and Change in the Soviet Union* (New York: Cambridge University Press, 1980), pp. 127–205.

28. Kissinger, *The White House Years*, p. 1227.

29. Stephen F. Cohen, "Hard-Line Fallacies," the *New York Times*, August 22, 1980, p. A23.

30. On the concept of political culture, see Sidney Verba, "Conclusion: Comparative Political Culture," in Lucian W. Pye and Sidney Verba, eds., *Political Culture and Political Development* (Princeton: Princeton University Press, 1965), pp. 512–60.

31. Proverbs quoted in John S. Reshetar, Jr., "Russian Ethnic Values," in Cyril E. Black, ed., *The Transformation of Russian Society: Aspects of Social Change Since 1861* (Cambridge: Harvard University Press, 1967), p. 560, and Richard Pipes, *Russia Under the Old Regime* (New York: Charles Scribner's, 1974), p. 160.

32. Bialer, *Stalin's Successors*, p. 81.

33. *Ibid.*, p. 104; Jerry F. Hough, *Soviet Leadership in Transition* (Washington: Brookings Institution, 1980), pp. 149, 167–68.

34. See, for example, Alexander Yanov, *Detente After Brezhnev: The Domestic Roots of Soviet Foreign Policy* (Berkeley: Institute of International Studies, 1977), Yanov, *The New Russian Right: Right-Wing Ideologies in the Contemporary USSR* (Berkeley: Institute of International Studies, 1978), and George W. Breslauer, *Five Images of the Soviet Future: A Critical Review and Synthesis* (Berkeley: Institute of International Studies, 1978), pp. 53–61.

35. Bialer, *Stalin's Successors*, pp. 107, 229–30, 265.

36. I am grateful to Robert C. Tucker for clarifying this option. See also his "United States-Soviet Cooperation: Incentives and Obstacles," *The Annals of the American Academy of Political and Social Science*, vol. 372 (July 1967), pp. 1–15.

37. Some of the problems involved in any spheres-of-influence arrangement in

the Middle East are suggested by the case of Europe in 1945. George Kennan recalls that in 1945 he was "an advocate—the only such advocate, I suppose, in the higher echelons of our governmental service—of a prompt and clear recognition of the division of Europe into spheres of influence and of a policy based on the fact of such a division." Kennan thought the Western public was deceiving itself by "clinging to the hope that what the foreseeable future held in store for most of these [East European] countries could be anything less than complete Communist domination and complete isolation from the West, on the Soviet pattern." But the Truman administration continued to cling to this hope and did not finally yield to what Kennan took to be realities for some time to come. The likelihood of an American administration's accepting a Soviet sphere of influence in the Middle East is suggested by Washington's harsh reaction to the Soviet Union's attempt to create one in Afghanistan. See Kennan, *Memoirs: 1925–1950*, p. 266.

Index

Acheson, Dean, 159–60, 198–99, 201, 212, 215, 218
"Action Program of the Bloc of Militant Democracy," 80–81
Afghanistan, Soviet intervention in, 228, 229, 230, 239, 240, 241–42, 245, 246
Akhmatova, Anna, 140
Allied Control Commission, 79, 110–11, 113, 154
Allied Control Council (ACC), 115, 119, 123, 125, 148, 183, 213
Alliluyeva, Svetlana, 197–98, 205
Allison, John, 217
Alperovitz, Gar, 6–7
Anglo-Soviet Treaty (1942), 50–51, 156
Angola, Soviet-Cuban intervention in, 236, 238
Arbatov, Georgi A., 238, 239, 240
Argentina, United Nations and, 104–5
Atlantic Charter, 47, 48, 102
atomic bomb, 110, 169, 176, 178, 198, 209, 211
Australia, at Paris Peace Conference, 161
Austria, Allied peace treaty with, 154, 155, 232

Badoglio, Pietro, 79
Baillie, Hugh, 143, 163
Baltic states, Soviet relations with, 28, 47–48, 50, 65, 67, 69, 70, 171
Barghoorn, Frederick, 144
Barnes, Maynard, 102, 145–46
Baruch Plan, 143
Beaverbrook, William Aitken, Lord, 42–46, 48, 49, 57
Belgium, 81, 103, 124
Beneš, Eduard, 54, 55, 61, 69, 77, 101
Beria, Lavrenti, 205
Berlin blockade (1948), 9, 166, 182, 187–92, 207, 215, 234
Bern peace talks, 95, 96
Berry, Burton, 102, 146

Bevin, Ernest, 117, 119, 120, 125, 126, 136, 137, 150, 152, 156, 160, 169, 179, 215
    Berlin blockade and, 187, 188
    Marshall Plan talks and, 173, 174
Bialer, Seweryn, 251–53
Bidault, Georges, 120, 169, 173, 174, 179
Bierut, Boleslaw, 77
Biryuzov, S. S., 113
Bohlen, Charles, 35, 45, 65, 66, 120, 157, 158, 163, 199, 201, 209, 215
    at Potsdam Conference, 108, 110
Bolshevik, 185
Bolshevik Revolution (1917), 12–13, 249
Brest-Litovsk, Treaty of (1918), 13, 15, 20, 168
Brezhnev, Leonid, 43, 46, 237–38, 239, 241, 242, 246, 247, 249–50
"British Plan for a Western European Bloc," 108
Browder, Earl, 74, 98
Brussels Pact (1948), 182–83
Brzezinski, Zbigniew, 239
Bukharin, Nikolai, 16
Bulgaria, 151
    Nazi occupation of, 29
    Soviet relations with, 29, 74, 75, 90, 91, 93, 102, 111, 112–13, 145–46
    U.S. relations with, 102–3, 109, 111, 112, 113, 115, 118–19, 145–46
Bullitt, William C., 25
Byrnes, James F., 99, 101, 130, 143, 148, 149, 162
    German question as viewed by, 154, 158, 161
    at London Conference (1945), 116–20
    at Moscow Conference (1945), 125, 126–27, 129, 132, 152, 159
    at New York Conference, 154, 160, 163
    at Paris Peace Conference, 161, 163
    at Potsdam Conference, 109, 110, 111–12

Cachin, Marcel, 206
Campbell, Thomas W., 19–20

283

capitalism, 39, 84, 87
  contradictions of, as viewed by Stalin, 16–18,
    21–22, 24, 75, 224–25
  imperialism related to, 7, 12, 16–18, 21–22
  Leninist views of, 10–11, 12, 16, 75
  postwar economic crisis predicted for, 129,
    131, 135–39
Carter, Jimmy, 45, 56, 101, 238–40, 242, 247
Carter Doctrine, 194, 242
Central Intelligence Agency (CIA), 155, 169,
    173, 194, 202, 205, 245
Central Intelligence Group (CIG), 155
Changes in the Economy of Capitalism (Varga),
    84
Chiang Kai-shek, 23, 63, 82, 122–23
China:
  Communists vs. Nationalists in, 22, 23, 82,
    122–23, 148
  as great power, 63, 88, 89
  at London Conference, 116, 119, 120
  Soviet relations with, 22, 63, 81, 82, 122–23,
    148
  U.S. relations with, 138
China, People's Republic of, 198
  Korean War and, 213, 214, 216, 217, 221, 222
  Soviet relations with, 10, 209–10, 214, 228,
    229, 233–34, 246
  United Nations and, 210, 215, 216, 217, 221
  U.S. relations with, 214, 228, 229, 236, 239,
    240–41, 253
  Vietnam invaded by, 240, 241
Churchill, Sir Winston, 42–43, 46, 47, 49, 50,
    59, 68, 77, 91, 102, 103, 130, 151
  aid to Soviets promised by, 33, 34
  anti-Communism of, 34, 41, 133, 140–41,
    144–45
  "Iron Curtain" address of, 133, 140–41,
    144–45
  Polish question and, 61, 65, 71, 76, 79, 90, 92,
    94
  at Potsdam Conference, 107–8, 110, 111
  Roosevelt's communications with, 62, 90
  Roosevelt's relationship with, 39, 83
  Stalin's attacks on, 140, 141, 143, 144–45
  Stalin's communications with, 45, 61, 71
  Stalin's meeting with (Oct. 1944), 91
  Stalin's views on, 40, 41, 77, 93, 141
  at Tehran Conference, 39, 65–66, 68, 69, 71,
    80, 82
  Truman's relationship with, 107, 108
  United Nations and, 65, 90, 92
  at Yalta Conference, 82, 90, 92, 93, 94
Clay, Lucius, 154, 168, 187
Clifford, Clark, 130, 131
coal shortage, after World War II, 136, 137
Cohen, Benjamin V., 146, 162
Cold War, 84, 98, 151, 193–227, 240, 243
  Berlin blockade in, 9, 166, 182, 187–92, 207,
    215, 234
  Cuban missile crisis in, 233, 234

détente vs., 5, 6
globalization of, 9
origins of, 5, 6–9, 35–37, 74, 102, 107, 110,
    166–92
post-Stalinist reduction of, 231–40
Riga axioms and, 35–37
Soviet image of capitalism in, 135
Soviet policy in, 197, 203–8
Soviet self-image in, 208–11
Stalin's psyche as factor in, 197–98
U.S. image of Soviet policy in, 197, 198–203
see also Korean War
collectivization, 16, 23, 134
Colmer, William M., Stalin's meeting with
    (1945), 115–16
Cominform, 172, 175, 176–78, 214
Comintern, 51, 247
Communist parties, see specific countries
Congress, U.S., 44, 45, 49, 62, 66, 69, 85, 87,
    164, 169, 174, 194, 236, 253, 254
  see also Senate, U.S.
Connally, Tom, 212
Constitution, Soviet (1936), 43, 44, 67
Constitution, U.S., 62
Council of Foreign Ministers (CFM), 111,
    154–55, 159, 161, 167, 192, 207
  London meeting of, 99, 115, 116–20, 121
  Moscow meeting of (1943), 60–61, 63–64, 69
  Moscow meeting of (1945), 125–27, 129, 132,
    145, 152, 159
  Moscow meeting of (1947), 129–31, 136, 147,
    153, 155–57, 171, 179, 183
Cuba, 239, 242
  intervention in Africa of, 236, 238
  Soviet submarine base in, 236
Cuban missile crisis, 233, 234, 246
Curzon Line, 47, 50, 53, 55, 68, 71, 72, 92
Cyrankiewicz, Josef, 147
Czechoslovakia, 53, 55, 78
  Communist party in, 77, 101
  coup d'état in (1948), 166, 172, 180
  Marshall Plan and, 174–75
  Soviet relations with, 74, 75, 77, 101–2,
    147–48, 170, 175
  U.S. relations with, 148, 174–75
Czechoslovak-Soviet Treaty (1943), 77

Dallek, Robert, 7
Daniels, Jonathan, 100
Davies, Joseph, 35, 58–59, 62, 100, 101, 107
de Gaulle, Charles, 78–79, 92
Dekanozov, Vladimir, 29, 94–95
Democratic party, U.S., 19, 56, 83, 87
détente:
  advantages for Soviets of, 128–29
  defined, 5, 128
  entente compared to, 69
  under Khrushchev, 233
  in 1920s and 1930s, 5, 128–29

in 1970s, 5, 6, 69, 129, 140, 159, 164, 234–40, 246, 249–50
détente Stalinist-style (mid-1940s), 6, 8, 24, 74, 98, 122, 128–65, 197
    anti-Western propaganda in, 129, 134, 139, 140–45, 148, 150–51, 155, 172
    assumptions of, 133–45
    domination as policy of, 145–47
    duration of, 5, 129, 171–72
    Eastern Europe and, 129, 141, 145–48, 155
    economic factors in, 129, 131, 135–39
    intimidation as policy of, 145, 148–51
    moderation as policy of, 145, 147–48
    negotiation as policy of, 145, 151–65, 172
    nonliteral meaning of, 5, 128
    Soviet domestic crackdown and, 139–40
    transition to, 99–127
    U.S. policy transformed during, 129–31
Dewey, Thomas, 83
Djilas, Milovan, 40, 90, 134, 150, 153–54, 191
Dobrynin, Anatoly, 239
Douglas, William O., 133
Duclos, Jacques, 74, 75, 98
Dulles, John Foster, 120, 130, 168, 231, 232
Dumbarton Oaks Conference (1944), 73, 89–90, 124
Duranty, Walter, 21
Durbrow, Elbridge, 58, 143

East Germany, 154, 158
Economic Problems of Socialism (Stalin), 222–26
Eden, Anthony, 32–33, 63, 66, 91, 110–11, 203
    at Moscow meeting (1941), 46, 47–48, 49–50
Ehrenburg, Ilya, 140
Eisenhower, Dwight D., 81, 102, 226–27, 231, 232, 233
Engels, Friedrich, 12
Engen, Hans, 219–21
entente:
    condominium as form of, 254–55
    defined, 5
    détente compared to, 69
    in World War I, 13–15
    World War II origins of, 31–72
entente Stalinist-style, 8, 31, 73–98
    highpoint of, 68–70
    Hopkin's mission and, 101, 103–7
    international organization planned during, 88–90
    postwar economic assistance and, 85–88, 97–98
    Soviet aims in, 73–83, 90–96
    U.S. political scene and, 83
    Western economic prospects and, 84–85, 87–88
Eremin, I. A., 86–87
Ethridge, Mark, 122, 126, 132
expansionism, *see* Soviet expansionism
Export-Import Bank, 86, 236

Far Eastern Advisory Commission (FEAC), 115, 119, 123, 125, 148, 213
Finland:
    Soviet relations with, 48, 70, 180
    U.S. relations with, 112
Ford, Gerald, 238
Forrestal, James, 133, 170–71
Four-Power Declaration (1943), 63
France, 93, 129, 183, 225
    British competition with, 17
    Communist party in, 78–79, 98, 101, 134–35, 147, 172, 181, 206, 248
    at London Conference (1945), 116, 119, 120
    Marshall Plan and, 174, 175
    Poland compared to, 92, 93
    Soviet relations with, 18, 22, 24, 25, 64, 78–79, 147
    tsarist Russia and, 11
    in World War II, 64, 65, 71, 79

Gaddis, John Lewis, 7
Gagra meeting (1945), 121–25
German Empire, in World War I, 12, 13, 14
Germany, Nazi, *see* Nazi Germany
Germany, postwar, 138
    Allied partitioning of, 79, 81, 153–54
    Communist party in, 80–81
    negotiations on status of, 130, 145, 153–54, 155–59, 163–65, 179, 187–92, 207, 222, 234
    peace treaty and, 154, 155
    reparations made by, 48, 80, 108, 110, 111, 136, 155, 156–57, 158
    threat posed by, 134, 135
    unification of, 145, 153–54, 155
    see also East Germany; West Germany
Gilmore, Eddy, 141
Gomulka, Wladislaw, 53, 54, 205
Gottwald, Klement, 175
Great Britain, 183
    Atlantic Charter and, 47, 48
    Berlin blockade and, 187, 188
    Bulgaria and, 113, 114, 118
    détente Stalinist-style and, 129, 136, 140–41, 142, 144–45, 150, 156
    deterioration of Soviet relations with (1920s), 22, 23
    German zone held by, 154, 163
    Greece and, 91, 93, 103, 148, 150
    India and, 25, 64, 156
    Korean War and, 212, 215, 216, 218, 221
    Marshall Plan and, 174
    Nazi attack on Soviet Union as viewed by, 31, 32–33, 34, 38, 40
    Polish question and, 61, 65, 71, 76, 79, 90, 92, 94, 103–4
    as Soviet ally in World War II, 34, 39–41, 42–46, 47, 48–51, 57, 60, 61, 65–66, 70, 71, 76

Great Britain (*continued*)
  Soviet attempts at cooperation with (1930s), 24, 25
  Soviet trade agreement with (1921), 15, 18
  territorial interests of, 17, 25, 48, 49, 64, 65, 83, 91, 93, 103, 116, 117, 156
  tsarist Russia and, 11, 67
  U.S. competition with, 17, 19–20, 83, 107–8, 177–78, 225
Greece, 111, 117, 180, 232
  British role in, 91, 93, 103, 148, 150
  Communist party in, 80, 148, 149, 166, 180
  détente Stalinist-style and, 145, 148, 149, 150, 151
  U.S. relations with, 148, 151, 176, 180–81
Grew, Joseph, 103
Gromyko, Andrei, 211, 222, 231, 242, 247
  as ambassador to U.S., 59–60, 61, 82, 86, 89, 247
  Korean War and, 215, 216, 217

Haiphong harbor, U.S. mining of, 236, 237
Hammarskjöld, Dag, 231
Harriman, W. Averell, 34–35, 56, 63–64, 66, 69, 70–72, 95, 106, 113, 114, 115, 141
  at Gagra meeting, 121–25
  at London Conference (1945), 119, 123
  Moscow mission of (1941), 42–46, 48, 57
  Roosevelt's death and, 96–98
  Soviet policy developed by, 97–98, 99
  U.S. aid to Soviets as viewed by, 85, 86, 87, 88
Hazard, John, 86–87
Henderson, Loy, 180
Hickerson, John, 207–8
Hirohito, emperor of Japan, 114
historians, *see* revisionist historians; traditionalist historians
Hitler, Adolf, 42, 47, 77, 120
  Roosevelt compared to, 38, 68
  Stalin compared to, 168, 169, 193, 196
  Stalin's alliance with, 24–30, 39, 68
  Truman compared to, 175
Hobson, J. A., 12
Hodge, John R., 151, 211
Hoover, Herbert, 20
Hopkins, Harry, 41–42, 44, 66, 77, 226
  Moscow mission of (1945), 101, 103–7
Horthy, Miklós von Nagybánya, 55, 77
Hottelet, Richard C., 132–33, 153
Hough, Jerry, 252, 253
Howard, Roy, 21
Hull, Cordell, 35–36, 59–61, 63–64, 69, 70, 71
human rights policies, 145, 239
Hungary:
  Communist party in, 55, 77–78, 84–85, 122
  Soviet relations with, 74, 75, 77–78, 91, 102, 122, 134, 147, 167
  U.S. relations with, 102–3, 112, 167
  in World War II, 47, 55, 77

imperialism:
  capitalism related to, 7, 12, 16–18, 21–22
  Cominform Declaration and, 176
  of German Empire, 14
  of Great Britain, 17, 25, 48, 49, 64, 65, 83, 91, 93, 103, 116, 117, 156
  Lenin's theory of, 12, 14, 16, 83
  of Nazi Germany, 26–27, 29, 31, 46, 47, 48
  Stalin's views on, 14–15, 16–18, 22, 23–24, 83
  of U.S., 7, 83, 177–78
India, 124, 125, 148
  British control of, 25, 64, 156
  Korean War and, 216
Indo-Pakistan war (1971), 236
Iran, Soviet relations with, 82, 125–26, 130, 131–32, 141, 145, 148, 149–50, 169, 180–81, 229, 232
Italy, 111, 124
  colonies of, 82, 108, 109, 116–17, 133, 159, 162
  Communist party in, 79, 101, 147, 166, 172, 181, 183
  Marshall Plan and, 172, 175
  reparations made by, 159, 161
  Soviet relations with, 18, 28, 82, 108, 109, 147
Izvestia, 83, 186

Jacobs, Joseph E., 212
Japan, 130, 225
  Allied occupation of, 114, 115, 119–20, 123–24, 125, 148, 213
  Korean War and, 212, 213–14
  Soviet relations with, 10, 15, 18, 28, 29, 63, 81–82, 107, 114–15, 145, 148, 213–14
  U.S. relations with, 7, 110, 112, 114–15, 119–20, 124, 138, 213
  in World War II, 60, 63, 65, 81–82, 87, 93, 110, 114
Jernegan, John, 181
Jessup, Philip, 207
Johnson, Louis, 198–99
Johnson Act (1934), 86
Johnston, Eric, 87
Journal de Moscou, 204

Kamenev, Lev, 16
Kasaniev, Vasily, 219–21
Kelly, Sir David, 208
Kennan, George F., 6–7, 14, 35, 97, 116, 141, 153, 166–68, 169–71, 173, 181, 199
  fall of Molotov and Mikoyan as viewed by, 204–5
  German reunification plan proposed by, 192
  Korean War and, 193, 195, 201–2, 213, 214
  Long Telegram of, 130, 131
  on nature of Soviet threat, 170–71, 193, 198, 226
Kennedy, John F., 233, 234, 242

Khrushchev, Nikita, 212–13, 233–34, 242, 248
  Stalin as viewed by, 27, 32, 196, 197, 198, 205,
    231
  Stalin compared to, 233
Kim Il-sung, 212–13
Kirk, Alan, 202–3, 208, 211, 215, 222
Kissinger, Henry, 36, 46, 85, 191, 218–19,
    234–37, 244
  Carter compared to, 238, 239
  détente and, 69, 164, 236–37
  Soviet negotiating patterns encountered by,
    247–48
Kohler, Foy, 181, 207
Kolko, Gabriel, 6–7
Korea, East-West negotiations on, 145, 151–53
Korean War, 9, 193, 195, 201–2, 211–22
  armistice in, 231, 232
  China connection in, 213, 214, 216, 217, 221,
    222
  North Korean invasion in, 211, 212–16, 217,
    221, 234, 251
Kostov, Traicho, 205
Kosygin, Alexei, 46, 239–40, 247
Krzycki, Leo, 136

Labour party, British, 18, 94
Lane, Arthur Bliss, 147
Lange, Oskar, 54
Latin America, United Nations and, 89, 104–5
League of Nations, 89
Lenin, V. I., 32, 143, 210, 223, 248
  death of, 16
  foreign policy as viewed by, 5, 10–14, 15, 20,
    128
  imperialism as viewed by, 12, 14, 16, 83
  Stalin compared to, 14, 18
"Leningrad Affair," 205
Lie, Trygvie, 231
Litvinov, Maxim, 25, 26, 61–62, 83, 88, 94–95,
    107, 132–33, 153, 226
London Conference (1945), 99, 115, 116–20,
    121
London Conference (1948), 182–83, 187
Long Telegram (1946), 130, 131
Lovett, Robert, 168, 184
Lozovsky, Solomon, 36, 56, 57
Ludwig, Emil, 20

MacArthur, Douglas, 114, 120, 124, 213,
    217–18, 219, 220–21, 222
Mackintosh, Malcolm, 113
Maclean, Donald, 194
Maisky, Ivan, 32–33, 43, 49
Malenkov, Georgi, 176, 177, 205, 210–11, 231,
    232, 233
Malik, Yakov, 207, 217, 218, 222
Maniu, Julius, 146
Mao Tse-tung, 82, 122, 148, 210
Marshall, George, 129–31, 156–58, 161, 170,
    171, 187, 189

  Harvard commencement speech of, 173, 174
Marshall Plan, 131, 136, 147, 153, 158, 164,
    166, 167, 170, 172, 228–29
  Soviet reactions to, 173–79, 182, 224
Marx, Karl, 12, 223
Masaryk, Jan, 150, 174–75
Mastny, Vojtech, 7–8, 27, 51, 54, 79, 80–81, 95
Matthews, H. Freeman, 133
Memoirs (Kennan), 192, 193
Memoirs (Truman), 186–87
Michael, king of Rumania, 75, 113
Mikolajczyk, Stanislaw, 72, 77, 103, 114
Mikoyan, Anastas, 86, 203–5
Modzelewski, Zygmunt, 147
Molotov, Vyacheslav, 33, 47, 54, 56, 59, 70–72,
    85, 86, 91, 95–97, 101, 106, 107, 114, 115,
    123, 158, 162, 184–86
  Berlin blockade and, 188, 190–91, 215
  fall of, 203–5
  Korean question and, 152, 153
  at London Conference (1945), 116–20
  Marshall Plan talks and, 173, 174
  at Moscow Conference (1943), 60, 61, 63–64
  at Moscow Conference (1945), 126, 132, 152
  at Moscow Conference (1947), 155–56, 179
  at New York Conference, 154–55, 159–60,
    163, 179
  at Paris Peace Conference, 155, 161, 163
  at Potsdam Conference, 108–9
  speeches made by, 176, 177, 178
  at Tehran Conference, 66, 69–70
  Truman's meeting with (April 1945), 99–100,
    103
  United Nations and, 88, 95–96, 104–5
  at Yalta Conference, 79, 93, 94
Molotov-Ribbentrop Pact (1939), 24–30, 31, 32,
    39, 105, 167–68
  factors favoring passage of, 25–26
  secret protocol of, 26, 28
Montreux Convention (1936), 108–9
Morgenthau, Henry, 88
Moscow Conference (1943), 60–61, 63–64, 69
Moscow Conference (1945), 125–27, 129, 132,
    145, 152, 159
Moscow Conference (1947), 129–31, 136, 147,
    153, 155–57, 171, 179, 183
Moscow Daily News, 204
Moscow Summit (1972), 43, 46, 247–48
Muccio, John, 212
Murphy, Robert, 153, 155, 183, 187, 188
Mussolini, Benito, 25

Nagy, Ferenc, 147, 172
National Council of the Homeland (NCH), 53,
    54
National Security Council, U.S. (NSC), 198
  report 5 of, 180
  report 7 of, 168, 170
  report 20/1 of, 171
  report 68 of, 194, 198–202, 205

NATO, *see* North Atlantic Treaty Organization
Nazi Germany, 24–40, 181
 defeat of, 48, 49, 60, 61, 75, 87, 95, 104
 expansionism of, 26–27, 29, 31, 46, 47, 48
 Soviet pact with, *see* Molotov-Ribbentrop Pact
 Soviet Union invaded by (1941), 24, 27, 28, 30, 31, 32–38, 210
Nehru, Jawaharlal, 216
Nelson, Donald M., 85–86, 87
New Economic Policy (NEP), 15–16
New Times, 172
New York Conference (1946), 154–55, 159–60, 163, 179
New York Times, 132, 143, 187
Nixon, Richard, 43, 46, 85, 159, 164, 234–37
North Atlantic Treaty (1949), 206
North Atlantic Treaty Organization (NATO), 166, 173, 183, 202, 205, 206–7, 208, 210, 222, 228

oil interests, 17, 82, 131, 200, 229–30, 245
Orlemanski, Stanislaw, 54

Pakistan, Soviet relations with, 229–30
Papandreou, George, 80
Paris Peace Conference (1946), 130, 145, 148, 159, 161, 162–63
 as East-West brawl, 151
 procedures established for, 124–25, 154–55, 160
Pepper, Claude, 116
Perkins, Frances, 39
Philby, Kim, 194
Podgorny, Nikolai, 46
Poland:
 Communist party in, 51–52, 53, 76, 102
 government-in-exile of, 52–53, 54–55, 58, 61, 68, 72, 108
 Lublin government of, 53, 75–76, 92, 93, 108, 109
 Nazi occupation of, 26, 27, 31, 46, 47, 52
 unrest in (1980s), 229, 246
 U.S. aid to, 146–47
 U.S. recognition of, 108, 109, 146
Polish Council for National Liberation, 53
Polish-Soviet relations, 27, 39, 51–56, 58, 63–64, 66–72, 74–76, 92–96, 102, 103–7
 border question and, 47, 49, 50, 52, 53, 55, 61, 67, 68, 71, 72, 92
 "Czechoslovak solution" and, 54
 détente Stalinist-style and, 145, 146–47
Politburo, 203, 208, 244, 247, 251
Ponomarev, Boris, 247
Poskrebyshev, Alexander, 198
Potsdam Conference (1945), 99, 101, 107–12, 114, 116, 149, 153, 154
Powers, Gary, 233
Pravda, 70, 173, 174, 206, 209, 221, 231, 240

Rajk, Laszlo, 205
Rákosi, Mátyás, 78, 85

Rapallo, Treaty of (1922), 16–17
Reagan, Ronald, 253
Red Cross, 53, 61
Republican party, U.S., 19, 56, 83, 87
Reston, James, 226
"Review of Current Trends in U.S. Policy," 166
revisionist historians, 31–32, 77, 148, 158
 U.S.-Soviet relations as viewed by, 6–7, 74, 98, 100, 113, 129, 145, 151, 199
Rhee, Syngman, 151–52, 211, 212
Ribbentrop, Joachim von, 25, 26, 28–29, 32, 95
Ribicoff, Abraham, 239
Riga axioms, 35–37, 63
Robins, Raymond, 20–21
Rockefeller, Nelson, 104
Romanov, Grigori, 239, 240
Roosevelt, Elliott, 143–44, 155
Roosevelt, Franklin D., 19, 47, 61, 151
 accommodationist Soviet policy of, 7, 8–9, 49, 51, 55–56, 68, 85, 91, 92–93, 102
 Churchill's communications with, 62, 90
 Churchill's relationship with, 39, 83
 death of, 74, 96–101, 144
 domestic policies of, 21
 Polish question and, 39, 55–58, 62, 65, 66–68, 69, 76, 79, 90, 92–94, 95, 96
 presidential elections of, 44, 66, 67, 83
 revisionists' views of, 6–7, 74, 98, 100, 113, 129, 145, 151, 199
 Soviets aided by, 34–35, 42
 Soviet Union as viewed by, 21, 38
 Stalin as viewed by, 38–39, 56, 95, 106–7
 Stalin flattered by, 64–65
 Stalin's correspondence with, 75–76, 90, 95–96
 Stalin's praise for, 21, 42
 Stalin's views on, 9, 39, 40, 41, 44–45, 56, 62, 69, 93
 at Tehran Conference, 39, 45, 55, 62, 64–69, 71–72, 80, 86, 89
 United Nations and, 65–66, 88–90, 92, 93, 96
 at Yalta Conference, 79, 82, 90, 92–94
Rostow, W. W., 6–7
Rumania, 124
 anti-Communist coup planned in, 146
 Roosevelt's protest on, 90
 Soviet influence in, 55, 74, 75, 90, 91, 93, 102, 111, 117–18, 145, 146
 Soviet territorial interests in, 28, 29, 47, 48
 U.S. relations with, 102–3, 109, 111, 112, 115, 118–19, 145, 146
Rusk, Dean, 168, 212
Russia, tsarist, 11–12, 67, 180
Russia: Market or Menace (Campbell), 19
Russian Revolution (1917), 12–13, 249
Russia's Road to the Cold War (Mastny), 7–8

SALT II agreement, 238, 239, 240, 241
San Francisco Conference (1945), 95–96, 104, 123
Schlesinger, Arthur M., Jr., 7

Schulenberg, Count Werner, 29
Semenov, Vladimir, 247
Senate, U.S., 89, 208, 239–40
Sforza, Count Carlo, 169
Shulman, Marshall, 197, 214
Sikorski, Wladislaw, 52, 53, 61
Smith, Kingsbury, 206
Smith, Walter Bedell, 132, 139, 149, 153, 155,
    162, 175, 179–80, 183–86
  Berlin blockade and, 189–90
  Stalin's meetings with, 141–42, 149
Snow, Edgar, 88, 94, 132
Sokolovsky, Vasily, 187, 188, 191, 211
Solzhenitsyn, Aleksandr, 243
Sonnenfeldt Doctrine, 235
Soviet expanionism, 3, 35, 143, 168–69
  entente Stalinist-style and, 74, 75–83, 90–96
  Molotov-Ribbentrop Pact and, 26, 27, 28–29
  roots of, 7, 11, 28
  in World War II, 47–56, 58, 61, 63–64, 66–72
Soviet foreign policy:
  dualistic approach to West in, 9, 10, 25, 27,
    37, 131–32
  from 1917–1941, 10–30
  insecurity as factor in, 10, 24, 25, 27, 133
  "peace policies" in, 5, 15, 18, 22, 23–24, 128,
    232
  tsarist legacy in, 11–12
  see also Cold War; détente; entente; Polish-
    Soviet relations; U.S.-Soviet relations;
    specific countries
Soviet-French treaty (1944), 79
Soviet-Iranian treaty (1921), 126
Soviet Union:
  Allied intervention in, 13–15
  Civil War in, 14–15
  Communist party of, 15, 17, 23, 24, 109,
    237–38
  current change of leadership in, 251–53
  economy of, 15–16, 17–18, 172, 228, 233,
    245
  elections in, 133, 139
  Great Terror in (1930s), 16, 25, 35, 51, 251
  increased pluralism in, 243–44, 250
  military power of, 10, 35, 40, 129, 171,
    245–46
  opposition in, 16, 23, 36, 133, 140, 241, 243
  stability and confidence of, 245
  "stability of cadres" in, 251
  trade of, 15, 18, 19–20, 23, 27, 85–86,
    115–16, 143, 245
Spaak, Paul Henri, 81, 169
Stalin, Joseph:
  as Americanophile, 18–20
  as "bastard," 39
  Berlin blockade and, 188–92, 234
  crimes of, 16, 25, 35, 39, 51, 61, 134, 251
  death of, 197, 227, 230, 231, 246–47
  at Gagra meeting, 121–25
  interviews with, 19–21, 38, 42, 141–45, 163,
    206

  at Moscow Conference (1943), 60–61
  Moscow Conference (1947), and, 130–31
  political legacy of, 246–49, 251–52
  at Potsdam Conference, 99, 107–12
  revolutionary war as viewed by, 13, 15, 22
  as role-player, 45–47
  speeches made by, 14, 17, 22, 23, 32, 73–74,
    133–34, 139, 204
  suspiciousness of, 5, 8, 27, 31–32, 74–75,
    106–7, 182, 197–98, 205–6, 211, 246, 250
  at Tehran Conference, 39, 45, 62, 64–70, 71,
    79, 80, 82, 86, 89
  Trotsky vs., 14, 16, 22
  as "Uncle Joe," 38–39, 62, 108, 116
  United Nations and, 65–66, 88–90, 92, 96,
    104–5, 143
  U.S. as viewed by, 8–9, 17, 18–21, 31–32,
    43–44, 54, 87, 94, 106, 137
  World War II aims of, 47–56, 58, 61, 63–64,
    66–72
  at Yalta Conference, 79, 82, 90, 92–95
  see also Cold War; détente Stalinist-style; en-
    tente Stalinist-style
Standley, William, 56, 57, 58–59
Stassen, Harold, Stalin's meeting with (1947),
    137–39, 157, 172
State Department, U.S., 33, 35, 58, 97, 102,
    103, 108, 131, 132, 145, 147, 166, 171,
    188, 192, 198, 202, 208, 213
  Division of European Affairs in, 37–38, 133
  telegram to Smith from (1948), 183–84
Steinhardt, Lawrence, 33, 36–37, 56
Stettinius, Edward, 89
Šubašić, Ivan, 40–41
Sulzberger, C. L., 132
Supreme Soviet, 76, 96, 133
Suslov, Mikhail, 247

TASS, 209
Tehran Conference (1943), 39, 45, 62–63,
    64–72, 79, 80, 82, 86, 89, 98
  as high point of East-West cooperation, 68–70
  Polish question and, 39, 55, 64, 65, 66–68,
    69–72
Third World, Stalin's views on, 21–22
Thorez, Maurice, 79, 134–35, 177, 206
Tito, Marshall (Josip Broz), 40, 90, 101, 181–82,
    205
Togliatti, Palmiro, 79, 172, 206, 214
Toon, Malcolm, 56
traditionalist historians, 14, 74, 140, 153
  U.S.-Soviet relations as viewed by, 6–7, 35,
    98, 133, 151, 166–68
  Yalta Conference as viewed by, 93, 94
Tripartite Pact, 28–29
Trotsky, Leon, 13, 14, 16, 22
Truman, Harry S, 34, 96, 97, 100, 114–15, 129,
    140, 221
  anti-Communism of, 133, 164, 175
  Berlin blockade as viewed by, 182, 188
  Clifford Memorandum and, 130

Truman, Harry S (*continued*)
hard-line Soviet policy of, 7, 8–9, 85, 98, 99–101, 103, 107, 109–10, 145, 164, 253
Harriman's influence on, 98, 99, 106
inconsistent foreign policy of, 100–101
Marshall's communications with, 156–57
Moscow Conference (1945) and, 126–27
Polish question and, 103, 106, 107
at Potsdam Conference, 107–10, 111
renewed war feared by, 168–69
Soviet Union as viewed by, 148
speeches made by, 133, 146, 151, 153, 168
Stalin as viewed by, 100, 106–7, 186–87
Stalin compared to, 100
Stalin's communications with, 103, 119, 123
Stalin's quarrels with, 114–15
Truman Doctrine, 7, 133, 148, 151, 153, 176–77, 181, 242
Tucker, Robert C., 47
Turkey:
British relations with, 50
Soviet relations with, 82, 108–9, 126, 130, 145, 148, 149–50, 232
U.S. relations with, 148, 151, 176, 180–81
in World War II, 63

Ulam, Adam, 22–23, 24, 27, 158, 176, 233
Ulbricht, Walter, 80–81
Umansky, Konstantine, 33–34, 44
Union of Polish Patriots (UPP), 53
United Nations, 45, 49, 58, 88–90, 92, 93, 100, 111, 141, 143, 162, 203, 208
China and, 210, 215, 216, 217, 221
East-West confrontations in, 148, 149, 151, 155, 207, 215
founding conference of, 95–96, 104
General Assembly of, 220
Korean War and, 212, 214, 216, 217, 218, 219–21
Security Council of, 88, 92, 124, 150, 215, 216
Tehran discussions on, 65–66, 89
United Nations Relief and Rehabilitation Administration (UNRRA), 146–47
United Nations Temporary Commission on Korea (UNTCOK), 212
United States:
anti-Communism in, 41, 94, 133, 164, 175, 238, 242
Communist party of, 20, 74, 83, 98
economy of, 7, 17, 21, 84, 85–88, 108, 115–16, 136–39
elections in, 44, 56, 66, 67, 83
foreign policy of, *see specific countries*
military spending of, 171, 194, 198–99, 242
political parties in, 19, 56, 83, 87, 94, 186
Stalin's views on advantages of, 17, 20
U.S.-Soviet relations:
arms race and, 110, 129, 169, 176, 178, 194, 198, 209, 211, 228, 229, 230, 240, 242, 250, 253
economic factors in, 7, 18, 19–20, 32, 33, 74, 136–39, 147, 253
future of, 249–55
lend-lease aid and, 34–35, 43–44, 86, 105
"linkage diplomacy" and, 85, 112, 119–20, 147, 254
Nazi invasion of Soviet Union and, 31, 32, 33–38
in 1940s as compared to 1970s, 5, 36, 45, 46, 56, 85, 112, 121, 140, 159, 164
in 1940s as compared to 1980s, 3–6, 228–29, 250–51
in 1950s as compared to 1970s, 218–19
possible types of, summarized, 5–6
post-revisionists' views of, 7–8
Roosevelt's death as turning point in, 97–101
Soviet misperceptions and, 8–9, 44–45, 54, 69, 83, 85, 87–88, 94–95, 195–96
Soviet nastiness and, 35, 41–42, 45, 46, 47, 247–48
Soviet public opinion and, 61, 104, 114
after Stalin, 228–55
traditionalists' views of, 6–7, 35, 98, 133, 151, 166–68
U.S. misperceptions and, 9, 38–41, 69, 149, 195–96, 202, 203
U.S. public opinion and, 43, 44–45, 49, 51, 54, 55–56, 61–62, 67–68, 83, 87, 92, 94, 95, 97, 103, 104, 170, 184, 230–31, 254
see also Cold War; détente; entente

Vance, Cyrus, 197
Varga, Eugene, 84, 135
Versailles Treaty (1919), 25
Vietnam War, 236, 237, 247
Vinson, Fred, 186, 187
Vyrianov, Colonel, 187–88
Vyshinsky, Andrei, 45, 57–58, 60, 94, 101, 146, 148, 155, 179–80
Korean War and, 215, 217, 220, 221, 222
at Potsdam Conference, 110–11, 150
relations with European Communist parties of, 75, 79, 113–14
as Soviet foreign minister, 204, 207, 208
United Nations and, 150, 217, 220

Wallace, Henry, 186
Warsaw Declaration (1948), 183
Watergate, 236
Watson, Thomas, 56
Welles, Sumner, 33, 34, 38, 62, 83, 132
Wells, H. G., 21, 38
Werth, Alexander, 142, 163
West Germany, 154, 182, 187, 205, 210, 225
Williams, William Appleman, 6–7
Willkie, Wendell, 56–58, 59, 70
Wilson, Woodrow, 19
Winant, John G., 48–49

Winiewicz, Jozef, 147
World Peace Congress, 210–11
World War I, 11–15, 40
    armistice in, 14
    as inter-imperialist war, 12, 13, 78, 83
World War II, 24–127
    as inter-imperialist war, 83, 134, 223–24
    Soviet aims in, 47–56, 58, 61, 63–64, 66–72
    threats of renewed war after, 134–35, 139, 140,
      166, 168–71, 175–79, 182–84, 187–227
    Western views of Soviet Union during, 41
    see also specific countries and conferences

Yalta Conference (1945), 45, 63–64, 75, 79, 82,
    92–95
    terms agreed upon at, 76, 77, 92–93, 101, 102,
      103, 105, 114
Yalta Declaration on Liberated Europe, 90, 102,
    109, 237

Yergin, Daniel, 35, 104, 110, 126–27, 130,
    131–32, 175, 179
Yugoslavia, 229
    Communist party in, 40, 51, 90, 151
    Nazi occupation of, 29, 40
    Soviet relations with, 29, 40–41, 90, 91, 171,
      181–82, 232
    Trieste claims made by, 101, 181

Zagladin, Vadim, 241, 242
Zamiatin, Leonid, 240
Zhdanov, Andrei, 139–40, 168, 176–77, 178,
    205
Zhemchuzhina, Polina, 205
Zhukov, Georgi, 32
Zhukov, Yuri, 207
Zinoviev, Grigori, 16
Zorin, Valentin, 241
Zorin, Valerian, 188–89